international VIDEO graphic design

Jack M. Beebe

The Library of Applied Design

PBC International • New York

Distributor to the book trade in the United States and Canada:

Rizzoli International Publications Inc.
300 Park Avenue South
New York, NY 10010

Distributor to the art trade in the United States:

PBC International, Inc.
One School Street
Glen Cove, NY 11542
1-800-527-2826
Fax 516-676-2738

Distributor to the art trade in Canada:

Letraset Canada Limited, Ltd.
170 Duffield Drive
Markham, Ontario, L6G1 B5 Canada

Distributed throughout the rest of the world:

Hearst Books International
105 Madison Avenue
New York, NY 10016

Beebe, Jack M.
International video graphic design/by Jack M. Beebe.
p. cm.
Includes index.
1. Computer graphics. 2. Videotape recorders and recording.
I. Title.
T385.B45 1991
791.45′0232′028566--dc20 90-26038
CIP

ISBN 0-86636-133-2

CAVEAT—Information in this text is believed accurate, and will pose no problem for the student or casual reader. However, the author was often constrained by information contained in signed release forms, information that could have been in error or not included at all. Any misinformation (or lack of information) is the result of failure in these attestations. The author has done whatever is possible to insure accuracy.

Color separation, printing and binding by
Toppan Printing Co. (H.K.) Ltd. Hong Kong

Typography by
TypeLink, Inc.

10 9 8 7 6 5 4 3 2 1

Dedication

With special love, I dedicate this book to Pamela McCormick, my partner and inspiration in many ventures, but most especially the adventure of love and life. It was Pam who originally thought of the idea for this book years ago.

Acknowledgements

This book couldn't have been written without these people and it is with gratitude and great pleasure that I acknowledge:

Rich Kearney
Dick Kopley
Two of my sturdy walls. Walls, that many ideas were bounced off.

Jim Simmonds, for always being there for me.

Garth Gentilin, for never forgetting.

Gerry Cantwell for ears, ideas and thoughtful application of knowledge.

Allen Schulman for wonderful words of wisdom.

David Breen, who came to the rescue.

James Biancardi, of Video Lab, for use of the hall.

Dominick D'Agostino for picking up the phone.

Raymond Seti of Seti Video Communications
Glenn Bodkin of C & C Visual
for early ideas and inspiration.

Barry Fialk,
Jacqueline Mauder
for always answering the call.

John Chris Jorgensen,
Steve Rutt
for talking technical talk that I could understand.

Mike McCall, Windsor Video
Joyce Feigenbaum, Feigenbaum Associates
Roy Sharp, Vanda Communications
Jim Tomlinson, Meta-Five
for great ideas and great suggestions.

Paul Krucik and Rich Bisignano of East Coast Video
for their technical proofing.

For taking the time to write the foreword;
Edgar E. Stevenson, Northeast Regional Manager,
Ampex Recording Media Corporation
Isaac Hersly, President, The Chyron Group
Patricia A. Portella, Senior Graphic Artist,
Harry/Paintbox, Quantel Inc.
Peter A. Dare, Vice President of Technology,
Sony Business Group, Sony Corporation of America

For the cover design:
From an idea by Carrie Abel
Developed by Allen Schulman
Created by Tony Caio of Data Motion Arts

My sister, June Dorer, who has always been my
sympathetic ear and my friend.

My daughter, Jean Beebe, who is the real writing talent
in the family and who has firmly encouraged this
project from its inception.

And last, because they were first, my parents
June and John Beebe, whose personal lives have
set positive examples for me and many others, and
who have inspired and encouraged every effort of my
own life from my very first breath onward.
And, who were the very first people who, long before
any of these and the following words were set down on
paper, called to find out where they could send a
check to order a copy of this book.

Contents

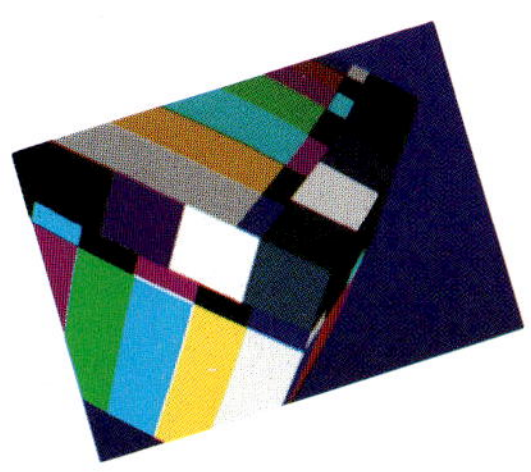

Foreword

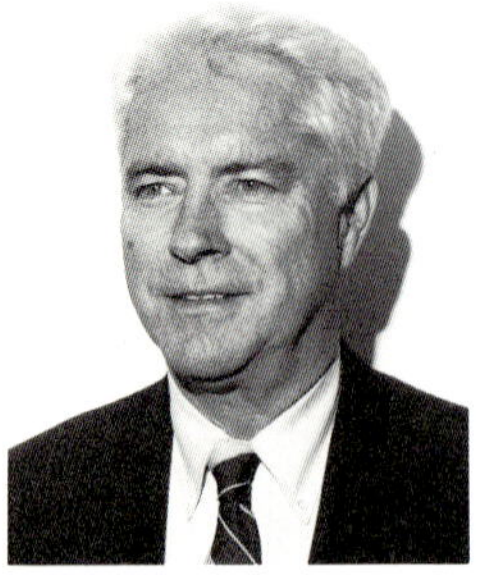

Edgar E. Stevenson
Northeast Regional Manager
Ampex Recording Media Corporation

In 1955, Ampex Corporation invented the video tape recording process as we now know it. From then on, an entire industry of production, post-production, syndication duplicators, and video graphic arts, have come on the scene, including electronic journalism, which has changed and enhanced our lives. The movie industry, with film-to-tape transfers, along with colorization, has improved our leisure time. Cable companies have added their contribution of the distribution of program material, most of which is on video tape.

Ampex has pioneered many of the newer formats directly or indirectly, including 1″, ½″, and the newest, digital recording. The libraries that the network, cable companies, broadcast journalism, and movie people depend on are well stocked in video tape. Even the Federal Government has many video centers, including their involvement in the Public Broadcast Corporation, all with extensive libraries of video and audio tape.

Video graphics was truly born with the Ampex Digital Optical System. This system has enhanced, enlarged, and developed to a fine art, the building of program material. We see it every day, especially in television commercials, when we remember what was delivered over 30 years ago in black and white, is done now in color and almost three-dimensional effects.

The Ampex Recording Media Research & Development team in Redwood City, are also looking to the future of the '90s, for newer formats. High-definition television, metal evaporated tape products, and refinement of the digital recording and broadcast processes are fast approaching. When our children look back at an industry a little over 40 years old and see what electronics have done to our lives compared to other industries, they can only say—amazing. The best may be yet to come, with the hand-held recorders and playback units, digital audio and video, videodiscs, and products on the drawing board for delivery in the '90s. Ampex Recording Media Corporation, a leader in magnetic tape research and development, has dedicated themselves with time and money to be there throughout this century with the latest technological developments, as it relates to magnetic tape, to better serve the worldwide market.

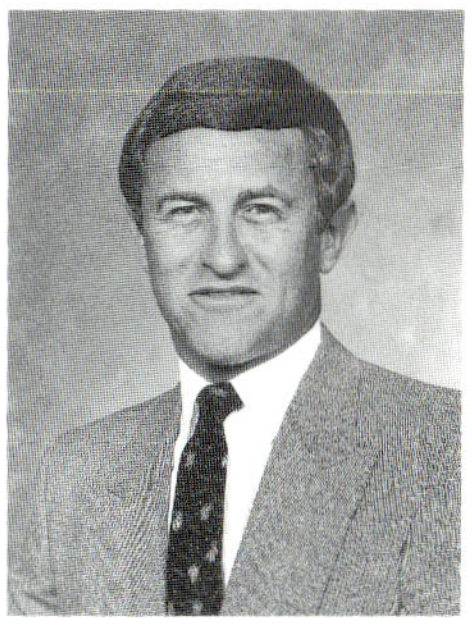

Isaac Hersly
President, The Chyron Group

The scene is a teleproduction facility in the '70s. Quad machines are buzzing as a live program from the studio reaches its final 30 seconds. The assistant director needs to cue the technician working a new machine that's going to do the credit roll. He's not sure he likes this. On previous shows, they had always keyed a camera shot of a moving scroll. But on this show, the producer didn't have a camera to waste. Now he has to give the new gizmo a cue to start. What should he call it? What was that brand? "Cue Chyron."

The name stuck and so did the technique of using electronically generated graphics in teleproduction. Today, Chyron is the generic word for character generation and the The Chyron Group is a manufacturer of an entire line of over 25 production and post-production products including Chyron character and graphics generators, CMX editing systems, DSC digital effects systems, and Aurora video graphic paint and animation systems.

Chyron's installed base of over 9000 units cover every state in the United States and over 50 countries around the world. In fact, if you watch television, you have better than a 50 percent chance that you are watching Chyron Group equipment at work.

Products like the Chyron IV, CMX 3600, and the Aurora 280 have been the workhorses of the business. New products such as the Chyron Scribe Infinit! and the CMX Omni and new enhancements and upgrades will keep our products the industry standard.

As for the future...The Chyron Group continues to invest in R & D to maintain our leadership position and keep those assistant directors saying "cue Chyron."

Introduction

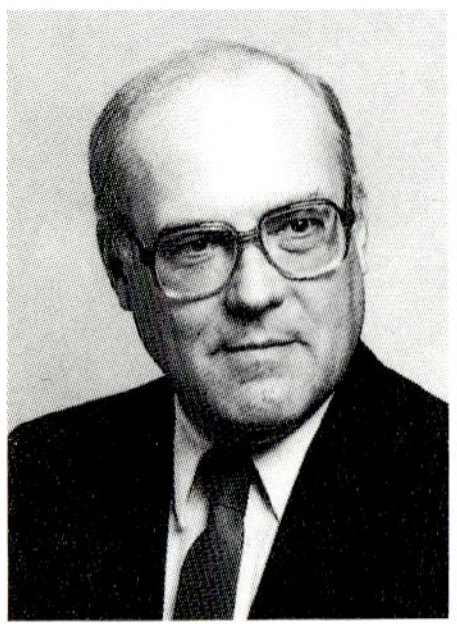

Jack M. Beebe

My first personal experience with, what then was a form of Video Graphic Design, was in 1953, when I was working for television station WPIX in New York City. A special graphic video effect was used on The Ted Steele Show, a live television show I later produced. Very simply, one live camera would shoot an object, sometimes even a moving object, such as a slide trombone, and the second camera would shoot a studio monitor screen containing that live shot. The two cameras were then superimposed over each other and the video images would chase each other into infinity. This live (there was no video tape in those days) video feedback was beautiful, especially when set to music. Today, we accomplish the same effect electronically, via computer.

In those early days of video, a split screen was accomplished simply by racking one camera lens turret so only half of a lens was used. A second camera turret was racked halfway in the opposite direction. The two cameras, each with different sides of their lenses half open, picked up two different subjects. They were then put on the air together. The result was a split screen. Now, we can electronically preview hundreds of various screens split or divided countless different ways, add some effects, and store everything. Then, when a desired effect is required, a simple push of a button provides the required result.

There were no video font or electronic character generators then either. Sport scores and other graphic information was done on lunch room menu boards or art cards, which were shot live. The menu board was very popular on sports programs. The teams and scores were physically spelled out, in advance, letter by letter and number by number, which took considerable time. When I went to WOR television in New York, our show was followed, in the same studio, by live sports and news done on TV, by radio announcers. Usually the radio announcer, who was not quite comfortable yet on the new medium of TV, would come on live and go quickly to the shots of the menu boards with the sports scores. On my first day, I was assigned to get our enormous pile of cue cards out of the studio before the start of the sports and news programs. With 10 seconds to go, before the sports came on live, I accidentally hit the sports show's menu boards with the pile of cue cards. Every football team in the United States, professional and collegiate, and their weekend scores, came cascading down onto the floor in one gigantic pile of letters and numbers. As I went through the door, the usually very deep voice of the announcer was heard in a very high squeal of, "Oh good God!! Oh good God!!"

That nightmare cannot happen now; the scores are electronically stored.

In those days, often closing credits were hand lettered on individual cards and then hung on notebook ring binders. At the end of the show, the stage manager would flip those cards live on the air, as a camera shot them. Now, we have sophisticated video font and electronic character generators or video typewriters, that do some dramatic non-typing things. This book contains some wonderful examples.

Interestingly enough though, a video graphic design effect that began in early days of television is still used today. One of the best ways to create a star or nighttime sky effect or background video bed continues to be to sprinkle common table salt on a black art card, and shoot it slightly out of focus.

Sports and news television programs began to widely use electronic video effects devices in the '60s. This paved the way for digital effect uses in all sorts of video.

Soon the innovative creators of other television programs, shows, commercials and music videos jumped on the band wagon. Electronic special video effects were used to make openings, closings, logos, and IDs. They were used on and in presentations, for data, in industry, at points of sale, on large screens, and on scoreboards. They were used to instruct and to inform, as well as to sell and to entertain.

Computers, electronic paint boxes, word and picture storage devices, and computer controlled animation stands soon were integrated making a wide variety of wonderful "toys" to create on and with. Some of the effects are seamless invisible video opticals. Invisible to the viewer because they are meant to be.

But, as unbelievable as the devices are today, even more unbelievable are the talents of the people who create on them. For machines are just that. Without human creativity, a machine remains a machine. For humans, creative boundaries do not exist. What follows in this book, are people who do this creating, and examples of the wonders and wizardry of their International Video Graphic Design.

Adtech Animation

8220 Commonwealth Drive, Suite 108
Eden Prairie, MN 55344

In business since 1981, Adtech is proud of its dedication to selection of the best of paint and 3-D animation systems which give them extensive flexibility for varied animation needs.

Chief animator, Kim Persons comes from a background in communications with a lifetime of fascination with and dedication to technology, especially in the computer graphics and animation industries. He has designed his own animation system.

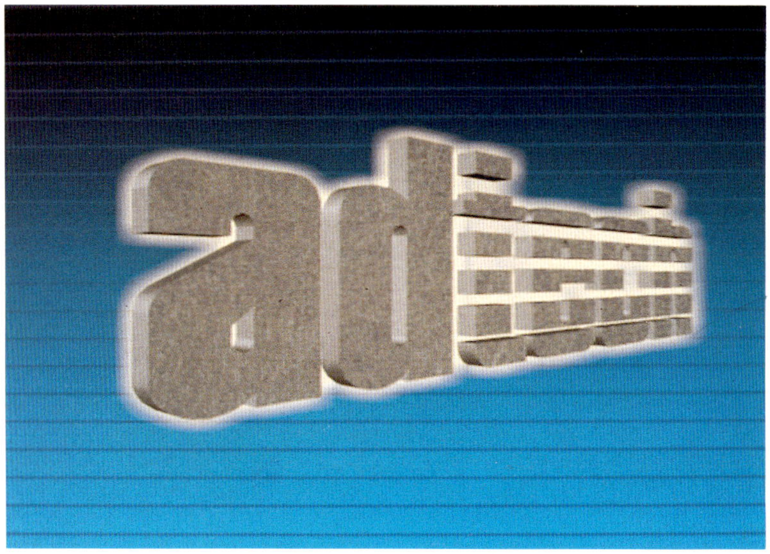

"Adtech in Stone"
Self promotional

After the animation moves, a piece of stone transforms into the Adtech logo. After the transformation, the rock glows.
Time to complete—7 days.

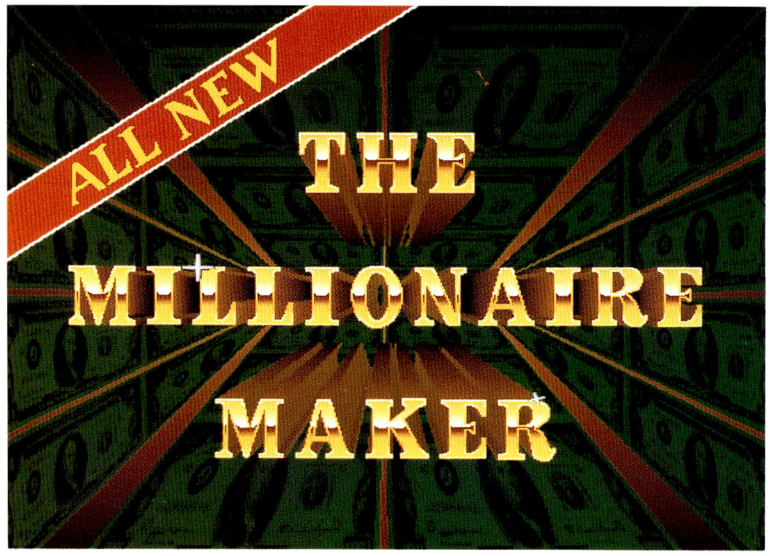

"The Millionaire Maker"
Open to television show for Ed Beckley, Fairfield, Ohio

The title moves across the screen and rests in place against a background of one hundred dollar bills.
Time to complete—14 days.

Both were totally designed, produced and animated at Adtech Animation by Kim Persons using the Vertigo V20-25, SGI, Cubicomp Picture Maker 60R, Paint Box systems, Image Capture devices, image output devices and 1" tape machine. Post production on "The Millionaire Maker" was completed at Beckley studios.

ANIMATION STATION, LTD.

633 South Plymouth Court
Chicago, IL 60605

Donnelly Directory Oscar

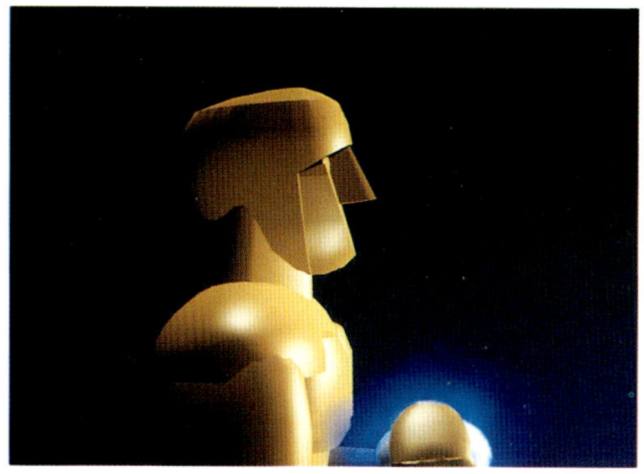

Created as a 15-second 3-D computer animated "Oscar" award for Donnelly Directory, Oak Brook, IL. It was designed to project on a large screen video to an audience of Donnelly Directory employees during their annual award meeting. As the statue appeared to throw the glowing ball toward the audience, the ball grew to full screen. The names of the awards and recipients were listed over the ball.

Two ArtStar 3D-Plus mainframe computers were used to compute and render 450 single key frames. Each frame was airbrushed to create the glowing ball effect.

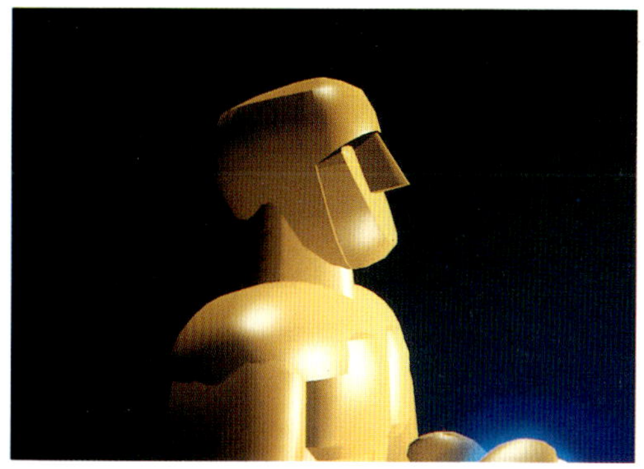

Produced by	Design Video Taping, Inc., Arlington Heights, IL.
Producer/Director	Paul Seitz
3-D Graphic Designer	Tim Knuth
Animation Director	Terry Choate
Graphics	Animation Station, Ltd.

Length of time to complete work: 3 weeks

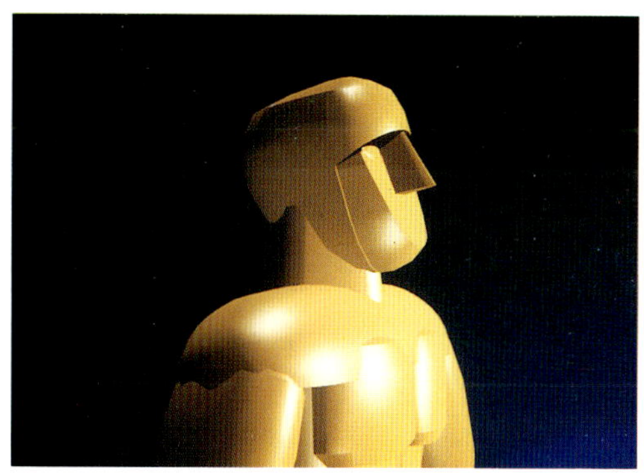

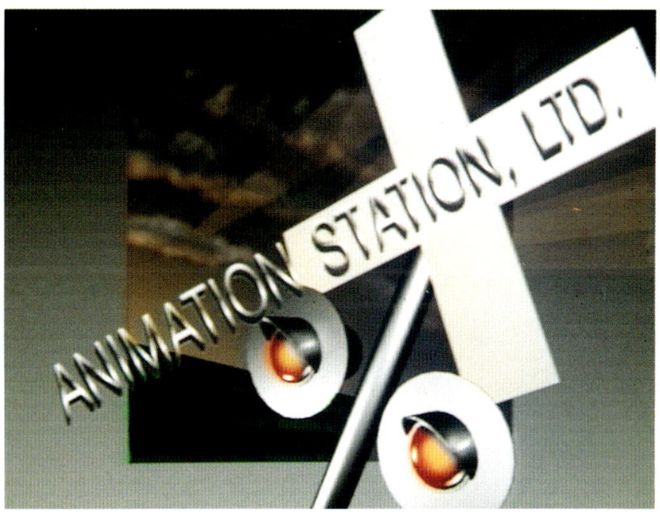

Animation Station Logo

Animation Director Terry Choate
2-D and Paintbox Artist
Terry Choate

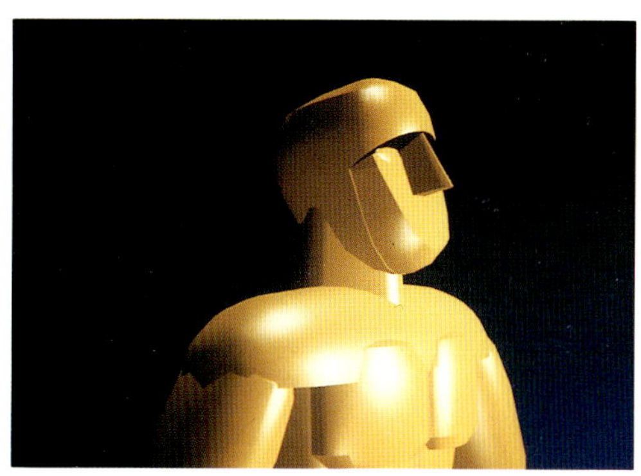

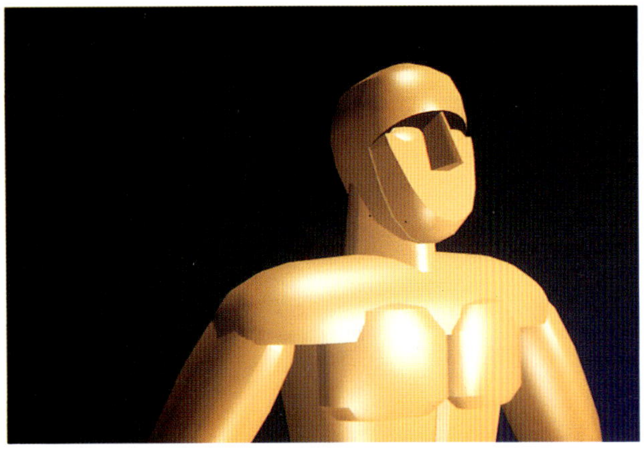
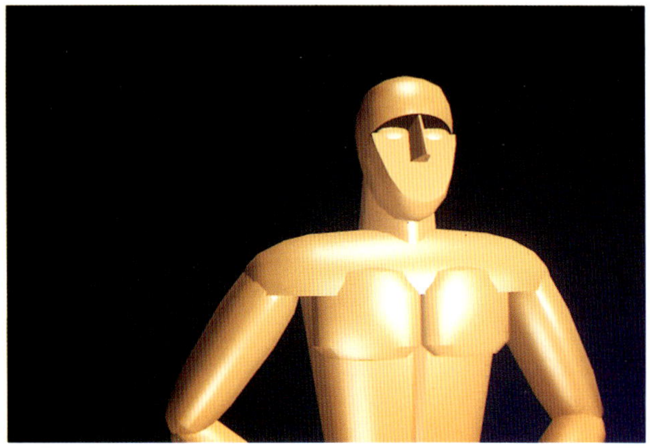
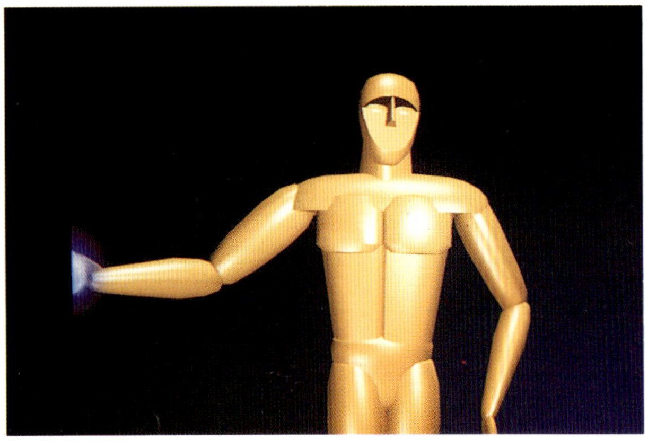
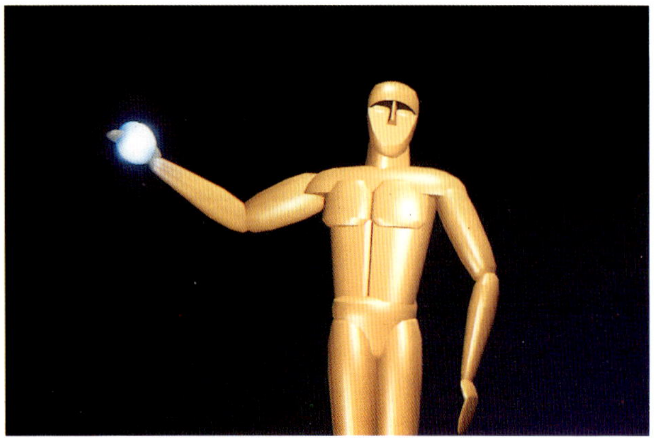

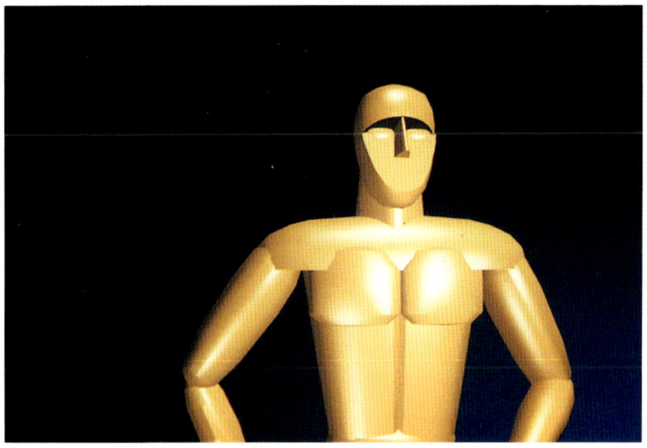

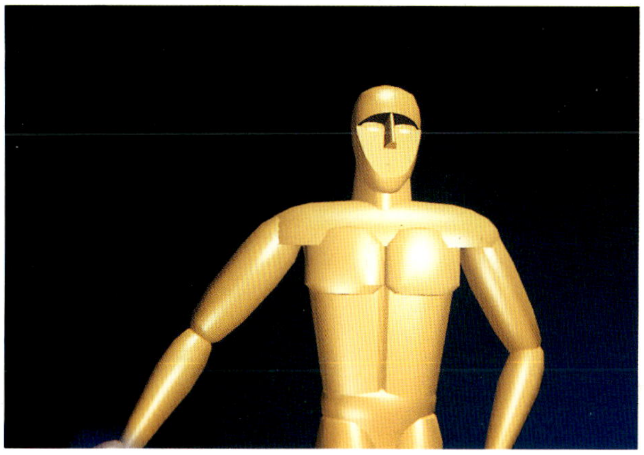

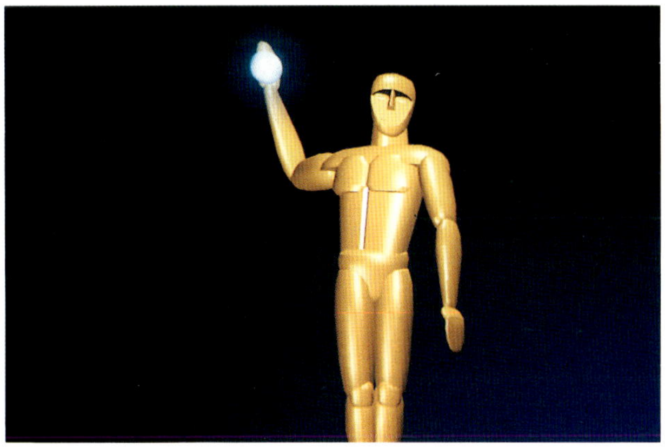

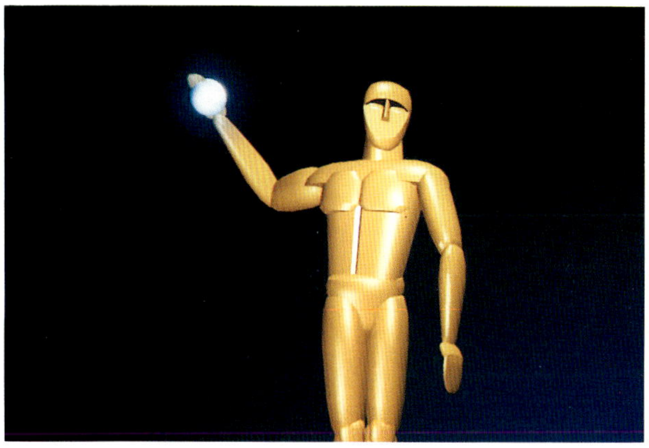

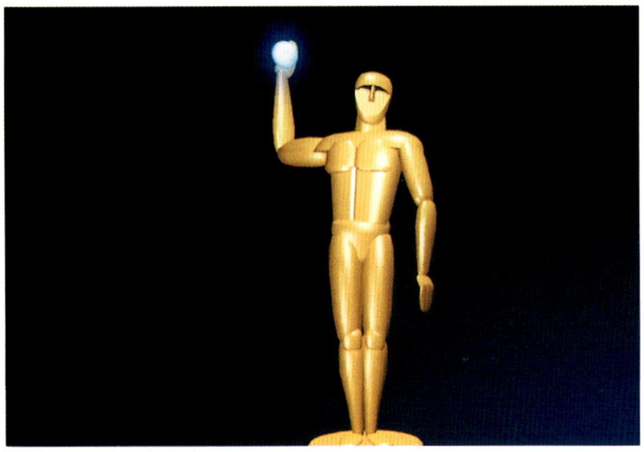

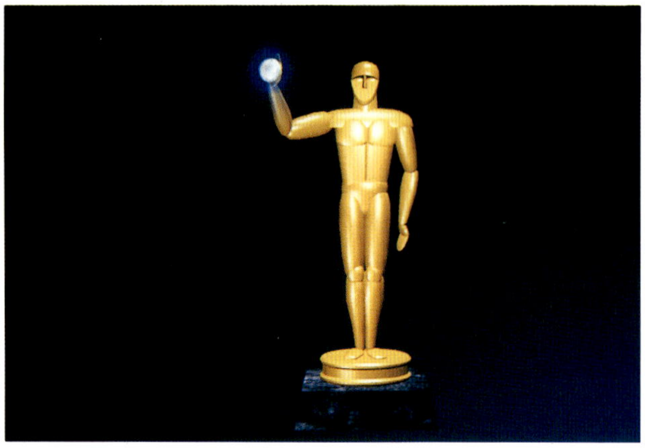

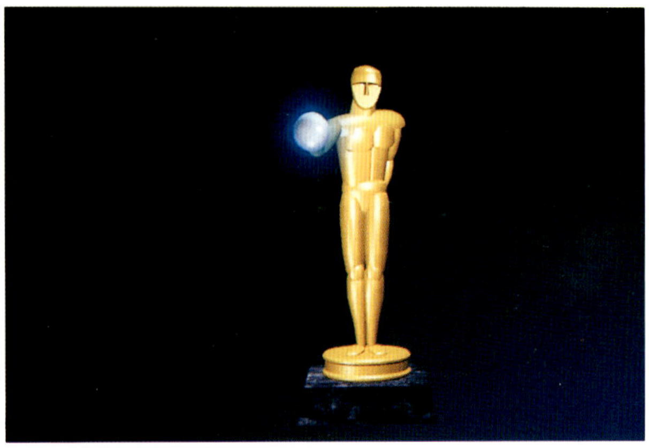

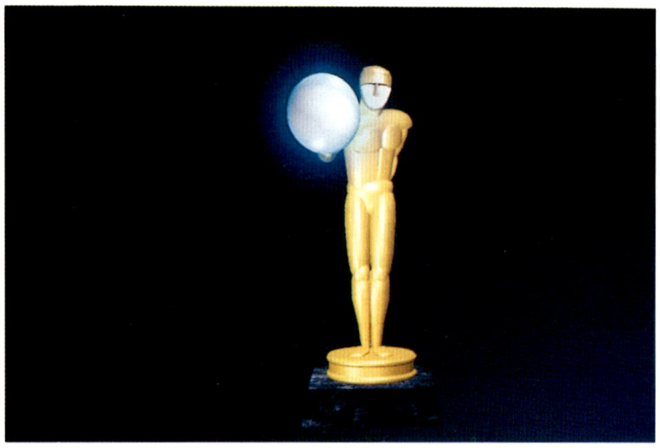

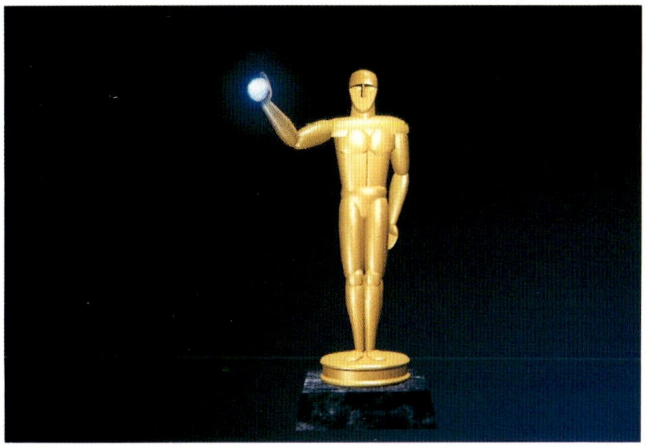
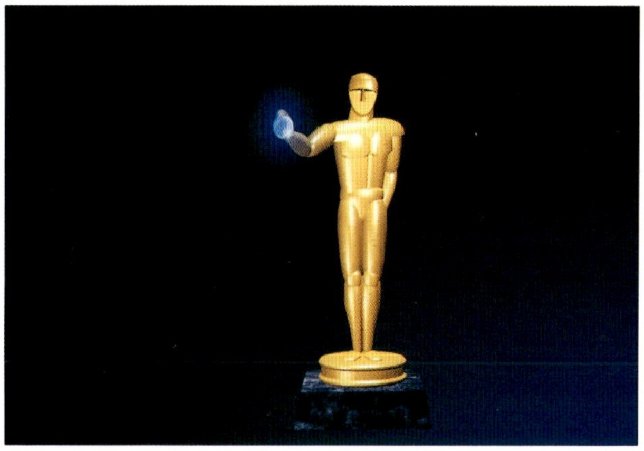
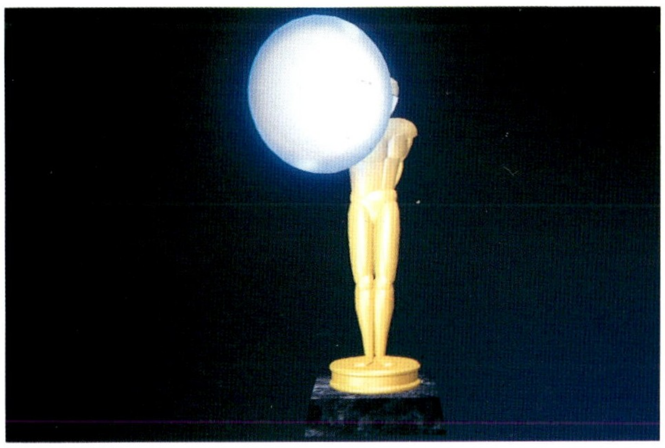
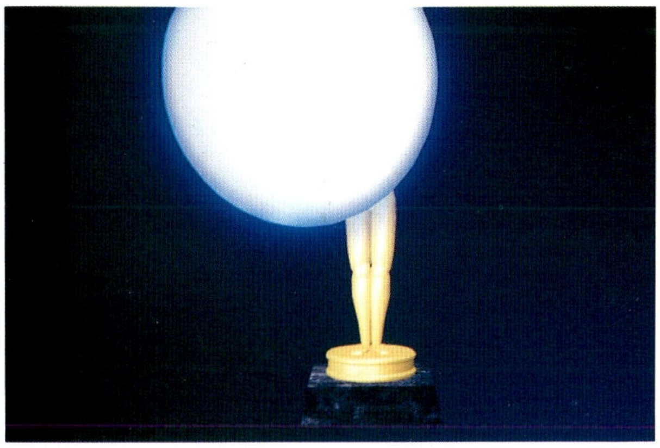

Santa Fe Train

Created as a part of a 30-minute animation segment for a training film for Santa Fe Railways, Chicago, IL.

The 3-D modeled train animation was used to instruct engineers on how their new locomotive worked. Some of the elements of this program were used in the interactive museum display at the Museum of Science and Industry, Chicago, IL.

Producer	Chuck Giehardt
3—D Designer	Tim Knuth
Animation Director	Terry Choate
Graphics	Animation Station Ltd.

Length of Time to Complete Training Segment: 2 months

Length of Time to Complete Museum Segment: 1 week

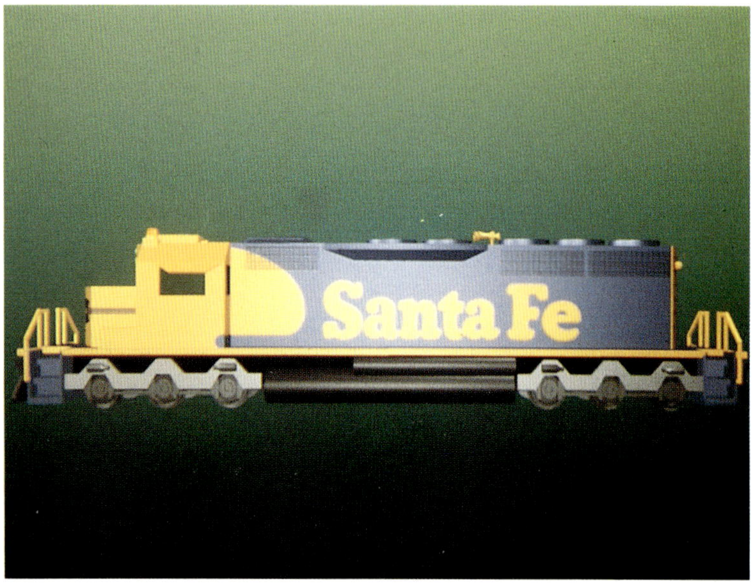

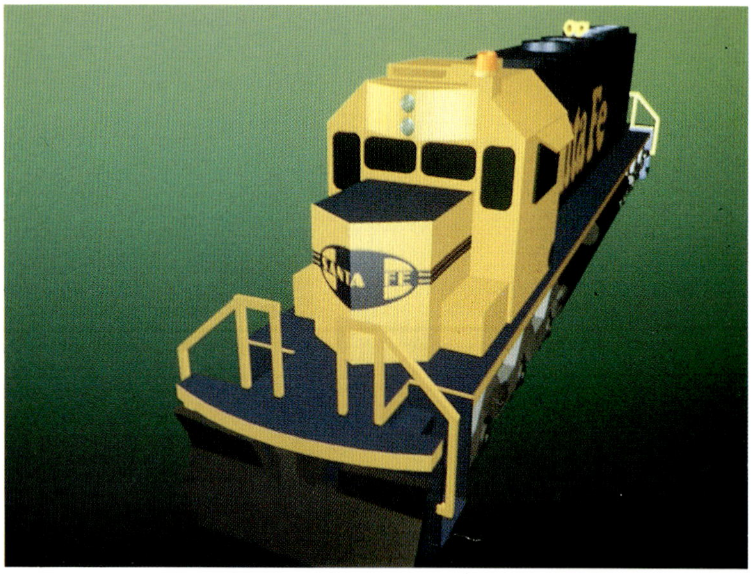

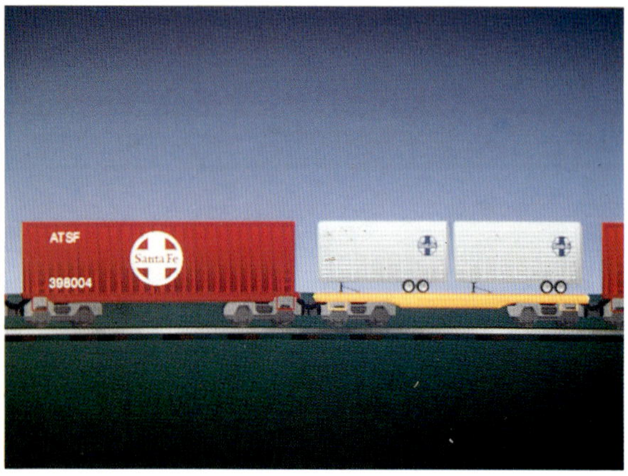

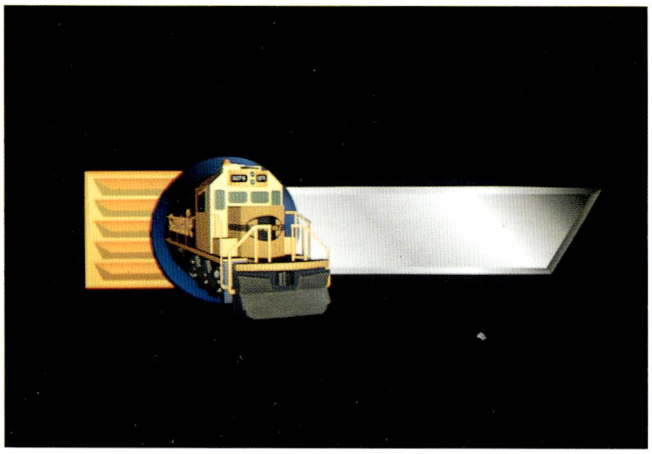

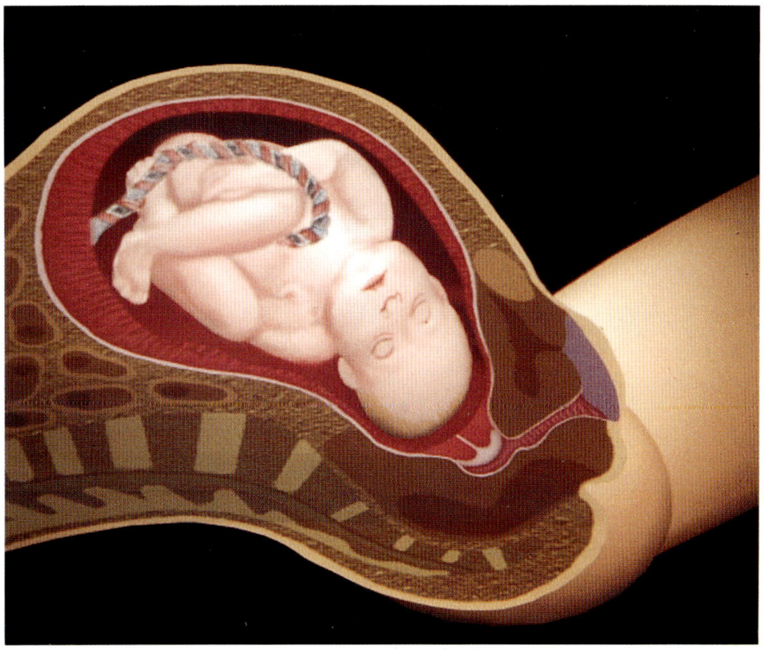

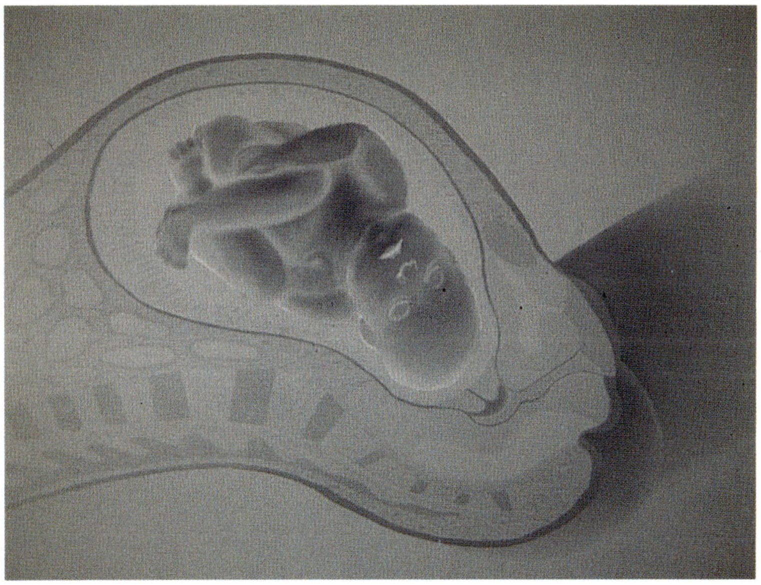

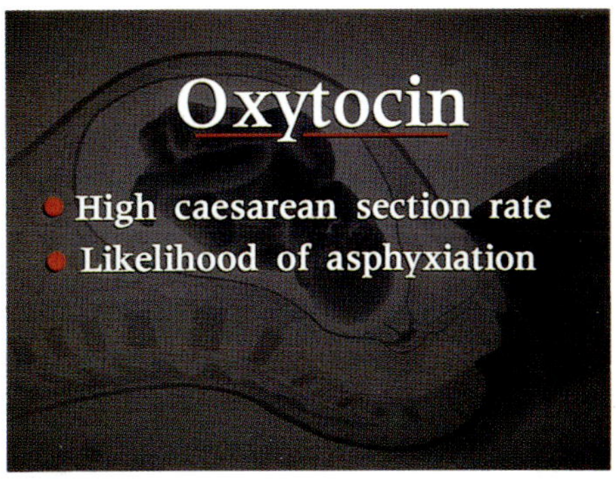

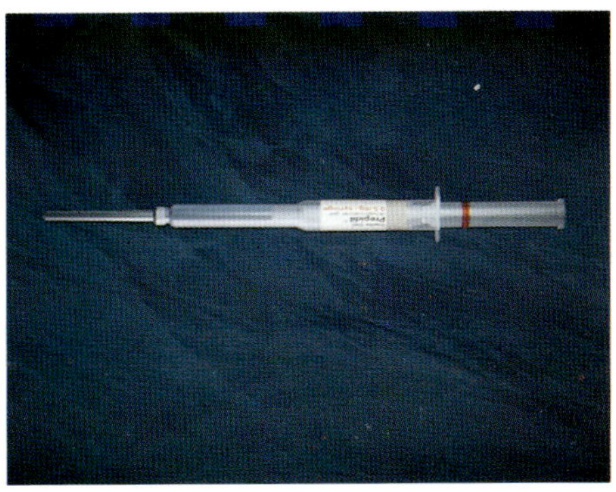

Upjohn Childbirth

Created for The Upjohn Company, Kalamazo, MI., to illustrate the assembly of a syringe for the product Prepidil and its insertion to assist childbirth. Stages of fetal development and cervical conditions were also shown.

Produced by	Jack Lieb Productions, Chicago, IL.
Producer/Director	Warren H. Lieb
Editor	Charles Kite
3—D Graphic Designer	Tim Knuth
Animation Director	Terry Choate
2-D and Paintbox Artist	Terry Choate
Graphics	Animation Station, Ltd.

Length of Time to Complete Work: 1 month

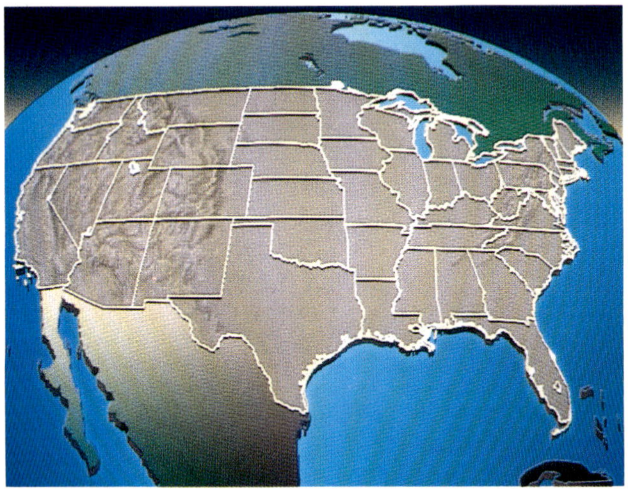

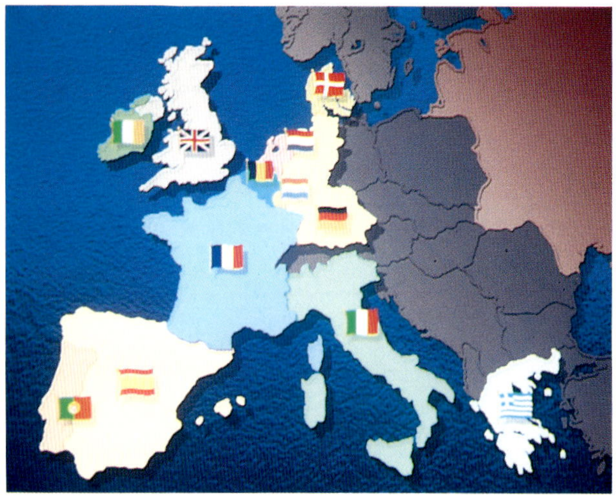

WABC Weather Map

Square D Europe Map

Created for Square D Company, Palatine, IL. The map of Europe is animated to show the company's facilities in the Common Market.

Designer Tamara Manning

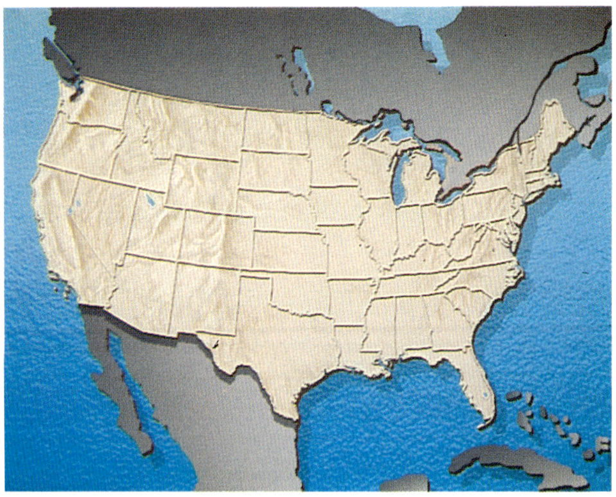

WFLD Weather Map

Shown as resembling examples of similar material for two different television stations. The clients are WABC-TV, New York, NY and WFLD-TV, Chicago, IL.

Designer Tamara Manning

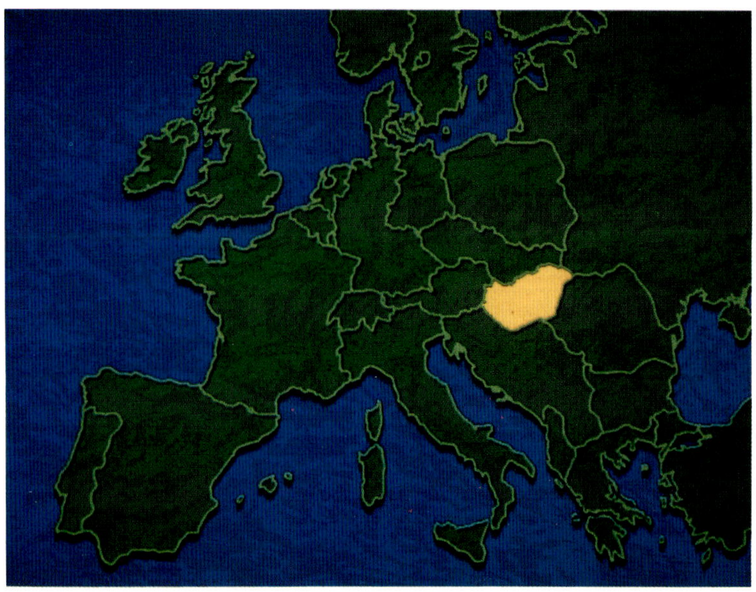

Hungary Coming Out

Created for Producers Group, Ltd., Hollywood, CA. The map was part of a spinning globe animation that zoomed to Europe and then Hungary. Part of a three program documentary project.

Producer/Director Lee Gluckman
Designer Terry Choate

Length of Time to Complete Total Project: 2 months

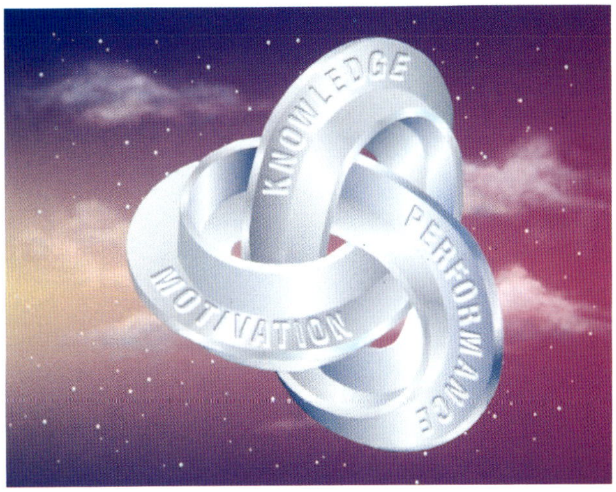

Sharp Mobius

Created as 15 seconds of 2-D animation as part of a training program for Sharp Electronics Corporation, Mahwah, NJ.

Producer Frank Fuchs
Designer Terry Choate

Length of Time to Complete Design and Animation: 2 weeks

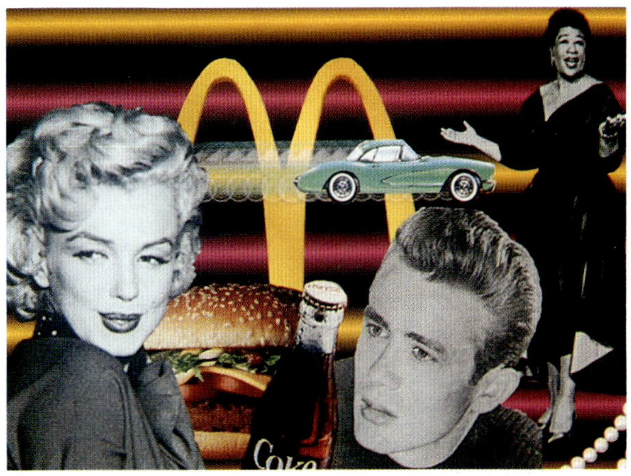

Rock of Ages

Created as an 8-minute program of animation and graphics dedicated to the class of 1959 Hinsdale, Illinois Township High School.

Producer/Designer Terry Choate

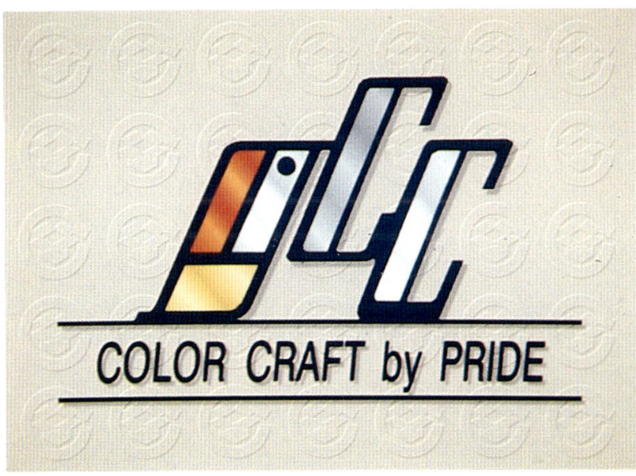

Pride Logo

Created as a logo treatment for the Pride Container Corporation.

Producer Chuck Hodes, Close Encounters Productions, Buffalo Grove, IL.
Designer Terry Choate

Currie Light

Created as logo treatment for a TV spot for Currie Motors, Chicago, IL.

Producer Steve Weiss, 1st Generation Film and Video Productions, Chicago, IL.

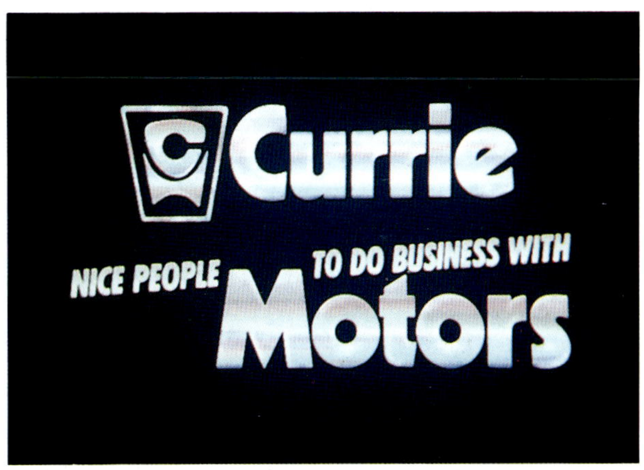

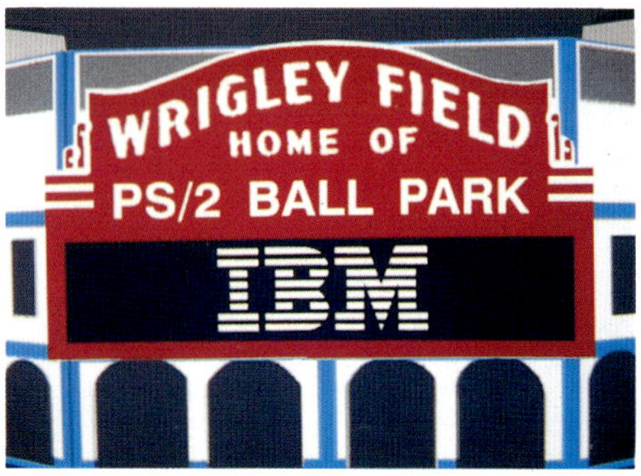

IBM Comdex

Created as three minutes of animation for IBM. Used as open, close and transitions on four video projection systems during a convention live show. The presentation includes a fly over Wrigley Field modeled in 3-D as well as scoreboard animations.

Producer	John Buckland, Caribiner, Inc., Chicago, IL.
3—D Designer	Tim Knuth
Animation Director	Terry Choate
Graphics	Animation Station, Ltd.

Length of Time to Complete Work: 2 weeks

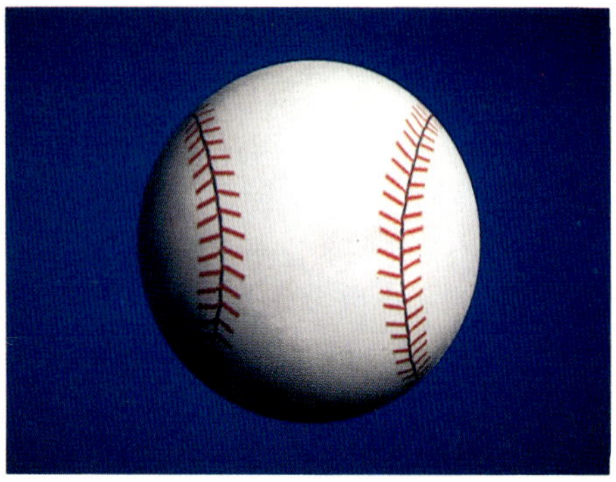

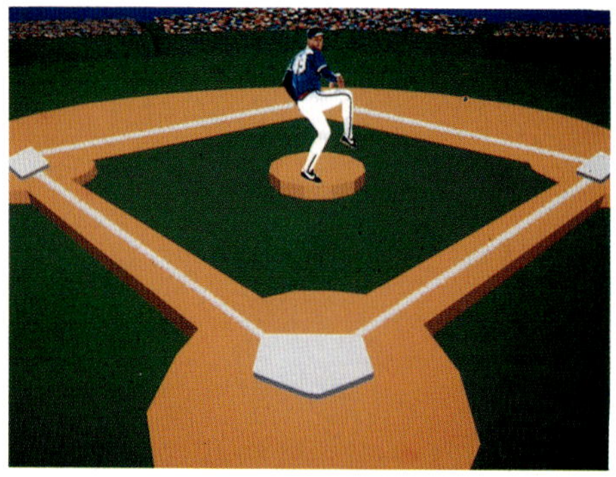

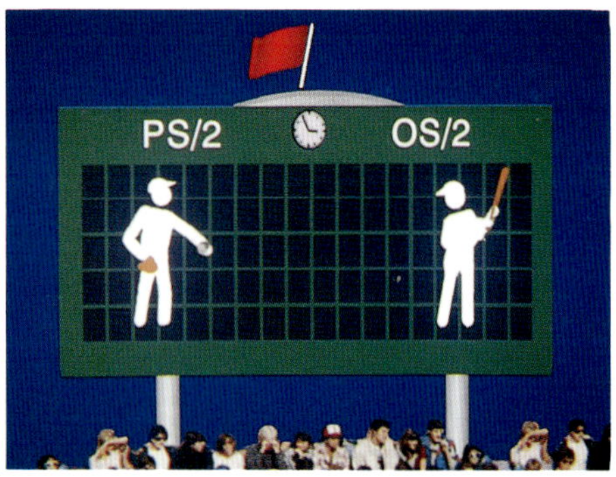

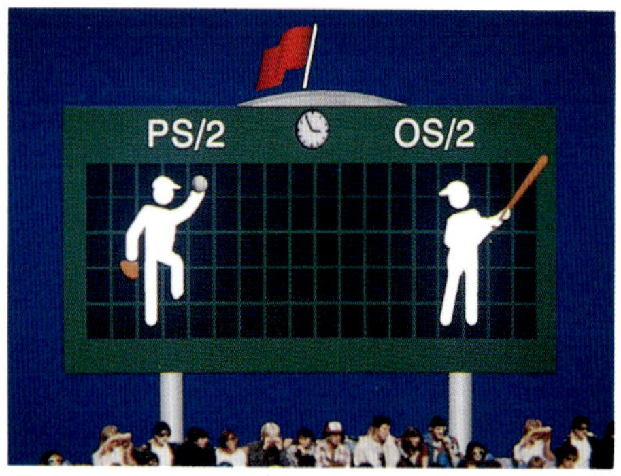

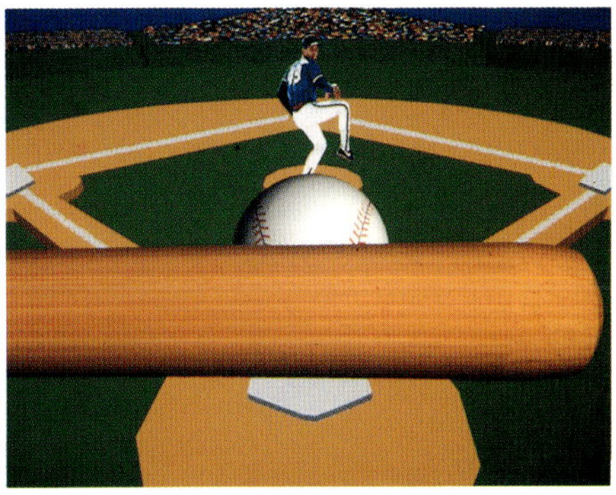

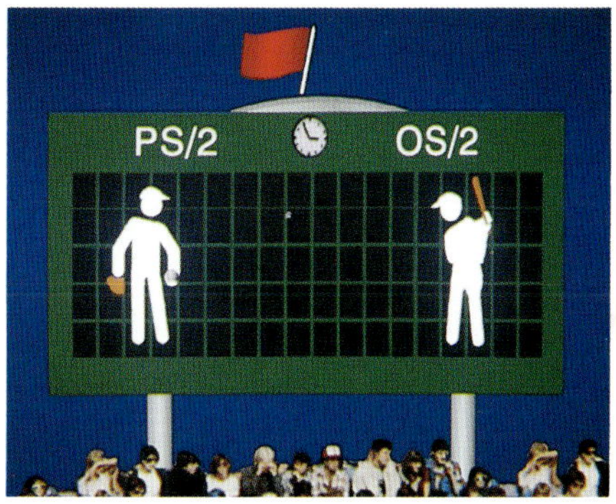

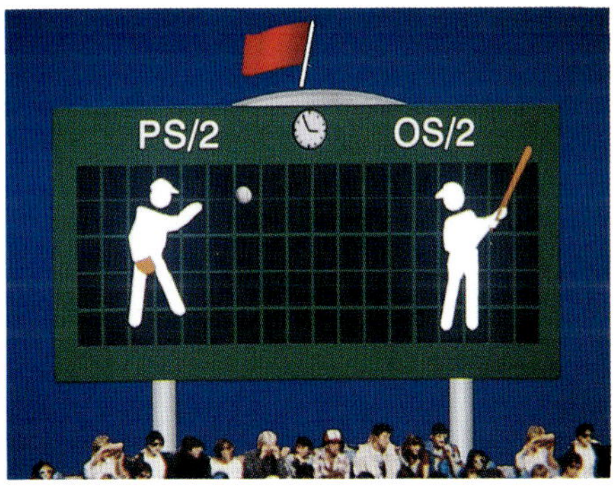

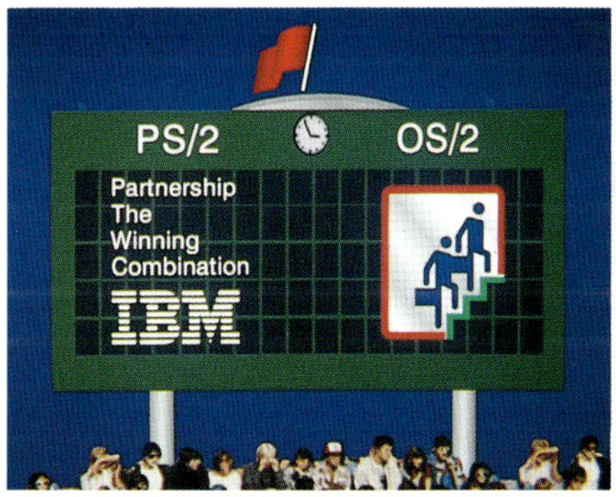

IBM Personal System/2

Windy City West

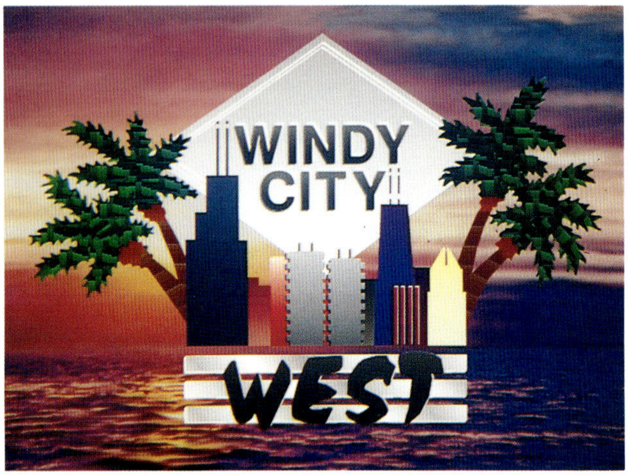

Created as a show logo, promo and transition graphic for an NBC one-hour special featuring Chicago talent now living and successful in Hollywood. The special effects on the program open shows the Hollywood sign becoming the Chicago sign at the snap of host Rob Weller's fingers.

Producer Paul Miller, Chicago Broadcast Communications, Chicago, IL
Designers Tamara Manning, Terry Choate

Length of Time to Complete Design and Production: 1 week

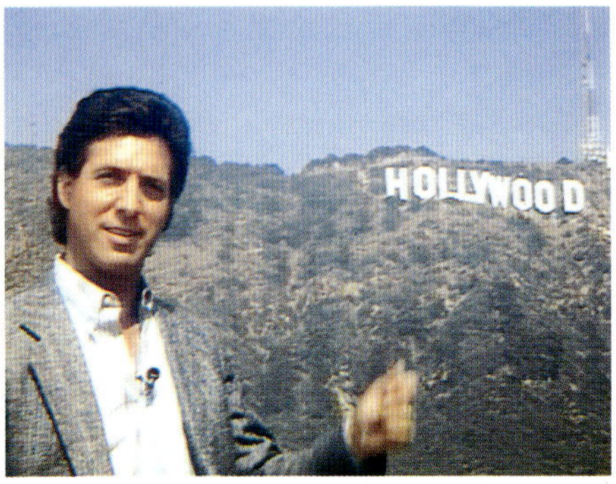

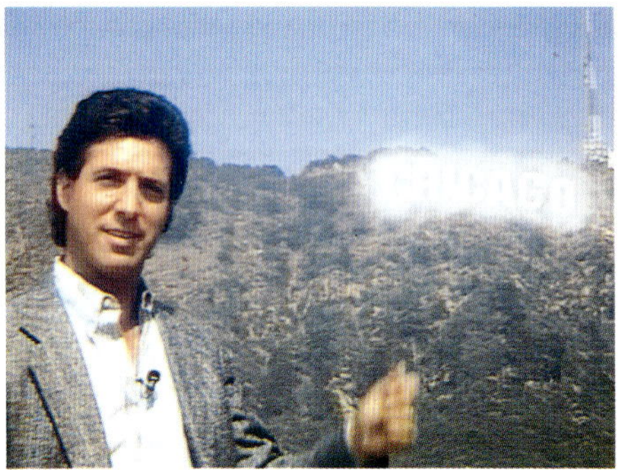

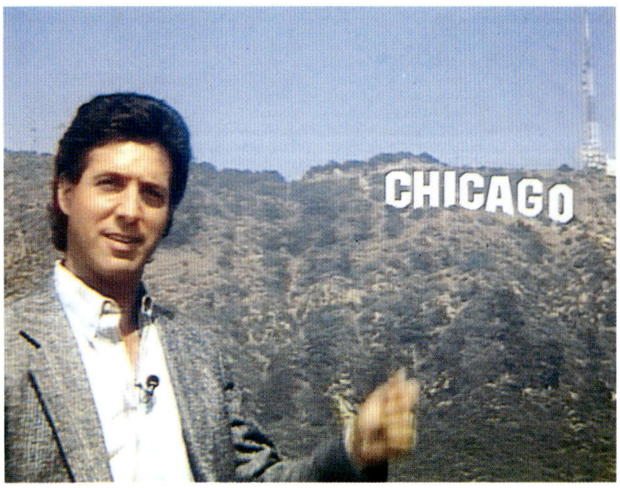

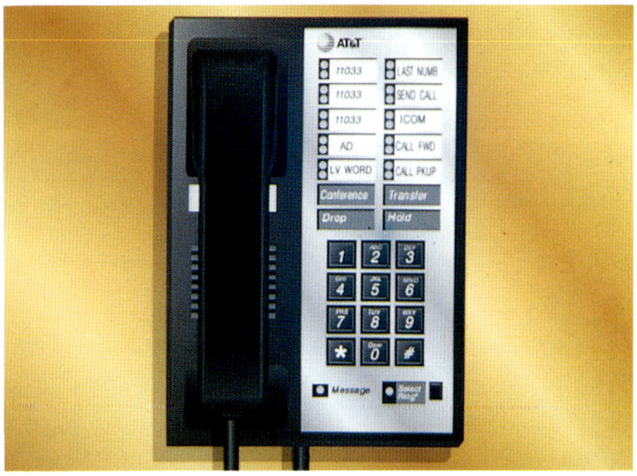

ATT Phone

Created for ATT as five minutes of animation to show how a phone system works.

Producer	Curt Cavnar, Cavnar and Company, Des Plaines, IL.
Animation Director	Terry Choate
2-D and Paintbox Artist	Terry Choate

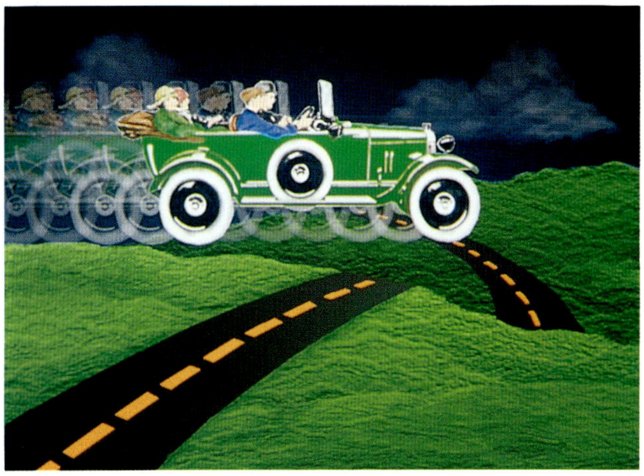

Drive By A Vision

Created as an element for a live show for the Eureka Corporation's annual sales meeting.

Producer	John Buckland, Caribiner, Inc., Chicago, IL
3-D Designer	Tim Knuth
Animation Director	Terry Choate
2-D and Paintbox Artist	Terry Choate
Graphics	Animation Station, Ltd.

Landfill

Created as cross view animation of a landfill.

Producer	Jim Benefield, Waste Management, Inc., Oak Brook, IL.
Designer	Terry Choate

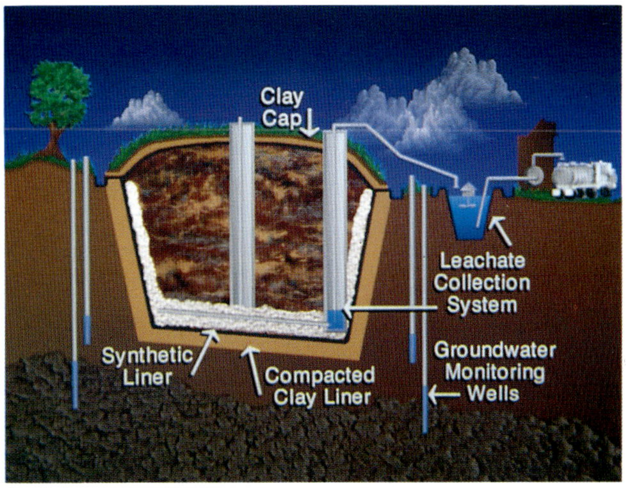

Meeting

Created as a minute of 3-D and 2-D animation on how to conduct a meeting.

Producer	Mark Stober, The John Volk Co., Chicago, IL
3-D Designer	Tim Knuth
Animation Director	Terry Choate
2-D and Paintbox Artist	Terry Choate
Graphics	Animation Station, Ltd.

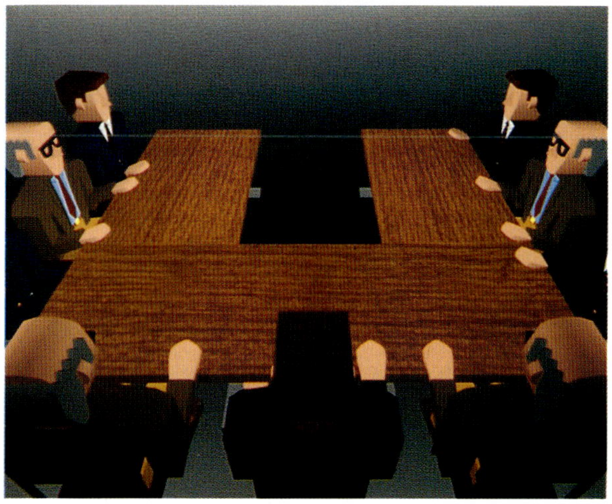

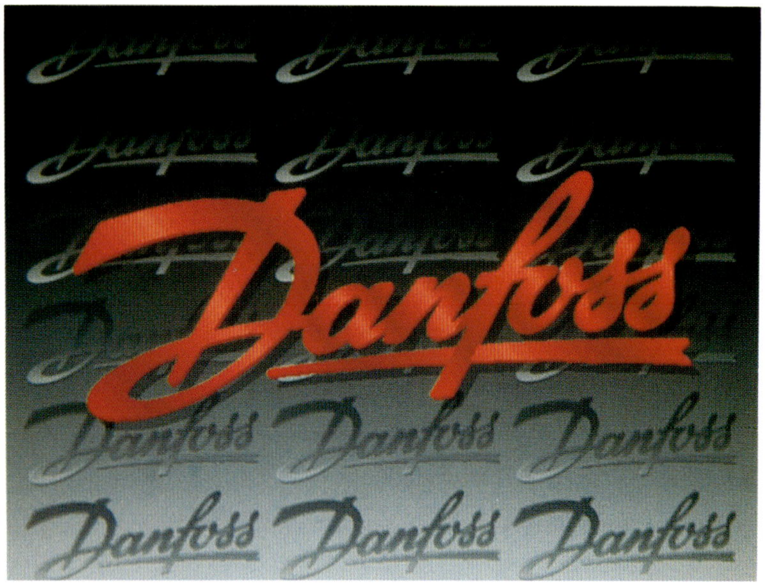

DANFOSS

Created as a logo treatment.

Producer	Dave Tucker, At The Post, Woodstock, IL.
Animation Director	Terry Choate
2-D and Paintbox Artist	Terry Choate

LEGENDS

Created as a show logo for Southwest Conference Awards which was a part of a three-minute animation piece.

Producer	Kevin Foley, KEF Media, Chicago, IL.
Animation Director	Terry Choate
2-D and Paintbox Artist	Terry Choate

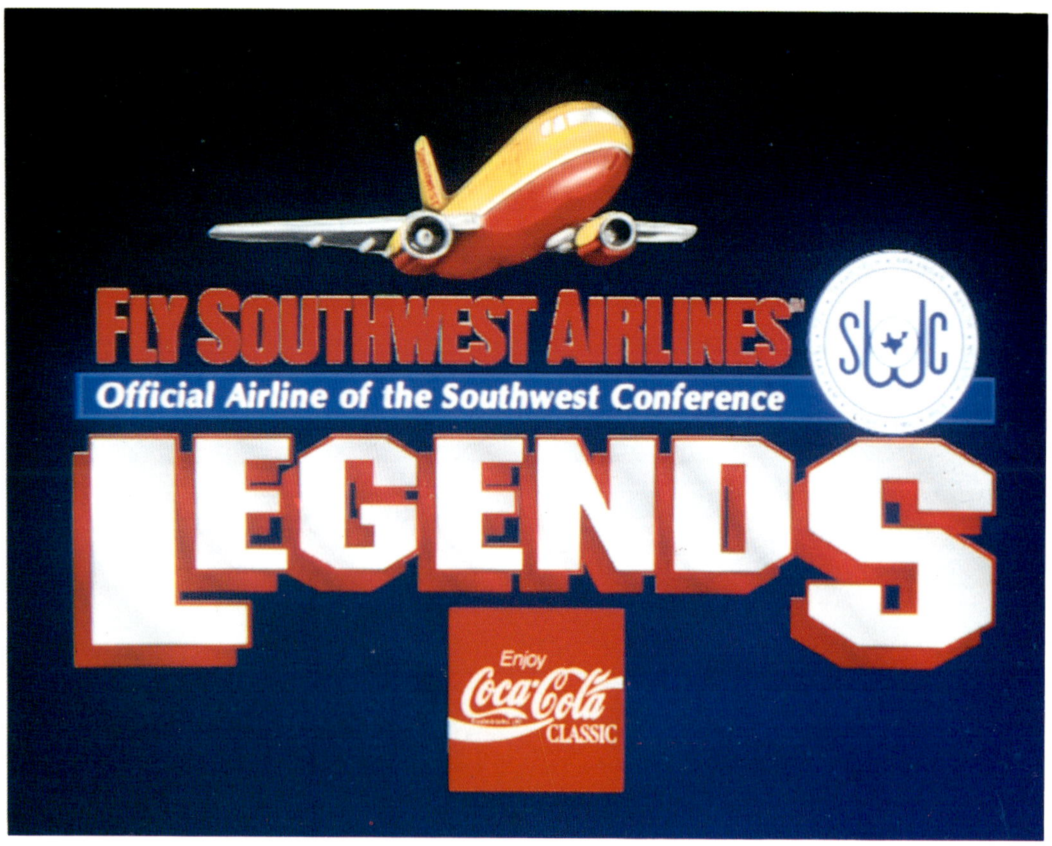

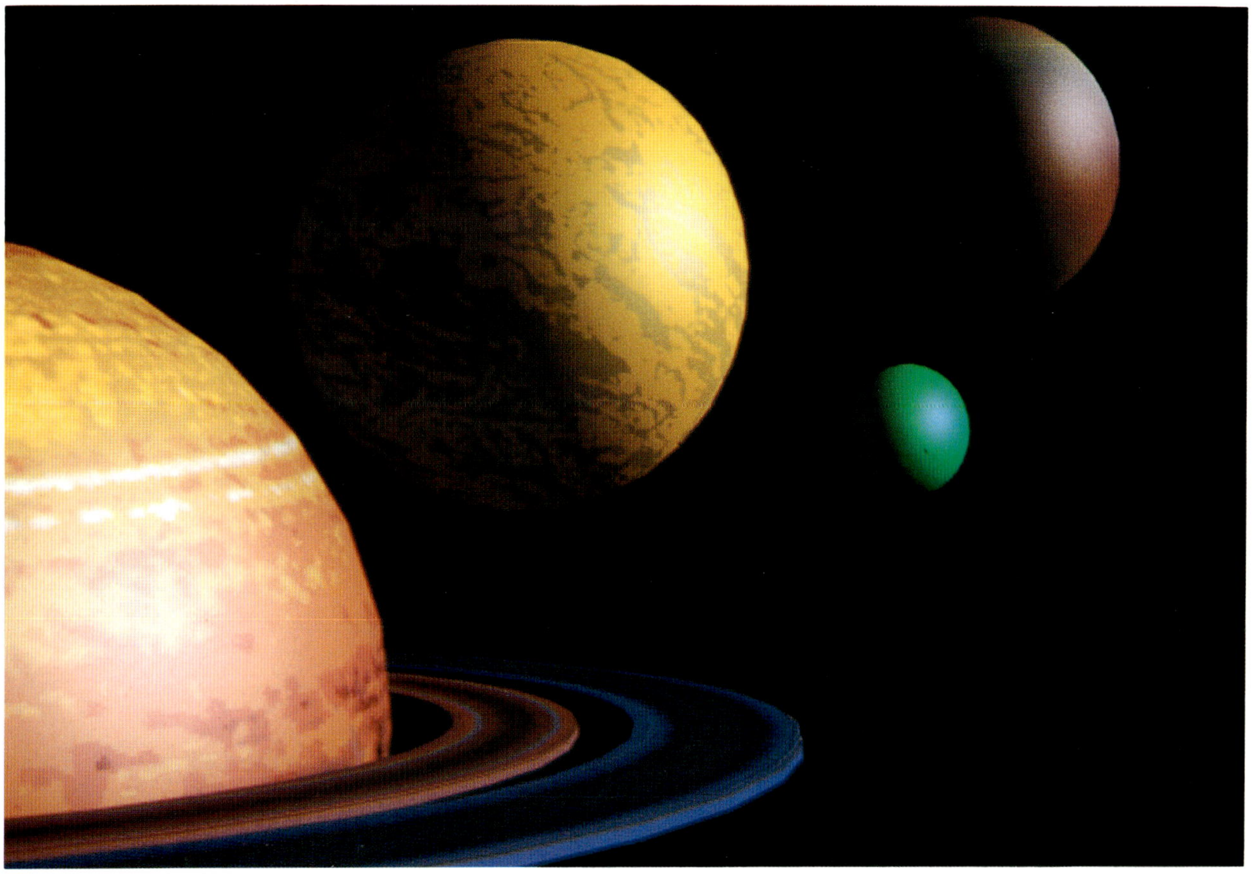

UNIVERSE

Created as a generic 3-D animation of the Universe.

3-D Designer	Tim Knuth
Animation Director	Terry Choate
2-D and Paintbox Artist	Terry Choate
Graphics	Animation Station, Ltd.

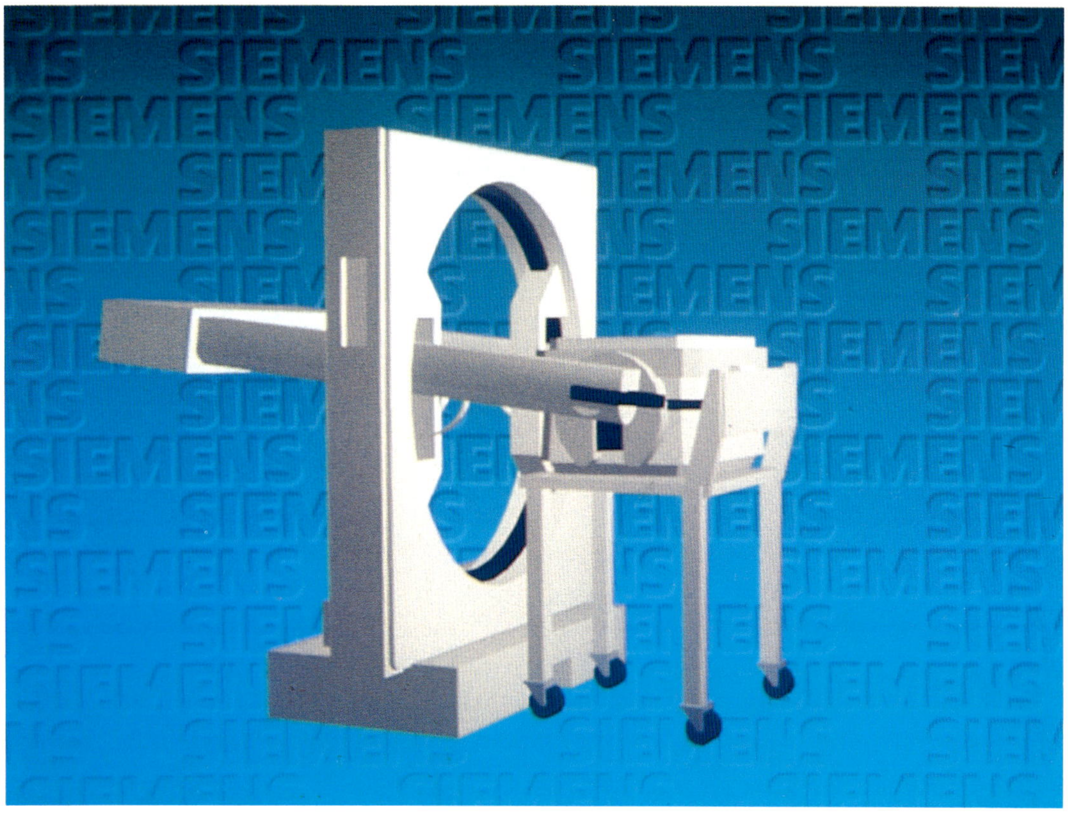

DIACAM

Created as 3-D animation of the movements of a diagnostics scanning machine (DIACAM) manufactured by the Siemens Corporation.

Produced by	Technigraph Studio, Inc., Elk Grove Village, IL
Producer/Director	Leo J. Cox
3-D Graphic Designer	Tim Knuth
2-D Paintbox	Terry Choate

Length of Time to Complete Work—1 month

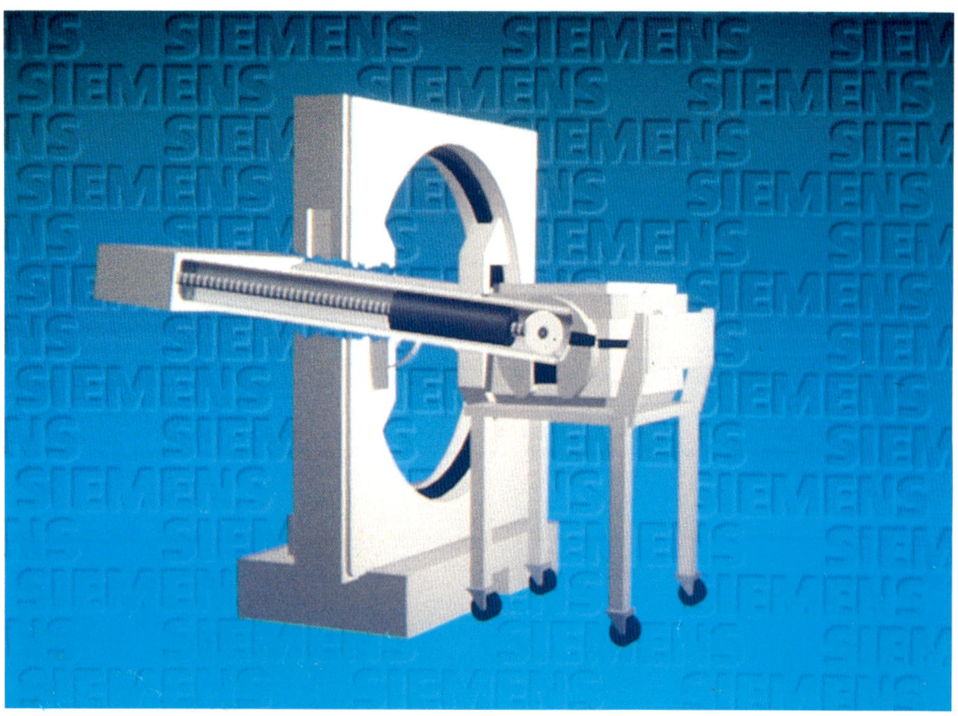

Siegal Strip Man

Created as a :04, 3-D Animation. Originally drawn for the head of Siegal Steel 42 years ago for $10 by man he met in a diner. Still used as a part of the corporate logo. Animation Station retained the original forties feeling in their high-tech design but was requested to remove an original cigar in the man's mouth.

Producer	Steve Weiss, 1st Generation Film and Video Productions, Chicago, IL
3-D Designer	Derek Chimenti

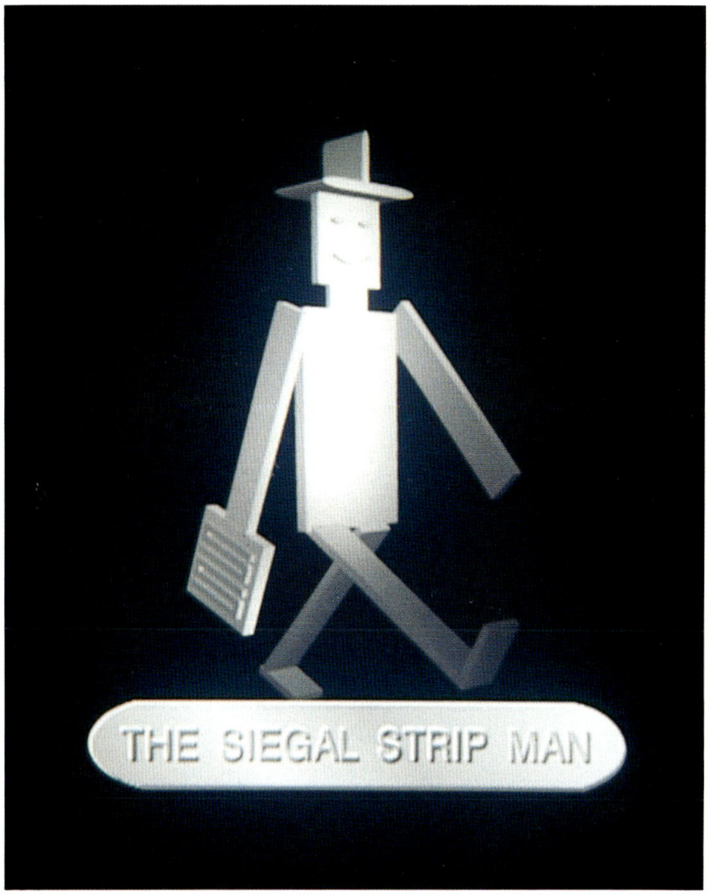

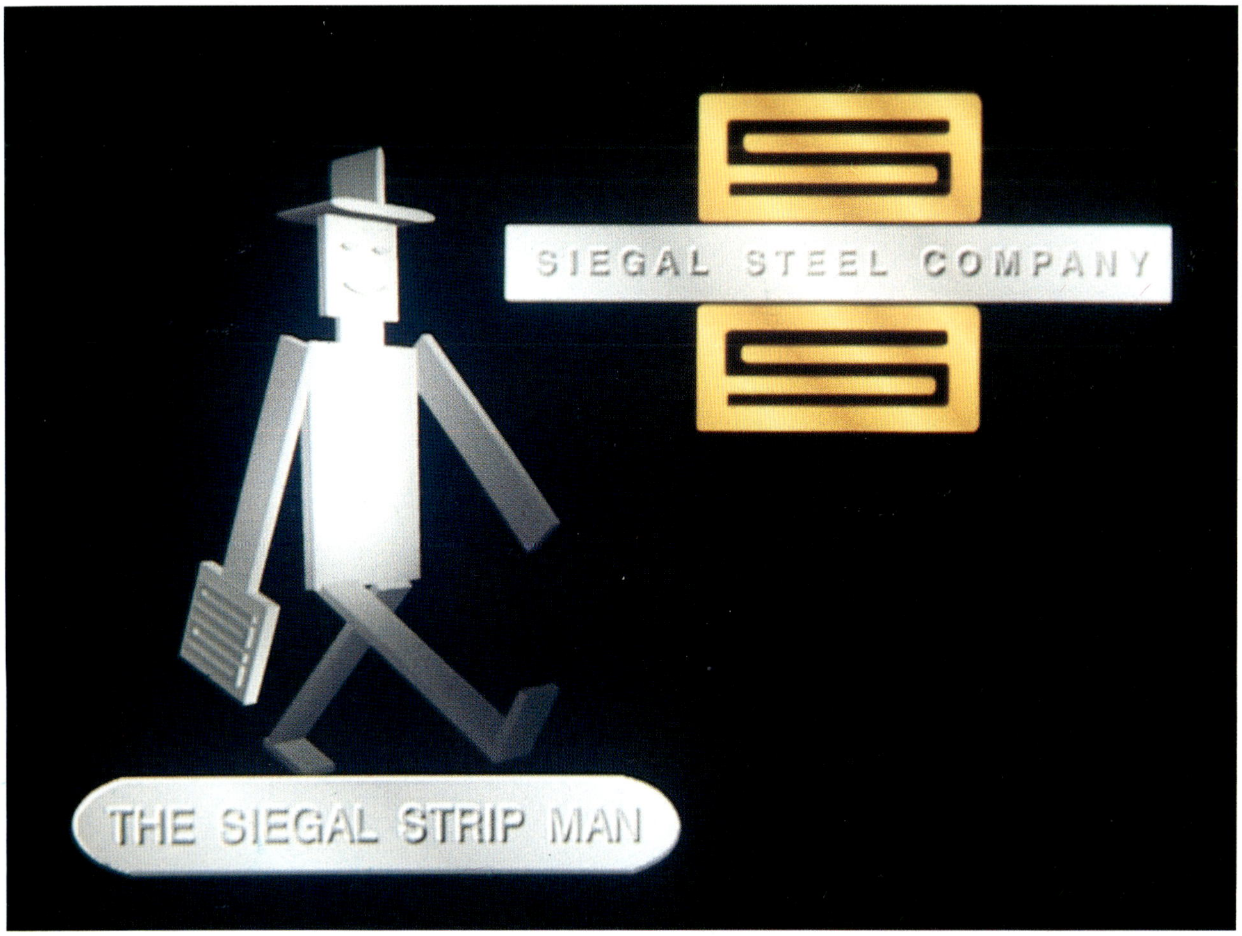

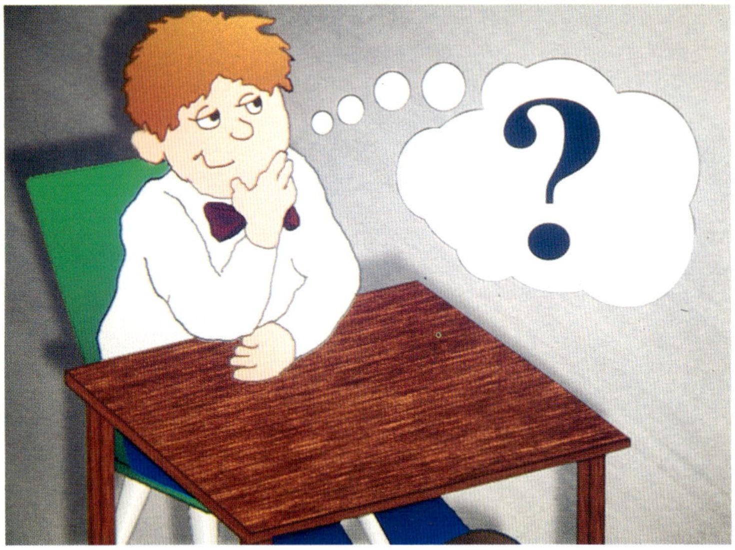

Canteen Corporation Recruitment

Created as a 4 minute opening animation for a recruitment video produced for the Canteen Corporation. Final picture shows rotoscoped electrical charges which were painted frame by frame over single images of digitized video.

Produced by	J. Cunningham Productions, Hinsdale, IL
Producer/Director	James Cunningham
3-D Animator	Tim Knuth
Animation Director	Terry Choate
Paintbox	Terry Choate

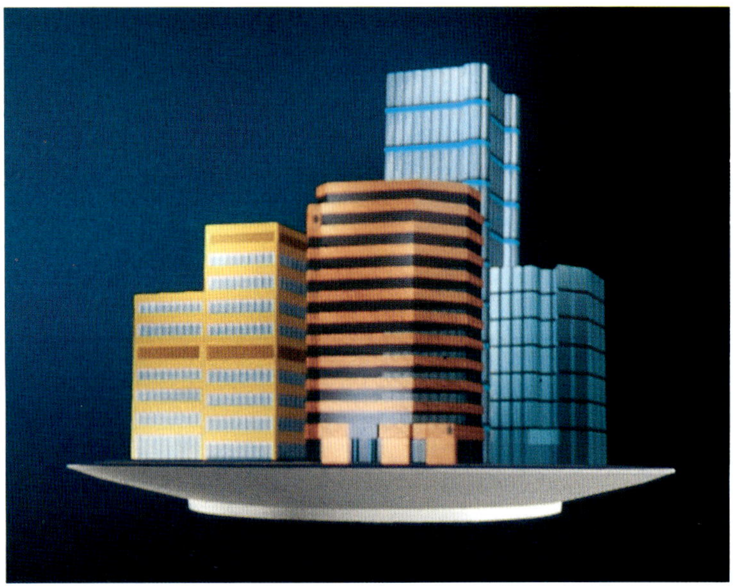

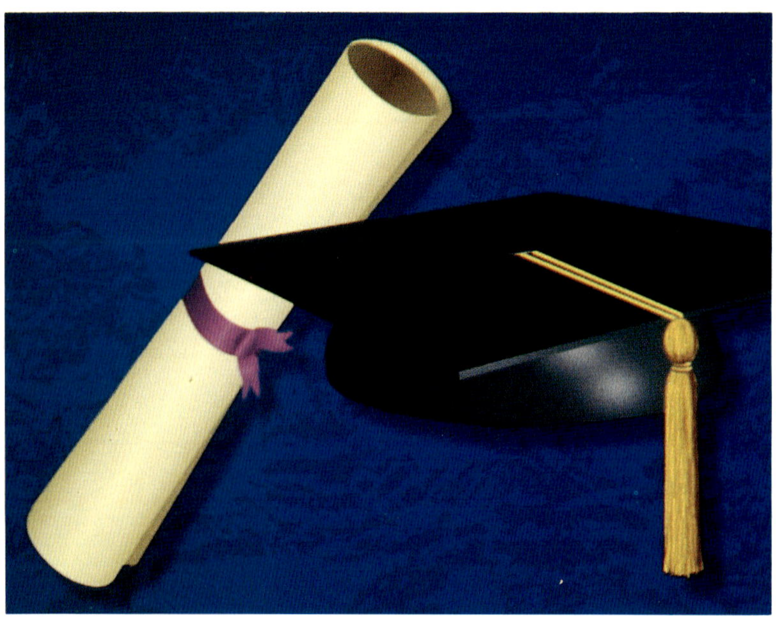

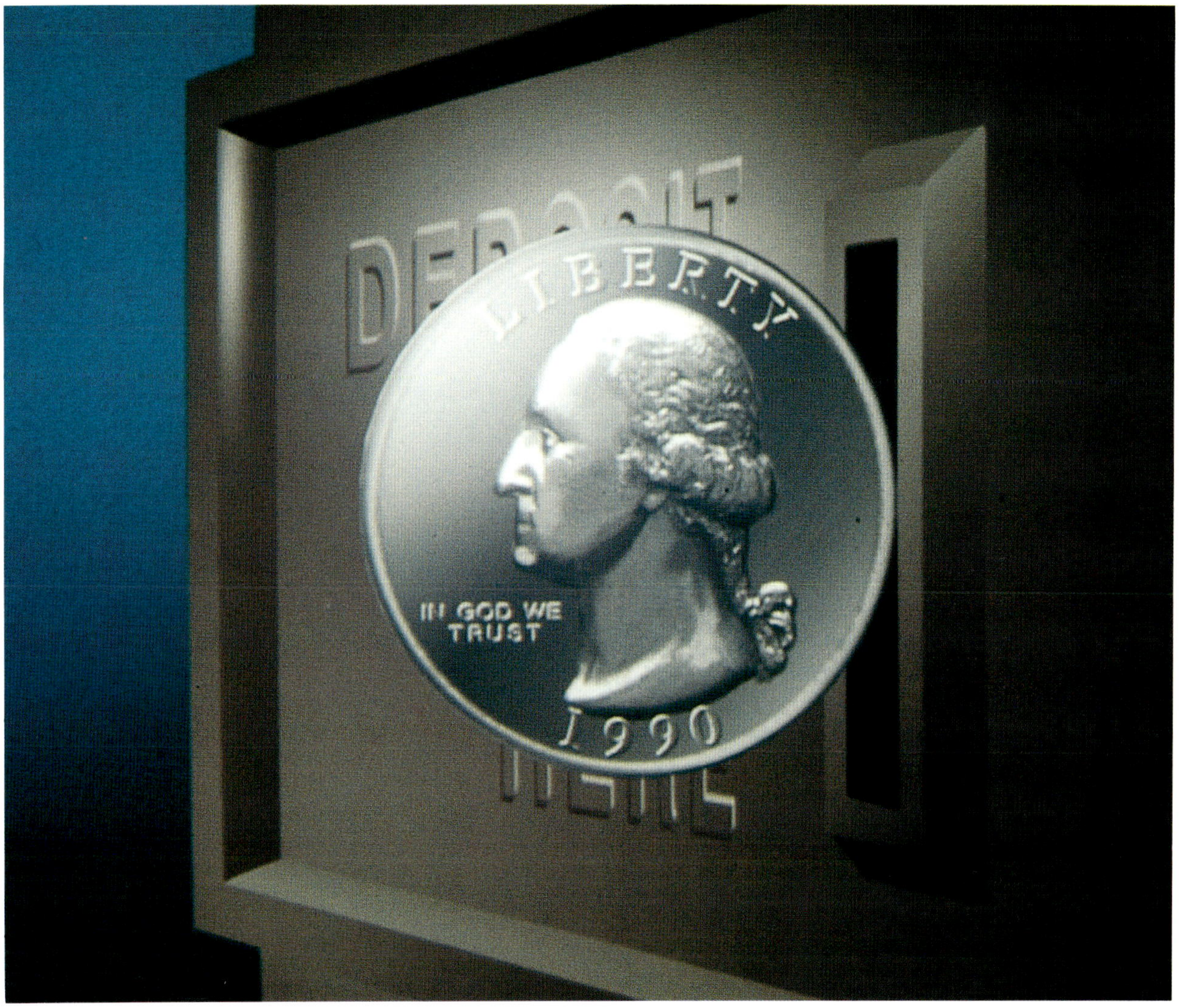
LIBERTY
IN GOD WE TRUST
1990

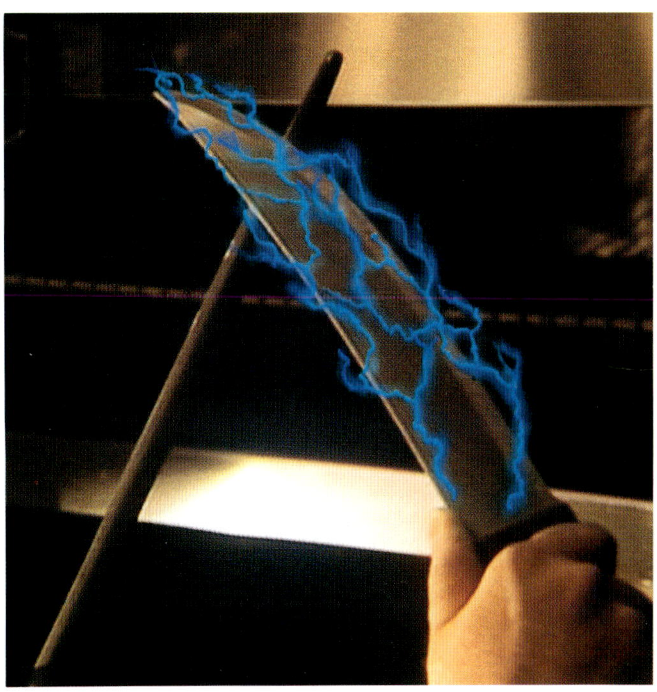

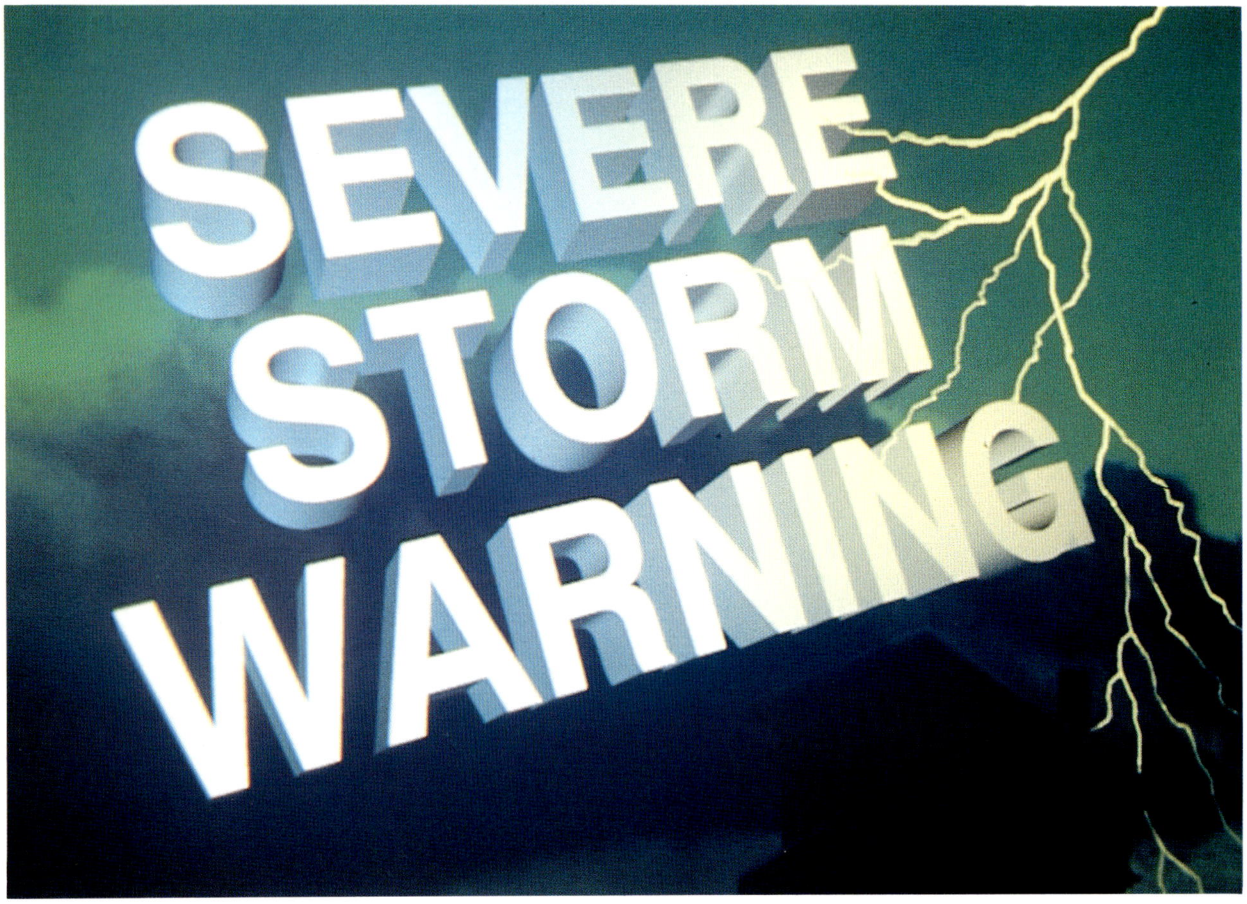

KTVI WEATHER

Created as bumpers for daily weather presentations for KTVI Television, St. Louis.

3-D Design	Terry Choate
Paintbox	Terry Choate

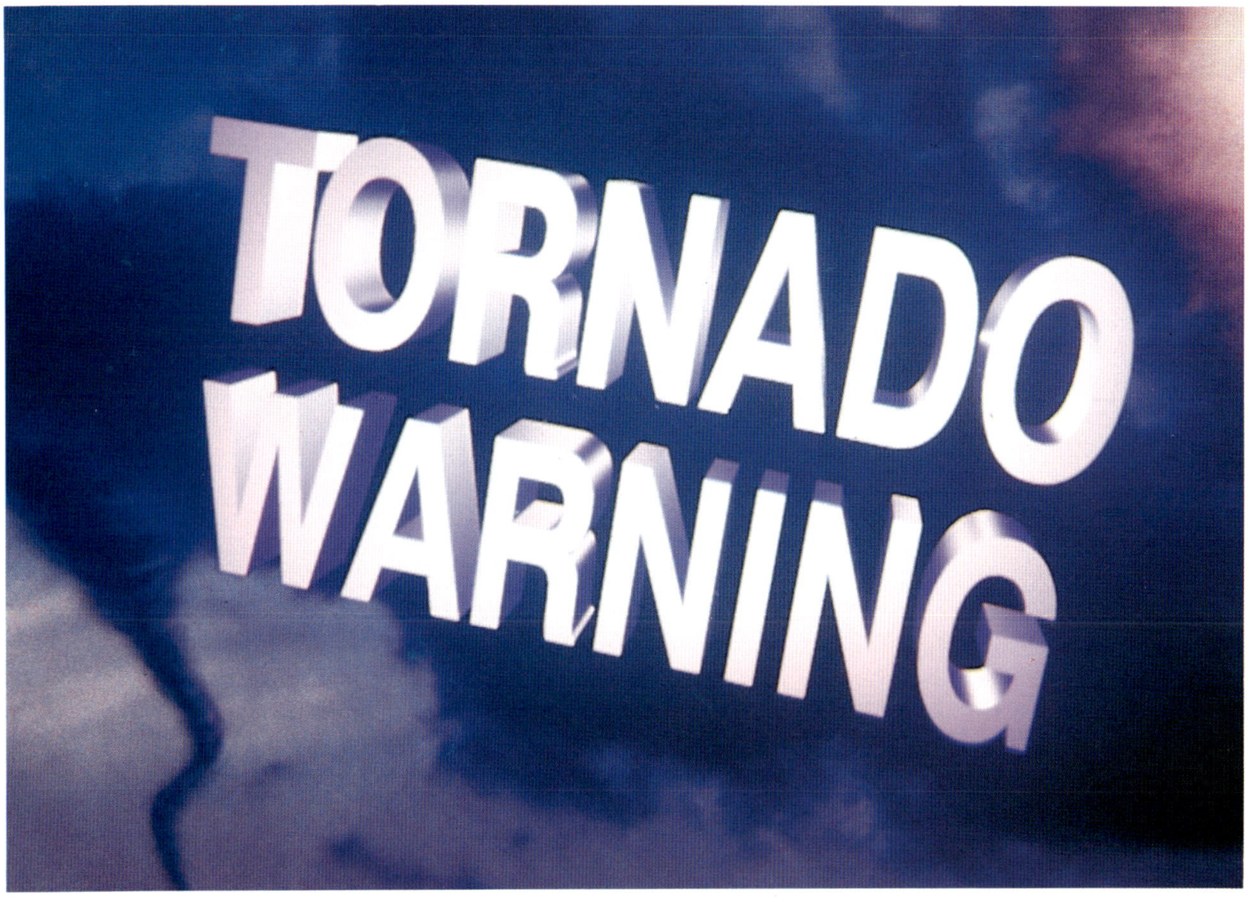

Animation Station Logo Opener

Created as a 3-D logo opener for demo reels for Animation Station Ltd.

3-D Designer Derek Chimenti

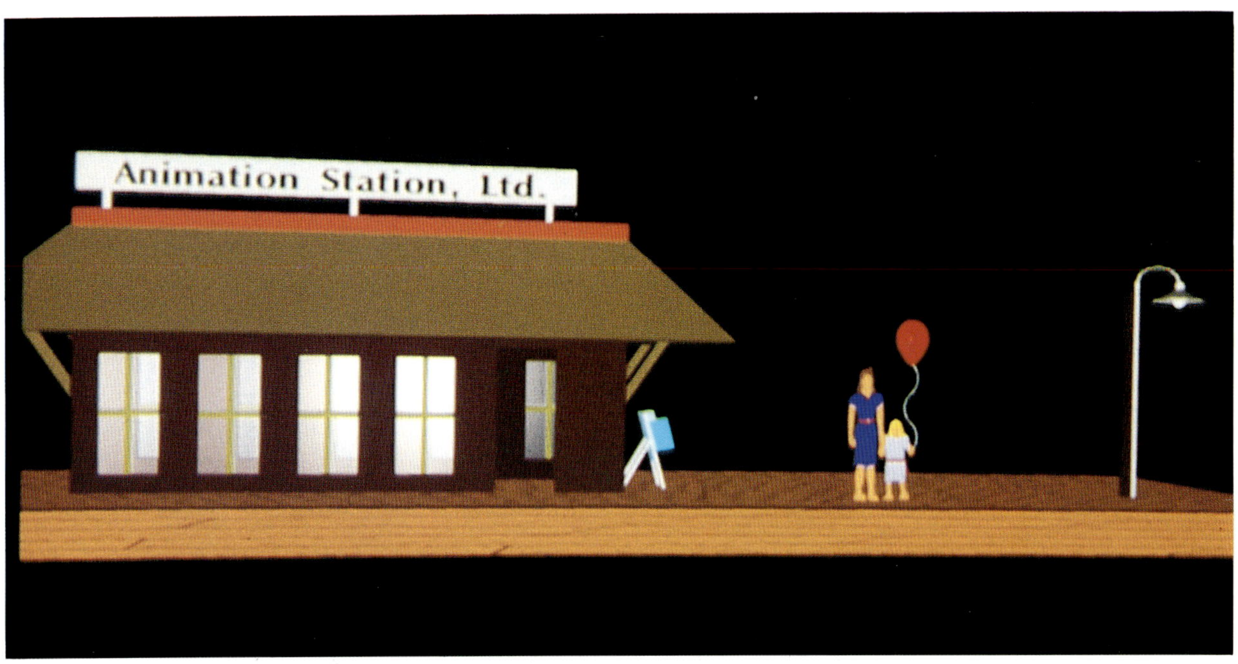

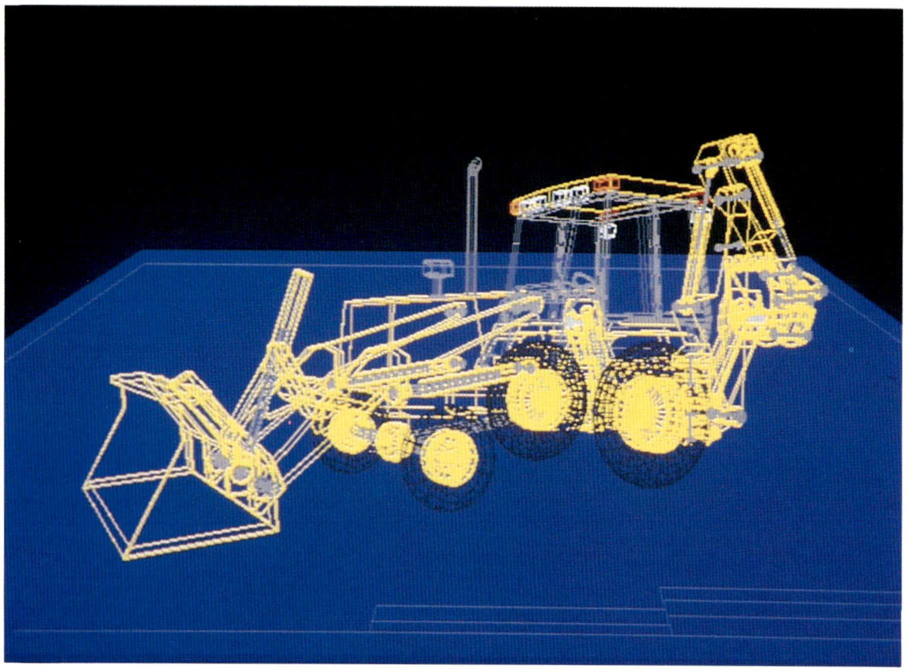

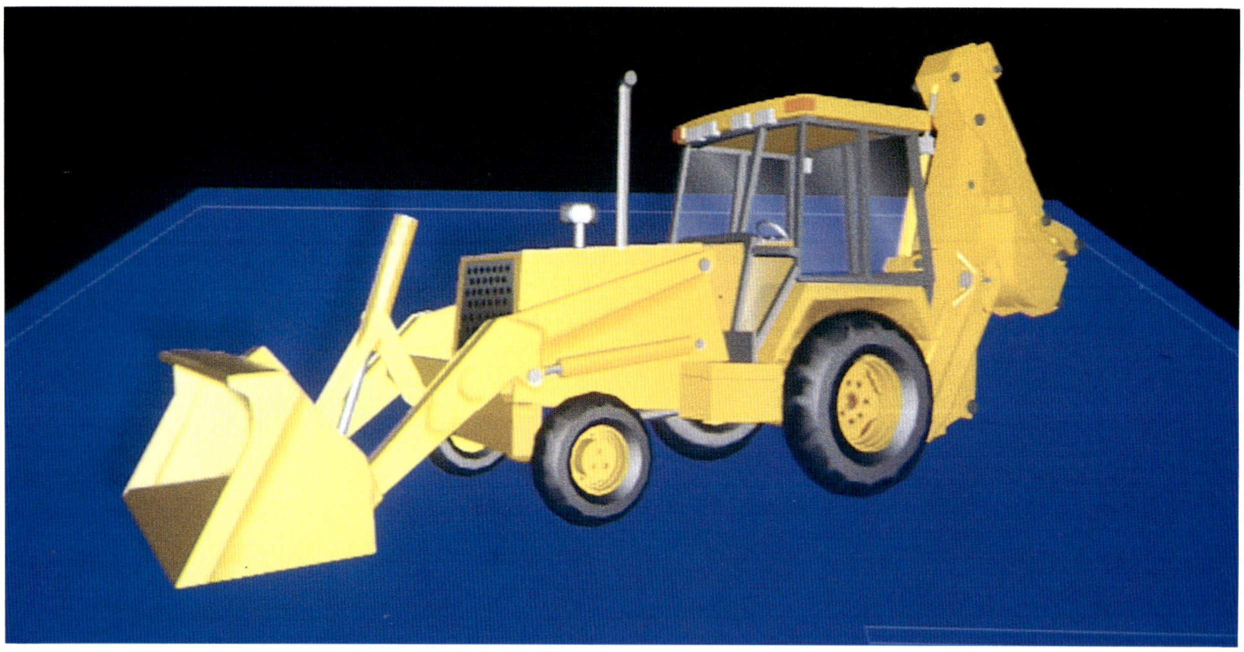

John Deere Videowall

Created as a 3-D animation for a videowall trade show presentation to introduce a new model John Deere tractor.

The animation was rendered in colored wire frame mode to create a unique look. The tractor rotated 360 degrees over a blueprint and then dissolved into a fully rotated frame showing the details of the tractor. The logo was also animated in 3-D with the box element tumbling in from the center while the deer leaped from the box from the right and the words from the left. The theme "Only the Best" was modeled and painted.

Produced by	AGS&R Communications
Producer	Ed Swain
3-D	Derek Chimenti
Paintbox	Terry Choate

Length of Time to Complete Work—4 weeks

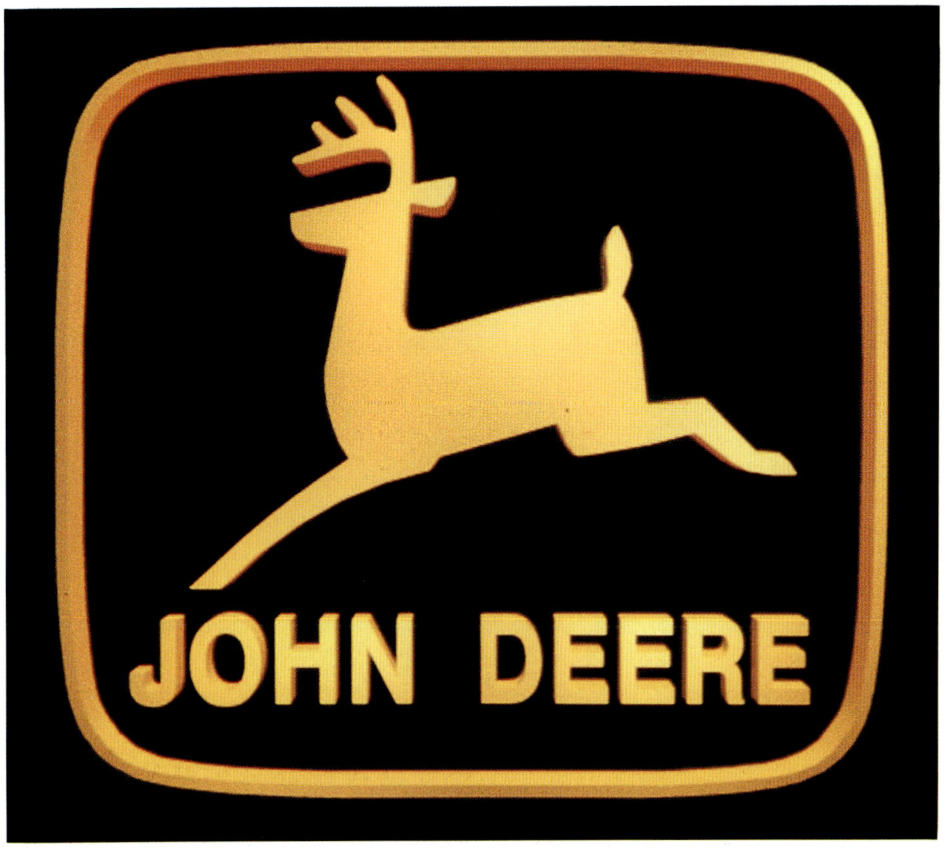
JOHN DEERE

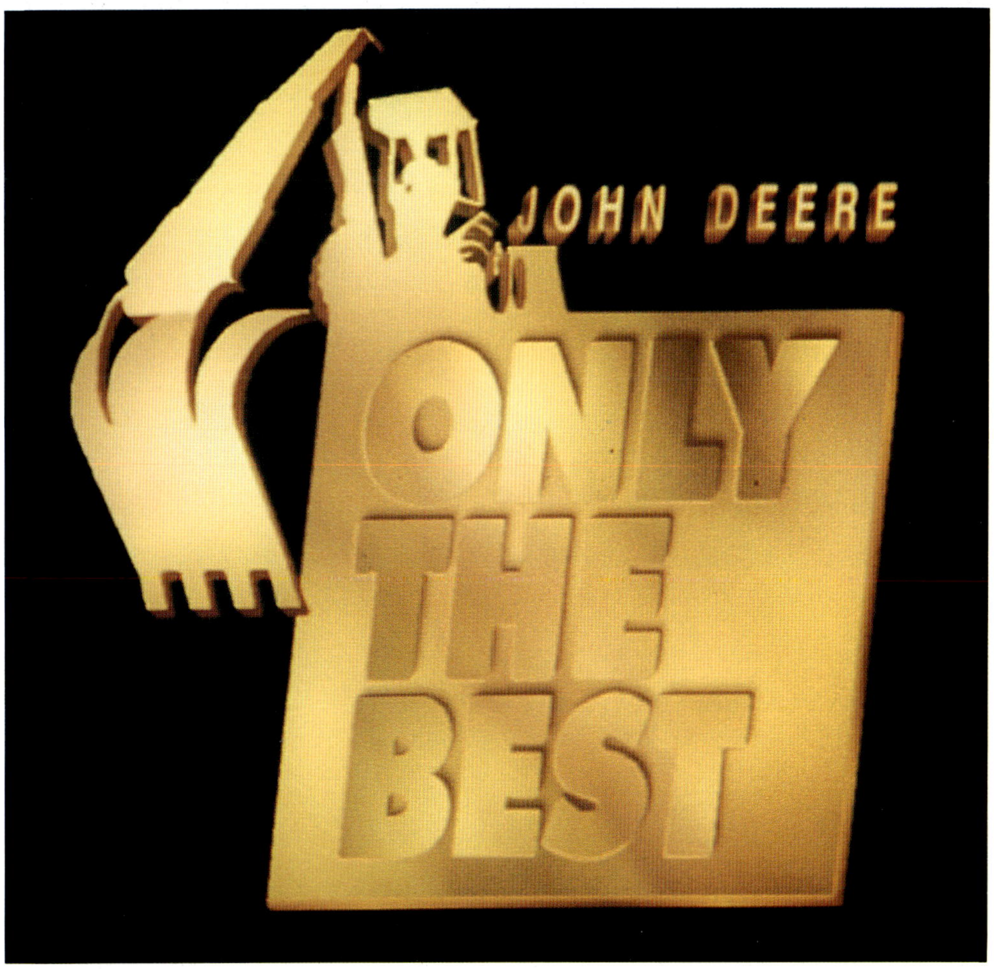
JOHN DEERE
ONLY
THE
BEST

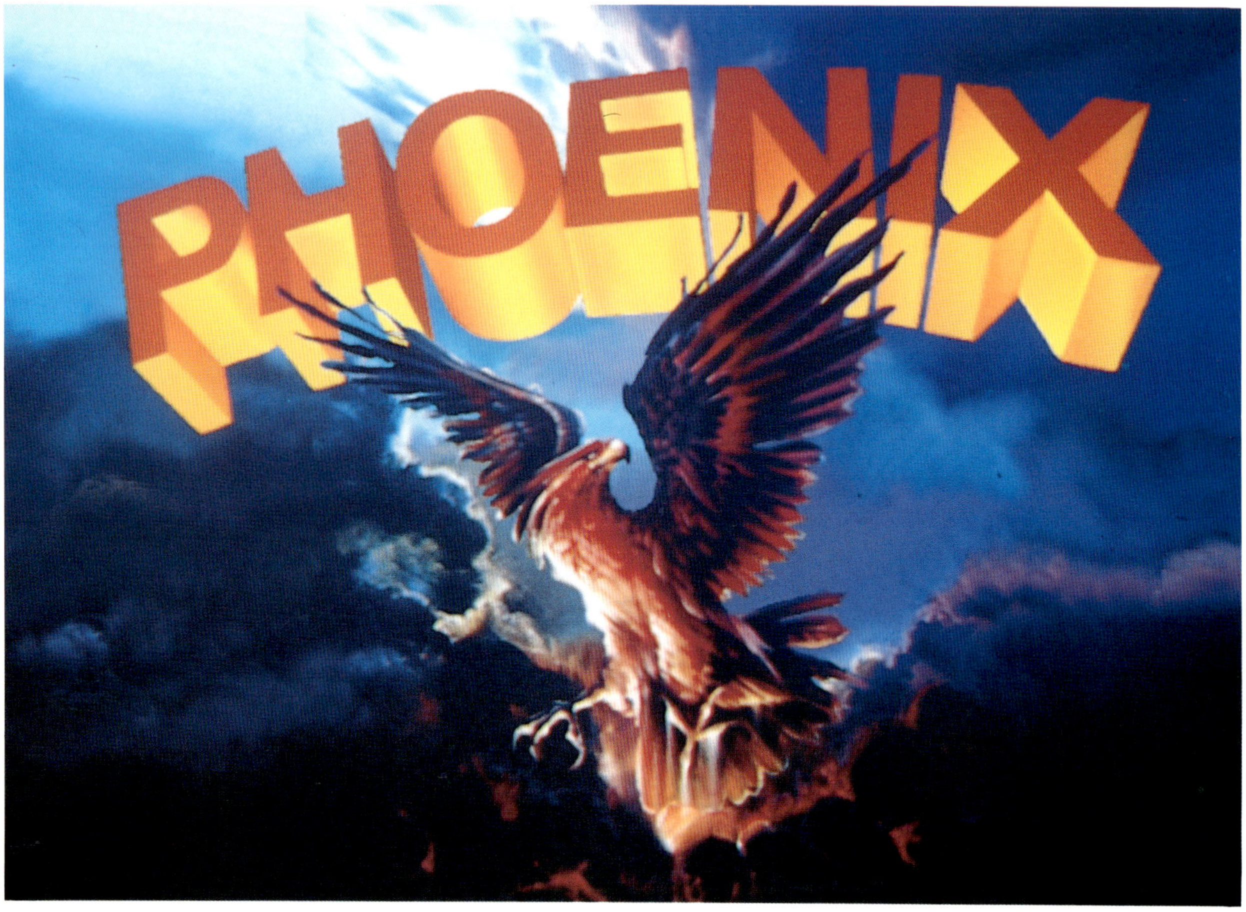

PHOENIX

Created as a 2-D animation of the company logo for Phoenix Concepts, Elk Grove, IL Used as an opening for a promotional video.

Rotoscope and cutout animation techniques were used.

Producer	Peter Hedlin
Animator	Terry Choate

Length of Time to Complete Work—3 weeks

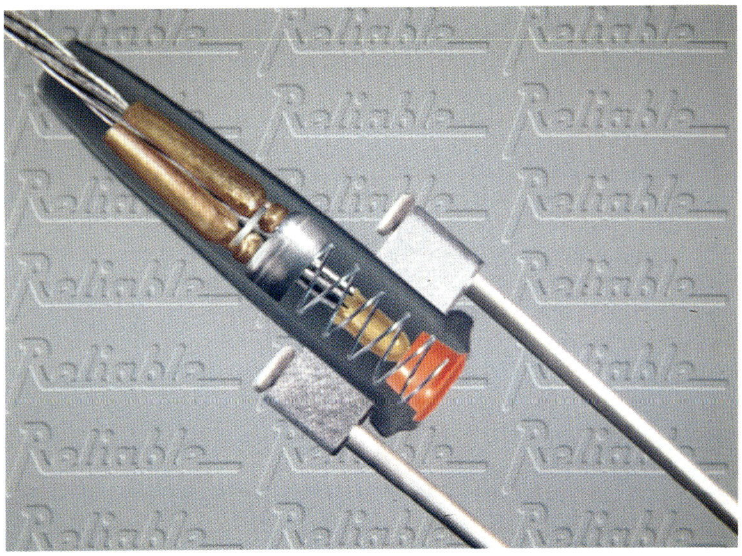

Reliable Power Products

Created as a program featuring Reliable Power Products.

Rotoscoping and color cycling overlays as well as 2-D cutout animation manipulated images of the digitized product were used.

Produced by	Reliable Power Product, Inc., Franklin Park, IL
Producer	Al Soell
Animator	Terry Choate
Graphic Designer	Terry Choate

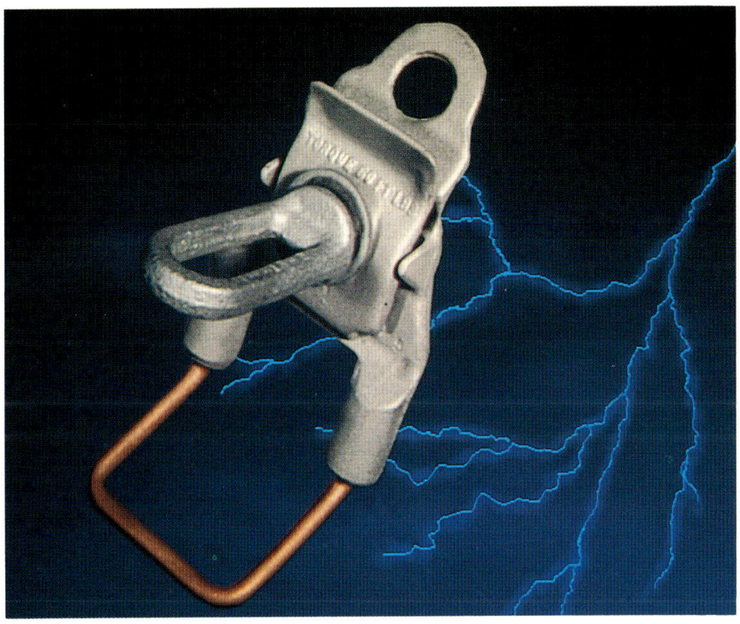

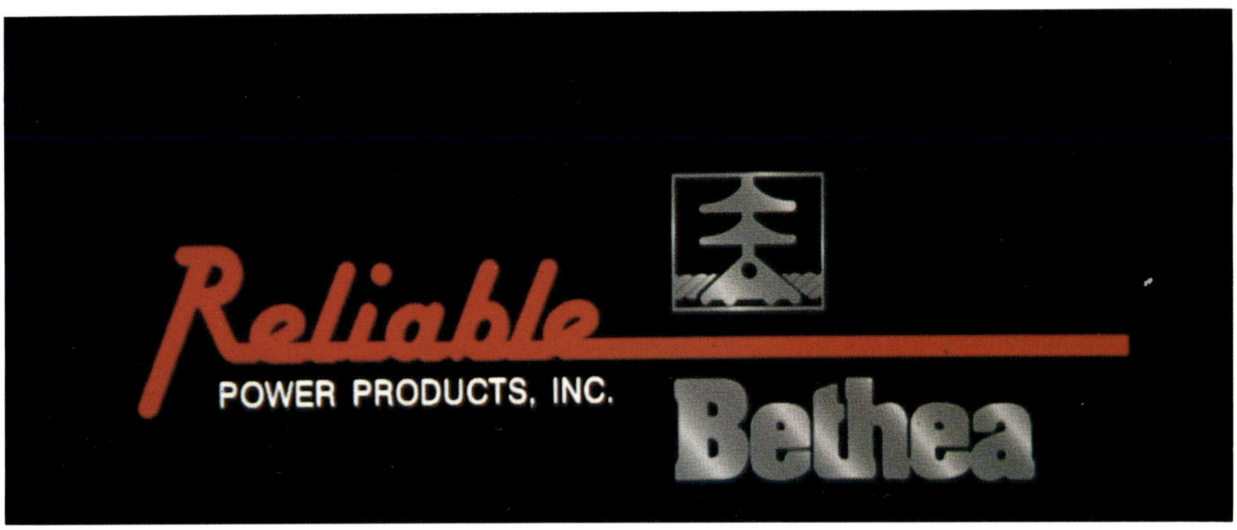

B × B, Inc.

120A East 23rd Street, New York, NY 10010

B × B, Inc. was formed in 1987 by Patty Bellucci and Henry Baker. The company specializes in graphics, effects, design and digital production as well as live action direction and consultation projects. B × B is located in HBO Studios, where they have access to the latest in digital and state of the art equipment.

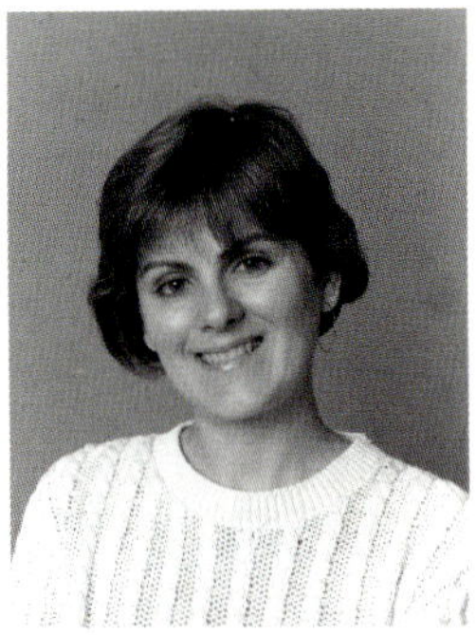

Patty Bellucci
Vice President and co-owner of B × B, Inc., New York, NY

Patty Bellucci, Vice President and co-owner of B × B has a lifetime of prestigious awards which include, among many others, Emmy; BDA—Gold, Silver and Bronze; International Film and TV—Gold, as well as numerous Monitor Awards. Ms. Bellucci is a graduate of the Fine Arts School of Visual Arts in New York.

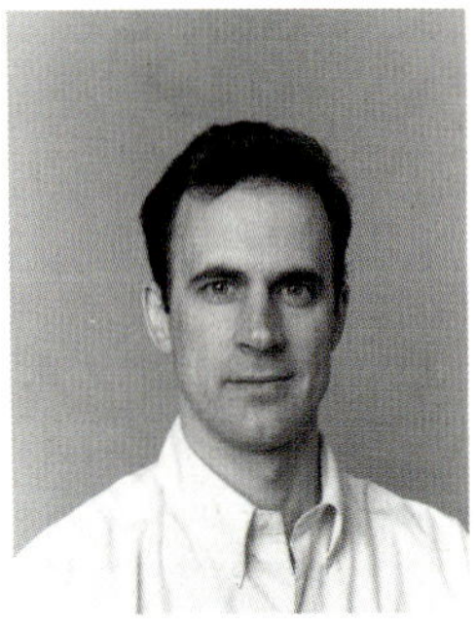

Henry Baker,
President and co-owner of B × B, Inc., New York, NY

Henry Baker, President and co-owner of B × B has had his designs for the digital suite seen in many award-winning productions. His designs for the graphic paint box have appeared in print advertisements and editorials for national magazines, as well as on posters and post cards. He lectures extensively. His extremely impressive lifetime awards include, among many others, BDA—Gold, Silver, Bronze and numerous Monitor Awards. He has a B.F.A. from Syracuse University, College of Visual and Performing Arts and an M.S. from Syracuse University, School of Education.

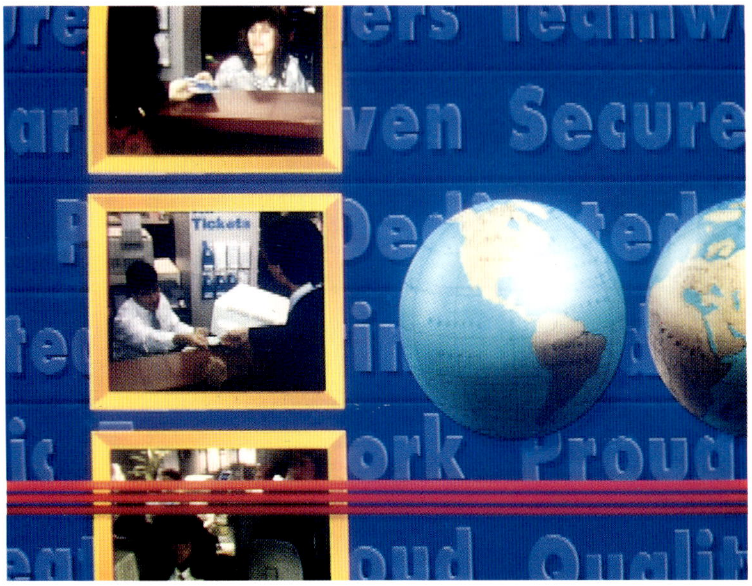

American Express—
TRS Express Television

Created as a show open for an American Express in-house program for Dean Thomson of Metro Productions.

Designed and illustrated on the Quantel Paintbox and composited in the Harry suite using the Kaleidoscope and D-1.

Created by	Patty Bellucci
Design Firm	B × B, Inc.
Designer	Patty Bellucci
Creative Director	Patty Bellucci
Art Director	Patty Bellucci
Effects Supervisor	Patty Bellucci
Graphic Artist	Patty Bellucci
Producer	Patty Bellucci
Video Editor	Patty Bellucci
Created and Completed at	Limelight Video

Length of Time to Complete Work—3 weeks

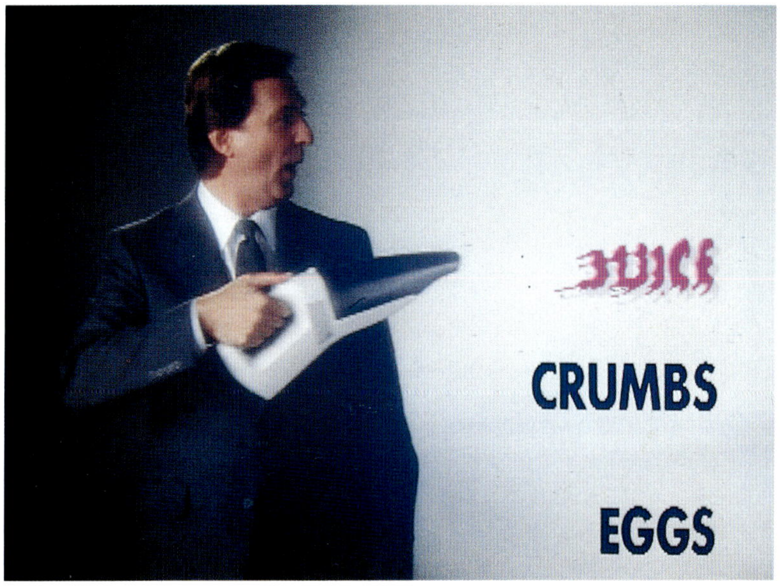

Dustbuster Power-Pro Plus

Designed as a national commercial for Black and Decker and Dan Lindau, Story, Piccolo, Guliner.

Created by compositing the Paintbox illustration and animation over live footage in the Harry Suite. Also used was Kaleidoscope and D-1.

Created By	Patty Bellucci, B × B and Ellen Kahn, Twin Arts
Design Firm	B × B, Inc.
Designer	Patty Bellucci
Effects Supervisor	Ellen Kahn
Graphic Artist	Patty Bellucci
Producer	Dan Lindau
Video Editor	Patty Bellucci
Created and Completed at	HBO Studios

Length of Time to Complete Work—2 Weeks

B × B Open

Designed as a promo reel for B × B

Created by using the Quantel Paintbox for design and illustrations and on the Harry-Encore for compositing, animation and editing.

Created By	Henry Baker and Patty Bellucci
Designer	Henry Baker, Patty Bellucci
Creative Director	B × B Inc.
Art Director	B × B Inc.
Effects Supervisor	B × B Inc.
Graphic Artist	Patty Bellucci
Producer	B × B Inc.
Video Editor	Henry Baker
Created and Completed at	HBO Studios

Length of Time to Complete Work—2 weeks

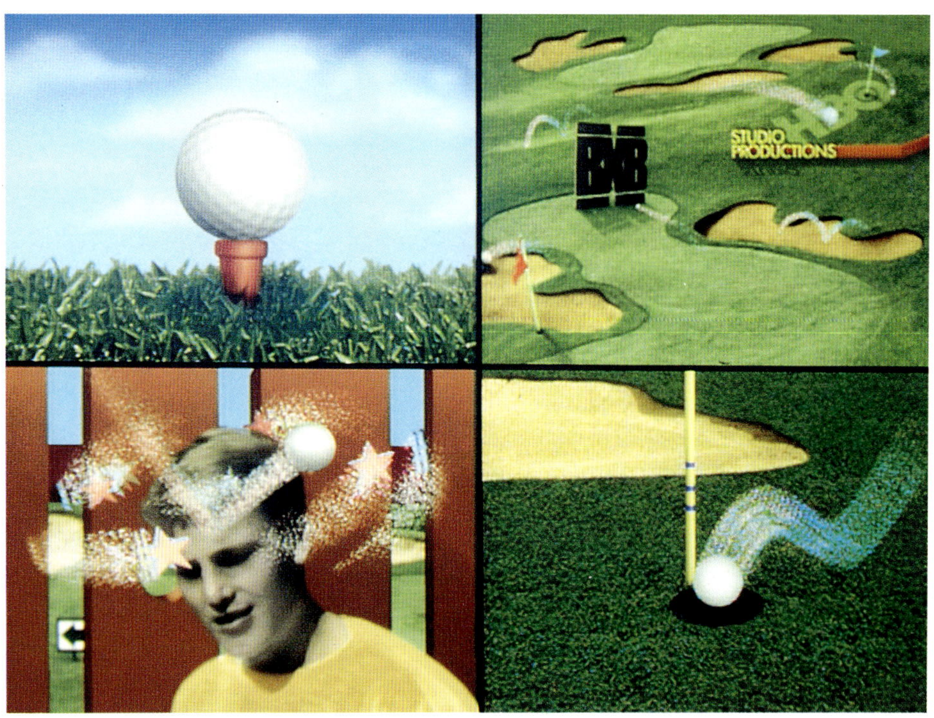

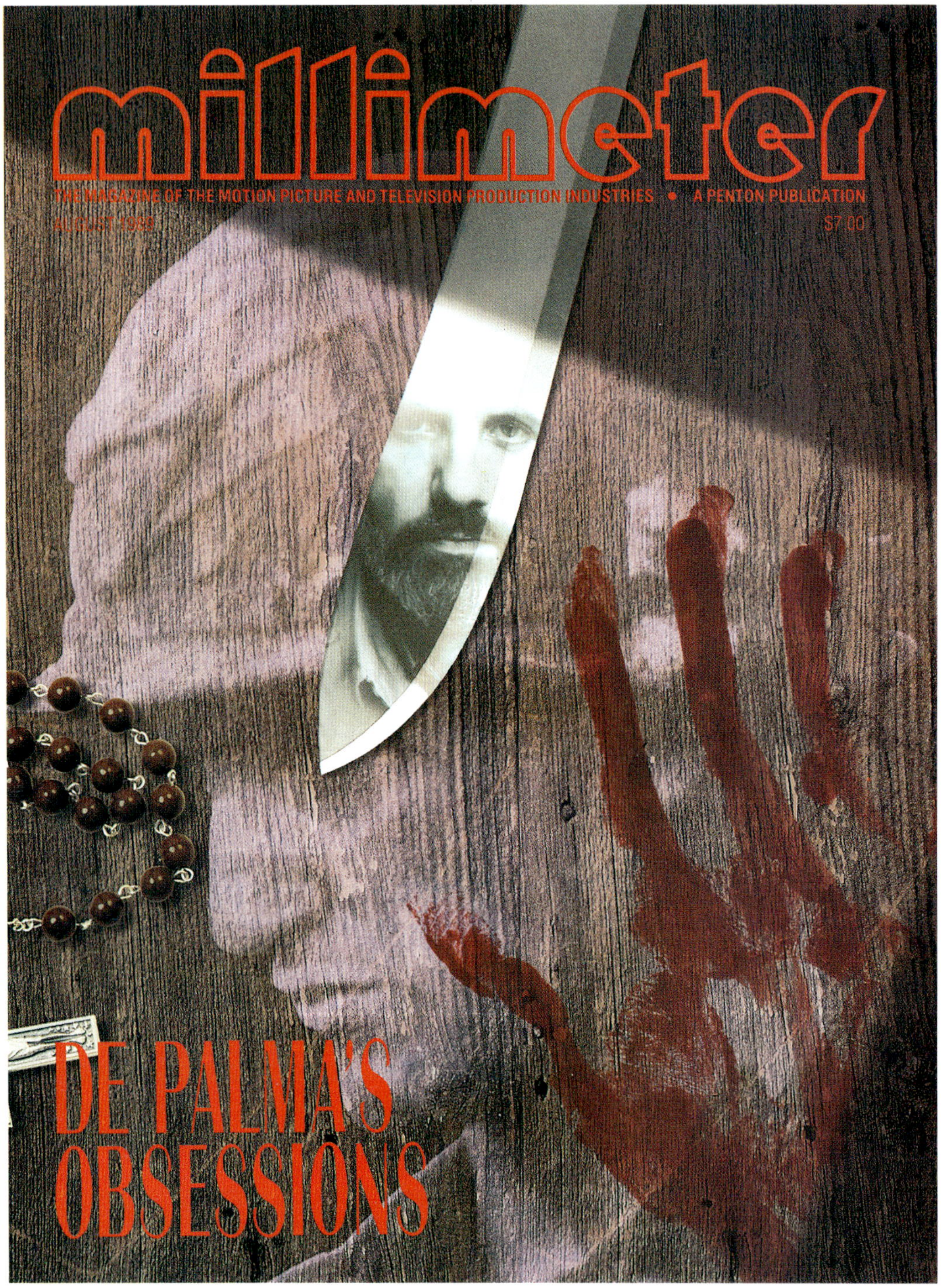

MILLIMETER COVER

Designed as a magazine cover for Millimeter Magazine's cover featuring Brian De Palma, for Stash Miller, Millimeter Magazine.

Designed on a video paint box which included still life elements. The work was finished on Quantel Video and Graphic Paintboxes.

Created By	Patty Bellucci, Sid Hoetzel, Marlo Bailey, Stash Miller
Design Firm	B × B, Inc.
Designer	Patty Bellucci
Art Director	Stash Miller
Graphic Artist	Patty Bellucci, Marlo Bailey
Created and Completed at	HBO Studios

Length of Time to Complete Work—1 week

Detroit '89

Designed for Scanlines Magazine Cover for the BDA

Created by first rendering the elements in the video Paintbox. Then compositing on the Quantel Graphic Paintbox and outputting to mag tape which then went to a printer for final output.

Created By	Henry Baker
Design Firm	B × B, Inc.
Designer	Henry Baker
Creative Director	Henry Baker
Art Director	Henry Baker
Graphic Artist	Henry Baker
Producer	Henry Baker
Created at	B × B, Inc.
Completed at	HBO Studio Productions

Length of Time to Complete Work—40 hours

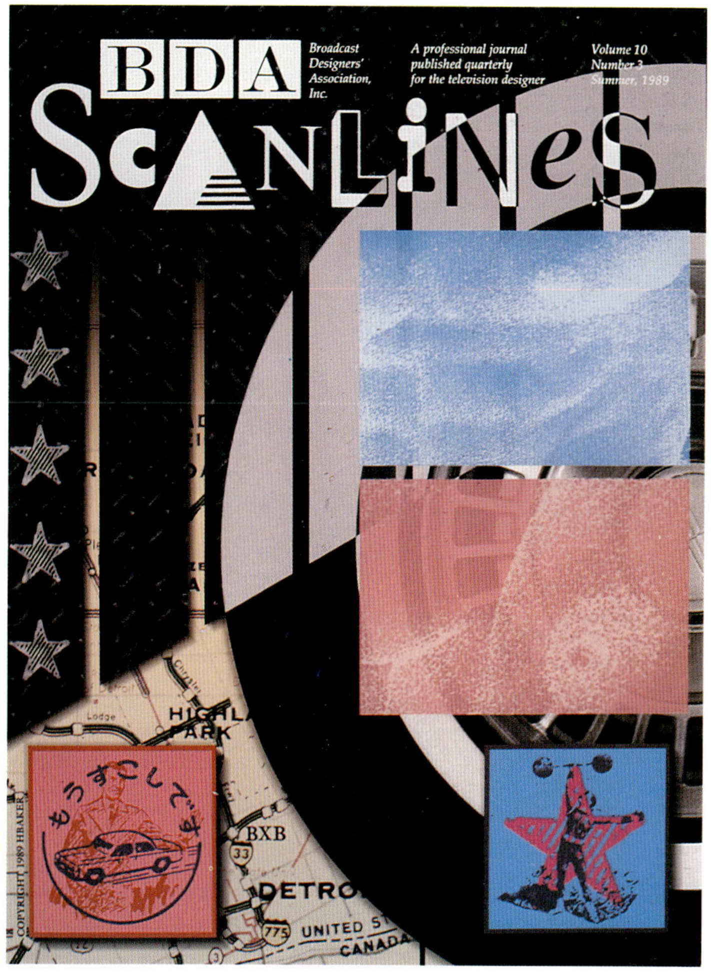

Graphic Paint Box Ad

Designed as a magazine ad to promote HBO Studio's Graphic Paint Box for Ralph Fumante, HBO Studios.

Created by retouching and re-compositing a classic painting in a Graphic Paint Box. Some original illustration was then added.

Created By	Patty Bellucci—B × B, Kathy Landman—K. Landman Assoc., Barry Blackman—photographer
Design Firm	K. Landman Assoc.
Designer	K. Landman
Graphic Artist	Patty Bellucci
Created and Completed at	HBO Studios

Length of Time to Complete Work—6 days

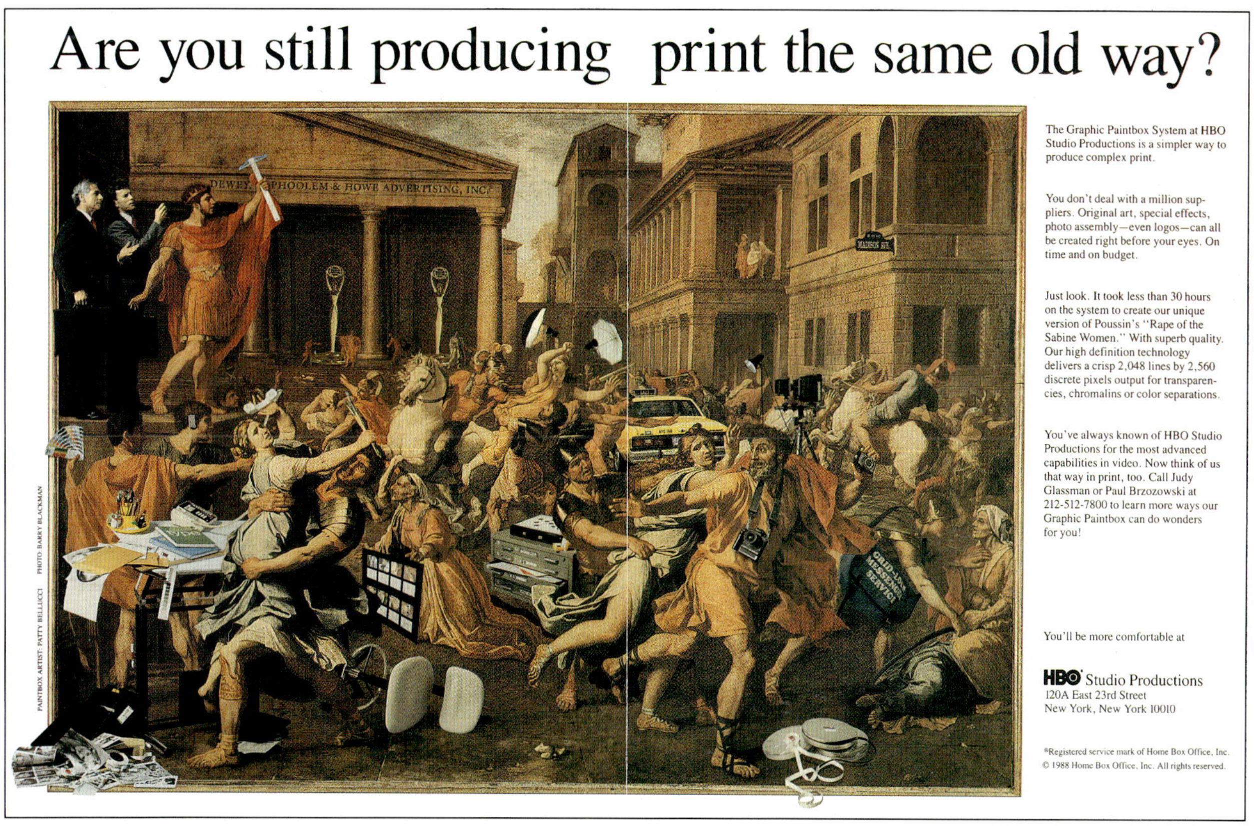

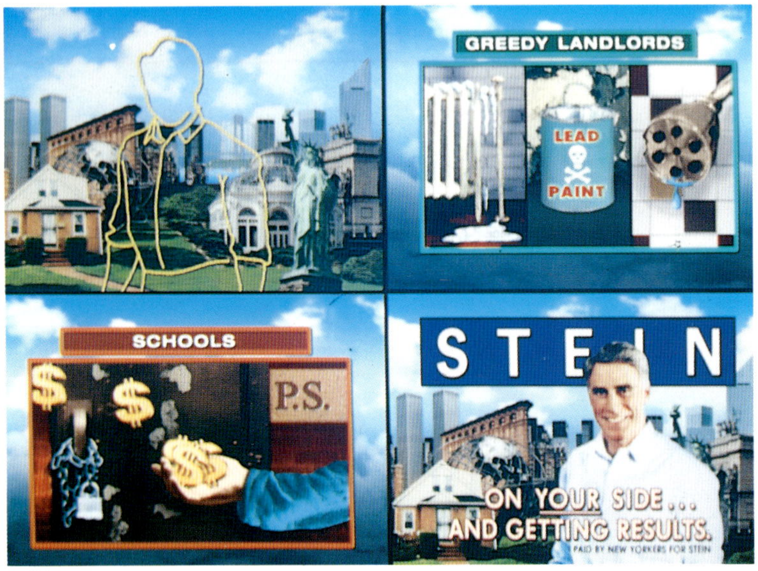

STEIN '89 CAMPAIGN

Designed as a political commercial for Press-Brenner, Inc.

Created by rendering the elements in the video Paintbox. Then compositing was done on the Quantel Harry with manipulation via the Grass Valley Kaleidoscope.

Created By	Henry Baker
Design Firm	B × B
Designer	Henry Baker
Creative Director	Judy Press-Brenner
Art Director	Henry Baker
Effects Supervisor	Henry Baker
Graphic Artist	Henry Baker, Patty Bellucci
Producer	Judy Press-Brenner
Video Editor	Henry Baker
Graphics Producer	Margo Halle
Created at	B × B, Inc.
Completed at	HBO Studio Productions

Length of Time to Complete Work—40 hours

RAYTHEON

Designed as a PBS Funding ID for D'Alessio Productions

The video paint box first rendered the elements, which were then manipulated on the Kaleidoscope and composited on the Harry.

Created By	Henry Baker
Design Firm	B × B, Inc.
Designer	Henry Baker
Creative Director	Henry Baker
Art Director	Henry Baker
Effects Supervisor	Henry Baker
Graphic Artist	Henry Baker
Producer	Clem D'Alessio
Video Editor	Henry Baker
Created at	B × B, Inc.
Completed at	HBO Studio Productions

Length of Time to Complete Work—40 hours

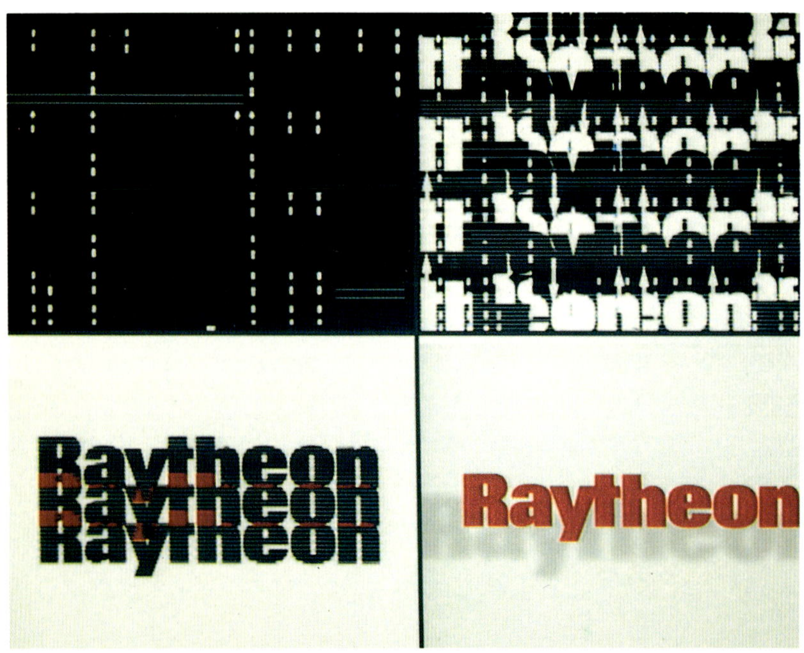

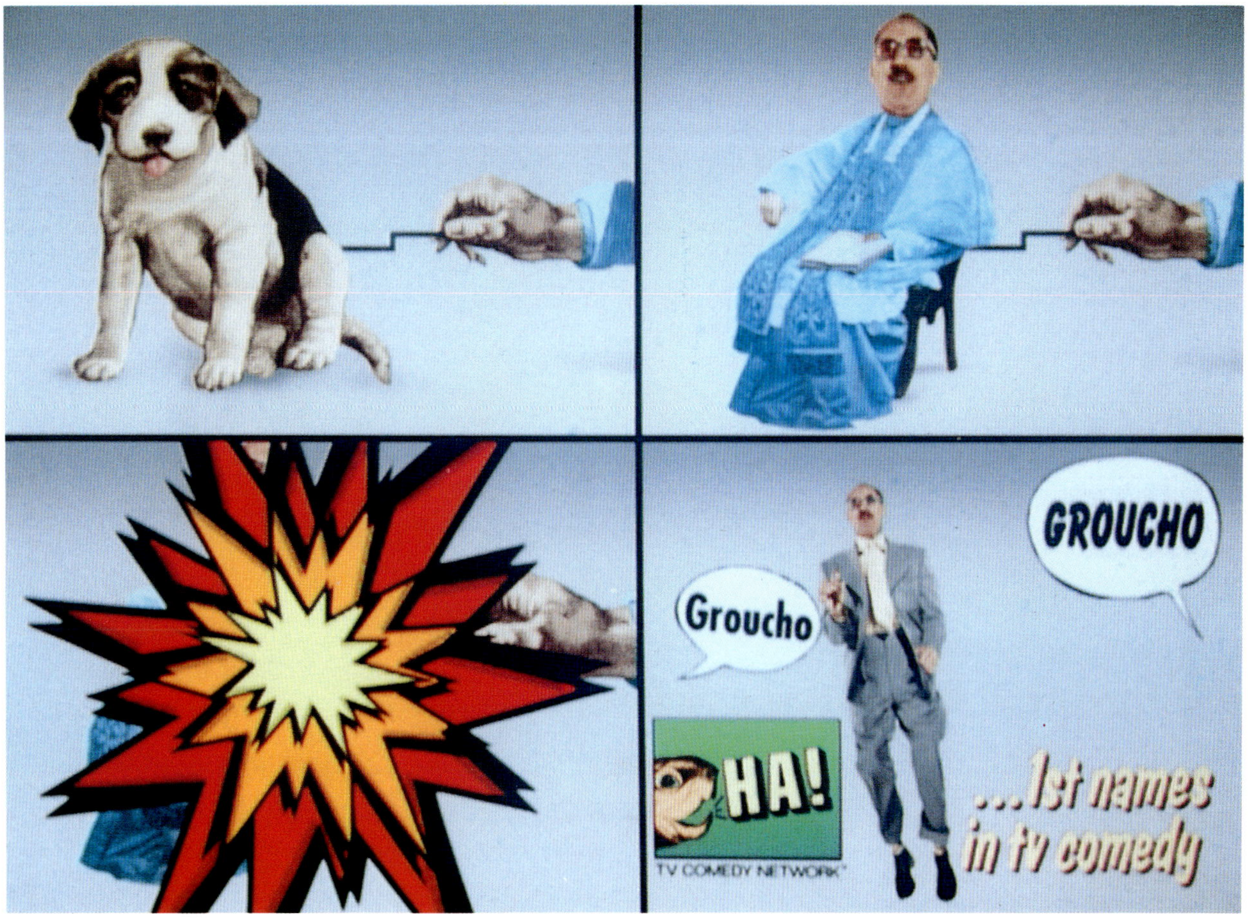

First Names in Comedy

Designed as a Cable Station ID for the HA! Network

The elements were first rendered in the video Paintbox, then composited on the Harry with manipulation by the Kaleidoscope.

Created By	Henry Baker
Design Firm	B × B Inc.
Designer	Henry Baker
Creative Director	Henry Baker
Art Director	Patty Bellucci
Effects Supervisor	Jeff Sargent
Graphic Artist	Patty Bellucci
Producer	Lee Hunt
Video Editor	Henry Baker
Created at	B × B, Inc.
Completed at	HBO Studio Productions

Length of Time to Complete Work—40 hours

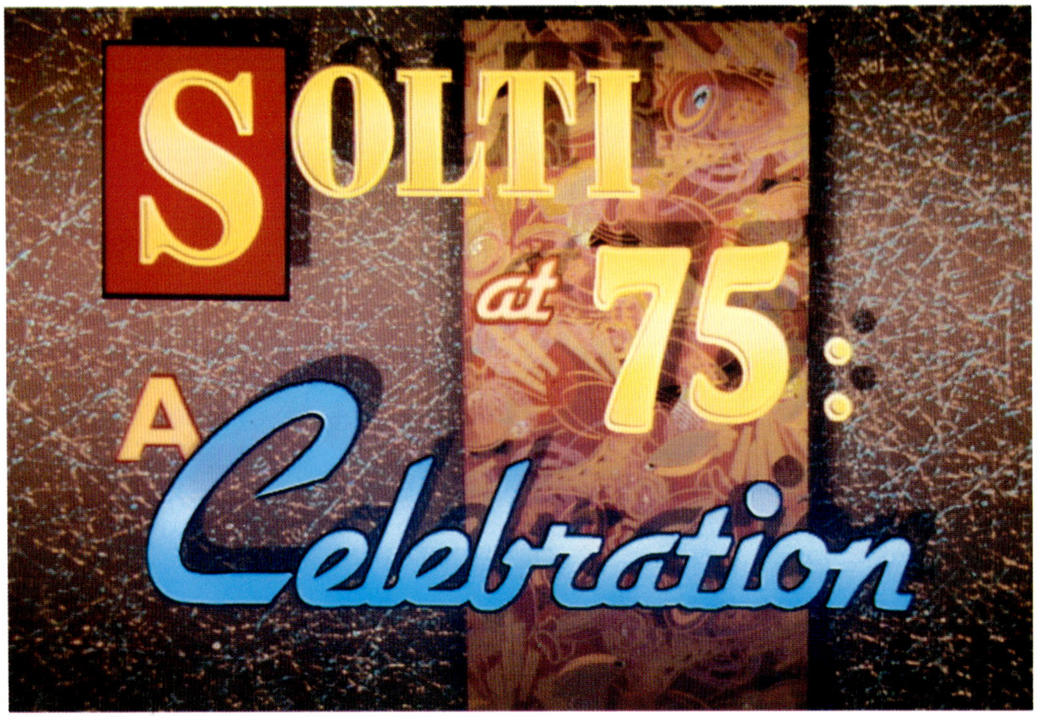

SOLTI AT 75

Designed as a show open for D'Alessio Productions

Electronic devices used to create the open were the Quantel Paintbox, Harry, Grass Valley Kaleidoscope and Sony D-1.

Created By	Henry Baker
Design Firm	B × B, Inc.
Designer	Henry Baker
Creative Director	Henry Baker
Art Director	Henry Baker
Effects Supervisor	Henry Baker
Graphic Artist	Henry Baker
Producer	Clem D'Alessio
Video Editor	Henry Baker
Created at	B × B, Inc.
Completed at	HBO Studio Productions

Length of Time to Complete Work—40 hours

COMEDY CHANNEL ID

Created as a cable station ID for the Comedy Channel.

The Paintbox was used to create the ID for its ability to render and create graphics and the Harry for its ability to composite digitally any video source.

Created By	Henry Baker
Design Firm	B × B, Inc.
Designer	Henry Baker
Creative Director	Henry Baker
Art Director	Henry Baker
Effects Supervisor	Henry Baker
Graphic Artist	Henry Baker
Producer	Sharon Gnoi
Video Editor	Henry Baker
Created at	B × B, Inc.
Completed at	HBO Studio Productions

Length of Time to Complete Work—40 hours

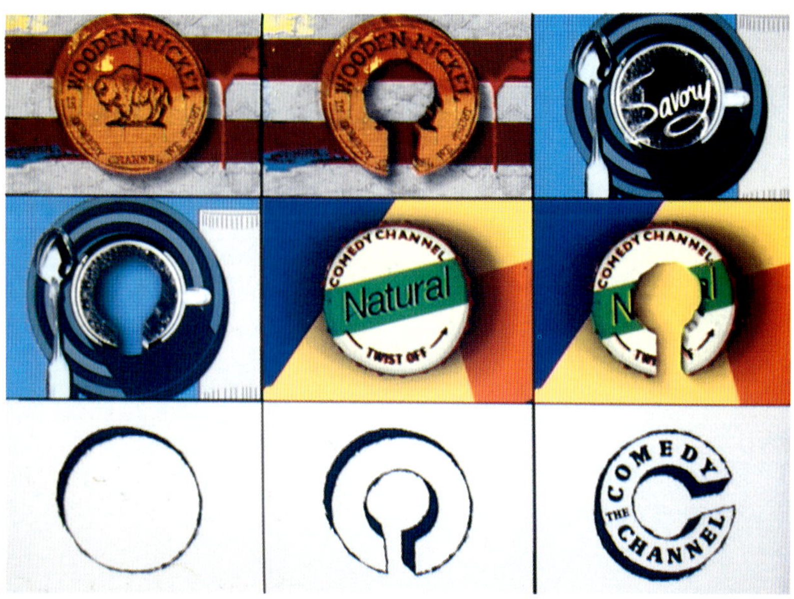

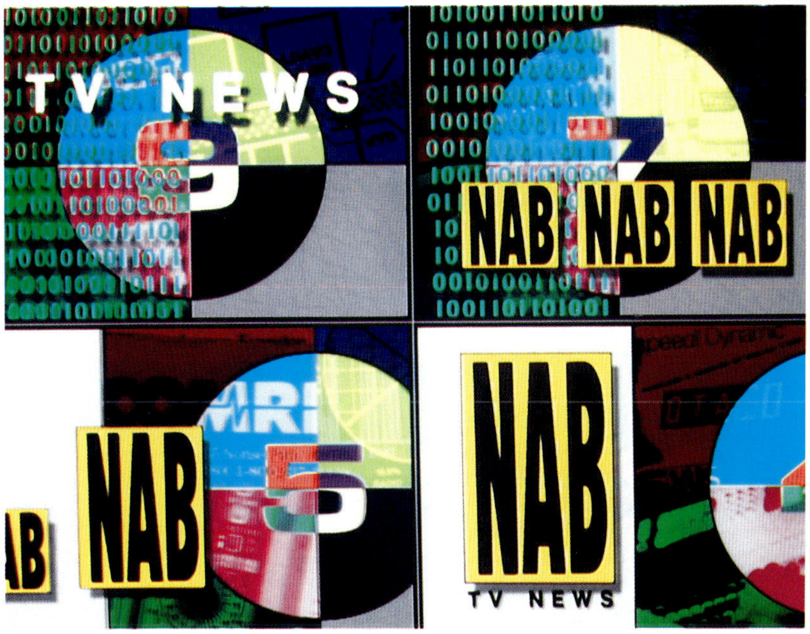

NAB TV News

Created as opening graphics for a news show for the NAB.

Created by using the Quantel Paintbox and Harry, Grass Valley Kaleidoscope and Sony D-1.

Created By	Henry Baker
Design Firm	B × B, Inc.
Designer	Henry Baker
Creative Director	Henry Baker
Art Director	Henry Baker
Effects Supervisor	Henry Baker
Graphic Artist	Henry Baker
Producer	Henry Baker
Video Editor	Henry Baker
Created at	B × B, Inc.
Completed at	HBO Studio Productions

Length of Time to Complete Work—40 hours

Play to Win

Designed as a commercial for the Maryland State Lottery and Trahan, Burden and Charles, Inc.

Created on the Paintbox, Harry and Kaleidoscope, using D-1.

Created By	Henry Baker
Design Firm	B × B, Inc.
Designer	Henry Baker
Creative Director	Henry Baker
Art Director	Terry Whistler
Effects Supervisor	Henry Baker
Director, Live Action	Alan Charles
Graphic Artist	Henry Baker
Producer	Ida Buffone
Video Editor	Henry Baker
Created at	B × B, Inc.
Completed at	HBO Studio Productions

Length of Time to Complete Work—40 hours

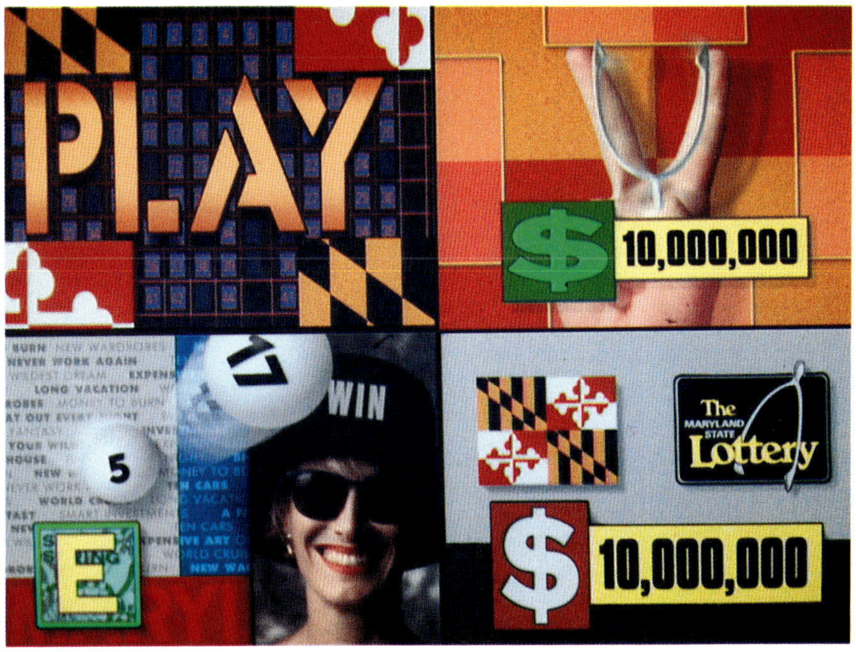

DAVID BERKNER

The Tape House, 216 East 45th Street, New York, NY 10017

David Berkner is the Digital Effects Designer for the Tape House in New York, NY. He is a graduate of The School of Visual Arts in New York, NY.

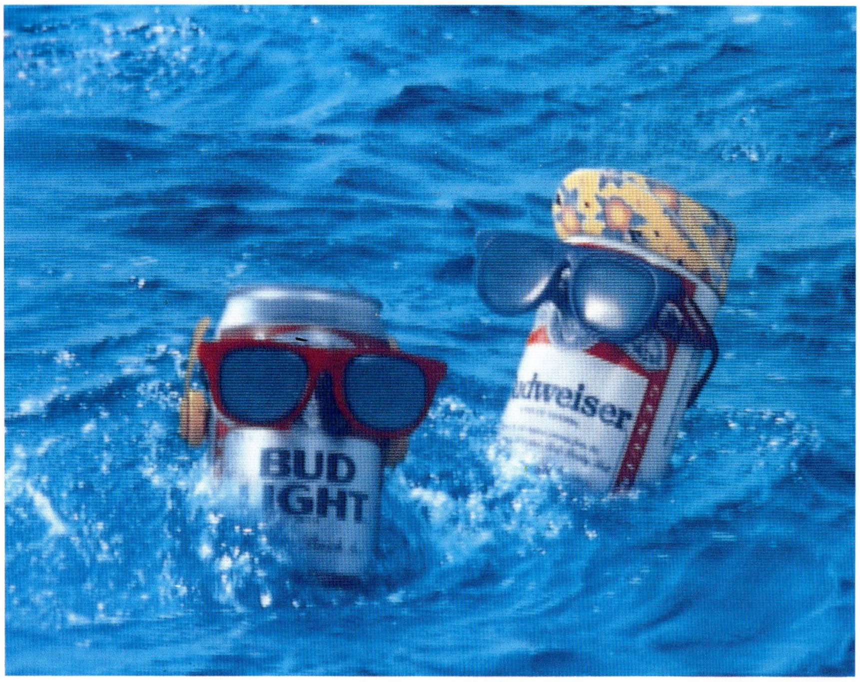

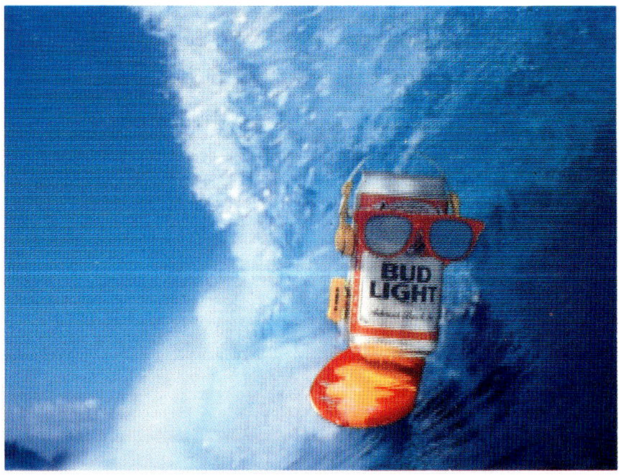

BUD TO THE BEACH

Designed as a commercial for Russ Dube at Broadcast Arts, New York, NY; DMB and B, St. Louis, MO; and Anheuser Busch.

The effect of cans surfing on real water was created by first selecting stock shoots of surfers. Then, stop motion cans were shot against green trying to mimic the surfers' motion. The original surfers were then removed using the Paintbox and Harry. The stop motion cans were then tracked over the surfers and the water was blended using the Harry. The Encore was used to move the cans on the surfboards.

Created By	Russ Dube, Ray McNallen, Milan Boncich, Darlene Ruess, David Berkner
Art Director	Ray McNallen
Graphic Artist	David Berkner, Darlene Ruess
Producer	Russ Dube
Colorist, Film to Tape	Milan Boncich
Created at	Broadcast Arts
Completed at	The Tape House

Length of Time to Complete Work—3 weeks

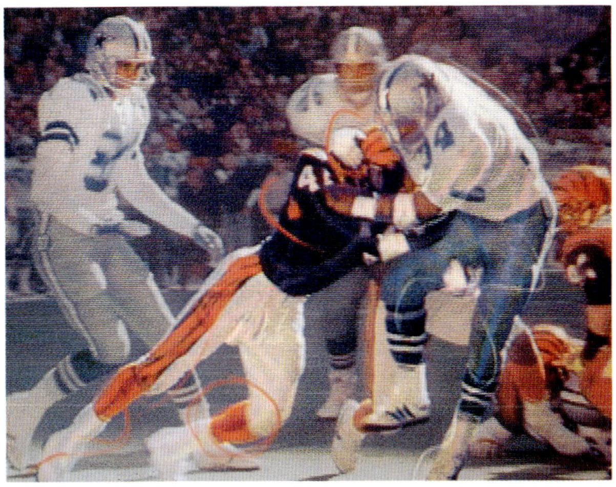

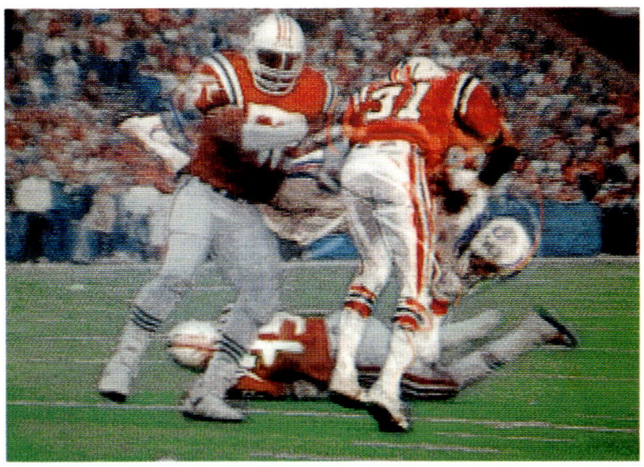

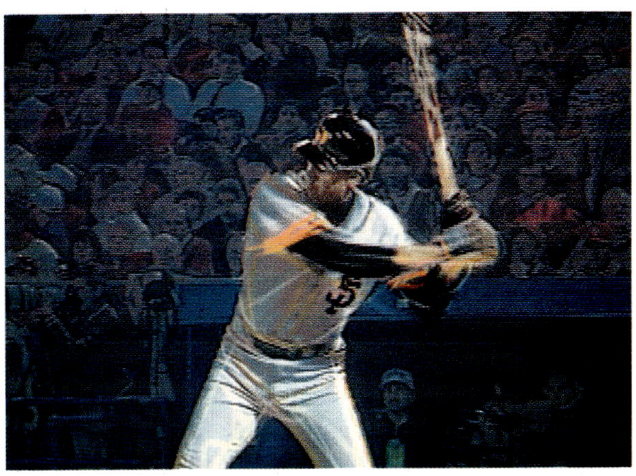

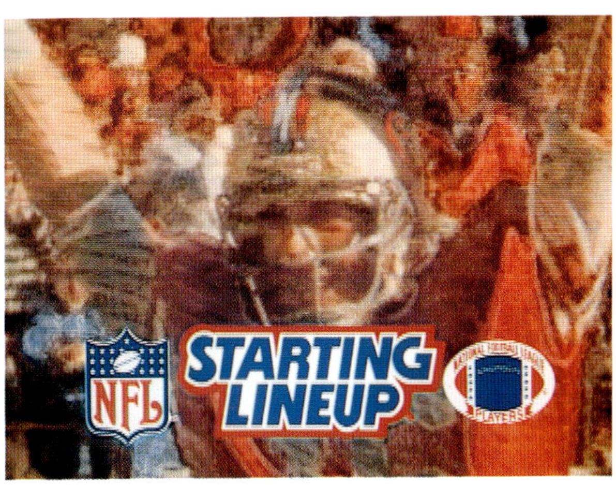

STARTING LINE-UP—FOOTBALL, BASEBALL

Designed as a commercial for Maureen Tobin and Grey Advertising, New York, NY.

To achieve a hand-painted animation look, every 4th frame was lifted from stock footage and inputted into the Harry, utilizing its Fettle function with mattes to build it. D-1 tape was processed in Harry and Paintbox.

Created By	Maureen Tobin, David Berkner, Darlene Ruess, Stacy Kless, Gary Covick, John Miller
Design Firm	The Tape House
Designer	David Berkner
Art Director	Maureen Tobin
Producer	Stacy Kless
Created and Completed at	The Tape House

Length of Time to Complete Work—11 days

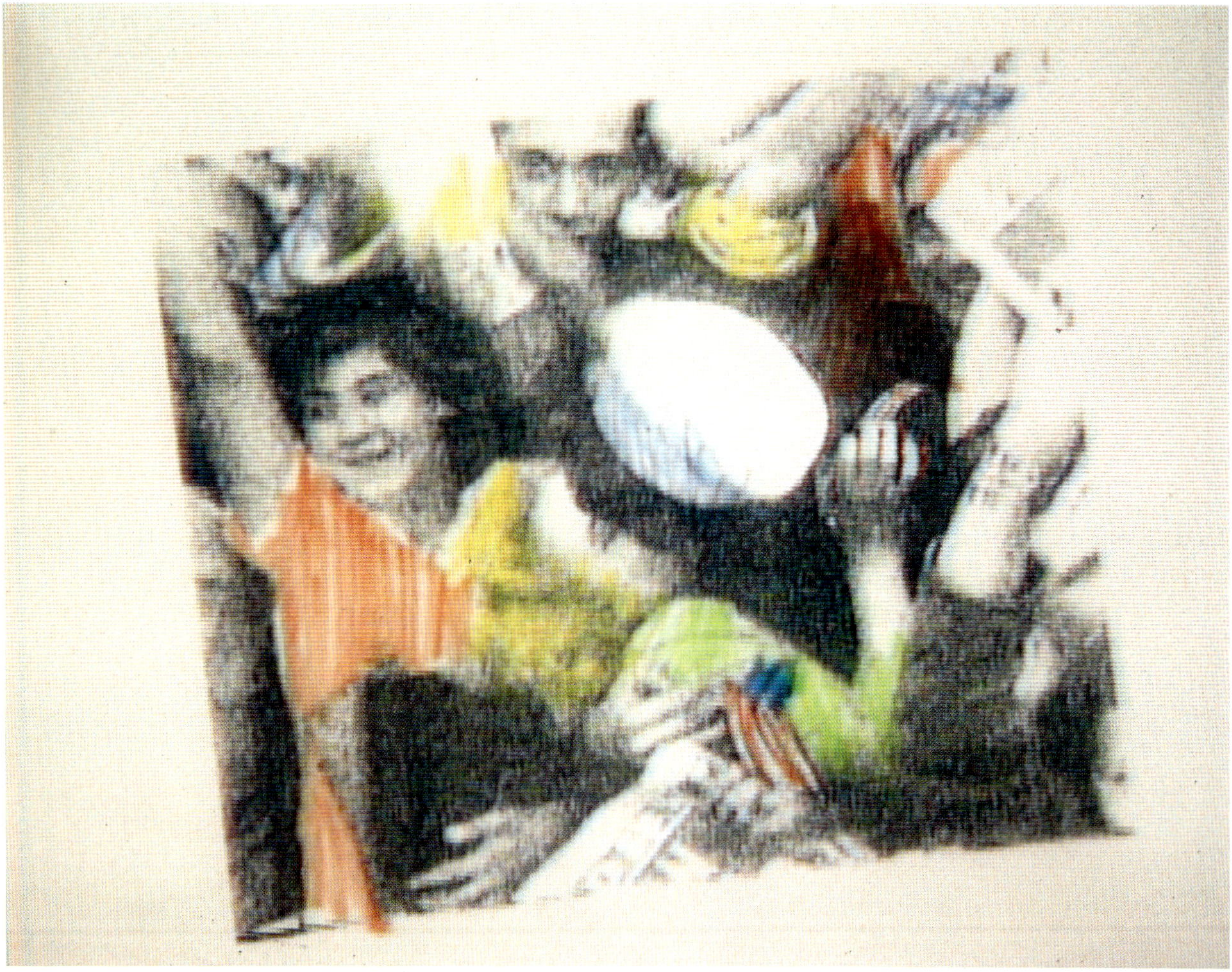

Classic Footage Times Square VJ Day

Created as a presentation for a possible look for a commercial.

Designed for a different look at this old stock footage, the material was first recorded onto a thermal printer. Then, each frame was Xeroxed. Each frame was hand-colored with pencil and then again with the Paintbox in Harry.

Designer	David Berkner
Graphic Artist	David Berkner
Created and completed at	The Tape House

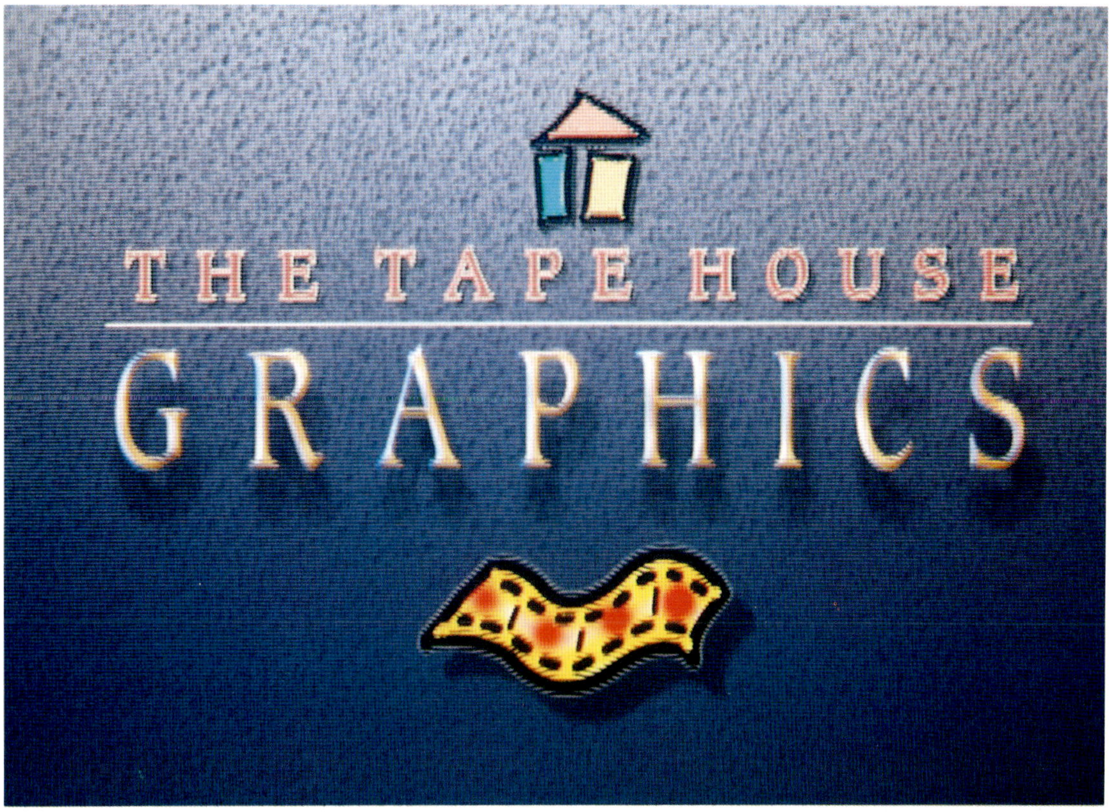

OPENING TITLES—GRAPHICS REEL-1

Electronic Devices Used—Paintbox, Harry and Encore.
Length of time to Complete Work—6 hours

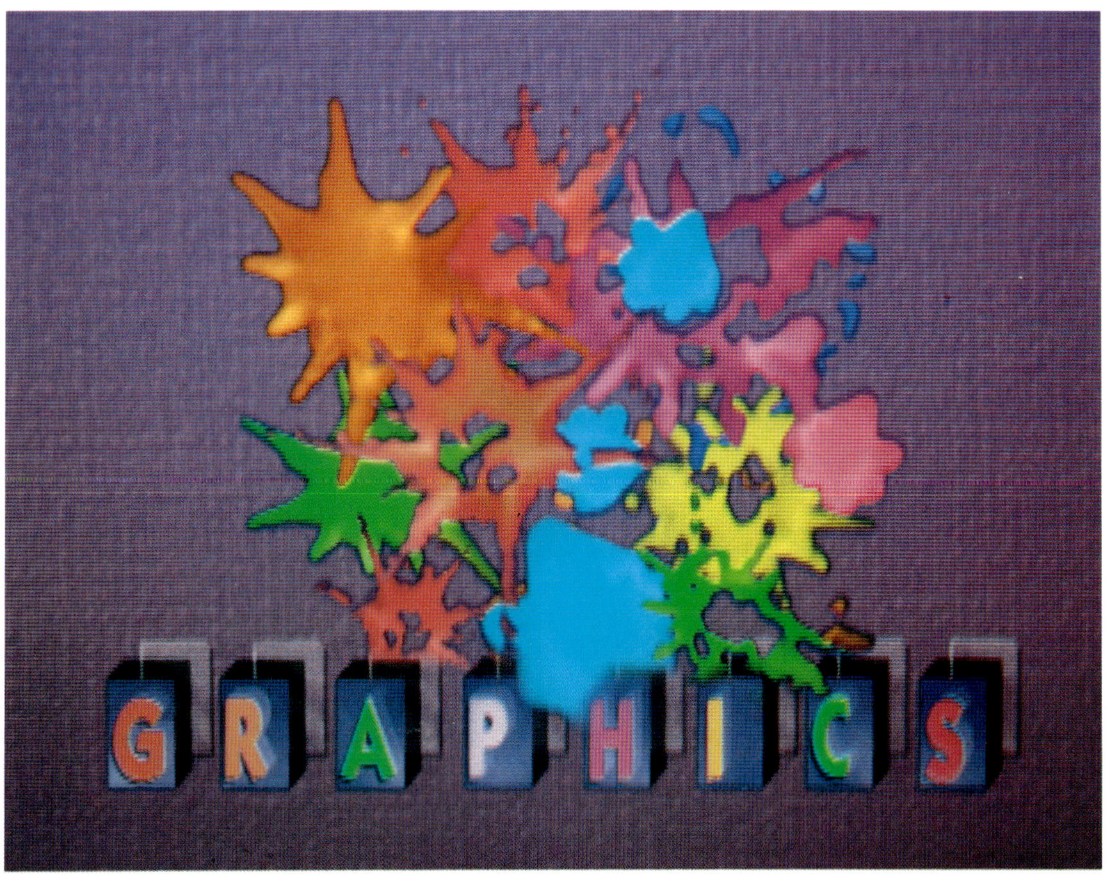

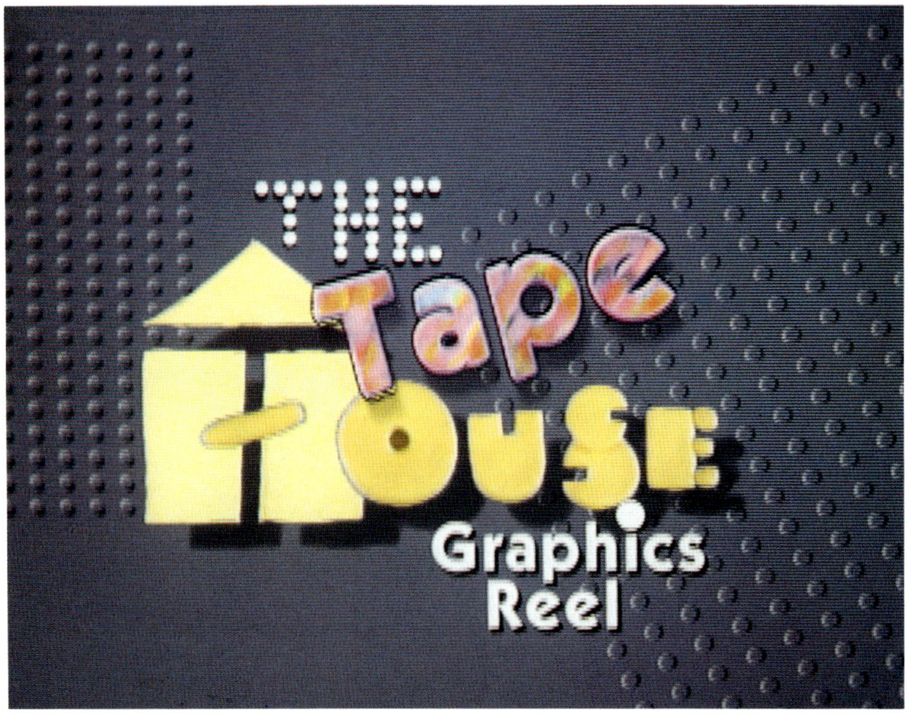

Opening Titles—Graphics Reel-2

Created by making a claymation transformation shooting a simple frame with a Harry and adding Paintbox, fonts and effects.

Length of Time to Complete Work—5 hours

Countdown—Graphic

Designed to keep a feeling of the tools used in the technology, and show them as beautiful and interesting to watch. Created by taking a frame of test chart and running footage of a test grid through Harry. Letterforms were built using the material as a base which were keyed into the Harry and Encore.

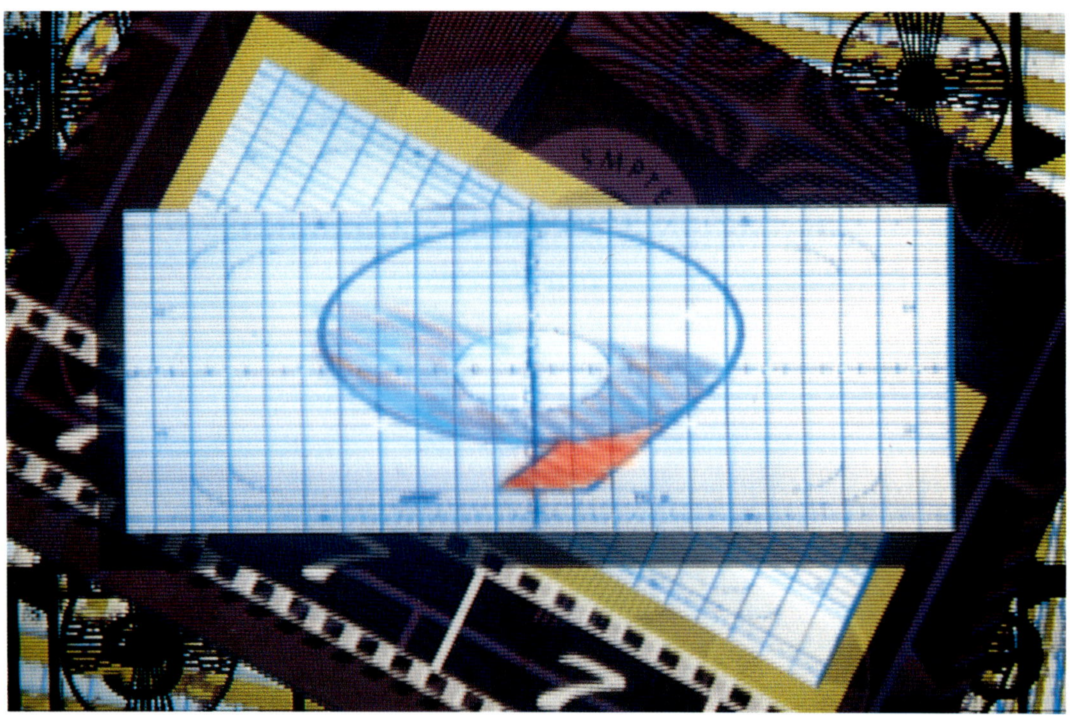

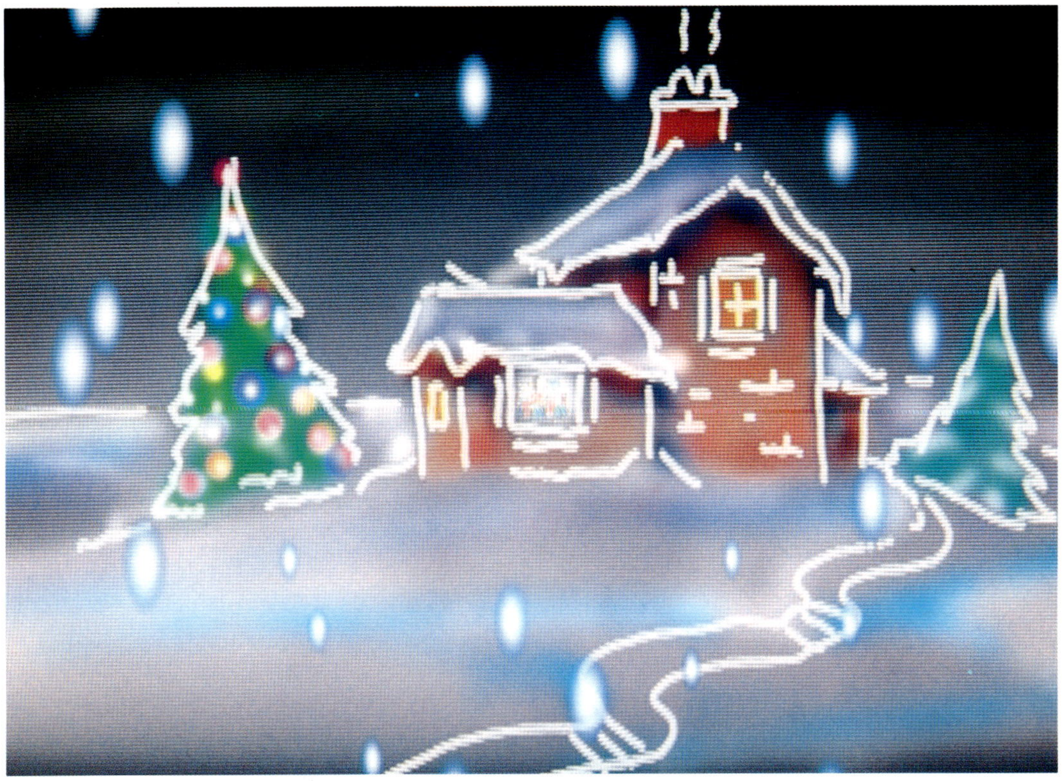

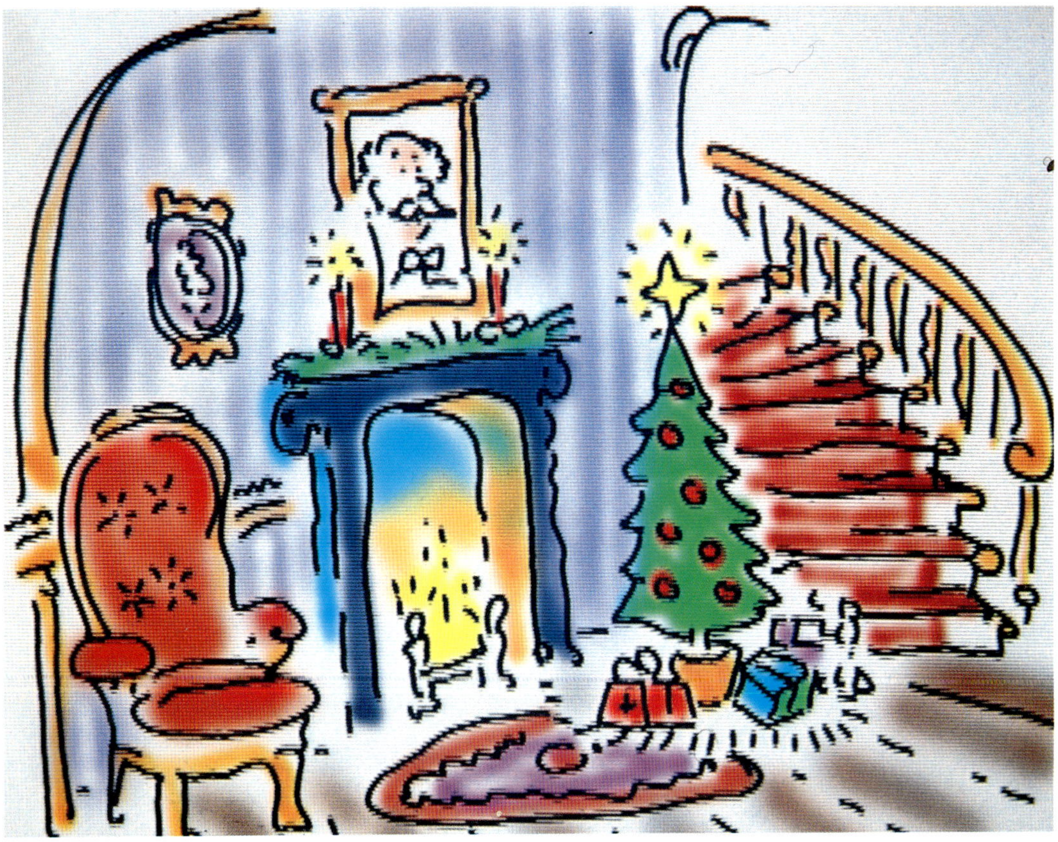

In-House Christmas Video

Designed to look like traditional cell animation with a light humorous mood, without having to shoot cells. The artwork was created in the Paintbox then moved and cycled with the Harry and Encore.

Length of Time to Complete Work—4 hours

Credits for the Graphics and In-House Work Are:

Designed for The Tape House self-promotion
Created by David Berkner
Designed by David Berkner
Graphic Artist David Berkner
Created and Completed at The Tape House

DAVID BOLINSKY

Advanced Imaging, Inc., 350 Center St., Wallingford, CT 06492

David Bolinsky's formal education includes a BS in Medical Illustration from Ohio State and non-degree Masters work in anatomy at Michigan State College of Human Medicine. He is the winner of numerous awards for his medical illustrations.

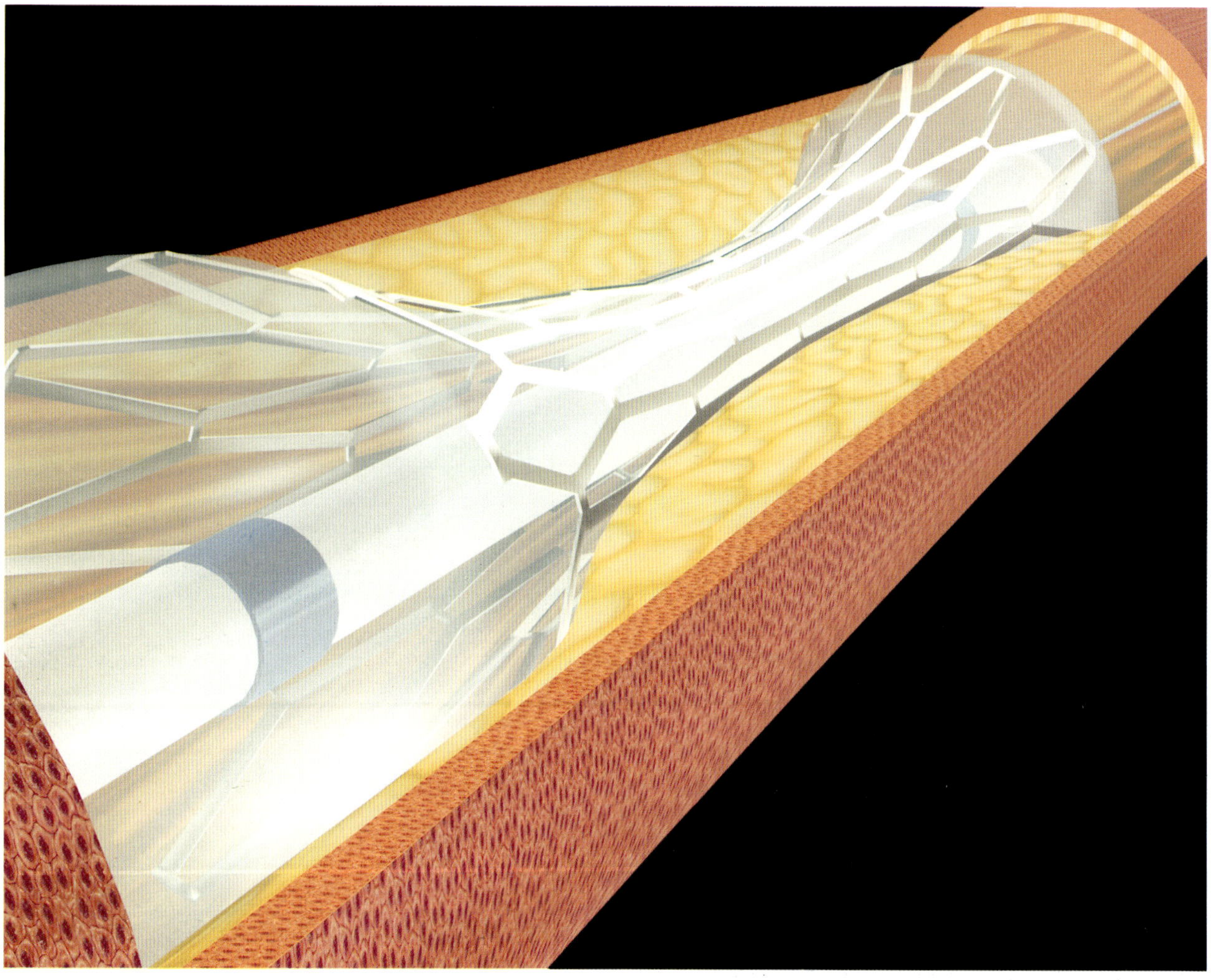

DEPLOYMENT OF THE PALMAZ BALLOON EXPANDABLE ARTERIAL STENT

Designed as animation for Jeremy Cole, J&J Interventional Systems, Inc./Varitech Corp., East Long Meadow, MA to help obtain FDA approval for their medical device.

Created on a Tektronix XD88 work station using Wavefront Technologies software. The texture maps were created by using Vista-Tips Paint software on a PC.

Created By	David Bolinsky
Design Firm	Advanced Imaging, Inc.
Designer	David Bolinsky
Creative Director	David Bolinsky
Art Director	David Bolinsky
Effects Supervisor	David Bolinsky
Graphic Artist	David Bolinsky
Producer	Jeremy Cole
Video Editor	Jeremy Cole
Created and Completed at	Advanced Imaging, Inc.

Length of Time to Complete Work—3 weeks

Color Dynamics

150 E. Bethany Road, Dallas, TX 75002

ColorDynamics Broadcast, Industrial, Corporate and Entertainment Composite

Broadcast, Industrial, Corporate and Entertainment Composite

Clients Represented:

Oryx	Oryx Industrial, Dallas, Texas
Texas Instruments	Texas Instruments, Fort Worth, Texas
Spirit of 8	WFAA Channel 8 ABC for opening newscast, Dallas, TX
Legends of the West	Channel 39 Western Weekends, Dallas, TX
Flax	Flax Art and Design, San Francisco, CA
Butterfly	Barney and the Backyard Gang video, "Campfire Sing Along"
Stamp and Teacup	ColorDesign in-house videos

Production and Design Credits:

Jerry Cadigan	WFAA Channel 8 ABC
Nelson Flanagan	Channel 39
Ed DeShields	Media Point
Dennis DeShazer	The Lyons Group
Michael Fleming	ColorDynamics Computer operator
Linda Hamil	ColorDynamics Computer operator

Design Firm: ColorDynamics

Production and Post Production created and completed at ColorDynamics

Length of time to Complete Work: From 3 days to 3 weeks

All of the animations were created on either the Symbolocs 3650, the Microtime IP4 or the Truevision with Targa 32.

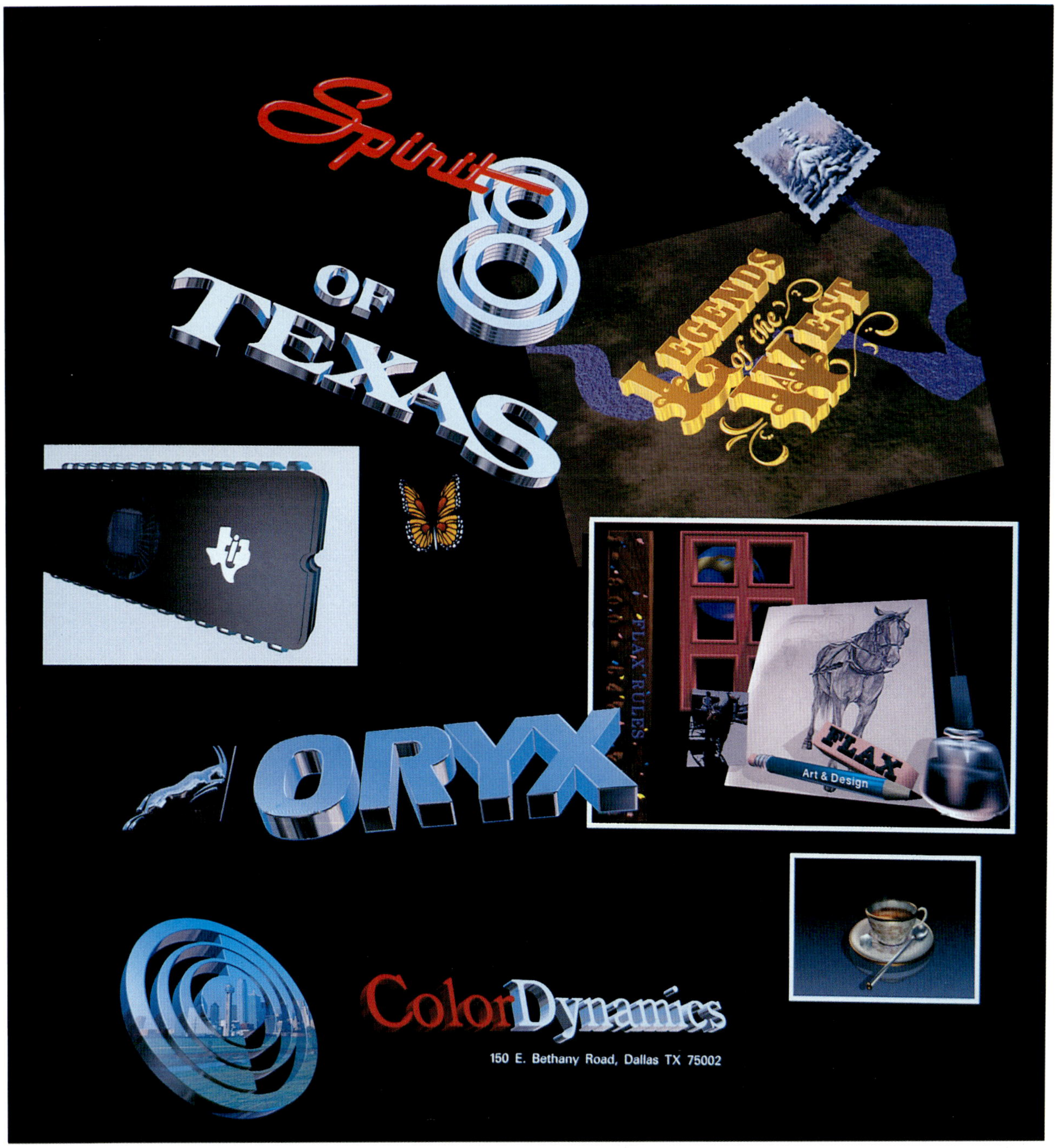

CONFERENCE EXPRESS

466 Lexington Avenue, New York, NY 10017

Conference Express was founded in 1986 as a joint venture of Olympia & York and US Sprint. It is the only company in the US dedicated to public use videoconferencing and has over 700 sites worldwide.

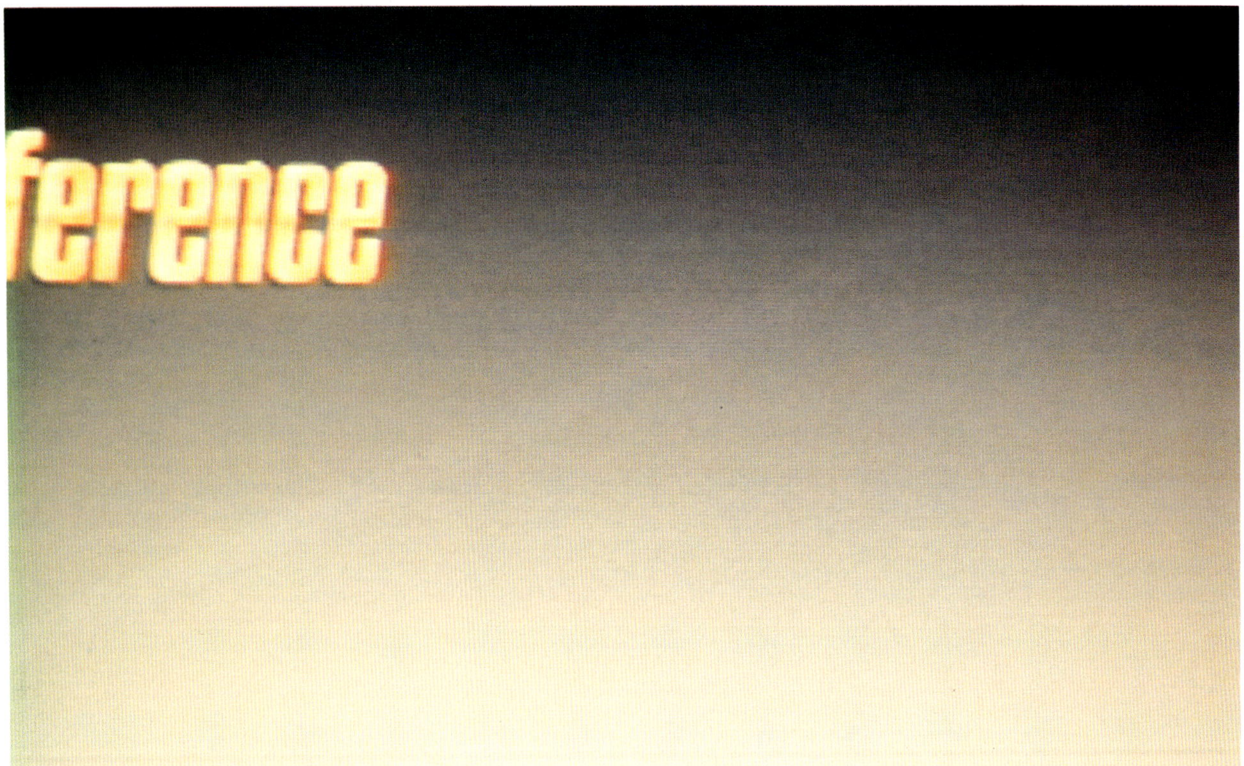

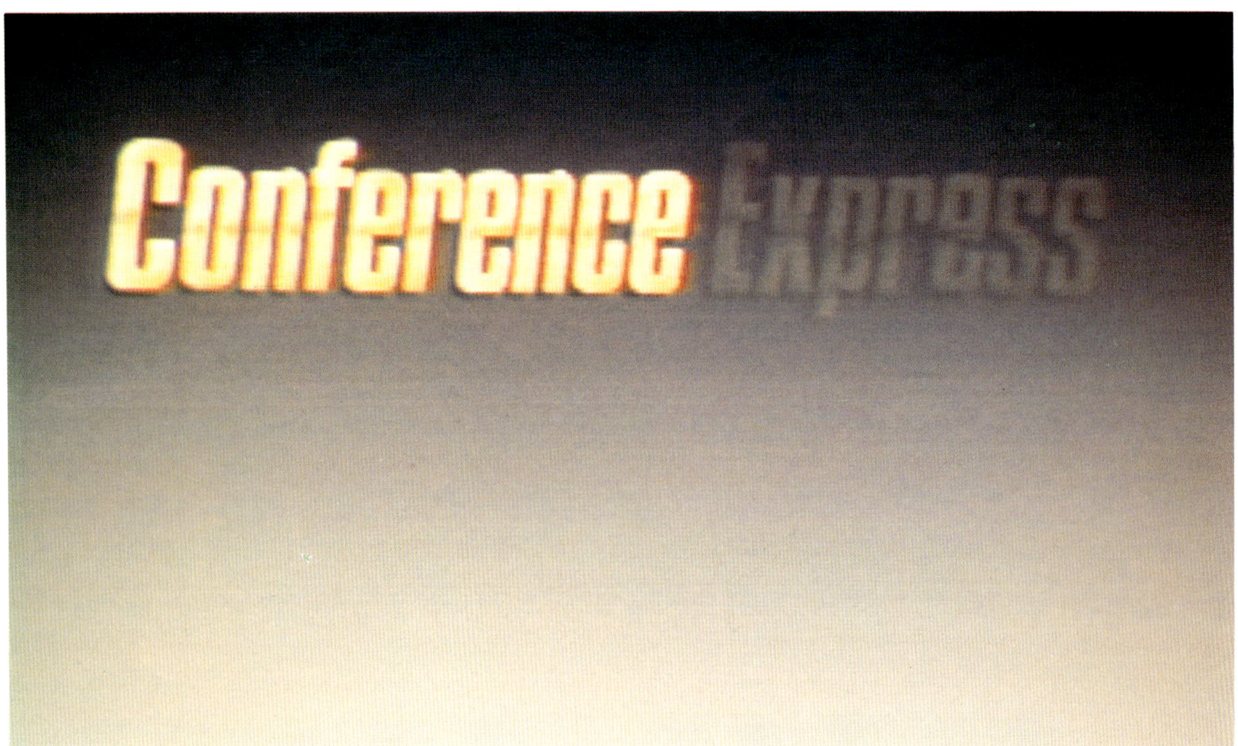

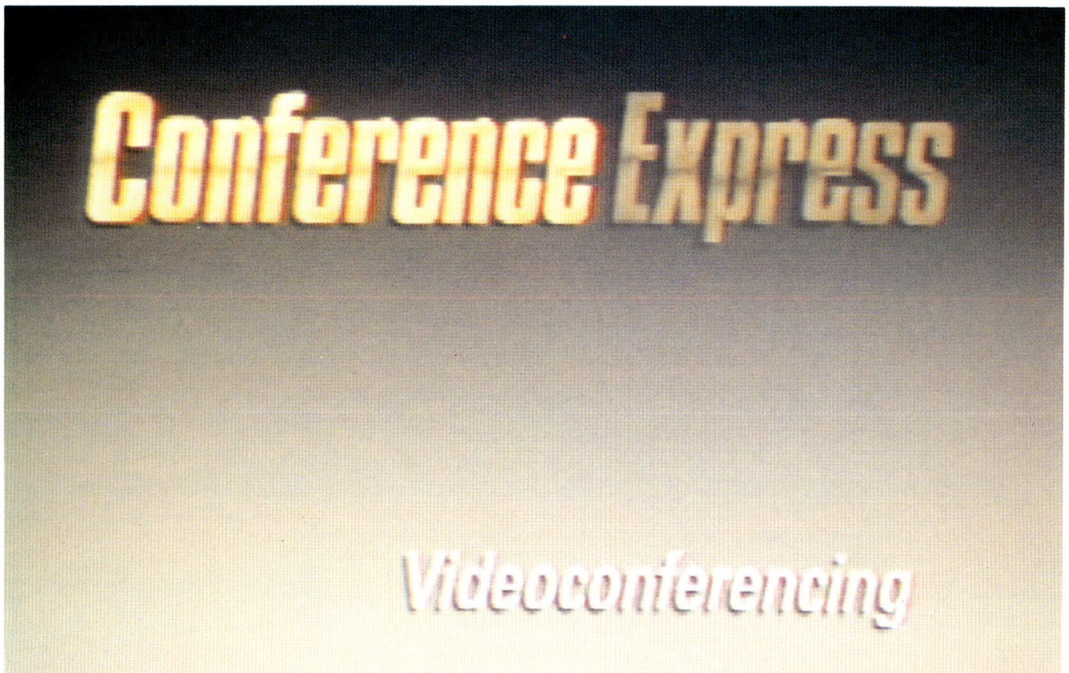

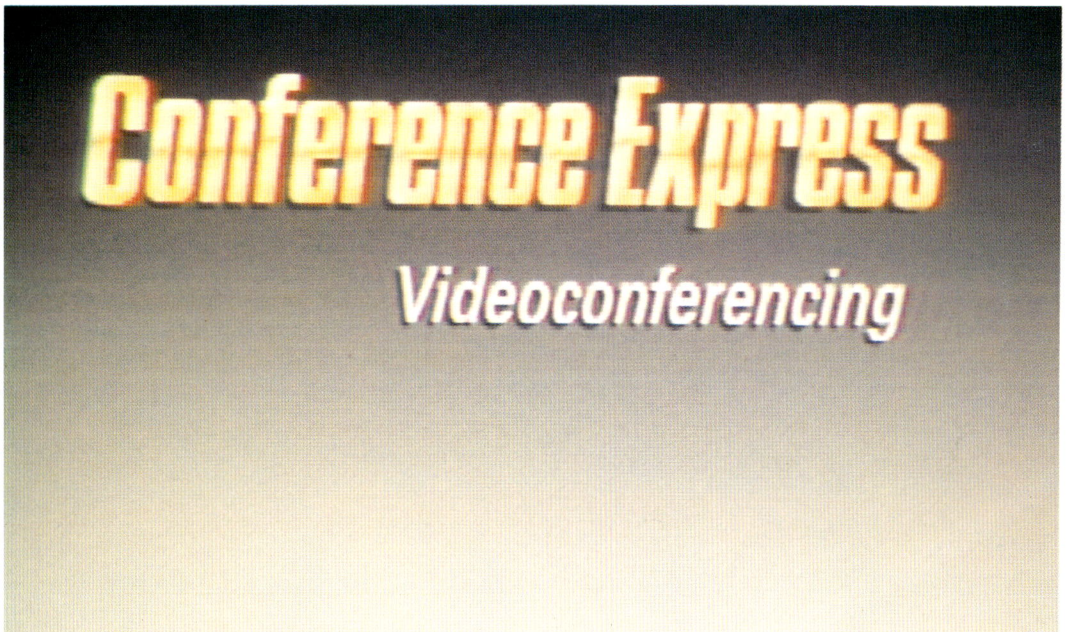

Its About Time

Designed as an opening/closing logo for a 5-minute demonstration reel for Conference Express.

Created on a PC compatible with Lumina software. It was recorded on a Betacam deck and re-recorded using an animation controller.

Created By	Chris Quilter, Anne McKay, Richard Marcus, Robert Bachalo, Rich Kearney
Design Firm	Richard Marcus Productions, Inc.
Creative Director	Chris Quilter
Effects Supervisor	Robert Bachalo
Producer	Chris Quilter
Video Editor	Richard Marcus
Created and Completed at	Richard Marcus Productions

Length of Time to Complete Work—3 hours

Lee Corey

Corey Design Studio, 42 E. 23rd Street, New York, NY 10010

Straight Talk With Joe Thursday

Designed for the Environmental Protection Agency for a 30-minute training video consisting of live action and animation which concerned leak detection for underground storage systems.

Design Firm	Corey Design Studios
Designer	Fillippo Giansante
Creative Director	Lee Corey
Art Director	Lee Corey
Effects Supervisor	Sal Malimo, Mimondo Productions
Animation Camera	Sal Malimo
Animator	John Dilworth
Graphic Artist	George Poladian
Producer	Debbie Goldberg, Mimondo Productions
Associate Producer	Julie Eisenberg, Environmental Media Center
Video Editor	Ed Kisberg
Created and Completed at	Corey Design Studios

Length of Time to Complete 3½ Minutes of Animation—6 weeks

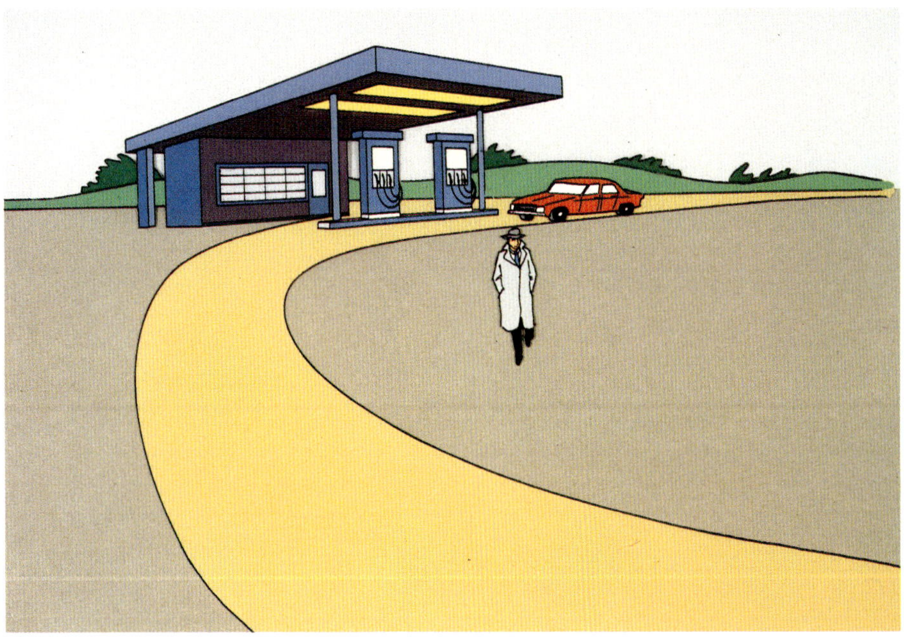

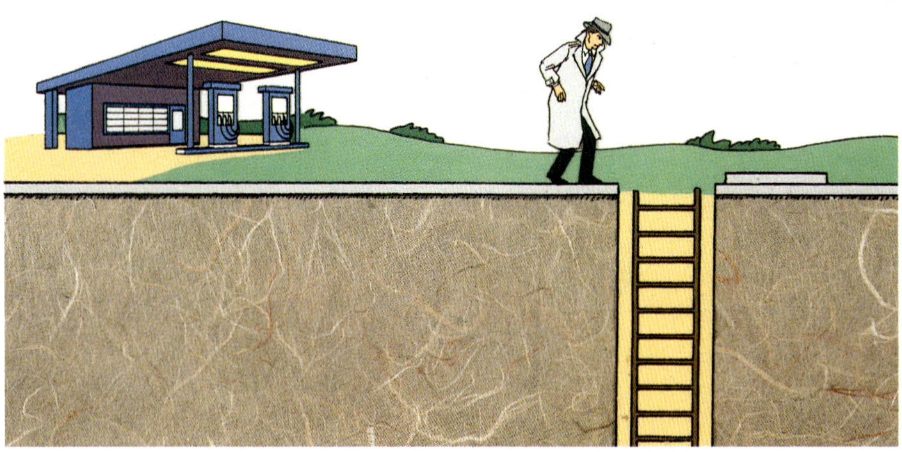

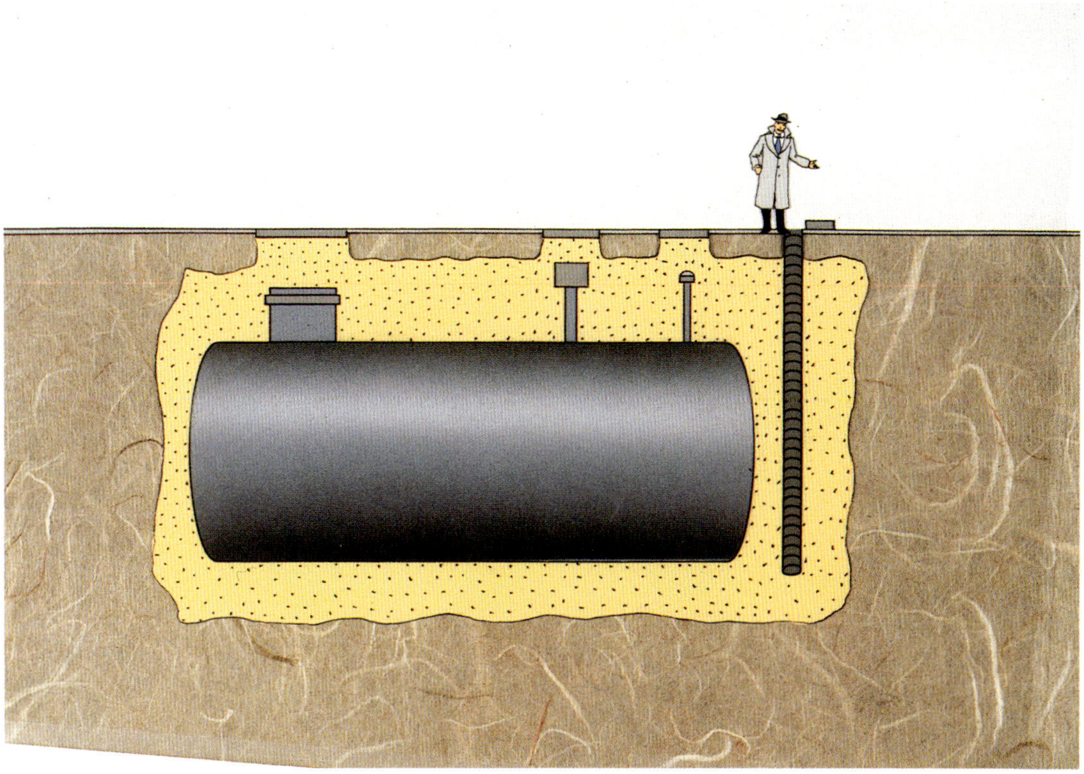

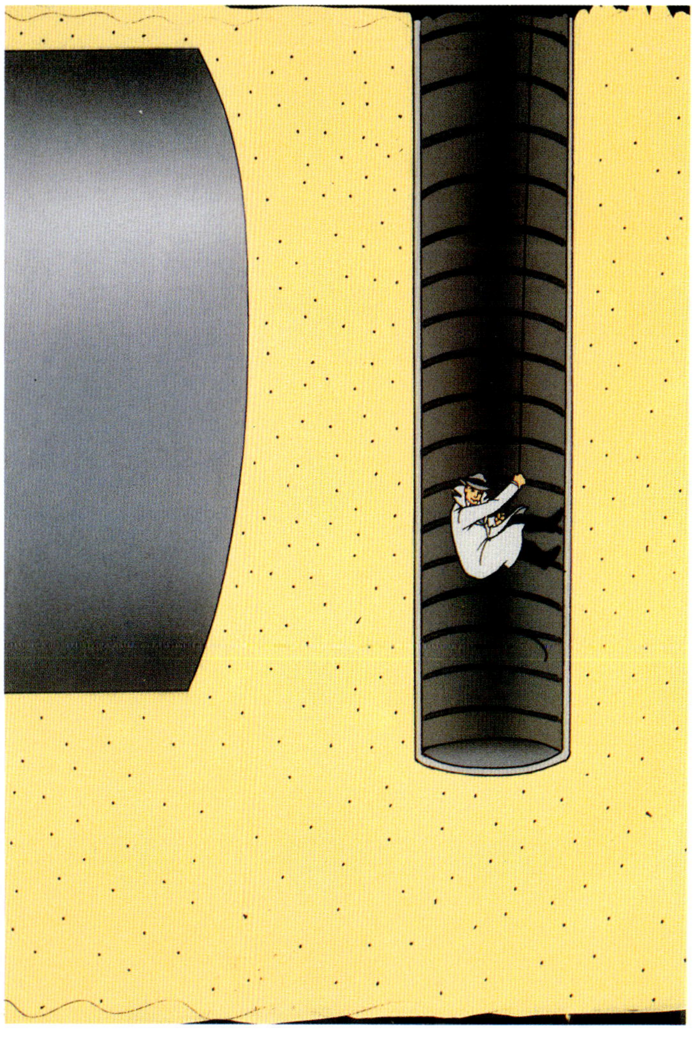

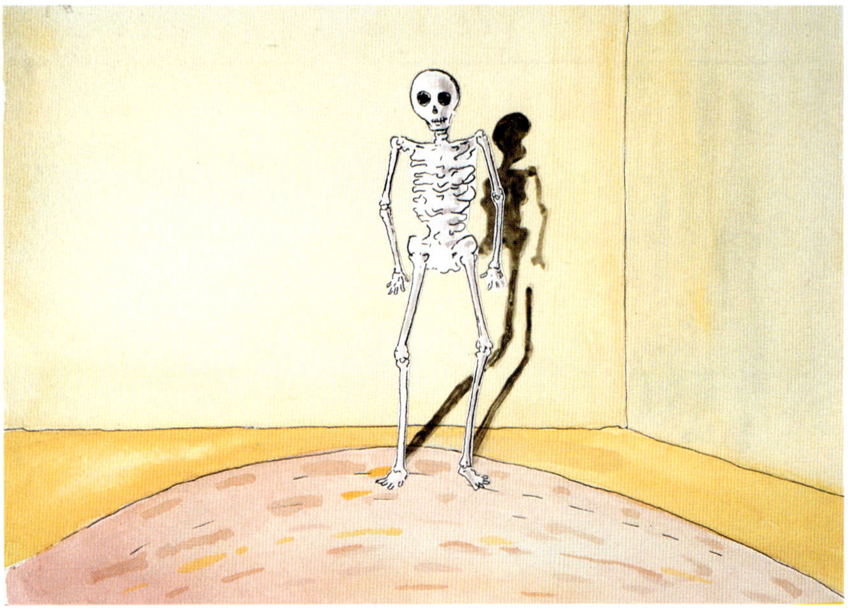

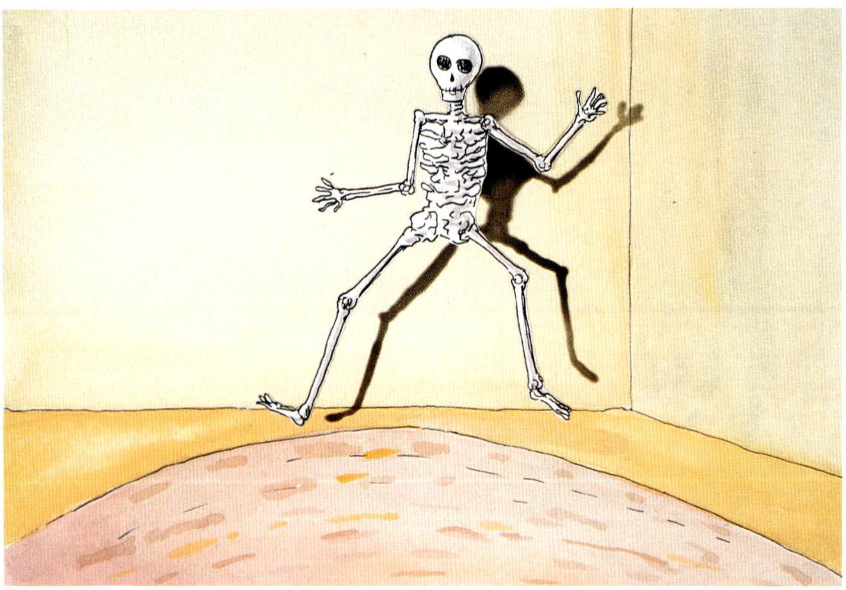

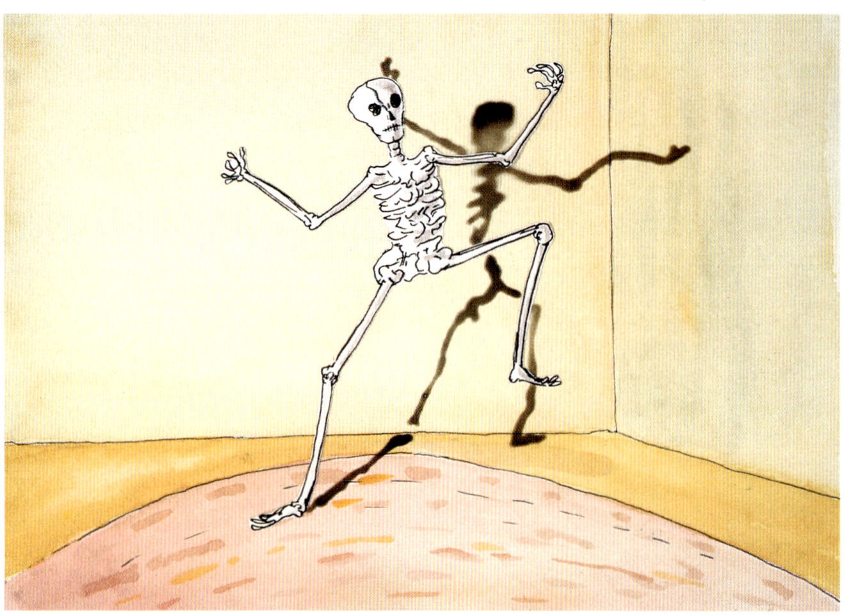

DANCING SKELETON

Created as a children's book video for McGraw-Hill/MacMillan, based on the book "The Dancing Skeleton" by Cynthia D. DeFelice, illustrated by Robert Andrew Parker.

Design Firm	Corey Design Studios
Designer/Artist	Robert Andrew Parker
Creative Director	Rosemary Killen
Art Director	Lee Corey
Animator	Lee Corey
Assistant Animator	David Spletzer
Production Artist	Michelle Bocklage
Producer	Rosemary Killen
Animation Camera	RB/Mavericks
Created and Completed at	Corey Design Studios

Length of Time to Complete Work—3 weeks

Data Motion Arts, Inc.

231 East 55th Street, New York, NY 10022

Data Motion Arts was founded in 1985 by Tony Caio who is also the firm's chief designer. Tony's first experience with computer imagery came while he was still a student at Syracuse University. He started Data Motion Arts because he saw the potential that low-cost work stations and personal computers offered the graphic artist. What began as a one-man operation, is now a firm of nine people which has moved several times in order to expand its facilities. DMA uses its commitment to the latest technology and design expertise to provide a full range of design services including video graphics, animation, print design, high resolution imaging and industrial simulation. Tony Caio and Data Motion Arts are responsible for the creation of this book's cover design.

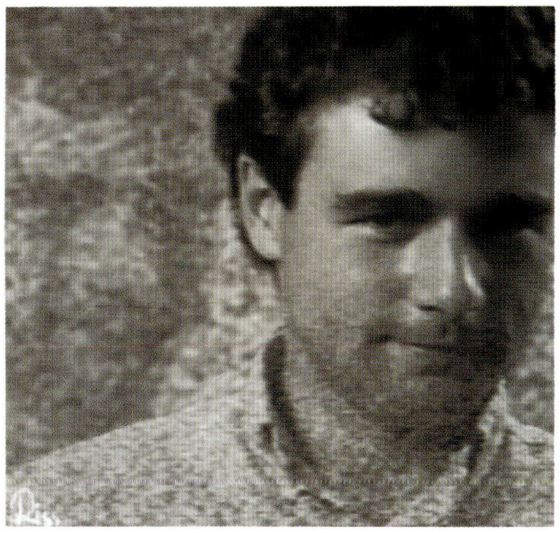

Tony Calo,
President,
Data Motion Arts, Inc.

International Banking

Client	Citibank
Project	International Banking
Producer	3D Communications
Application	Poster for international distribution
Designer	Tony Caio

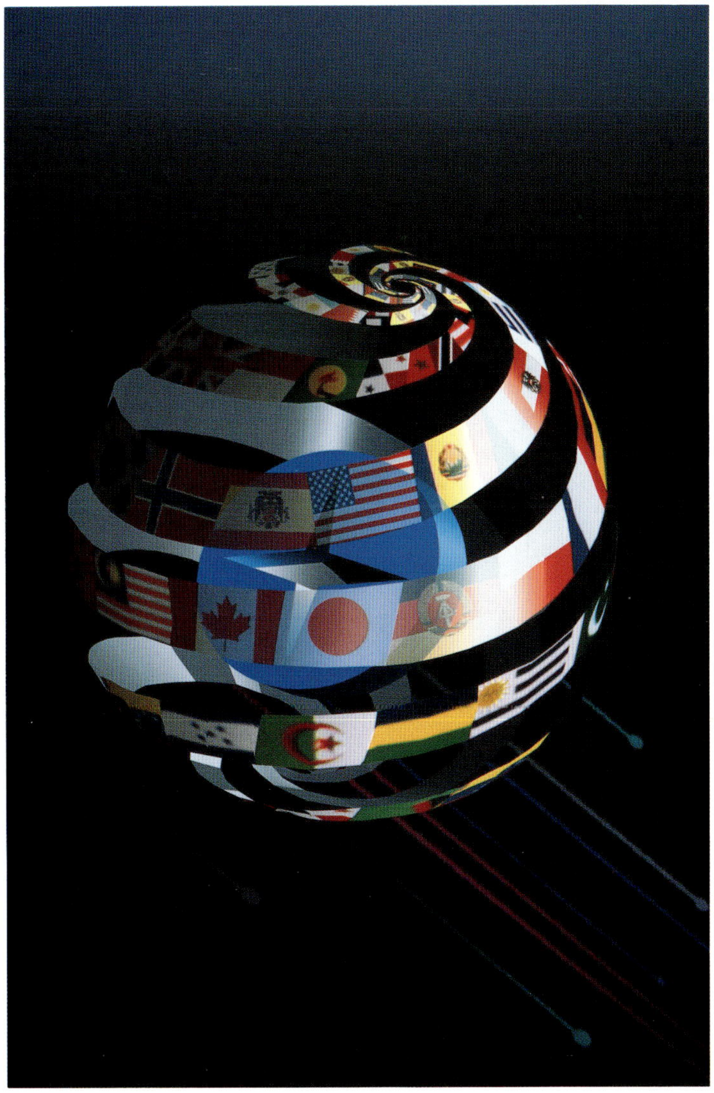

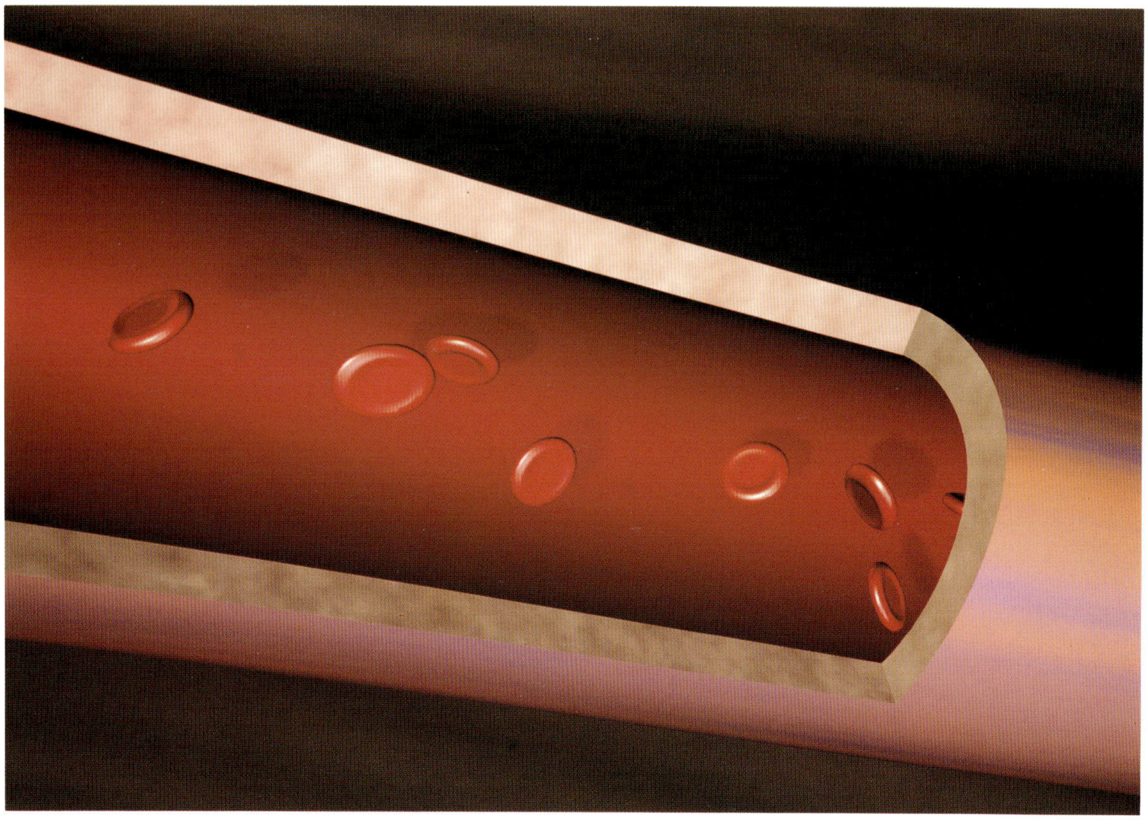

Blood Vessel Constriction

Client	Pfizer Pharmaceuticals
Project	Blood Vessel Constriction
Production Company	Dragon Medical & Scientific Communications
Art Director	Mark Miller
Application	Animation 10 seconds in length

NBA Entertainment

Client	Time Base Consoles
Project	NBA Entertainment
Art Director	Tony Caio
Application	Simulation
Animators	Saul Rubin, Rajesh Naiksatam

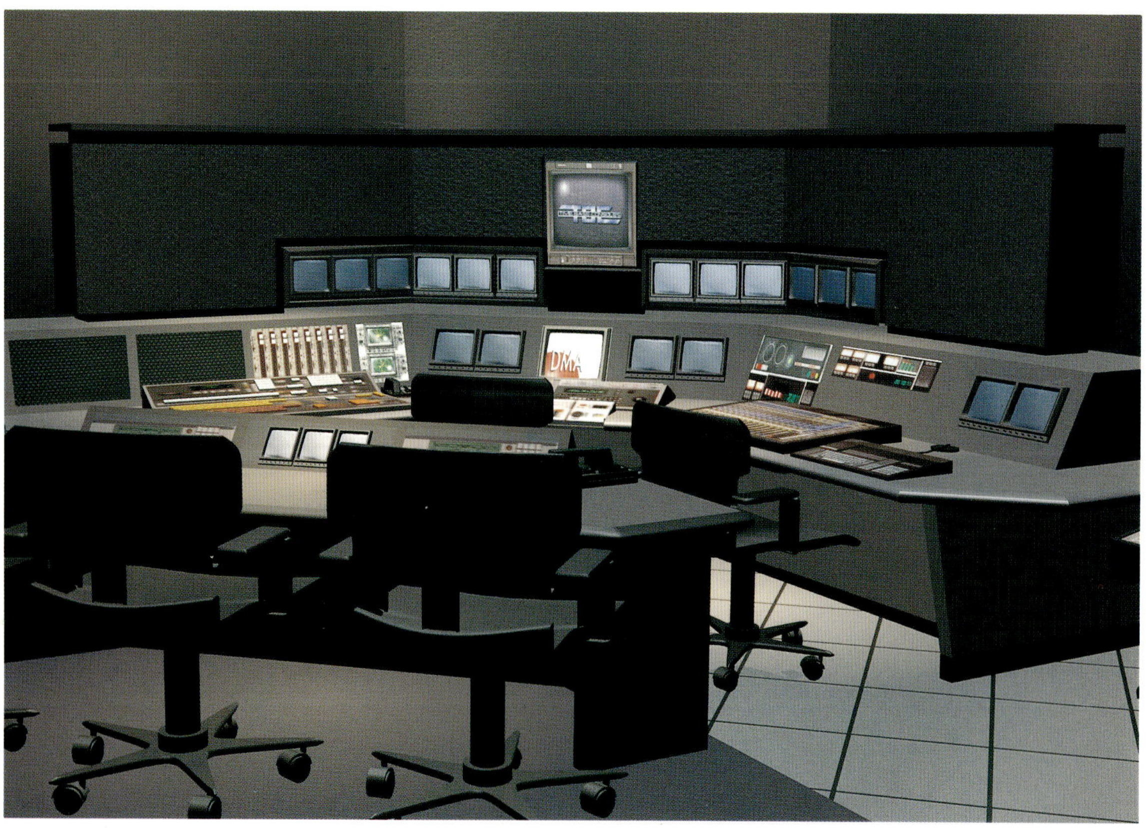

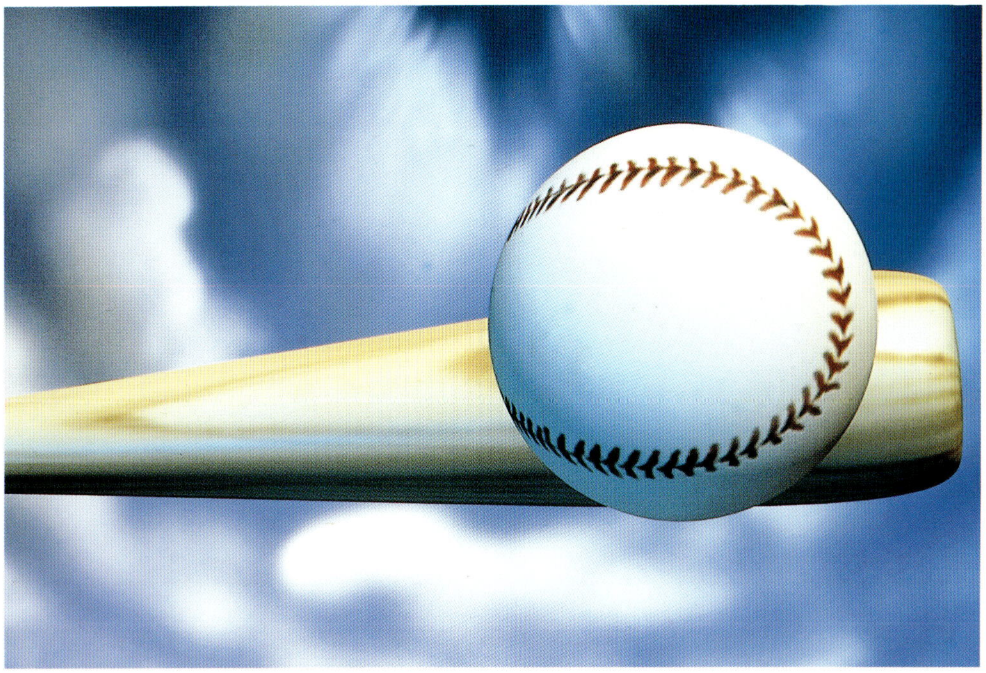

1990 CBS BASEBALL

Client	CBS Sports
Project	1990 CBS Baseball
Art Director	Tony Caio
Application	Animation 10 seconds in length
Animator	Saul Rubin
Designer	Tony Caio
Music	Saul Rubin, Data Motion Arts, Inc.

UNISYS BUSINESS TELEVISION

Client	Unisys
Project	Unisys Business Television
Producer	Steve Bob
Art Director	Tony Caio
Application	Animation open for global video conference 10 seconds in length
Animator	Saul Rubin, Steve Corin
Music	Saul Rubin, Data Motion Arts, Inc.

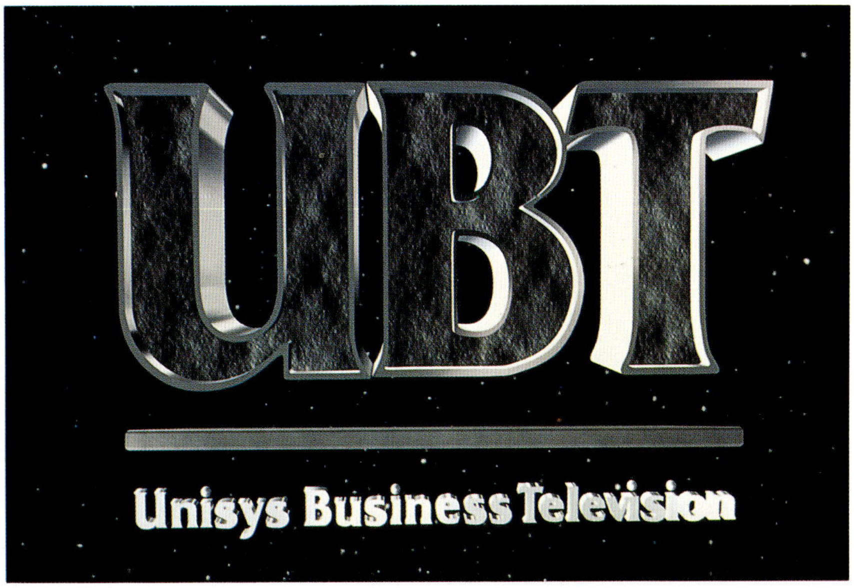

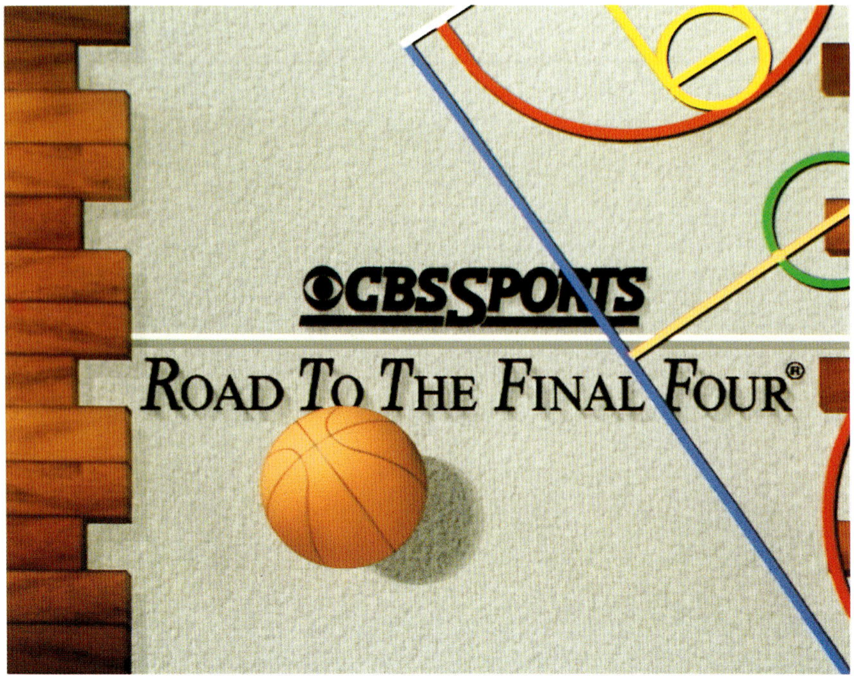

ROAD TO THE FINAL FOUR

Client	CBS Sports
Project	Road to the Final Four
Producer	Bob Mansbach
Art Director	Tony Caio
Application	Animation Show Open 5 seconds in length
Animators	Micha Riss, Tony Caio

ISLAND RECORDS LOGO IDENTITY TAG

Client	Island Records
Project	Island Records Logo Identity Tag
Producer	4 Front Video
Art Director	Tony Caio
Application	Animation 10 seconds in length
Animators	Saul Rubin, Steve Corin

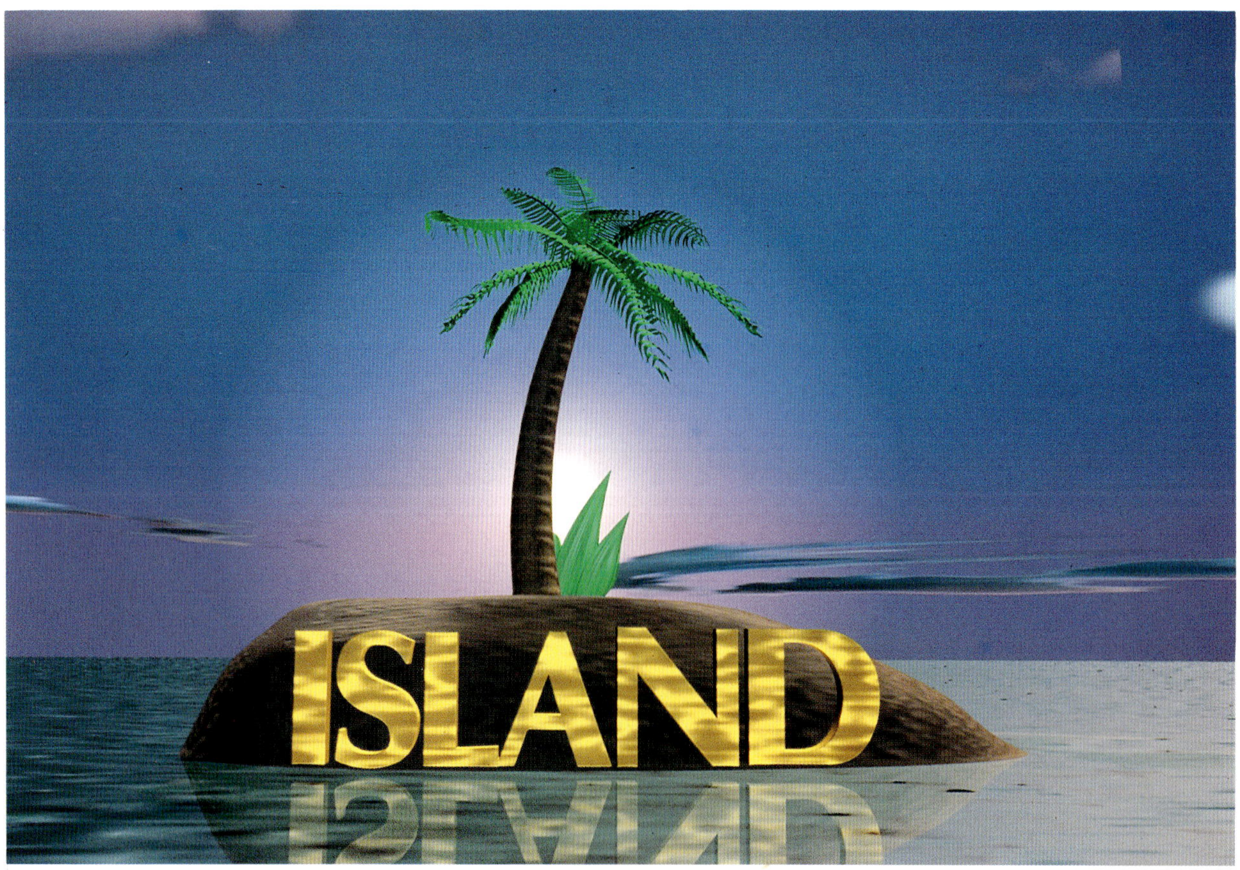

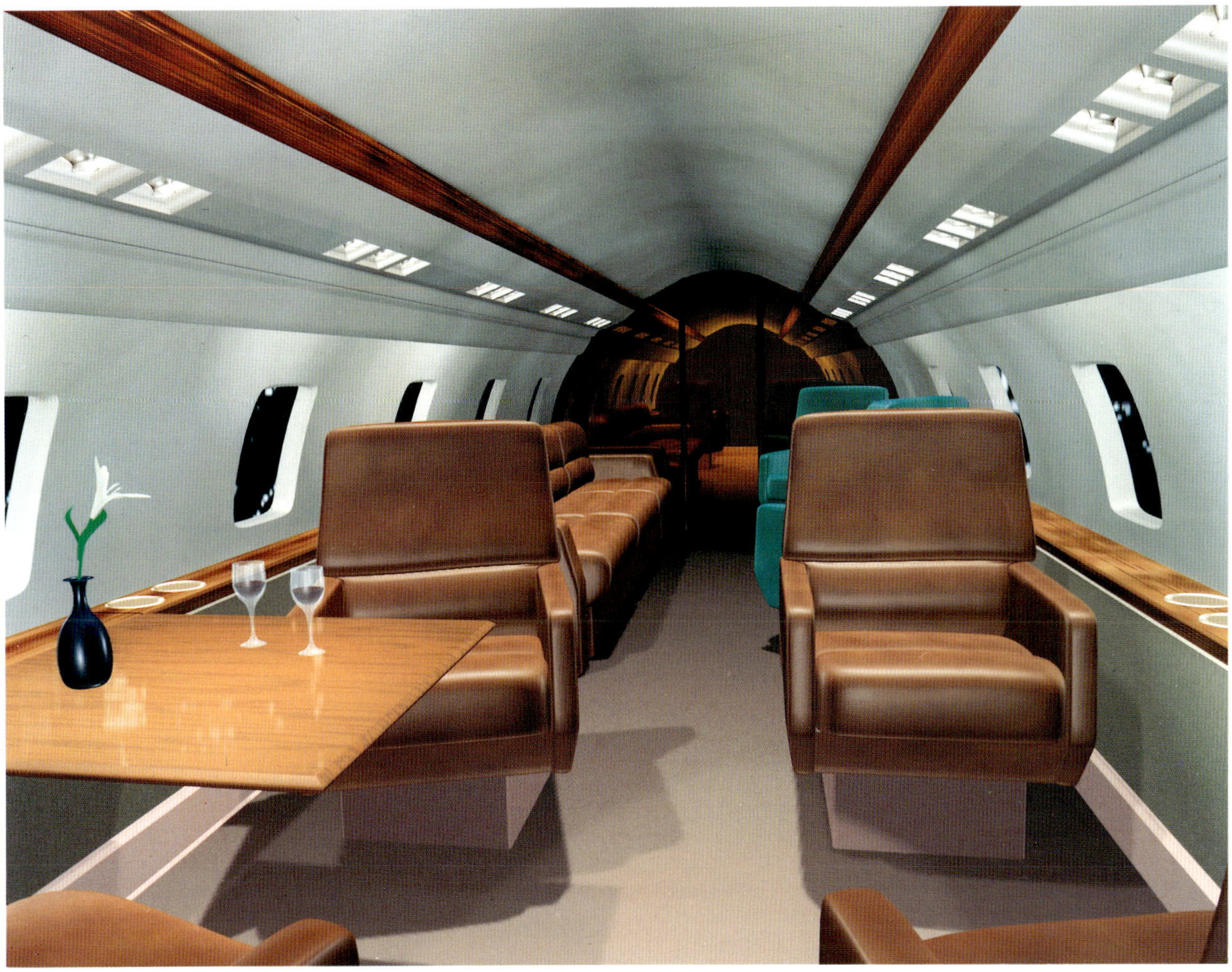

CHASE MANHATTAN CORPORATE JET DESIGN

Client	Falcon Jet
Project	Chase Manhattan Corporate Jet Design
Producer	Richard Nadeau Jr.
Application	Simulation
Animators	Tony Caio, Saul Rubin

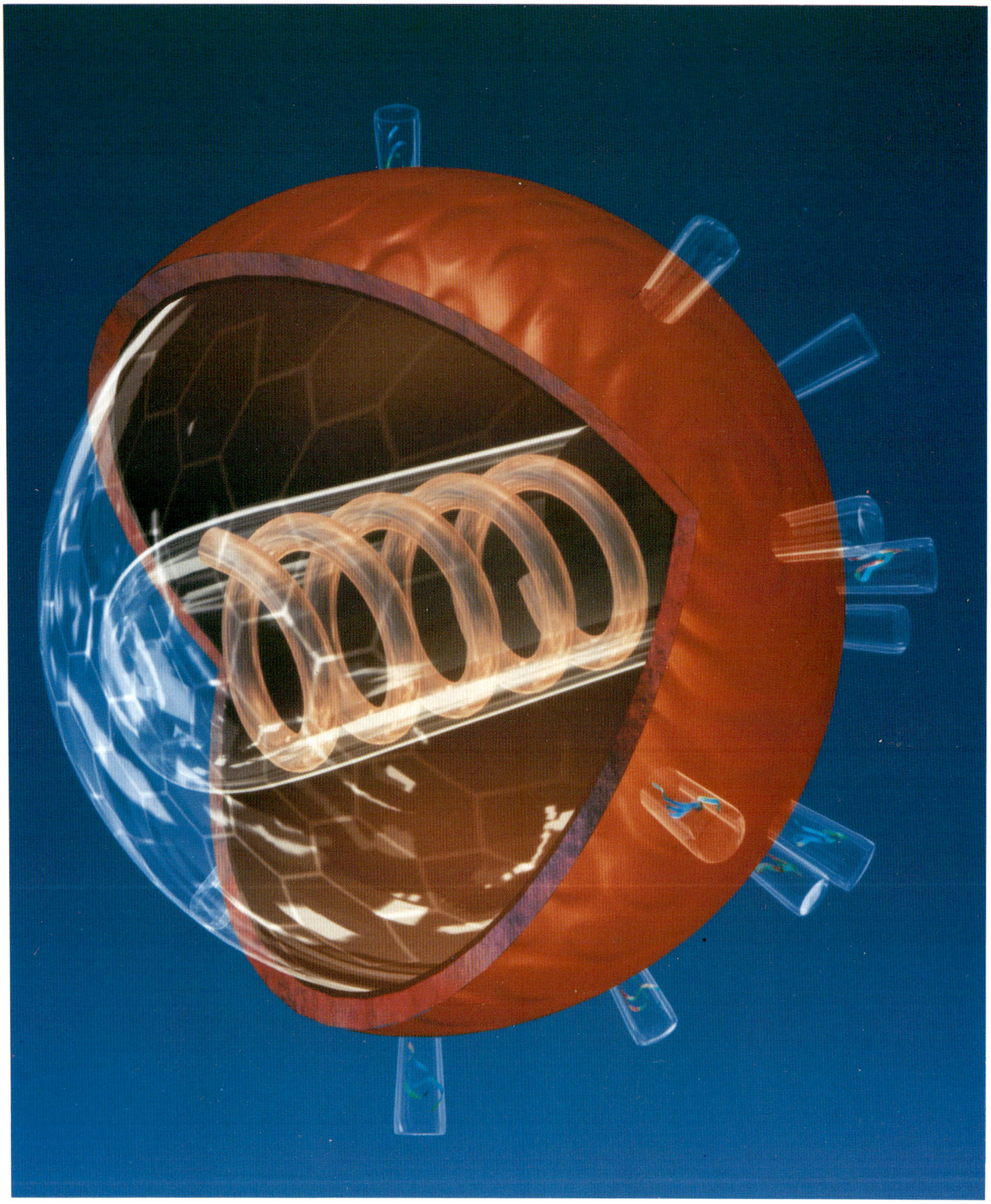

AIDS VIRUS

Client	DMA self promotion
Project	AIDS Virus
Producer	Tony Caio
Art Director	Saul Rubin
Application	Print/Illustration

Squibb Vitamin Product

Client	DMA self promotion
Project	Squibb Vitamin product
Producer	Saul Rubin
Art Director	Tony Caio
Application	Animation 5 seconds in length
Animator	Rajesh Naiksatam

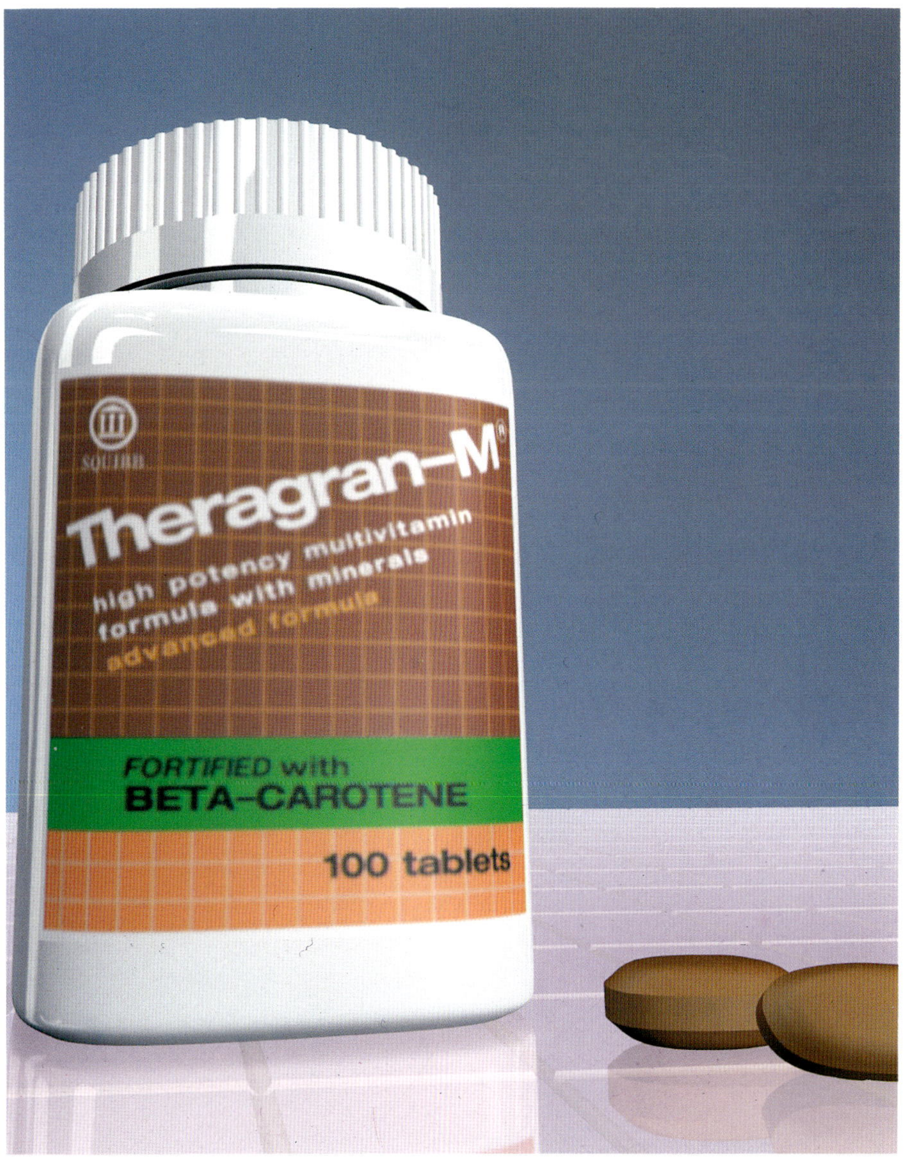

JOE DELCIAMPO

Frame: Runner, Inc., 1995 Broadway-Suite 1100, New York, NY 10023

Joe DelCiampo is the Design Director of Frame: Runner, Inc., an entirely component editing facility in New York, NY. He is a graduate of the Art Institute of Pittsburgh with a degree in commercial art. He has been a Demo Artist for both Quanta and Digital F/X.

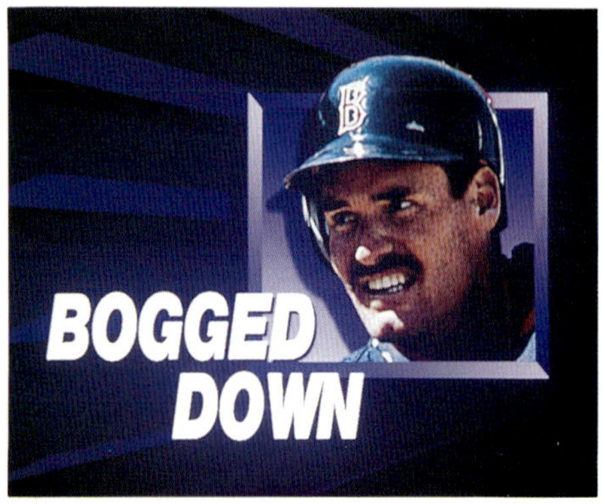

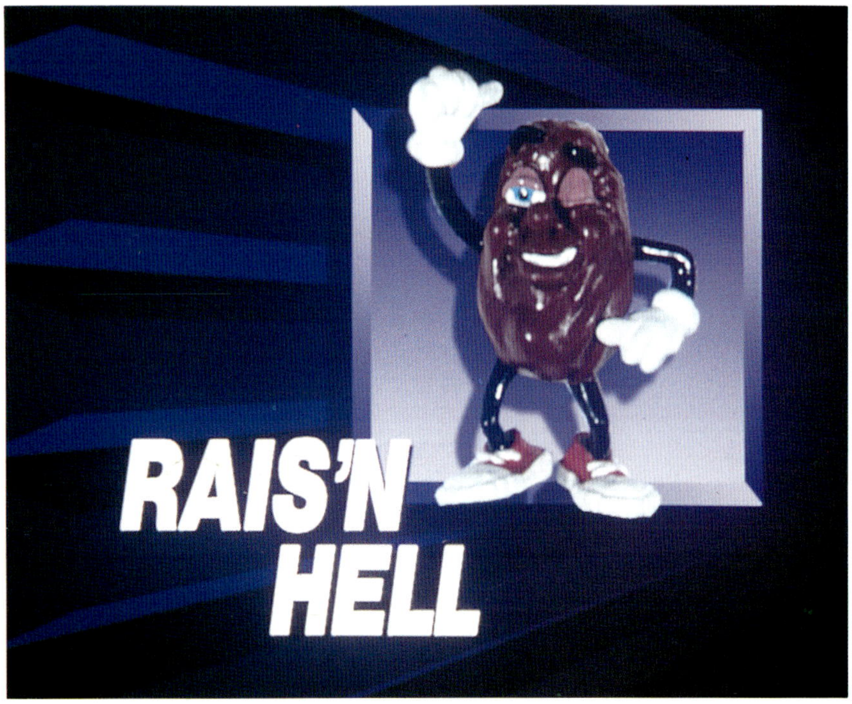

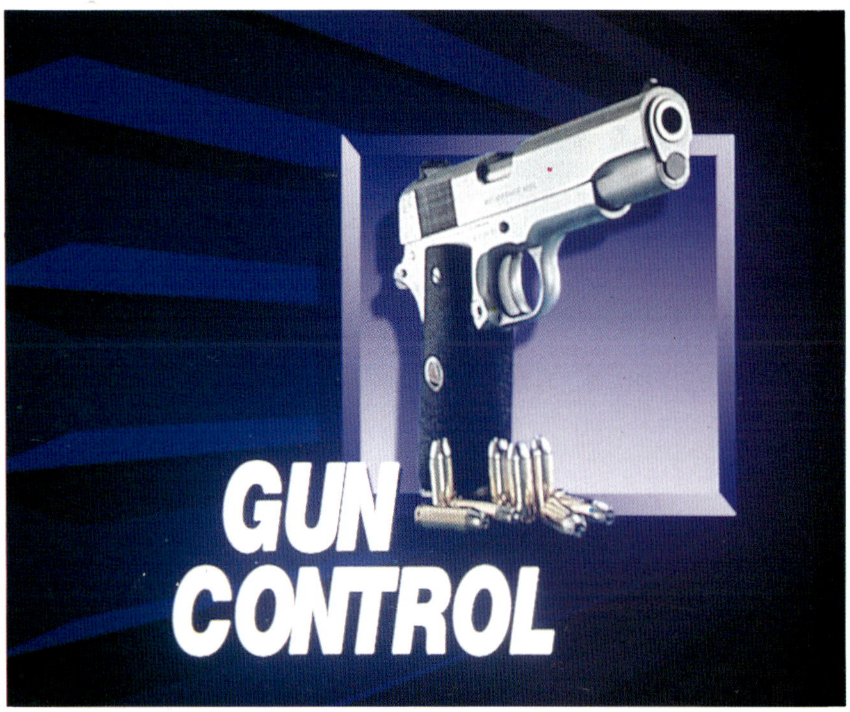

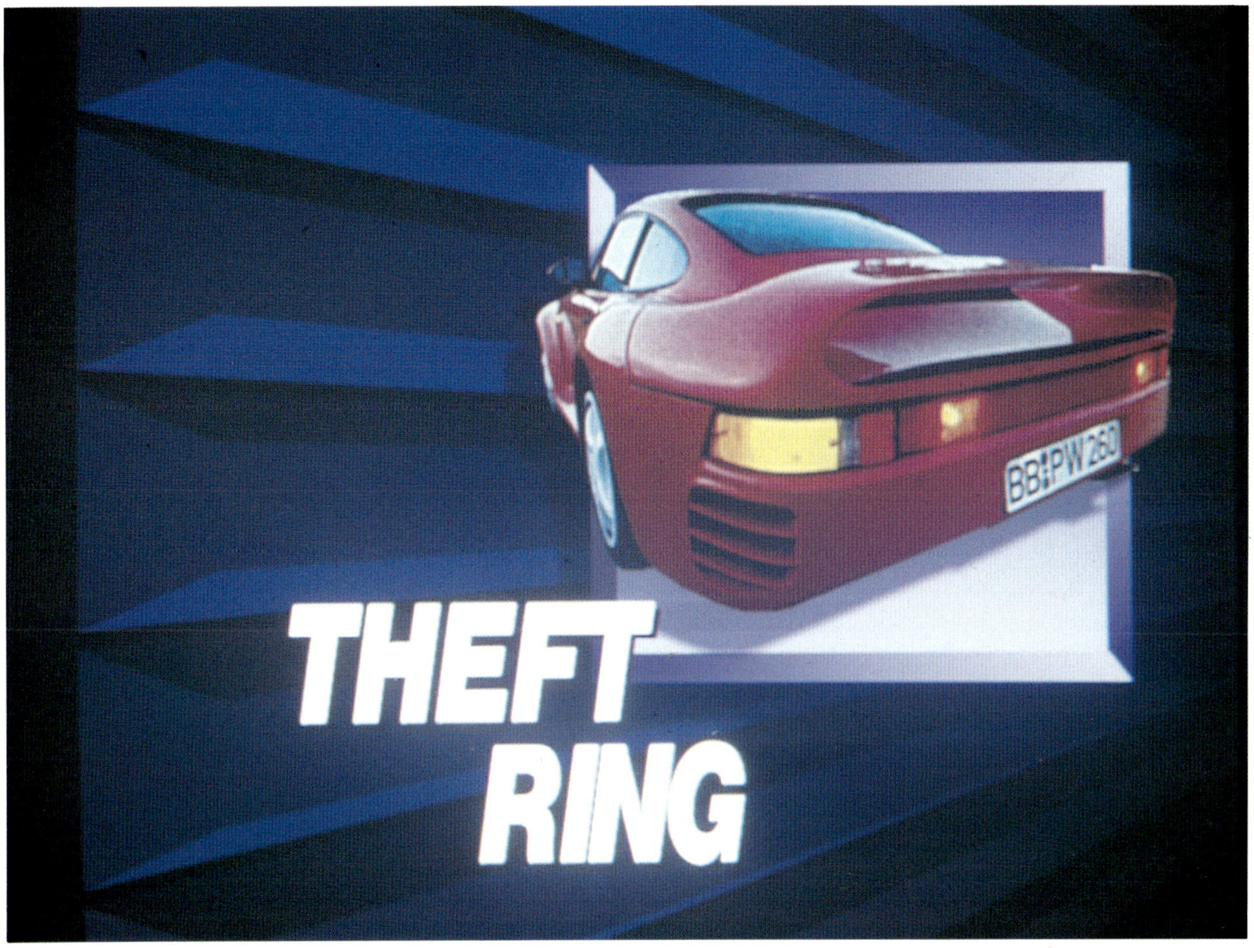

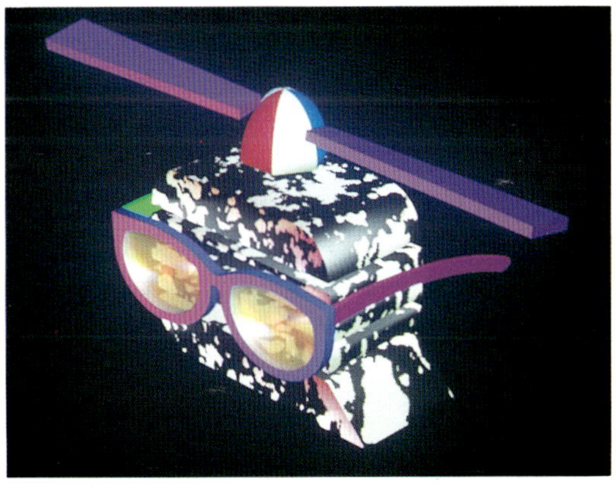

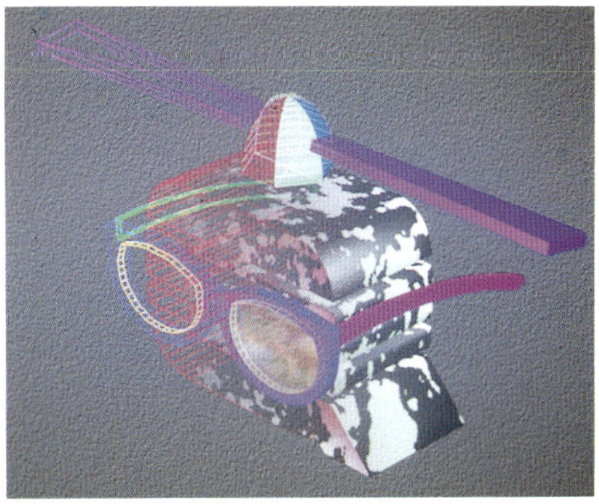

BOGGED DOWN
RAIS'N HELL
GUN CONTROL
THEFT RING
GLASSES

These images of over-the-shoulder graphics and 3-D animation were created with TOPAS 3-D and T.I.P.S. paint software from AT&T GSL (Graphics Software Labs, Indianapolis). Both were used to combine 3-D images with 2-D paint images.

FEIGENBAUM IN THE LIMELIGHT

219 E. 44th Street, New York, NY 10017

Bill Feigenbaum began his career in the early '60s as a cartoon animator, moving quickly into the design area. He is one of the developing pioneers of bottom lit graphics. Mr. Feigenbaum is the former Chief Art Director for NBC's On-Air Graphics and has co-authored and directed an animated feature film. He created some of the earliest 3-D broadcast openings. Bill was the winner of the first cable TV Emmy ever. In 1980 he and his wife Joyce formed Feigenbaum Productions. Bill attended the High School of Art and Design and the School of Visual Arts.

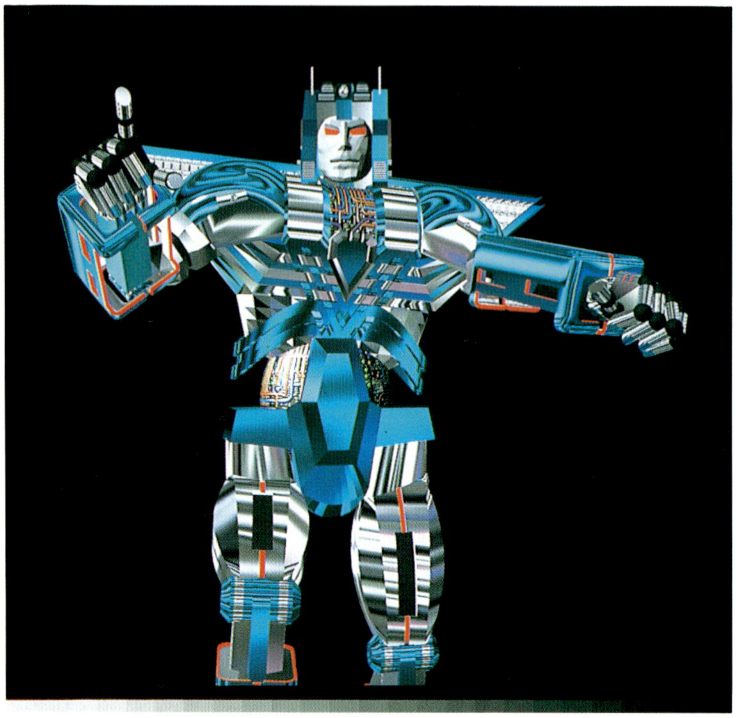

"ROBOT"—
Hasbro "G.I. Joe"—3-D insert

"ACTION MASTERS"—
Hasbro "G.I. Joe"—3-D insert

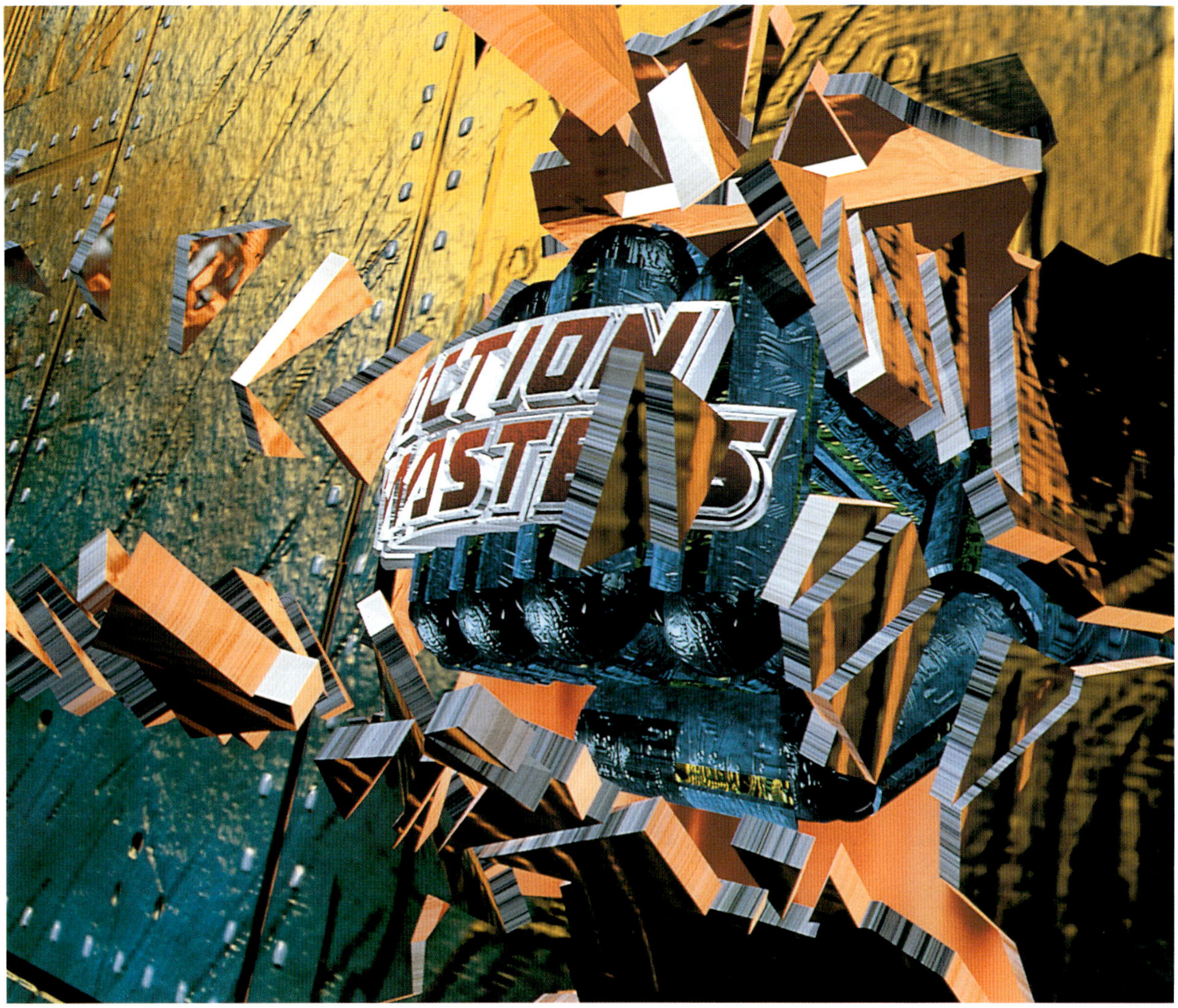

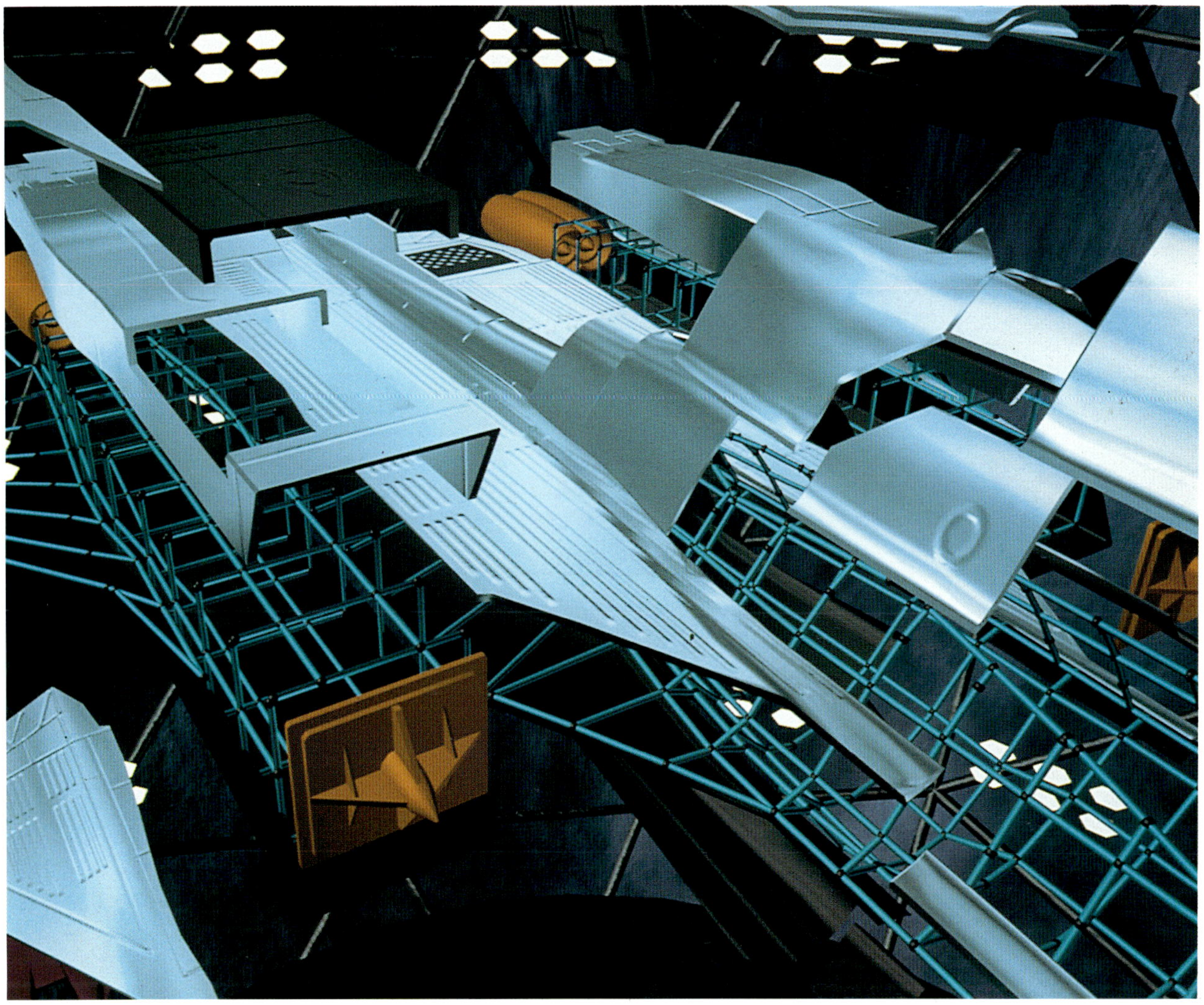

"Sky Raven"—
Hasbro "G.I. Joe"—3-D insert

Designed as commercial inserts for Joe Bacal, Jay Bacal and Tim Speidel of Griffith Bacal, Inc., New York, NY

Created on Silicon Graphics 3-D work stations. The client supplied full blueprint material on the Sky Raven to ensure detail and accuracy.

Designer	Bill Feigenbaum
Creative Director	Bill Feigenbaum
Art Director	Bill Feigenbaum
Effects Supervisor	Floyd Gillis
Graphic Artist	Tom Powers, Floyd Gillis, Michael Kanarek
Producer	Joyce Feigenbaum
Created at	Feigenbaum & Associates
Completed at	Unitel Video, Inc., Windsor Video

Length of Time to Complete Work—4 to 6 weeks each

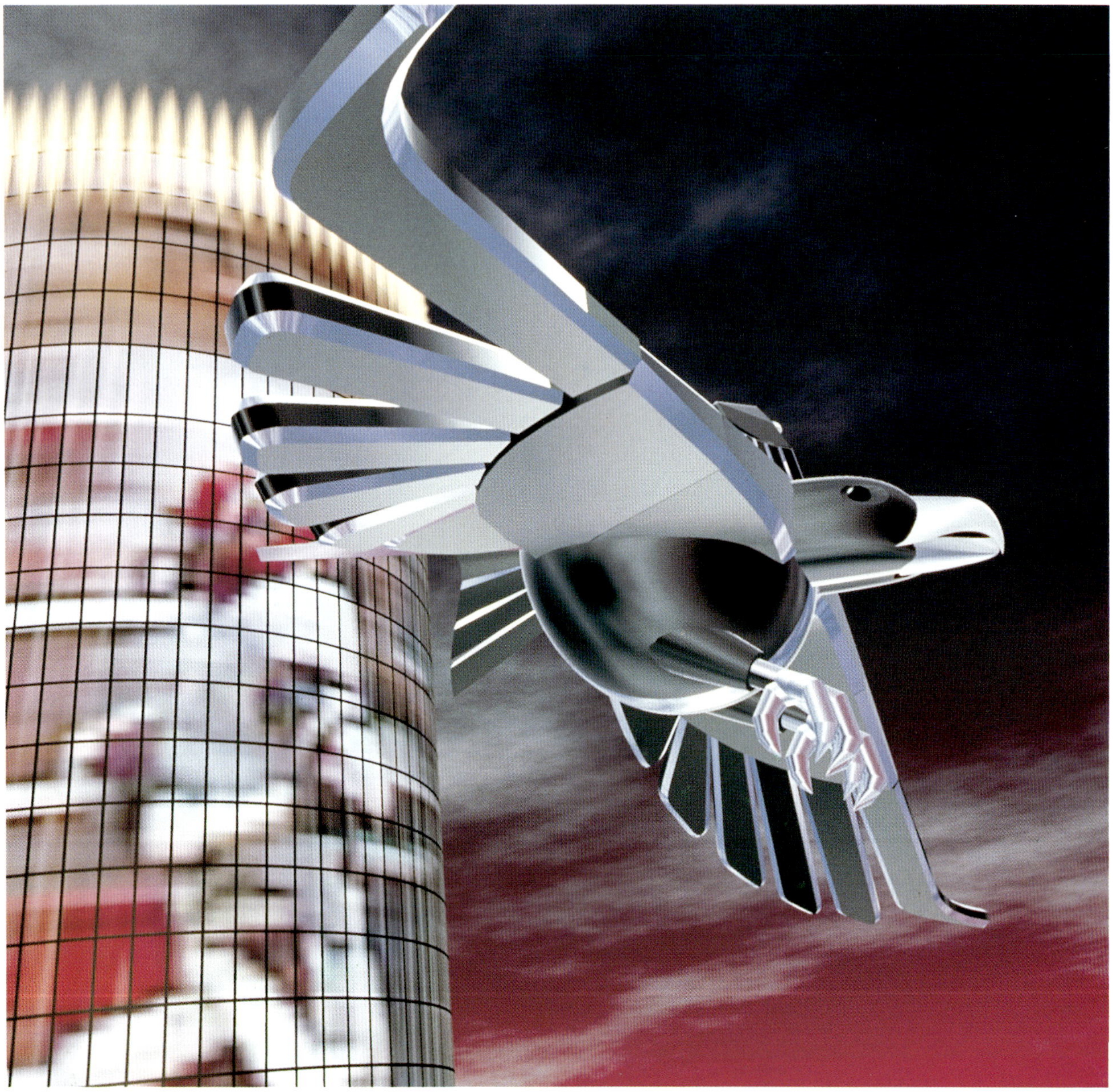

ESPN Sunday Night Football

Designed as show open and bumpers for John Wildhack, Fred Guadella, Bill Bonnell, Chip Dean and Mark Dayton of ESPN, Bristol, CT.

The entire project took 28 different graphic teams who created mostly in 3-D graphics which were combined with Paintbox textures, enhancements and motion control photography. Creative devices include Wavefront software, Proprietary software, Silicon Graphics, Iris work stations, Paintbox, motion control stand and CMX editing.

Design Firm	Feigenbaum in the Limelight
Designer	Bill Feigenbaum
Creative Director	Bill Feigenbaum
Art Director	Bill Feigenbaum
3-D Effects Supervisor	Floyd Gillis, Lester Weiss, Tim Richards, Rod Paul, Andy White, Karen Goulekas
Graphic Artist	Michael Kanarek
Producer	Joyce Feigenbaum
Video Editor	Joe Tavano, Dennis Deegen
Created at	Feigenbaum & Associates
Completed at	Unitel Video, Inc.

Length of Time to Complete Work—1 year

Big Apple N.I.T.

Designed as show open and bumpers for Mo Davenport and Chip Dean of ESPN, Bristol, CT.

Created in 3-D computer animation with data building on Wavefront/ Silicon Graphics Iris work stations, using Paintbox for textures and CMX editing.

Design Firm	Feigenbaum in the Limelight
Designer	Bill Feigenbaum
Creative Director	Bill Feigenbaum
Art Director	Bill Feigenbaum
Computer Animators	Rod Paul, Tim Richards
Producer	Joyce Feigenbaum
Video Editor	Joe Tavano
Completed at	Unitel Video, Inc.

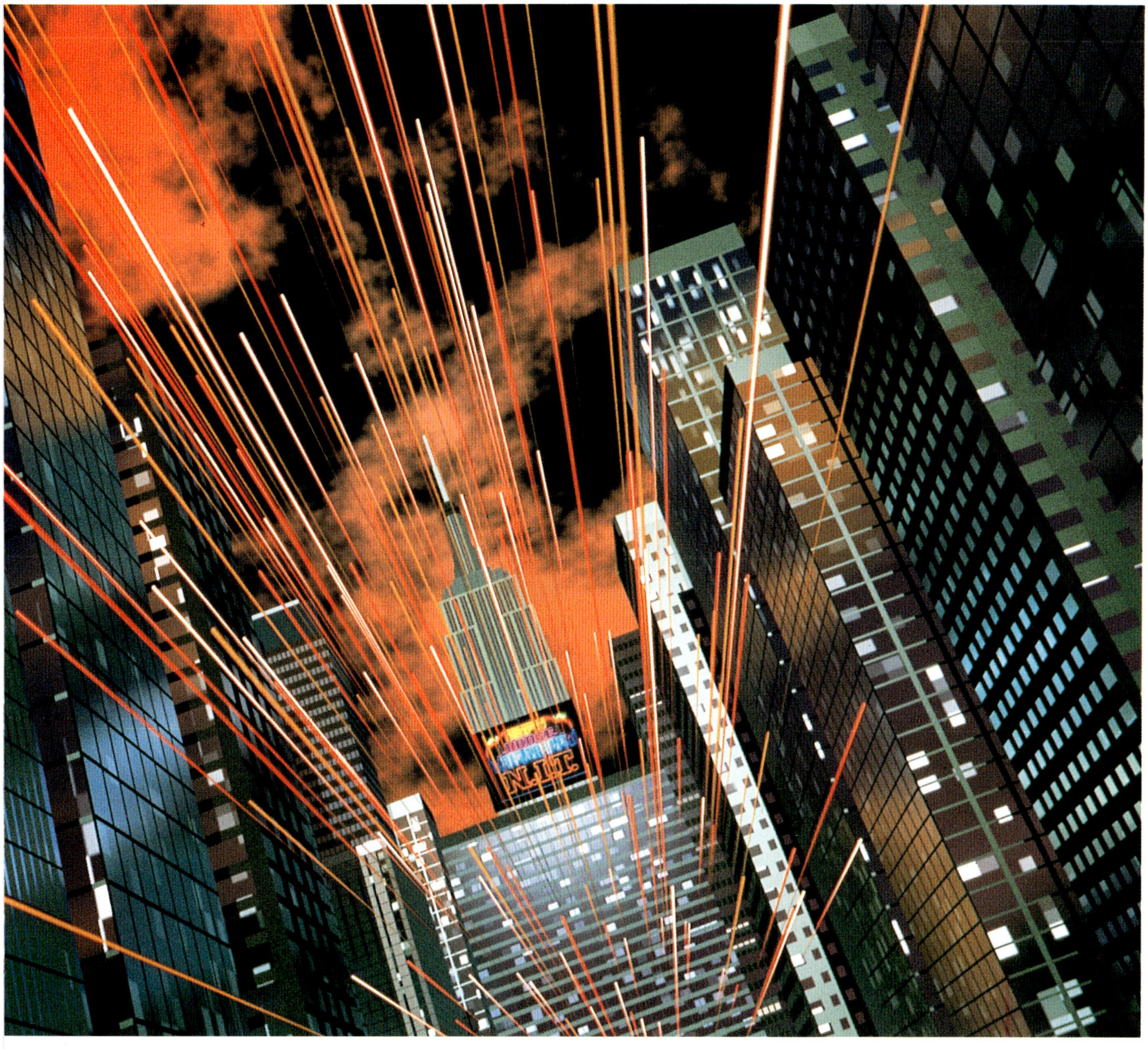

G Nine Productions

2030 Scott Street, San Francisco, CA 94115

G Nine Productions was started in 1987 by director Bill Groshelle. Bill was one of the creative leaders who developed the technique of sophisticated blending of computer graphics, animation, special effects, live action and motion control. He has a Bachelor of Arts in Film Studies from UC Santa Barbara, and a Master of Fine Arts from the School of Film/Video at Cal Arts. Bill's countless credits run the gamut from work on effects sequences for "Top Gun" to Christie Brinkley for Cover Girl Makeup. Some of Bill's selected professional awards include: ADDY—Silver; Broadcast Designers Association—Gold, Silver; Clio—Finalist; Emmy; Houston Int. Film Festival; IBA; International Monitor Award; San Francisco Show; and TELLY—Silver.

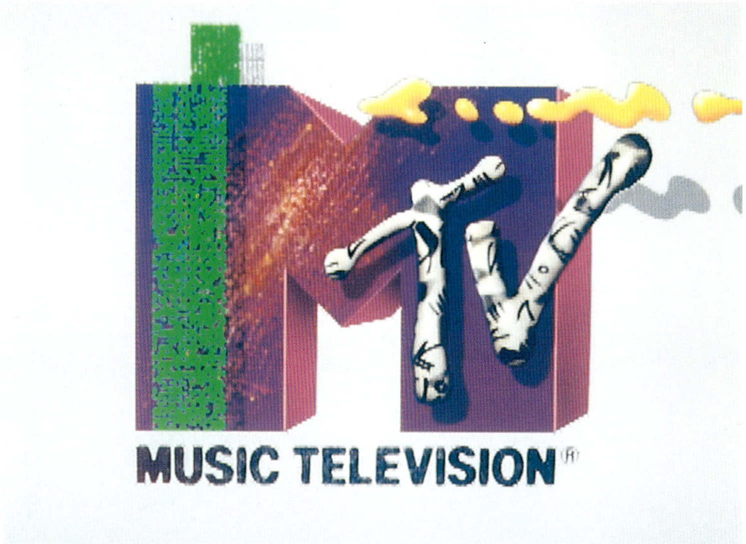

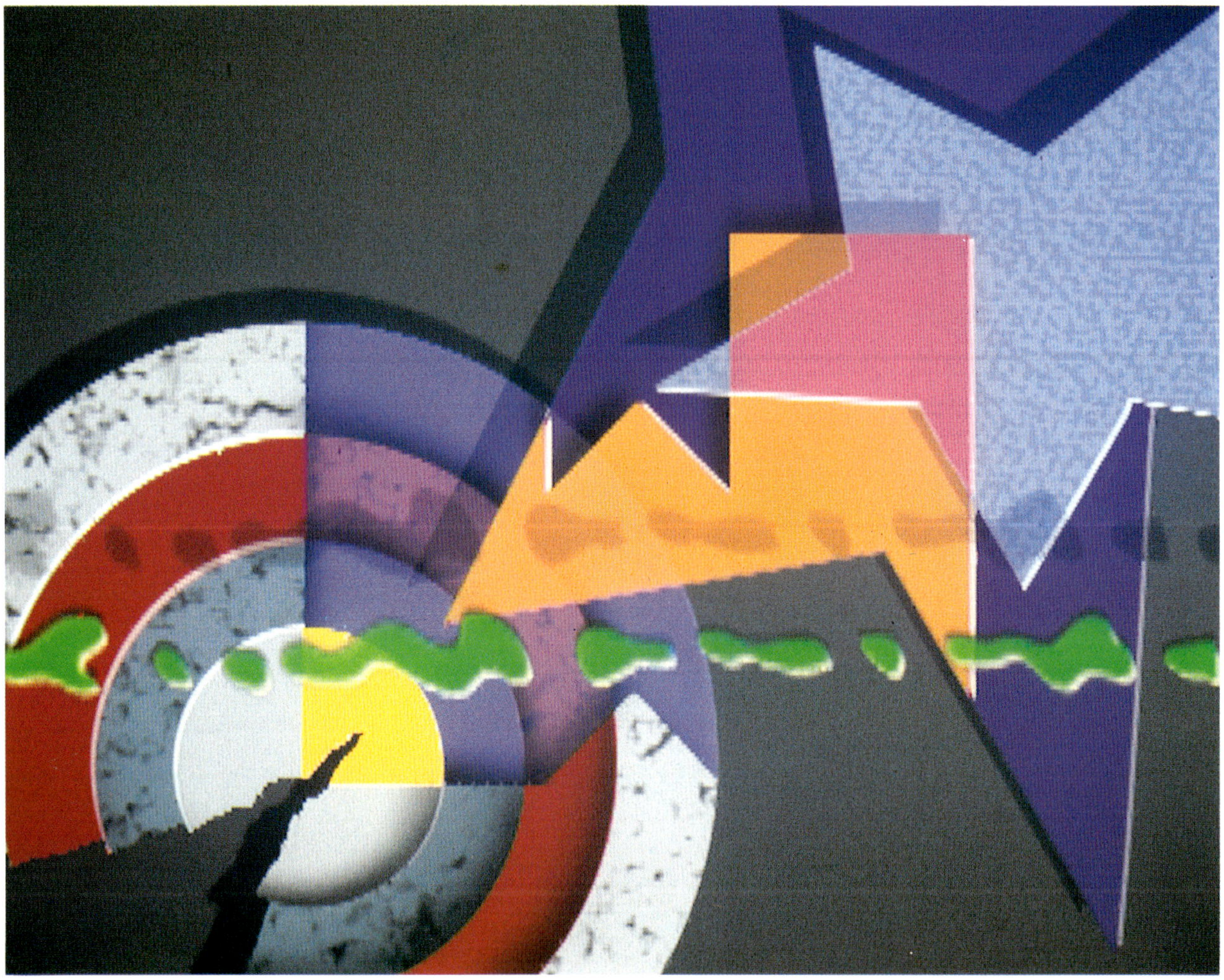

"Top of the Hour"
Station ID for MTV

The work was designed on an Amiga off line computer graphics system. The black-and-white art was created on a Macintosh with Linotronic output. The final color, motion and compositing were done on Quantel Paintbox with Harry and Encore.

Created By	William Groshelle, Kate Montgomery
Design Firm	G Nine Productions
Designer	William Groshelle
Creative Director	William Groshelle
Art Director	William Groshelle
Producer	Kate Montgomery
Created and completed at	One Pass Video

Length of Time to Complete Work—3 weeks

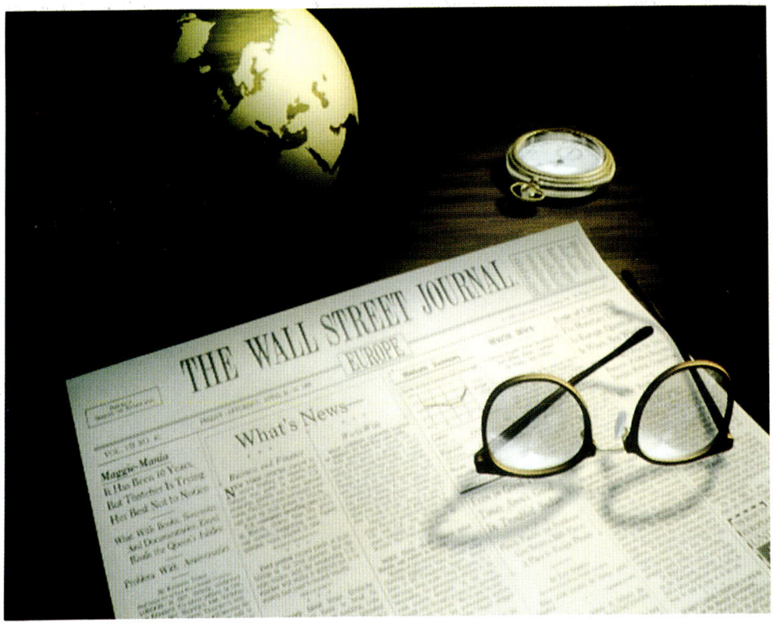

"ONLY ONE"

Commercial for Wall Street Journal, Europe

The work was created on Pacific Data Images silicon graphics system using their proprietary software. Standard computer graphics techniques were used with a high resolution scan of a real newspaper. The tabletop was computer simulated.

Created By	William Groshelle, Kate Montgomery, Theresa Ellis, Jim Friedlich
Design Firm	G Nine Productions
Designer/Director	William Groshelle
Creative Director	William Groshelle
Art Director	William Groshelle
Artist/Animator	Theresa Ellis
Producer	Kate Montgomery
Created at	Pacific Data Images
Completed at	AME, Los Angeles

Length of Time to Complete Work—4 weeks

"MACINTOSH PORTABLE, MACINTOSH ANYWHERE"

New product introduction for Apple Computer

Created using Super 8, 16mm and 35mm film animation along with live action footage. The combination was mixed with Paintbox and Harry. All type was set on a Macintosh. Live action images were layered with graphics and then additional type was added.

Design Firm	G Nine Productions
Designer/Director	William Groshelle
Creative Director	William Groshelle
Art Director	William Groshelle
Paintbox Artist	Darryl Vance
Executive Producer	Kate Montgomery
Producer	Jennifer Thomas
Video Editor	Mitra Tyree
On-Line Editor	Bill Weber
Created and Completed at	Western Video Tape

Length of Time to Complete Work—6 weeks

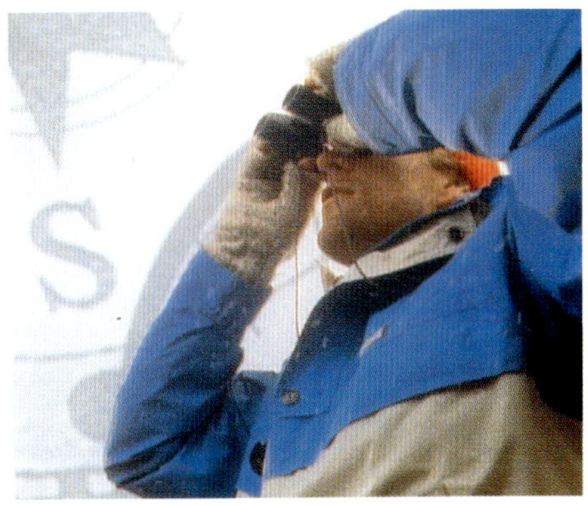

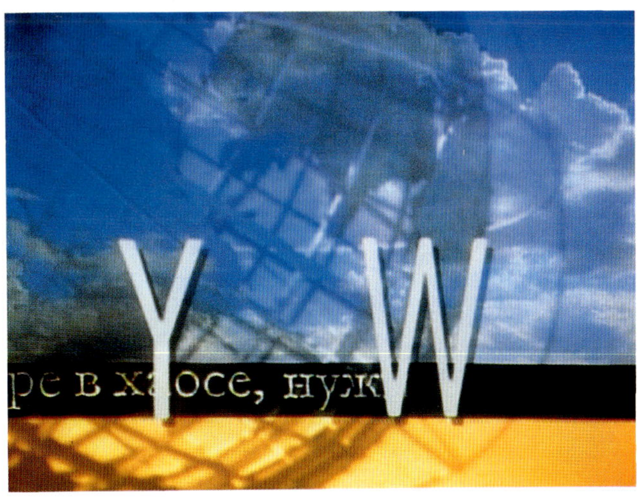

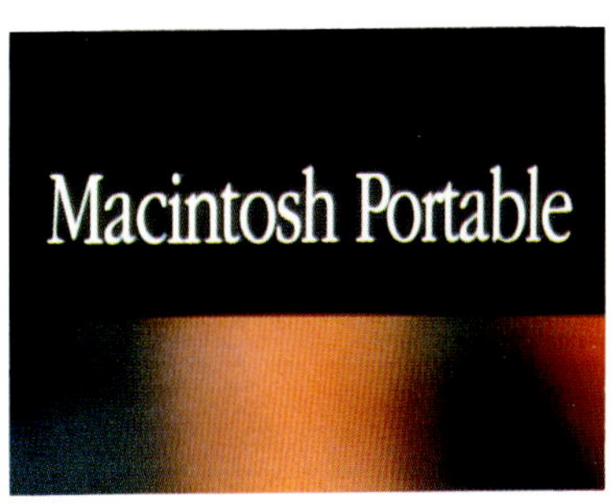

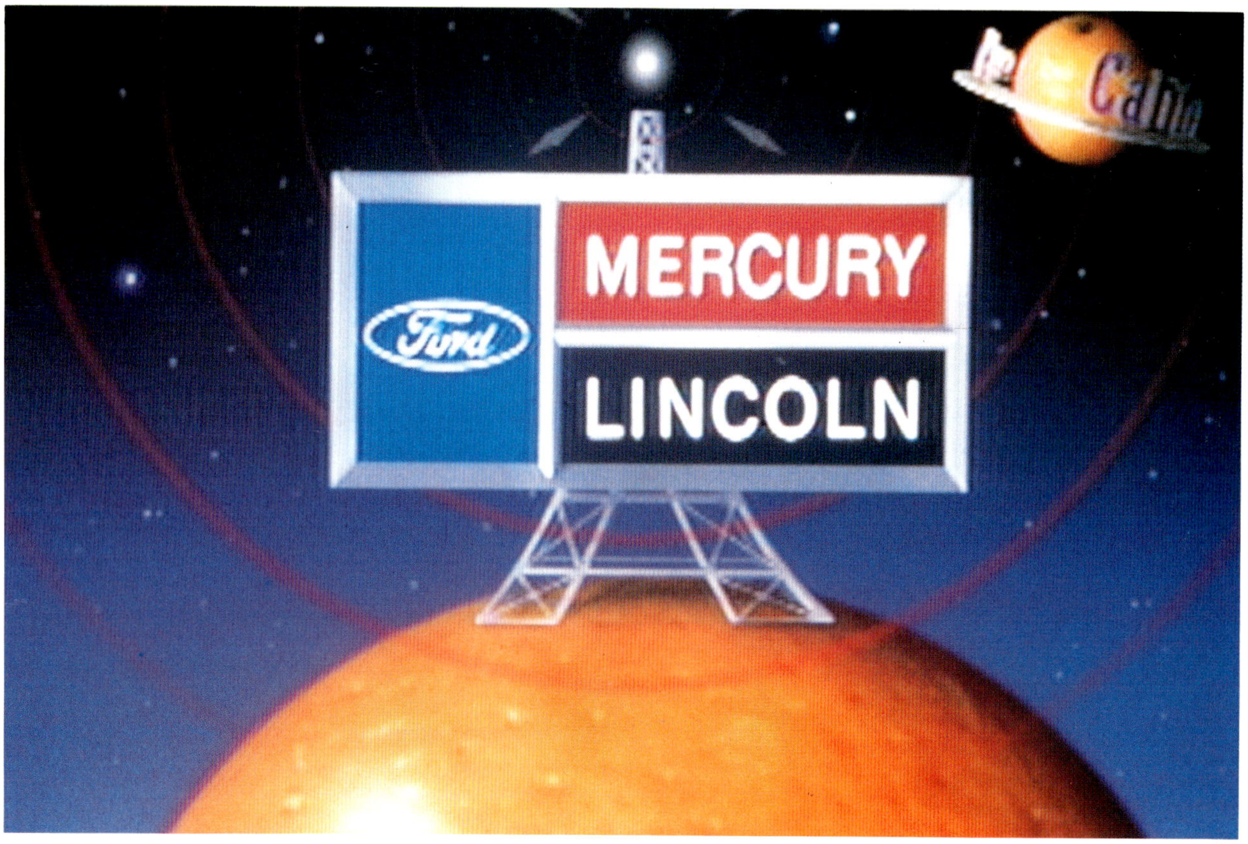

"CALIFORNIA CAVALCADE"
Advertisement for Lincoln Mercury automobiles

California Lincoln Mercury Dealers, Young and Rubicam

Created using a Vertigo computer graphics system, Paintbox, Harry and Encore.

Design Firm	G Nine Productions
Co-Designers	William Groshelle and Jon Lee
Creative Director	William Groshelle
Art Director	Jon Lee
Animators	Rick McKee and Kirk McInroy
Producer	Jadine Wu
Created at	San Francisco Production Group
Completed at	One Pass Video

Length of Time to Complete Work—6 weeks

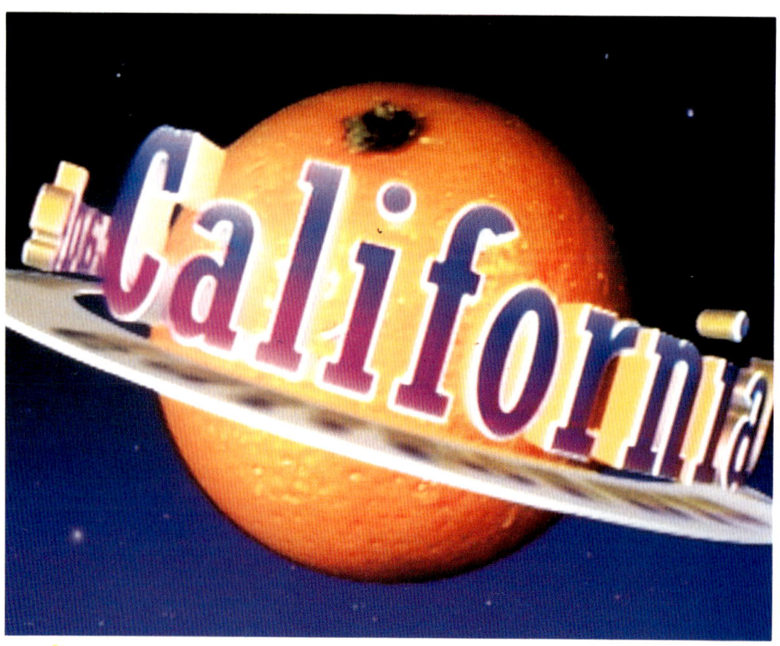

David Gieselmann

KSDK-TV, 1000 Market St., St. Louis, MO. 63101

KSDK-TV, St. Louis is committed to news. The television station broadcasts over 17 hours of local news weekly. David Gieselmann, the Director of Broadcast Design for KSDK, is totally committed to, and responsible for, the station's design and presentation of all on-air, print and display images for promotion, programming, sales and news. David's countless awards include ADDYS—Gold; NATAS—Emmy; Telly—Silver.

This work was designed for the image of Newschannel 5, KSDK-TV News.

The backgrounds were created by scanning the textures into an AVA-3 paintbox. This was combined with live action from news footage using a Grass Valley 200 video switcher and an Abekas A-62 recorder. Optical video effects were utilized for colorization and mixing 3-D elements from an Alias computer.

Electronic devices used were: Ampex AVA-3 paint box, Ampex 1" VTRs, Sony Beta VTRs, Grass Valley 200 switcher, Alias 3-D computer with Pixelerator BTS rendering platform, Abekas A-62 digital disk recorder, Ampex ADO, and Abekas A-53 digital video effects.

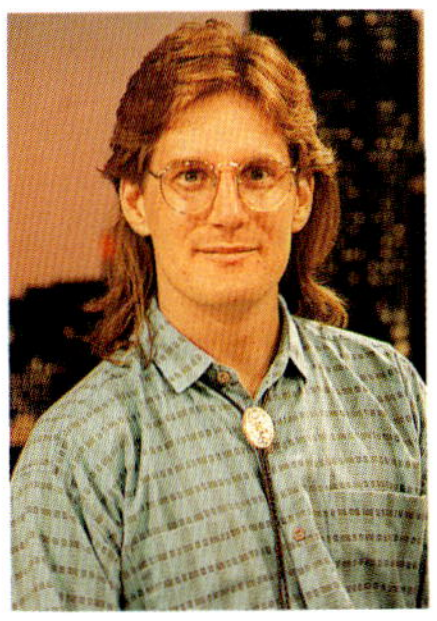

David Gieselmann,
Design Director, KSDK, St. Louis, MO

Newschannel 5 Open Sequence

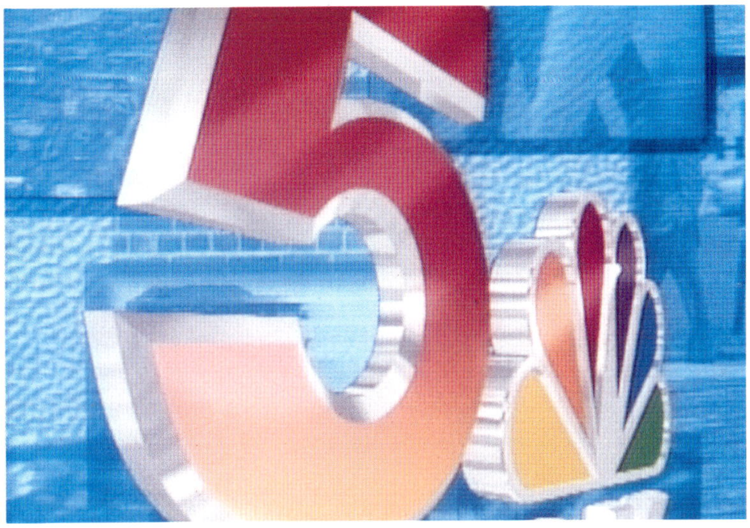

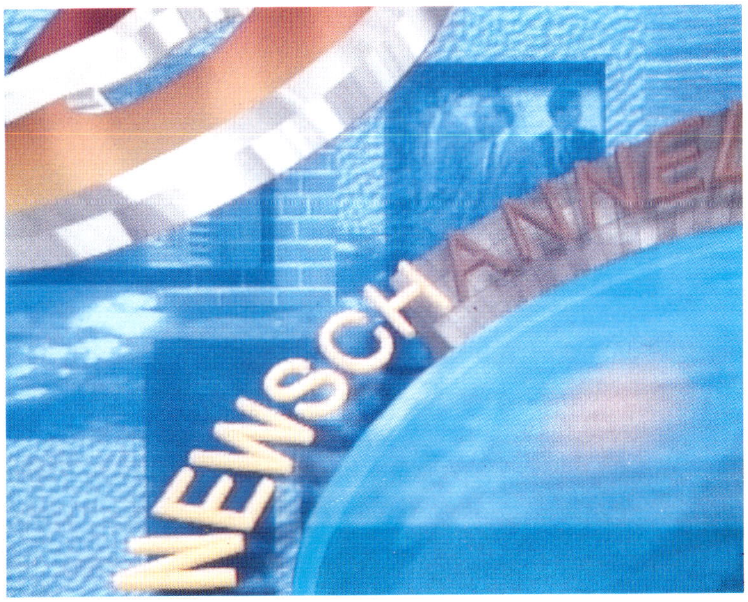

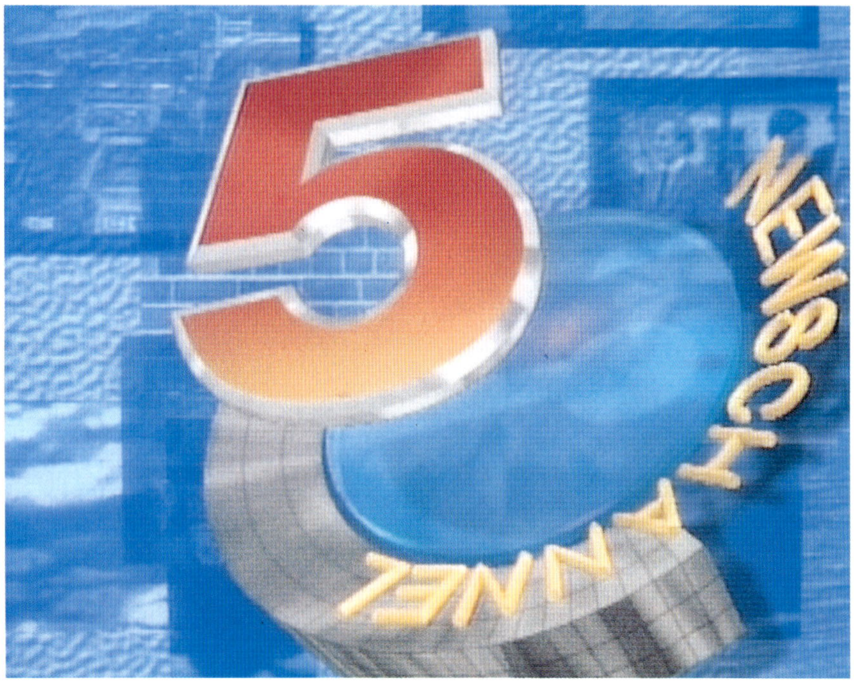

Created By	David Gieselmann, Mike Everhardt, Ken Yoder
Design Firm	KSDK Graphics Department
Designer	David Gieselmann
Creative Director	Rich Brase
Art Director	David Gieselmann
Effects Supervisor	Rich Haesemeyer
Graphic Artist	David Gieselmann
Producer	David Gieselmann, Gary Furlow
Video Editor	Mike Everhardt
Assistant Video Editor	Ken Yoder
Created and completed at	Multimedia Productions

Length of Time to Complete Work—2 months

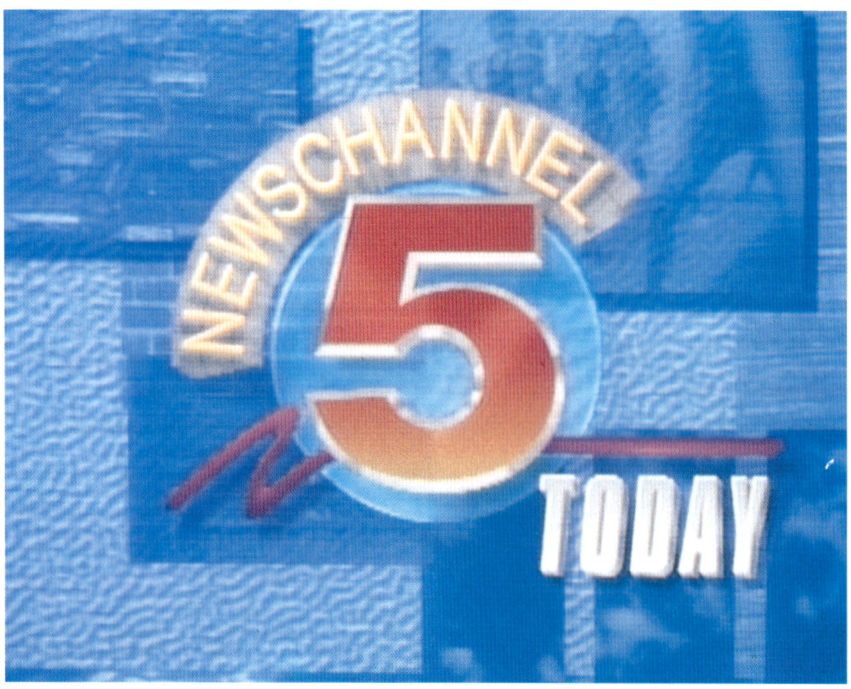

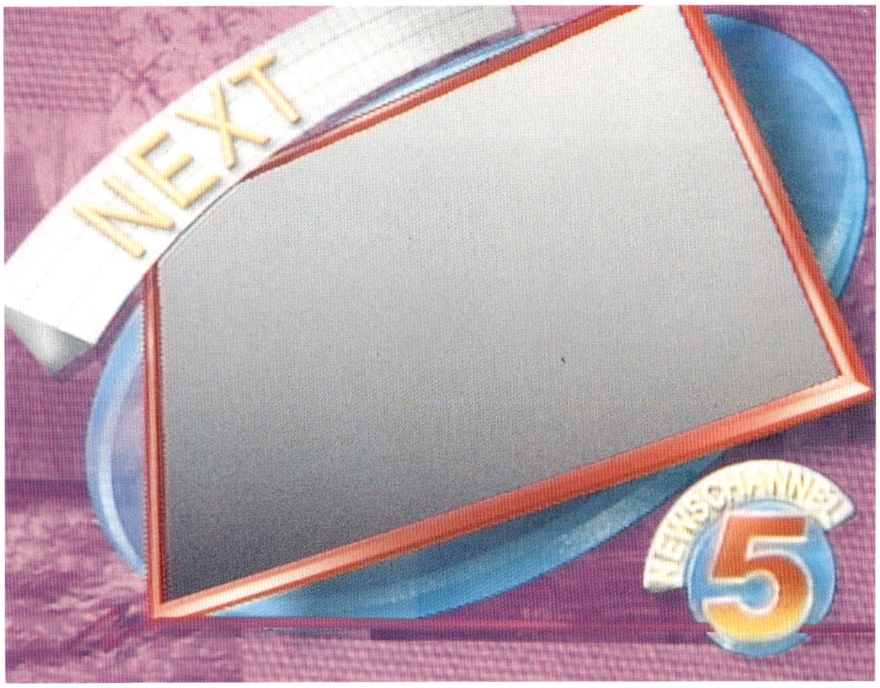

Newschannel 5 Bump

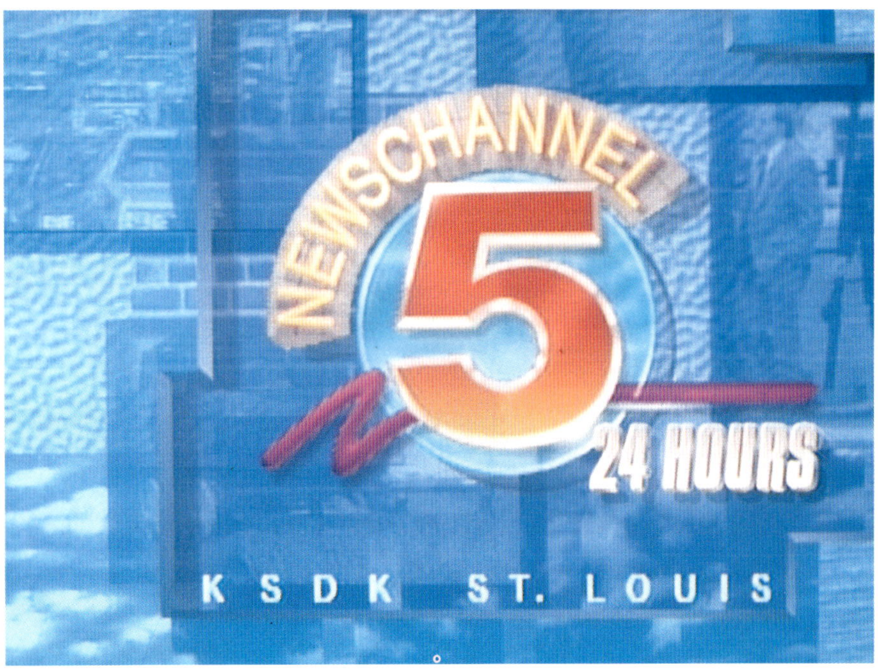

Newschannel 5 Update Sequence

Tama Alexandrine Goen

HBO, Inc., 1114 Avenue of the Americas, New York, NY 10036

Tama Alexandrine Goen has been with HBO since 1988. Prior to that, she held positions as Graphics Designer and Graphics Supervisor with major broadcast organizations in California. Her countless awards include BDA Silver and Bronze and numerous Emmy Award Nominations. Tama has a BA from San Diego State University, where she majored in art.

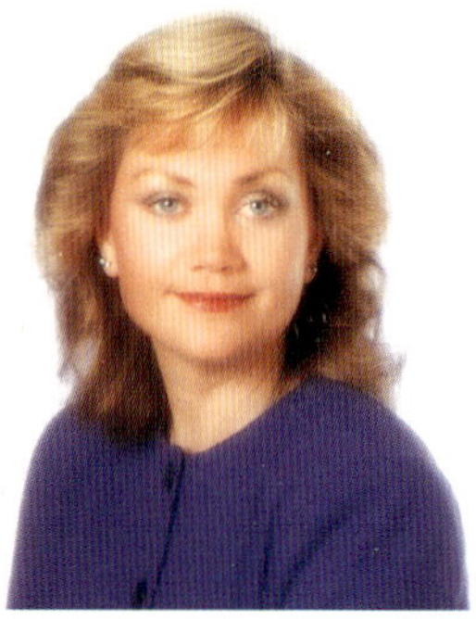

Tama Alexandrine Goen,
HBO, Inc., New York, NY

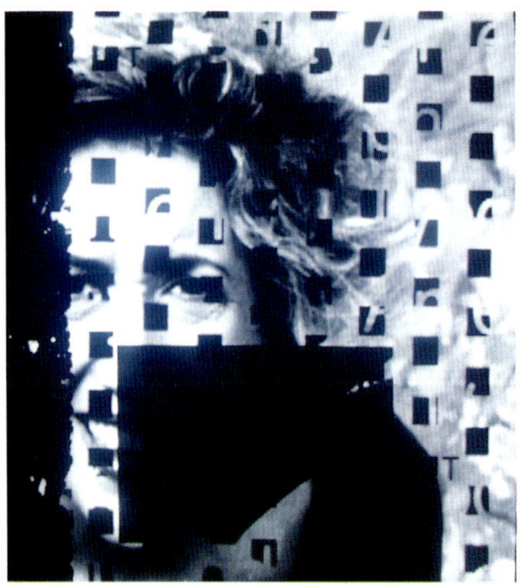

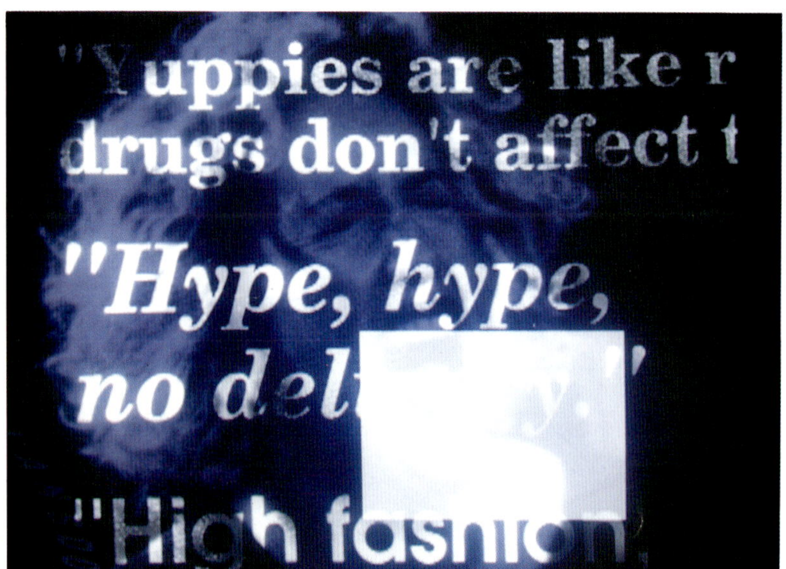

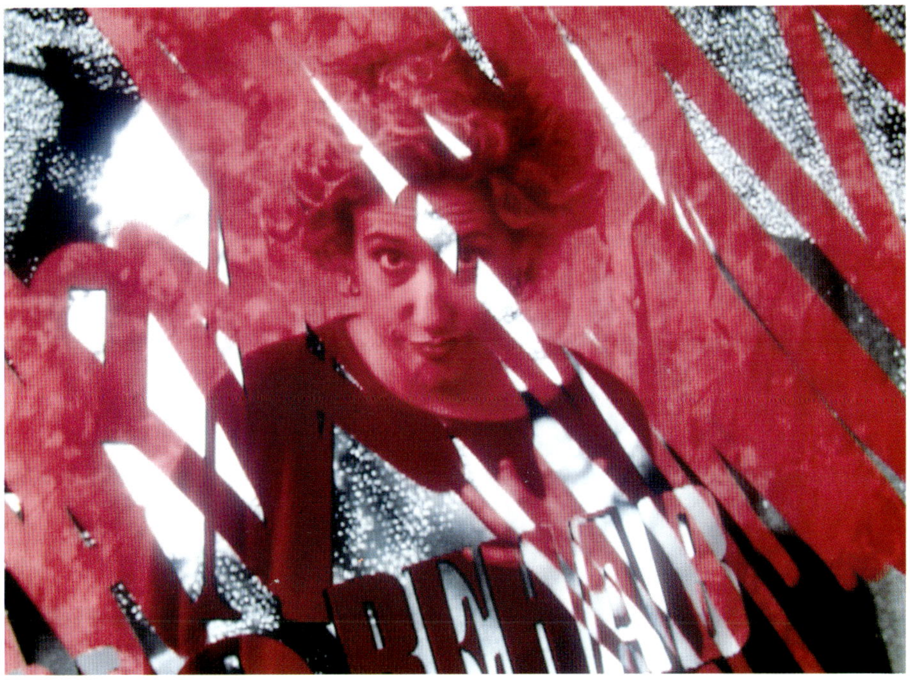

Reno in Rage & Rehab in New York City

Designed to promote an HBO comic discovery, Reno, for an exclusive one-hour adaptation of her hit one-woman off-Broadway show.

Created on a Quantel Paintbox and Harry.

Design Firm	HBO On Air Promotion
Designer	Tama Alexandrine Goen, HBO
Creative Director	Orest Woronewych, HBO
Animation	Patty Bellucci, B × B
Created and Completed at	HBO Studios, New York City

Length of Time to Complete Work—4 hours

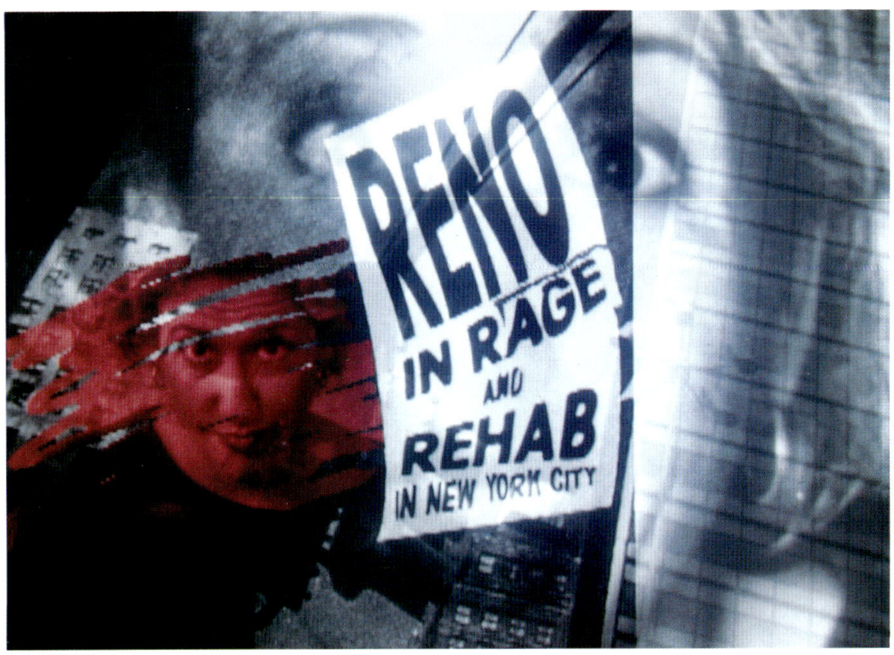

Graphics by Theresa

36 Iron Forge Square, Pompton Lakes, NJ 07442

Graphics by Theresa is a graphic design company providing computer graphic illustrations and animations for video productions. It was formed in 1984 by creative director and designer Theresa Nicholson. Her work has been seen nationally on such programs as "The Miss America Pageant," "Frank Fields Health Series" and "Earth 90." Theresa's graphic designs were featured in the Houston International Film Festival finalist award winning program, "Moods and Music" which aired on PBS. She is a fine arts graduate of Montclair State College.

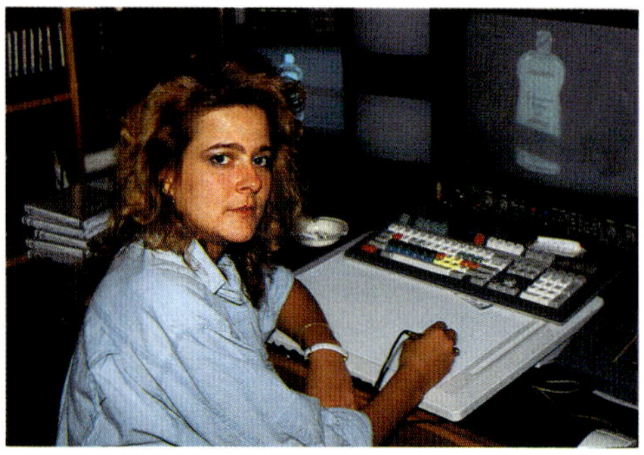

Theresa Nicholson,
President, Graphics by Theresa

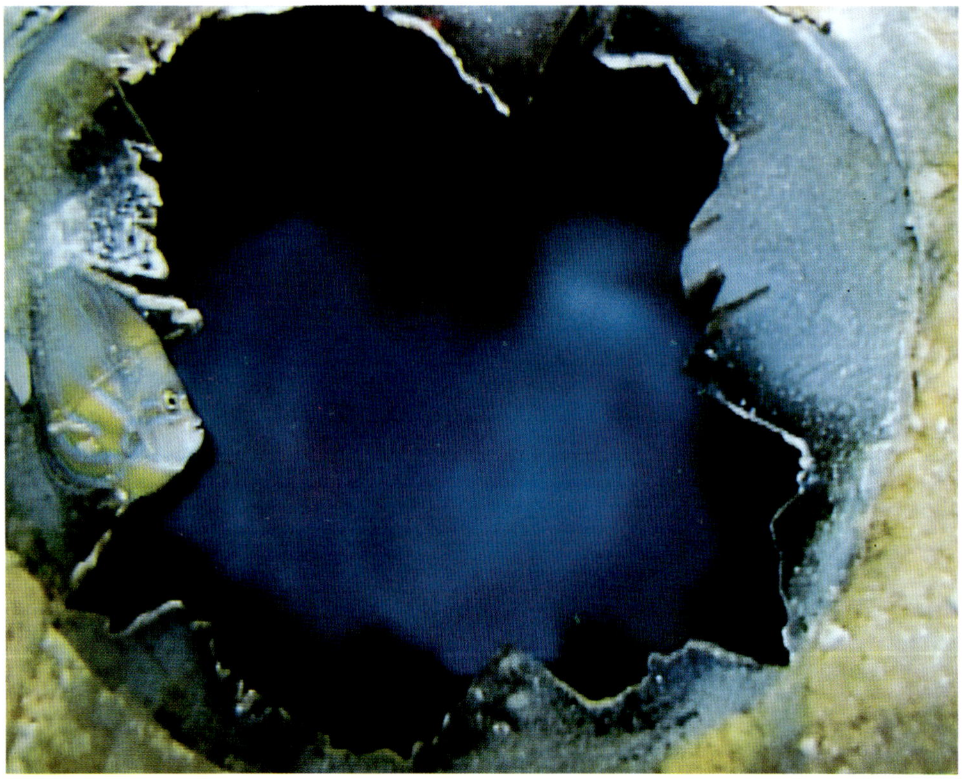

Porthole

Designed on the DFX Composium to exhibit the transluscent features of the system.

Created by shooting a live fish and port hole with a 35mm camera and then capturing the image in the DFX Composium. The fish image was then separated from the porthole image and the missing area painted in. The fish was then animated.

Created By	Theresa Nicholson
Designer	Theresa Nicholson
Graphic Artist	Theresa Nicholson
Created and Completed at	The VideoCenter of NJ.

Length of Time to Complete Work—3 hours

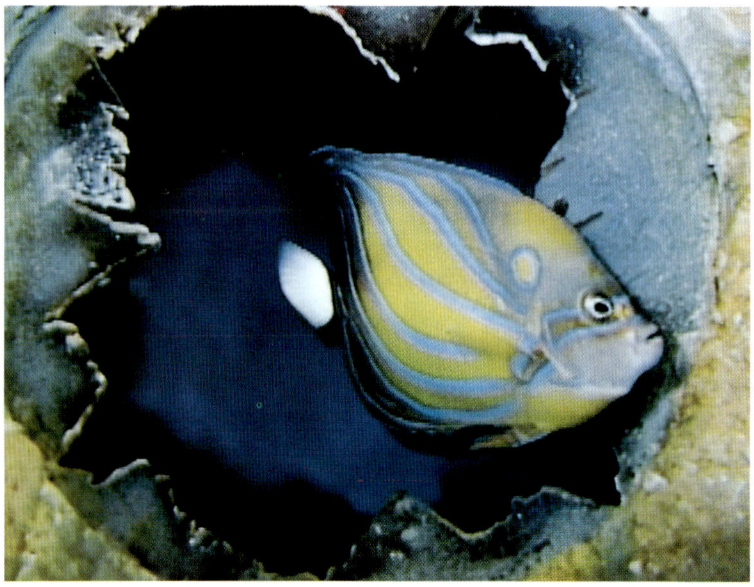

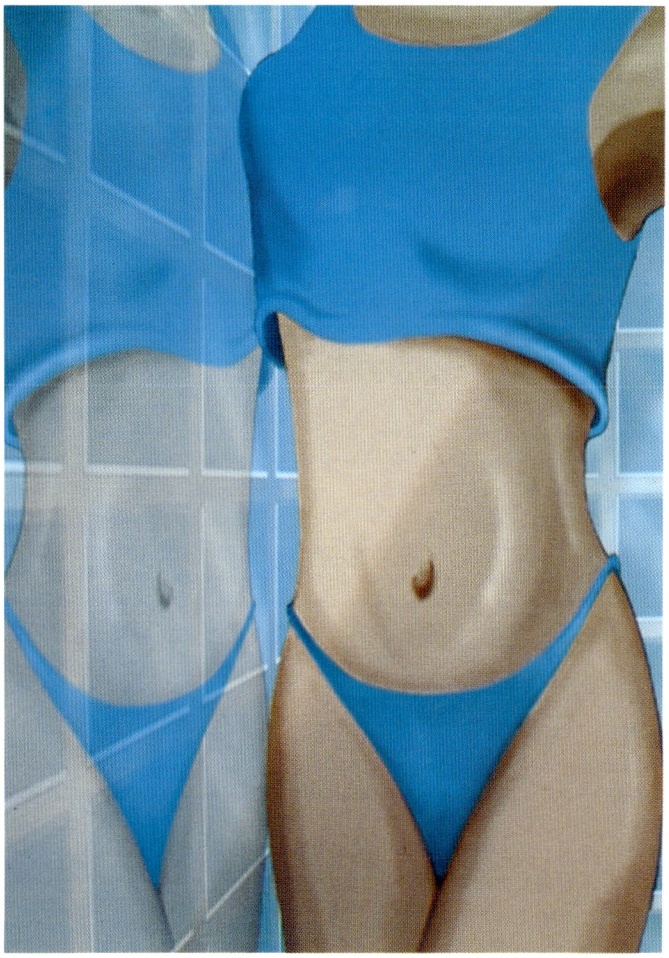

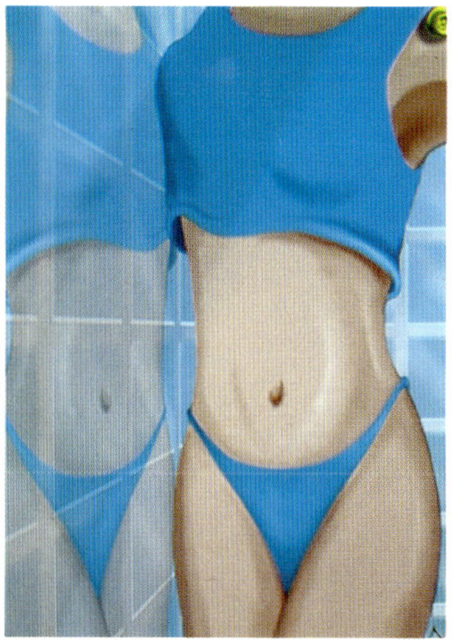

Tummies

Designed as an experimental illustration for art imaging on the computer paint system.

Created on the DFX Composium. The reflection was achieved by using the air brush feature in combination with a transparent cut out. The tile and glass effect was achieved by use of the draw line feature in the system. The entire piece was rendered manually.

Created By	Theresa Nicholson
Designer	Theresa Nicholson
Graphic Artist	Theresa Nicholson
Created and Completed at	The VideoCenter of NJ.

Length of Time to Complete Work—3 hours

Busy Fingers

Designed for Robert Schaffner and Frank O'Connell of The VideoCenter of NJ, East Rutherford, NJ.

Created on the DFX Composium as part of a 30-second segment of cell animated finger tapping.

Created By	Theresa Nicholson
Designer	Theresa Nicholson
Graphic Artist	Theresa Nicholson
Created and Completed at	The VideoCenter of NJ

Length of Time to Complete Entire Work—12 hours

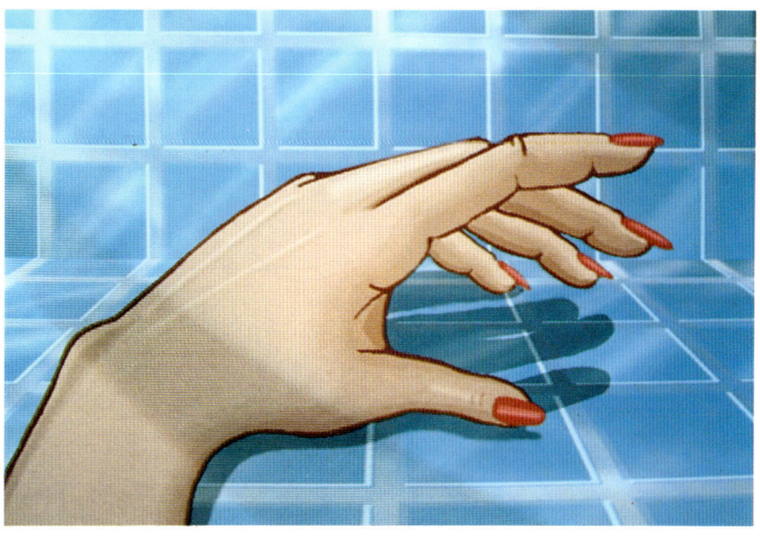

Image Resource Paris

27 Rue Blomet, Paris, France 75015

This work, submitted by Solly and Berti Dichy, from their prestigious Image Resource Paris, was created on the Paint Box, Harry, Kaleidoscope and DVR 1000.

Azantac Promos

Designed as a promotion of a new pharmaceutical product for Phillipe Courtin of Medication, Paris, France.

Created By	Medication and Image Resource
Design Firm	Image Resource
Designer	Philippe Courtin
Creative Director	Moshe Dichy
Effects Supervisor	Philippe Layani
Graphic Artist	M. Dichy
Producer	Medication
Video Editor	Michel Beaudreaux

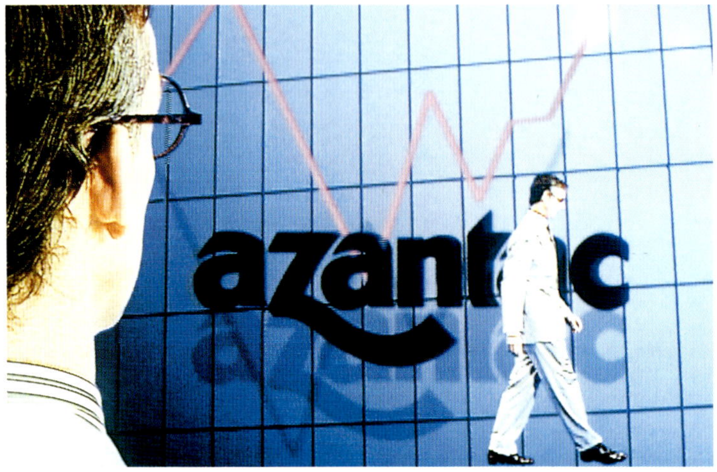

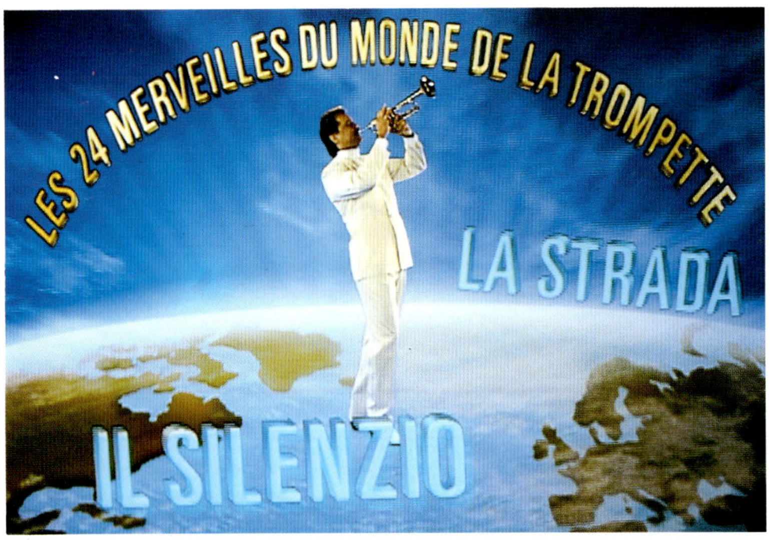

Jean Claude Borelli Promos

Designed as disk and CD promos for Flagrant-Delit

Created By	Flagrant Delit and Image Resource
Design Firm	Image Resource
Creative Director	Moshe Dichy
Art Director	Moshe Dichy
Graphic Artist	M. Dichy
Producer	Eric Mistler
Video Editor	M. Beaudreux

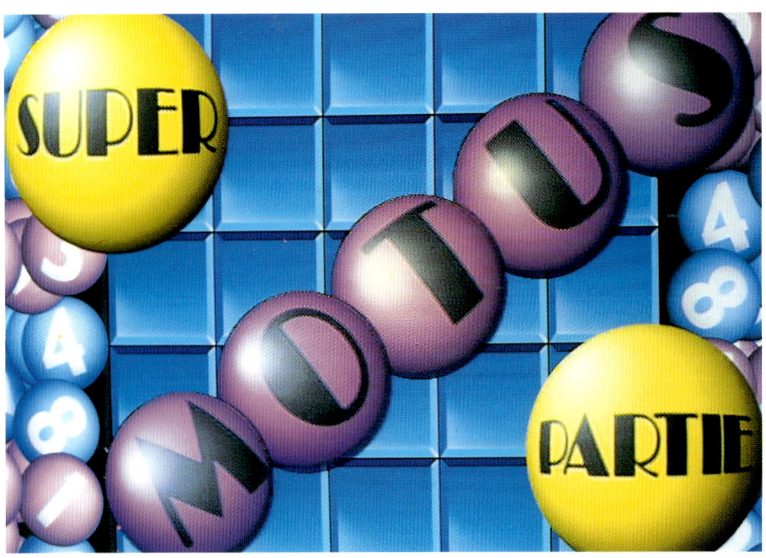

Motus

Designed as a TV open for the French Network, TF 1, Paris.

Created By	TF1 and Image Resource
Design Firm	Image Resource
Creative Director	M. Dichy
Art Director	Numa Rodagil
Effects Supervisor	Marc De Fourneaux
Producer	Veranda Productions
Video Editor	Philippe Layani

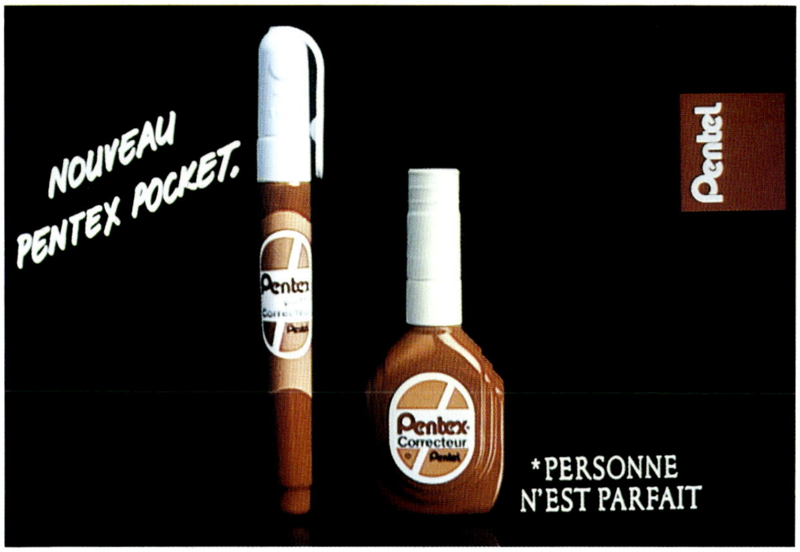

Spot for Pentex

Designed as a commercial spot for Lintas Paris.

Created By	Lintas and Image Resource
Design Firm	Image Resource
Creative Director	M. Dichy
Effects Supervisor	Claude Pegoraro
Producer	Les Filmes Du Sabre
Video Editor	Alain Goudet

Tina Turner in Concert in Paris

Designed as a promo for the French Network, Antenne 2., Paris.

Created By	A2 and Image Resource
Design Firm	Image Resource
Creative Director	M. Dichy
Art Director	Numa Rodagil
Effects Supervisor	Philippe Layani
Producer	Veranda Productions
Video Editor	J. P. Calduc

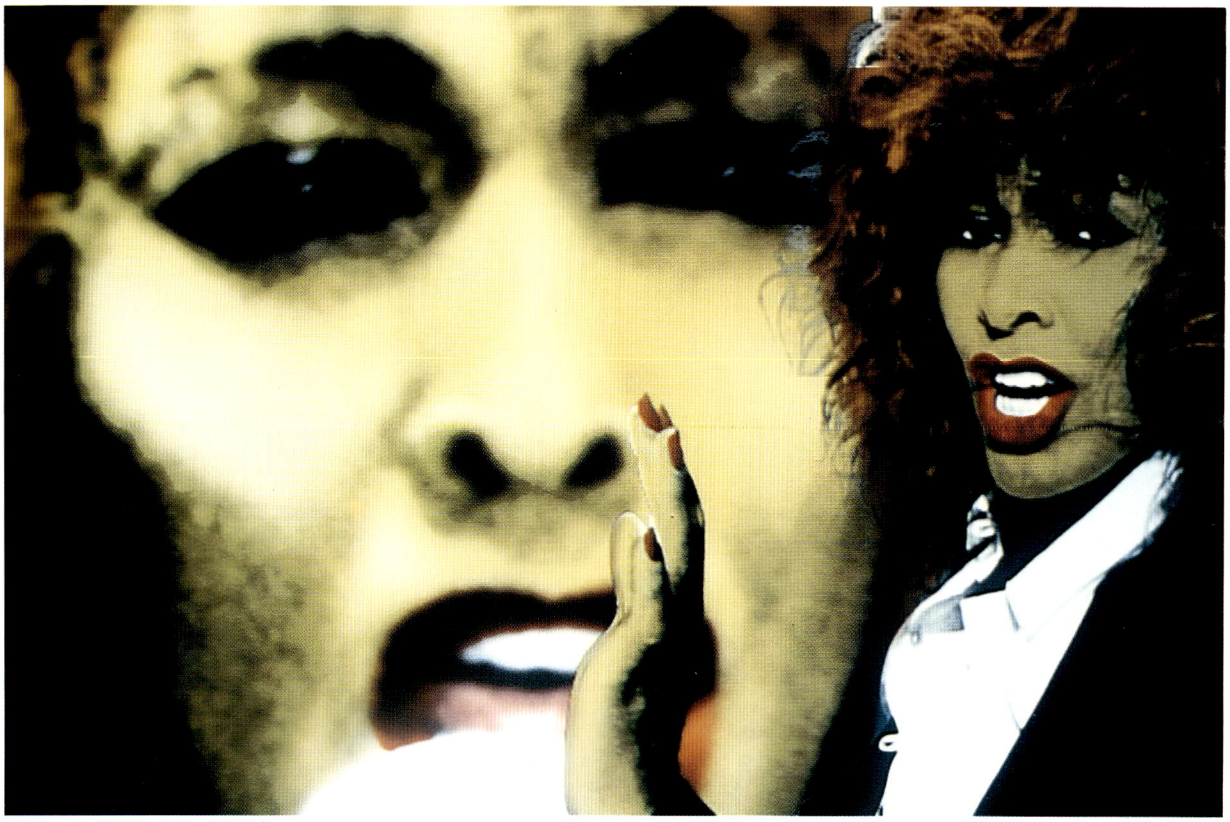

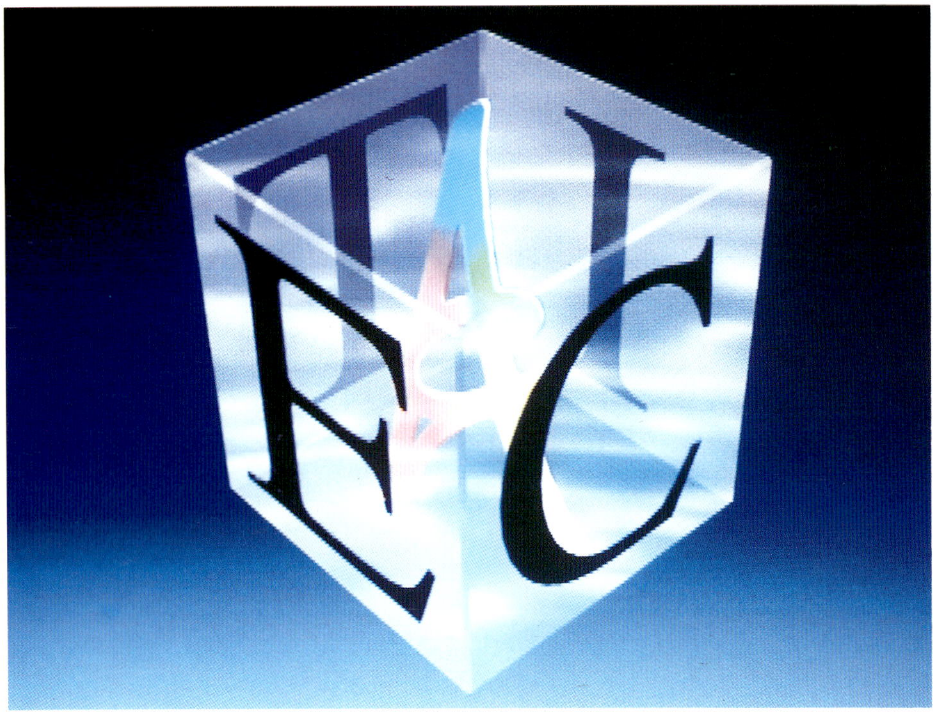

Spot for Cite Corporate

Designed for Cite and Fantome

Created By	Cite
Design Firm	Image Resource
Creative Director	Moshe Dichy
Art Director	Renato
Effects Supervisor	Phillipe Layani
Producer	Cite Fantome

Mag Max

Designed for Canal +, Paris and the French Network as a spot open for the TV Magazine—Mag Max

Created By	Canal + and Image Resource
Creative Director	Mose Dichy
Art Director	Jerome Revon
Producer	Canal +

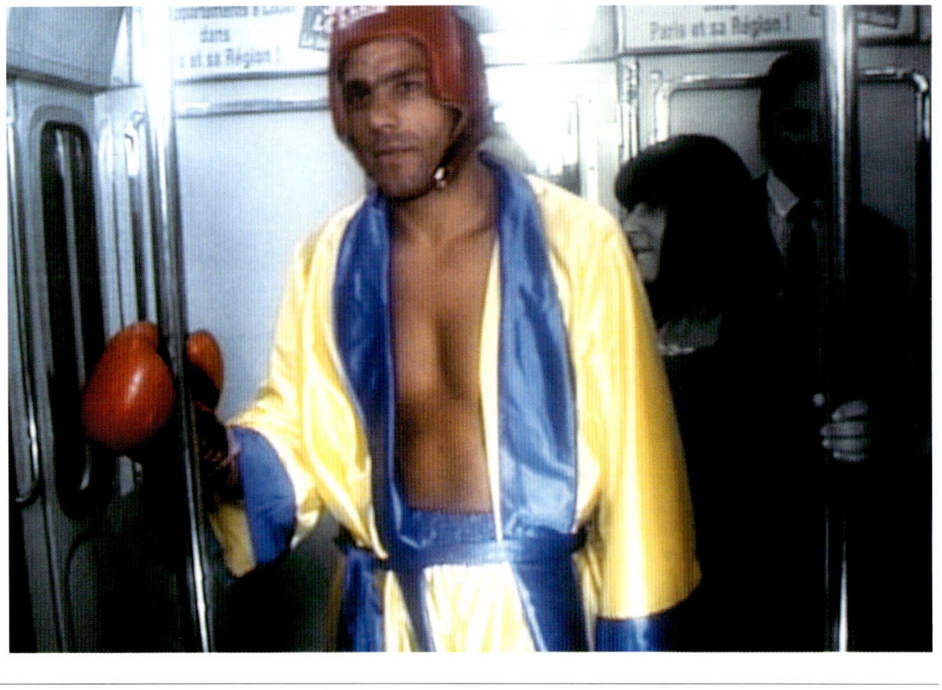

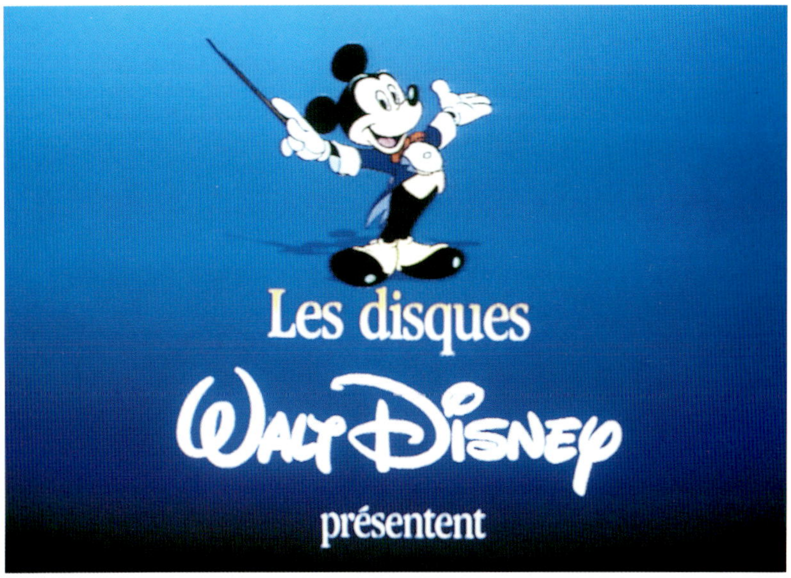

Mickey

Designed for Eclipsa, Paris as a spot for Music Walt Disney.

Created By	Walt Disney France and Eclipsa
Creative Director	Eclipsa
Art Director	Christophe Smith
Effects Supervisor	Michel Beaudreaux
Graphic Artist	Moshe Dichy
Producer	Christophe Smith
Video Editor	Phillipe Layani

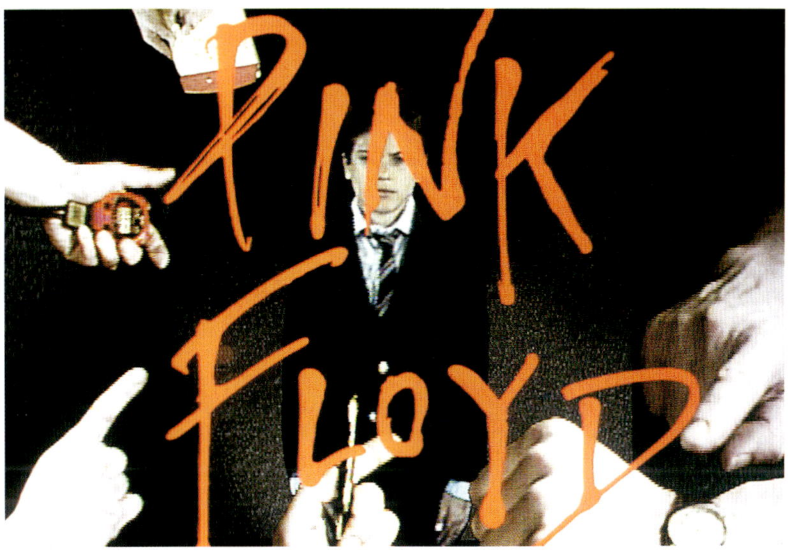

Pink Floyd in Concert in Paris

Designed for the French Network, Antenne 2., Paris as a promo for Pink Floyd.

Created By	Antenne 2 and Image Resource
Design Firm	Image Resource
Creative Director	Moshe Dichy
Art Director	Maxime Ruiz
Video Editor	J. P. Calduc

Baroque Music Bande

Designed for Flagrant Delit, Malakoff, France as a promo the Baroque Band.

Created By	Flagrant Delit
Design Firm	Image Resource
Creative Director	Moshe Dichy
Art Director	Maxime Ruiz
Producer	Flagrant Delit
Video Editor	Marc Defourneaux

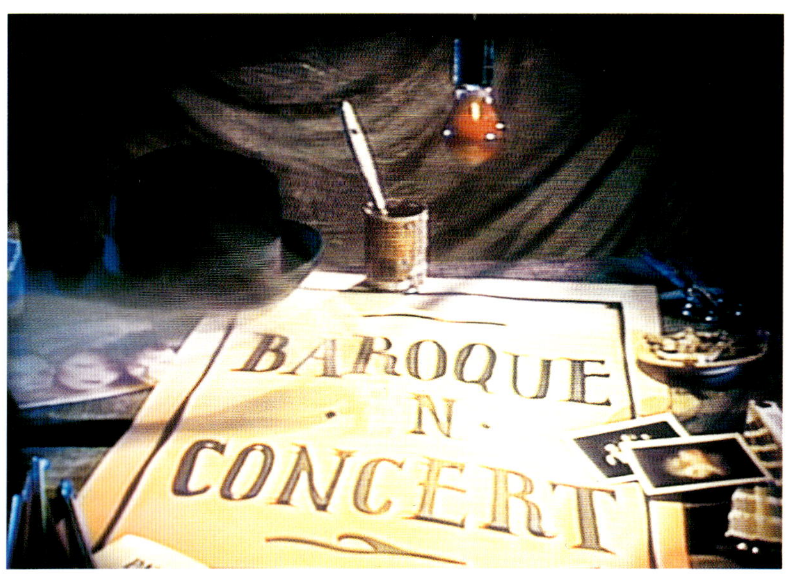

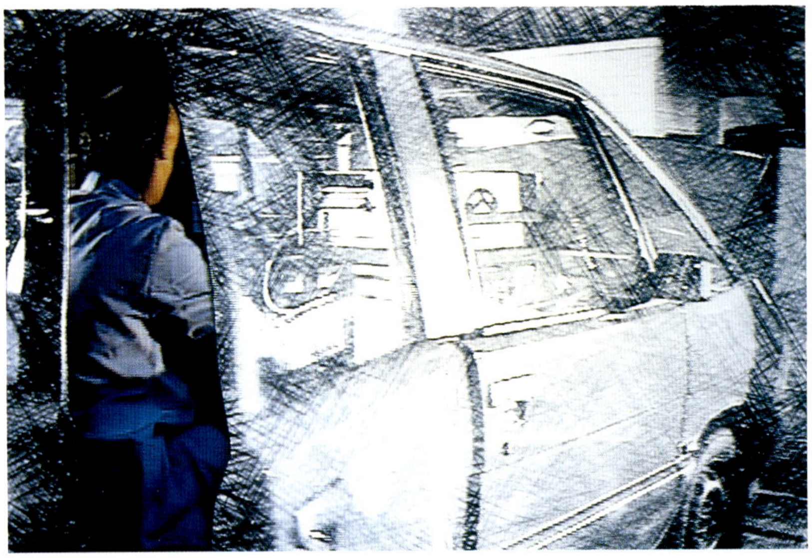

Matra Communications

Designed for Luminance, Paris as a corporate video.

Created By	Luminance and Matra
Design Firm	Image Resource
Creative Director	Moshe Dichy
Art Director	Jerome Auffret
Effects Supervisor	Michel Beaudreaux
Producer	Jerome Auffret

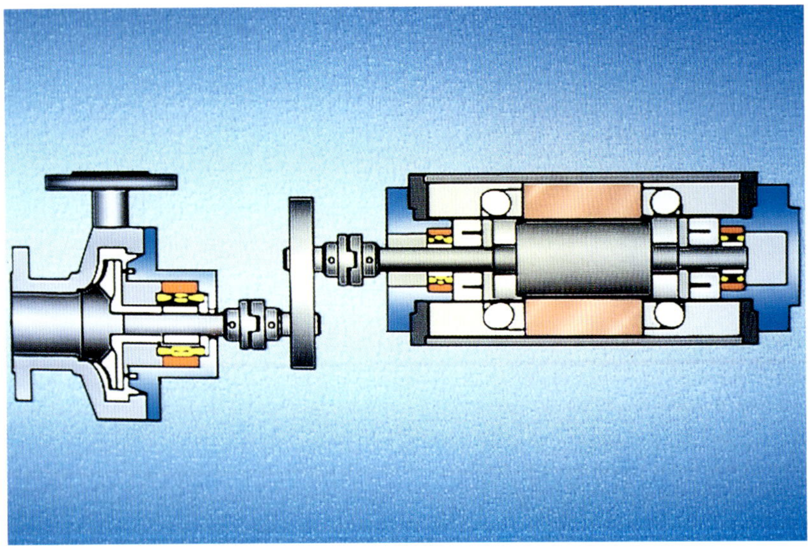

E.D.F.

Designed for Jacques Boumendil of Sodel and B.D.D.P. as a promo.

Created By	B.D.D.P. and Sodel
Design Firm	Image Resource
Creative Director	Moshe Dichy
Producer	Jacques Boumendil

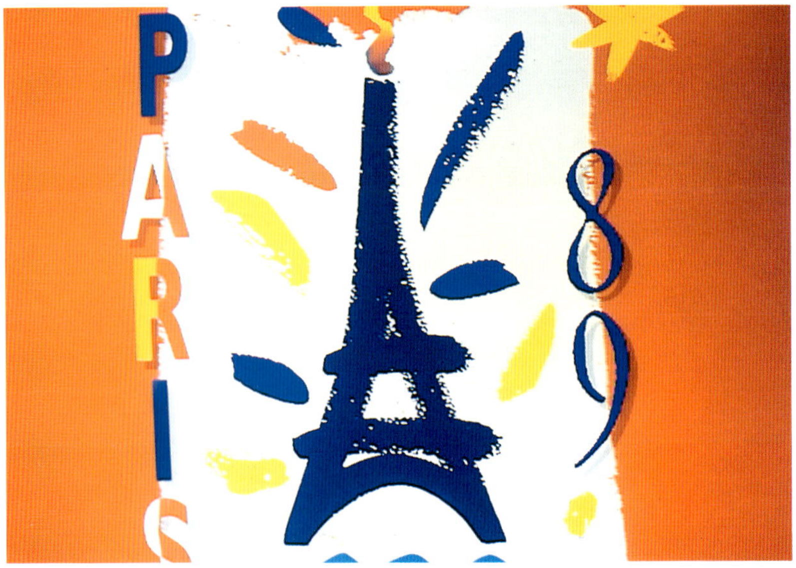

Bi Centenaire of the Eiffel Tower

Designed for Rockefeller Center Production, New York, NY for the Bi Centenaire of the Eiffel Tower.

Created By	Rockefeller Center Production
Design Firm	Image Resource
Creative Director	Moshe Dichy
Producer	Rockefeller Center Production

Aerospatiale Helicopter

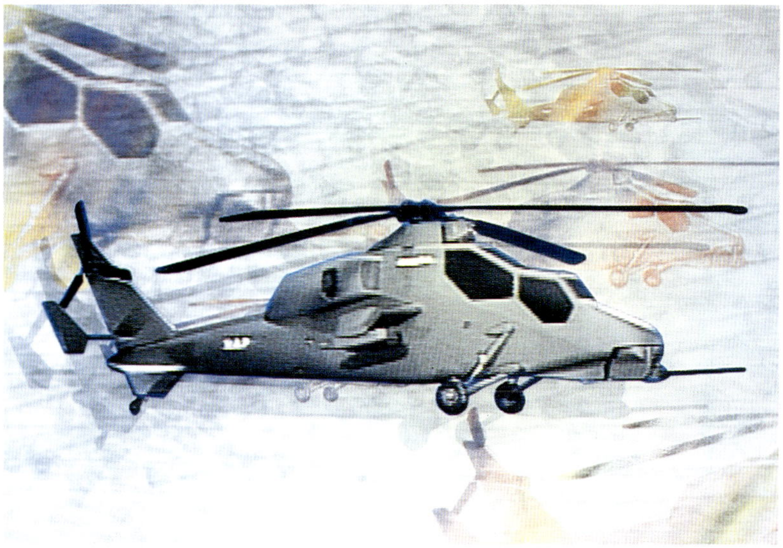

Designed for Aerospatiale, Paris and the Army.

Created By	Aerospatiale
Design Firm	Image Resource
Creative Director	Moshe Dichy
Art Director	Patrice Desenne
Effects Supervisor	Phillipe Layani
Producer	Patrice Desenne

TF 1 French TV Station

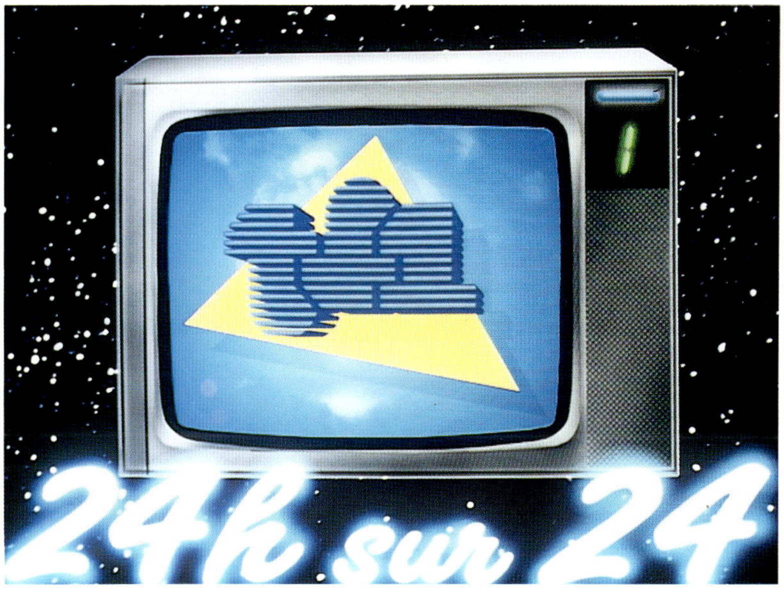

Designed for TF1, Paris as an open for television.

Created By	TF1
Design Firm	Image Resource
Creative Director	Moshe Dichy
Art Director	Eric Pages
Effects Supervisor	Michel Beaudreaux
Producer	Eric Pages
Video Editor	Alain Goudet

Smaïn Cafe De La Gare

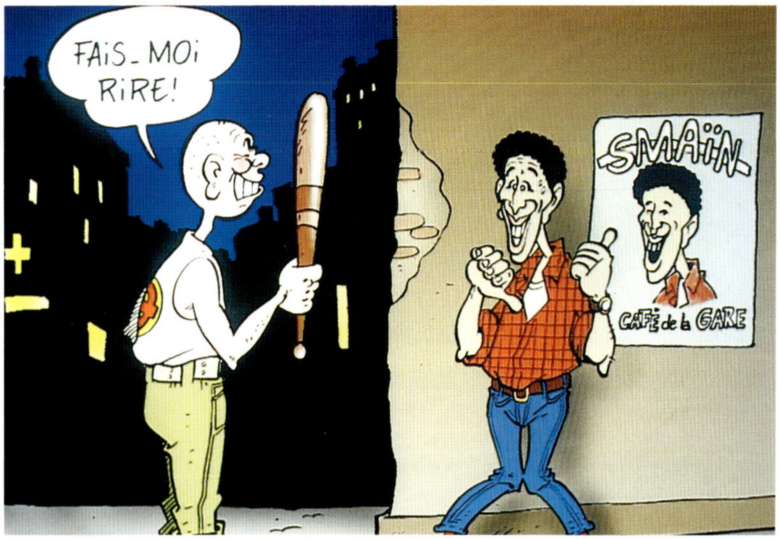

Designed for FR 3, French Network, Paris as a mini series animation.

Created By	FR 3 and Image Resource
Design Firm	Image Resource
Designer	Boudjella
Creative Director	Moshe Dichy
Effects Supervisor	Marc DeForneaux
Graphic Artist	Boudjella
Producer	FR 3
Video Editor	J. P. Calduc

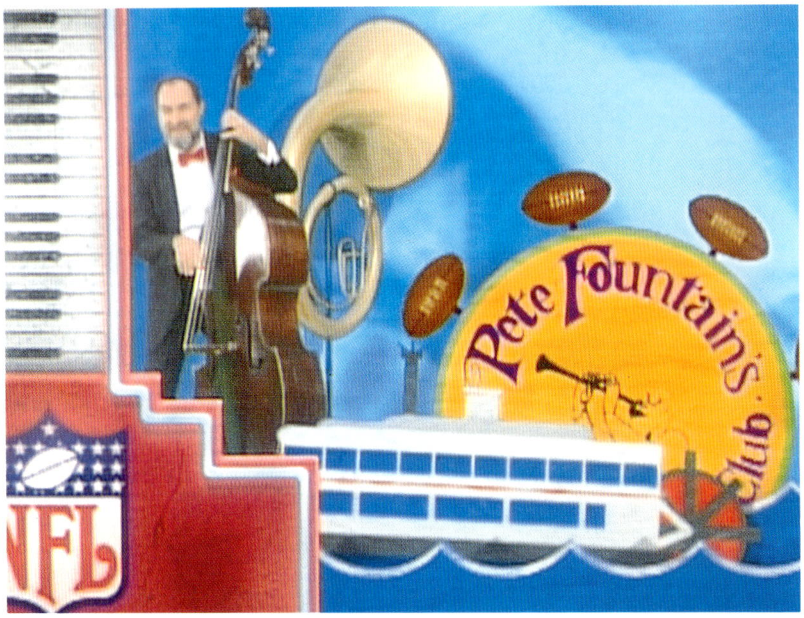
Pete Fountain's Club.
NFL

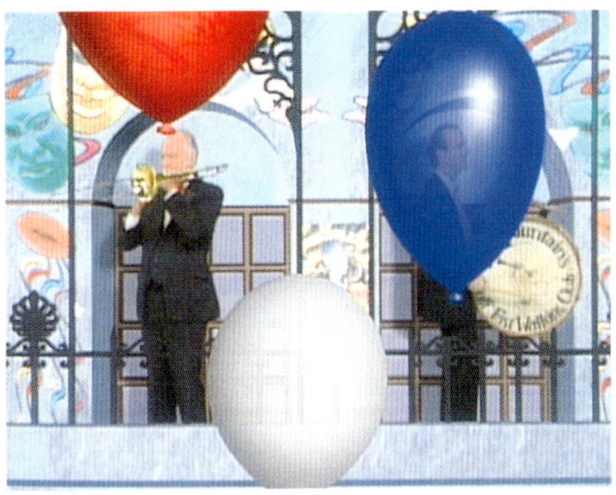

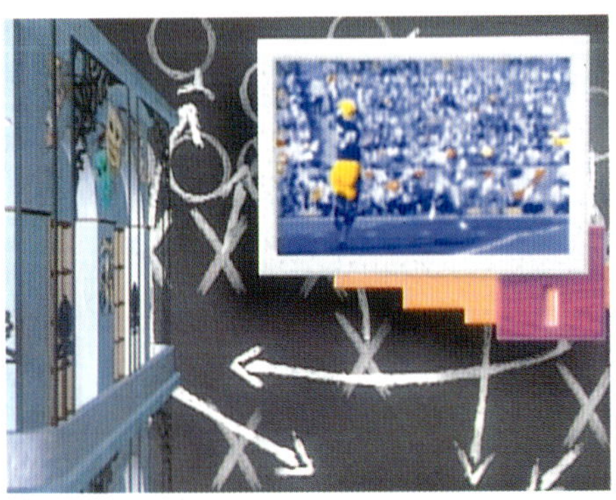

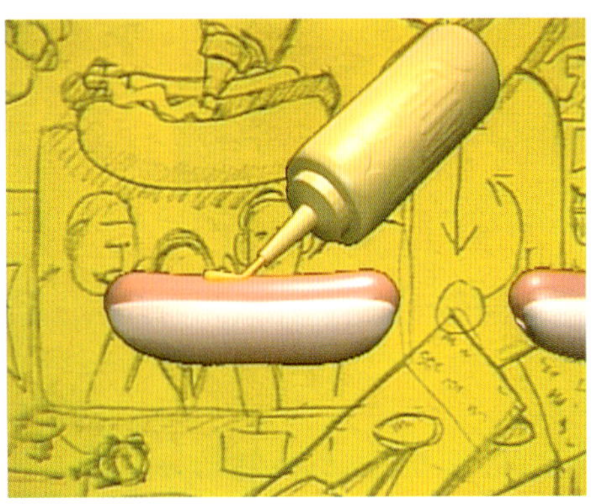

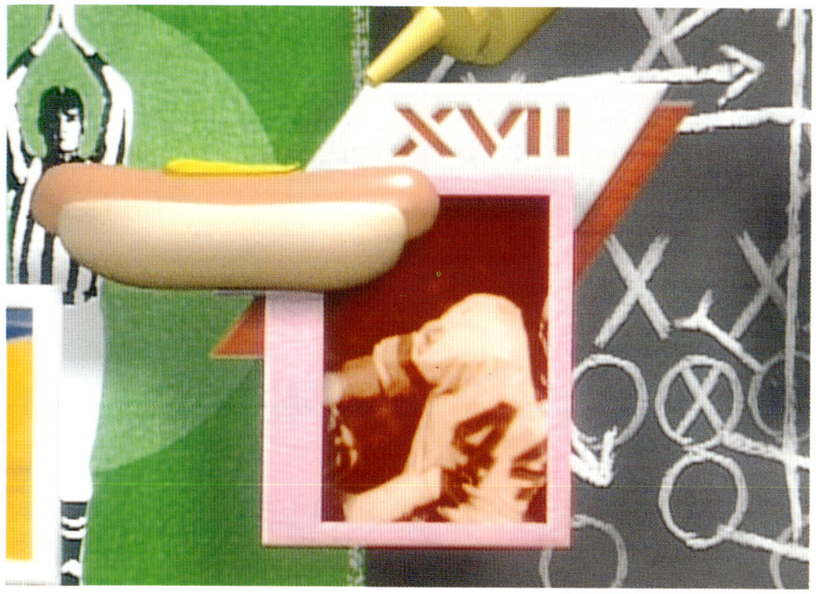
XVII

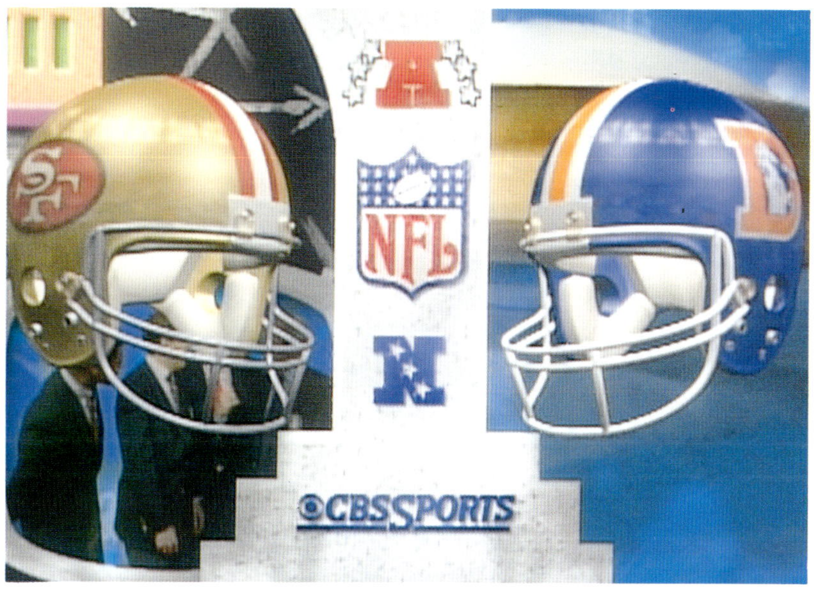
NFL
CBS SPORTS

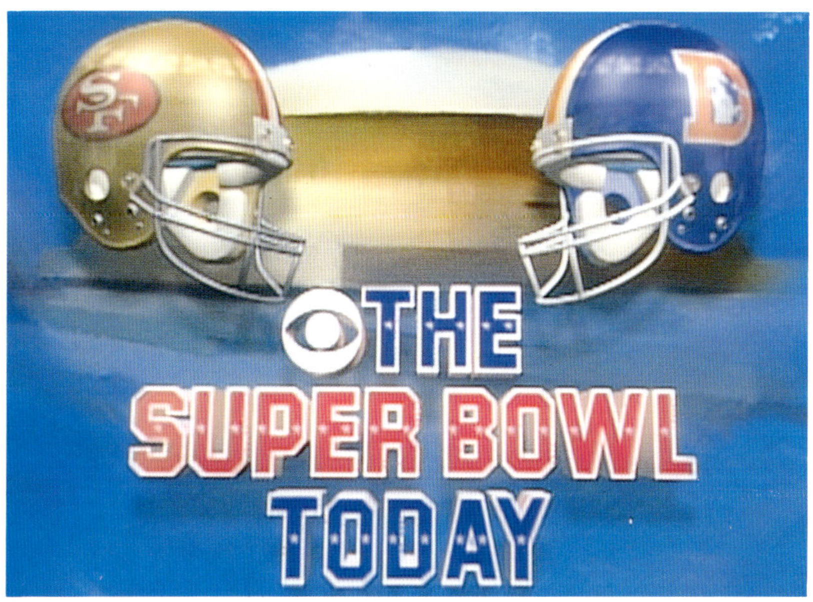
THE
SUPER BOWL
TODAY

Lisa Lloyd

Home Box Office, 1100 Avenue of the Americas, New York, NY 10036

Lisa Lloyd brings to the HBO Department of Design over 12 years of experience in the Video Graphics field. She has a BFA in Graphic Design from the California College of Arts and Crafts, Oakland, CA.

"From the Heart" Show Open

Designed to introduce a series of movies with strong emotional content for Cinemax, Home Box Office, Inc., New York, NY.

The storyboard and design were created on a Macintosh Computer. The video still elements were executed on the Quantel Paintbox. The work was done in D1 and the final composite on the Quantel Harry.

Created By	Lisa Lloyd, Henry Baker, Patty Bellucci, Ginny Jones
Design Firm	HBO On Air Promotion, Department of Design
Designer	Lisa Lloyd
Creative Director	Orest Woronewych
Art Director	Lisa Lloyd
Graphic Artist	Patty Bellucci, Ginny Jones
Producer	Lisa Lloyd
Video Editor	Henry Baker
Created and Completed at	HBO Studios

Length of Time to Complete Work—2 weeks

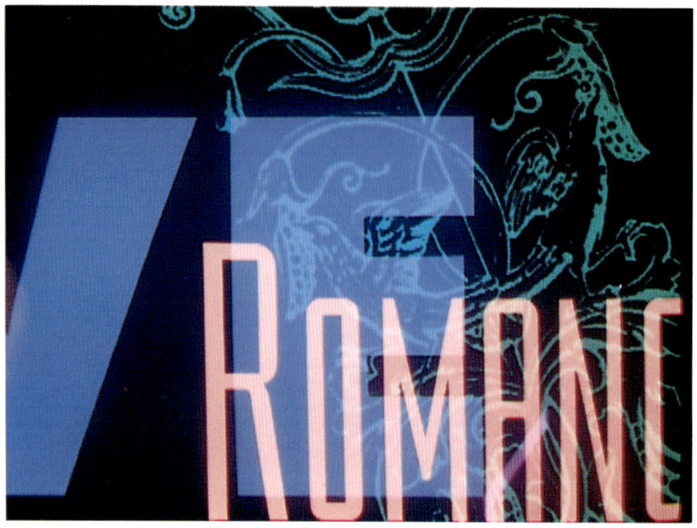

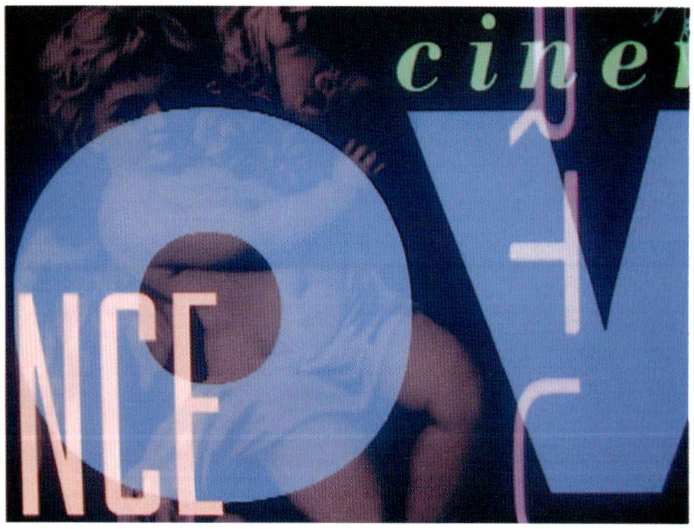

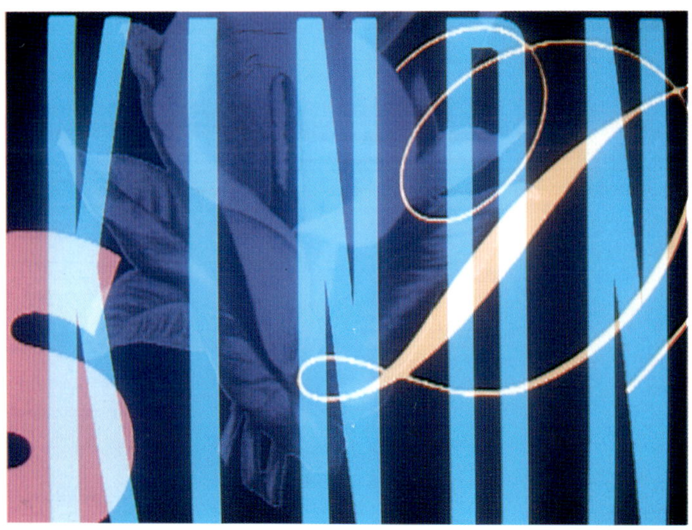

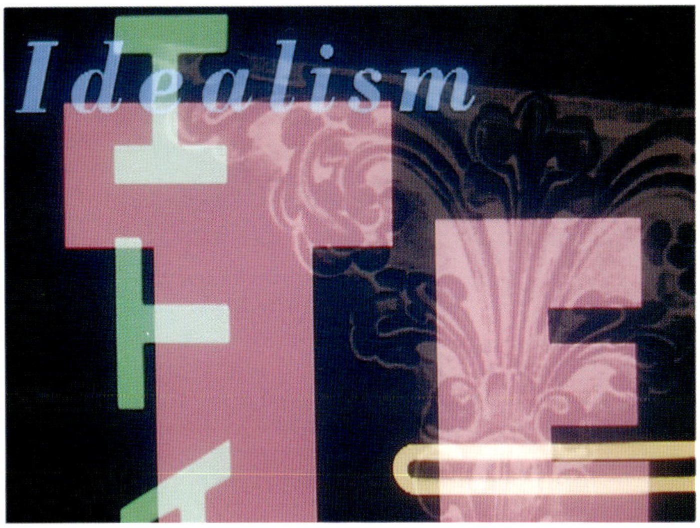
Idealism

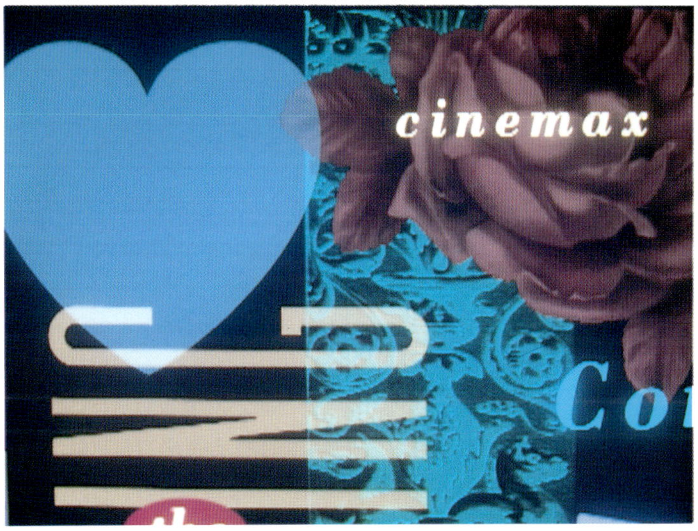
cinemax

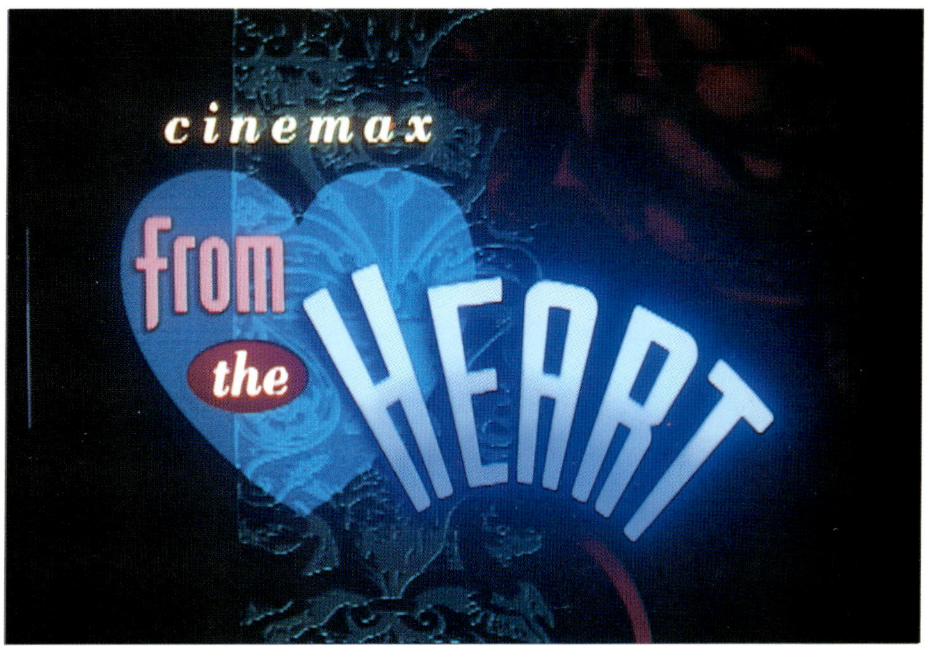
cinemax
from
the
HEART

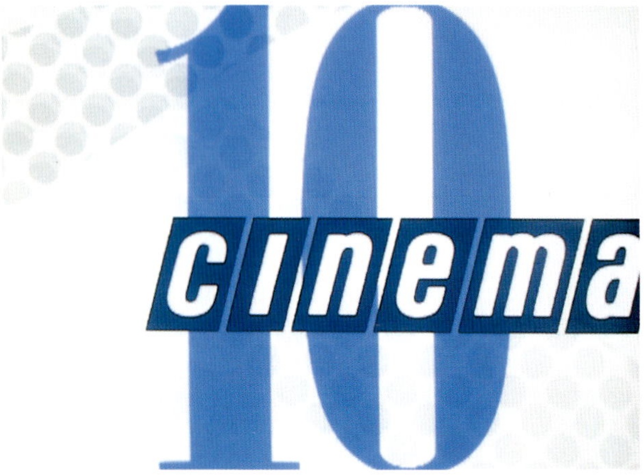

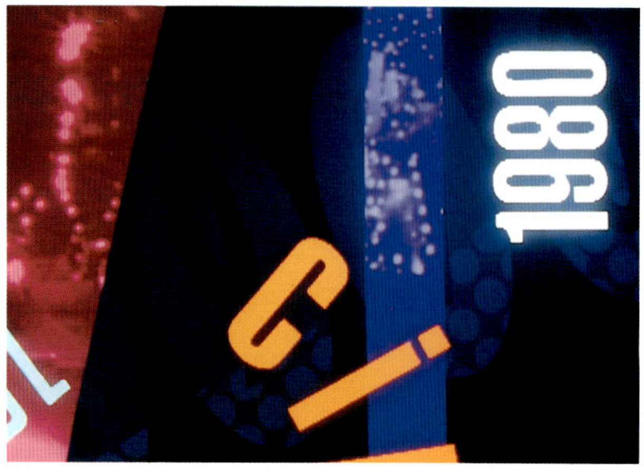

Cinemax 10th Anniversary

Designed to promote Cinemax's 10th year for Home Box Office, Inc., New York, NY

The storyboard and design were created on a Macintosh Computer. The video still elements were executed on a Quantel Paintbox with the final composite done in a digital editing suite on D1 and D2. A Grass Valley Kadenza with Kaleidoscope was used for keying and the layering was done with a Abekas A64.

Created By	Lisa Lloyd, Peter Consiglio, Patty Bellucci, Ginny Jones
Design Firm	HBO On Air Promotion, Department of Design
Designer	Lisa Lloyd
Creative Director	Orest Woronewych
Art Director	Lisa Lloyd
Graphic Artist	Patty Bellucci, Ginny Jones
Producer	Lisa Lloyd
Video Editor	Peter Consiglio
Created and Completed at	HBO Studios

Length of Time to Complete Work—10 days

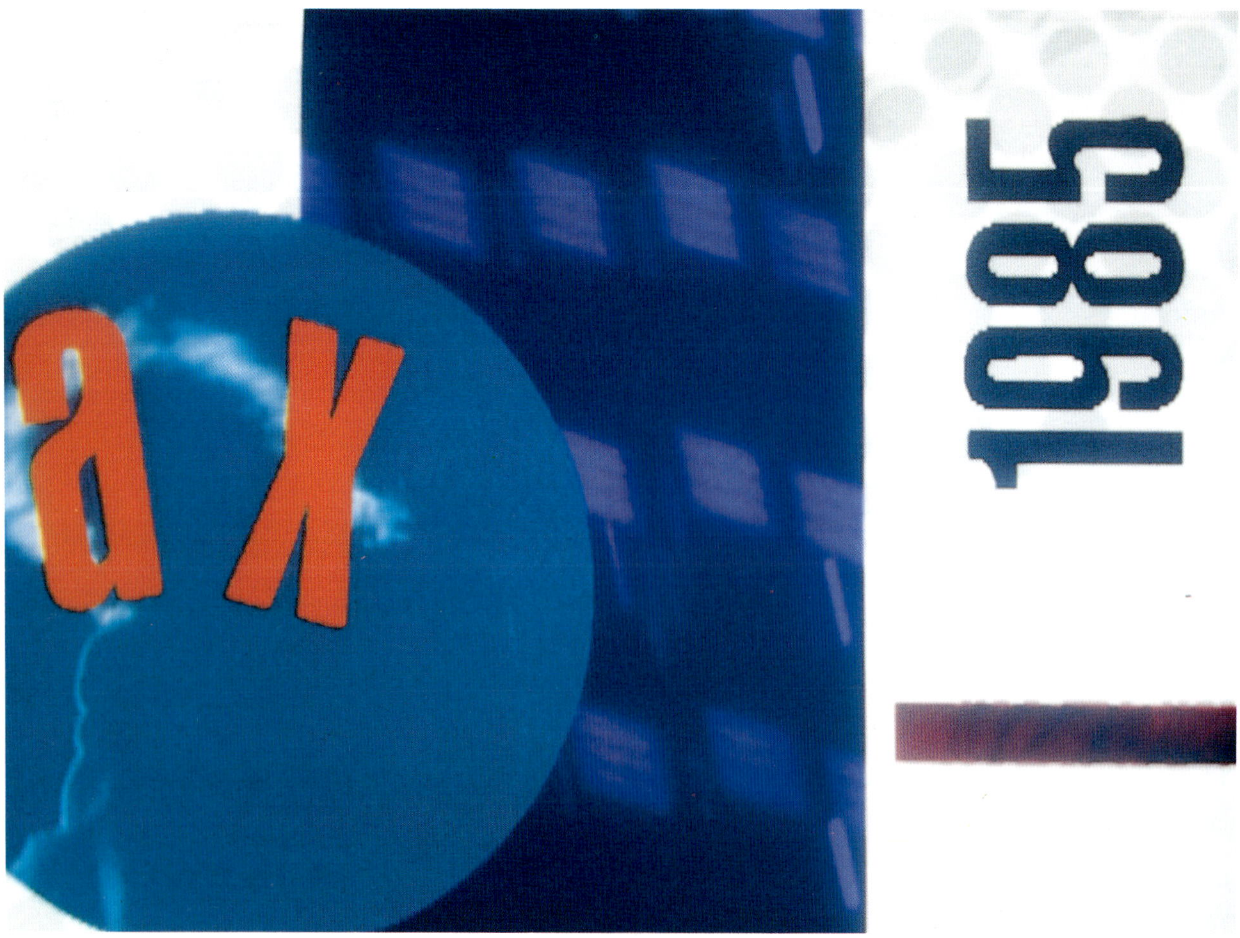

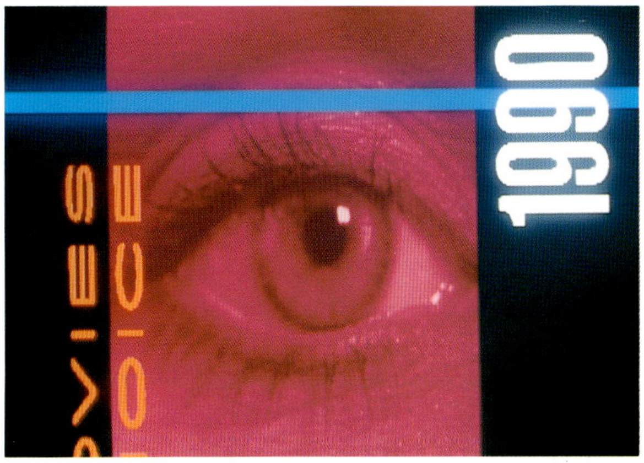
1990

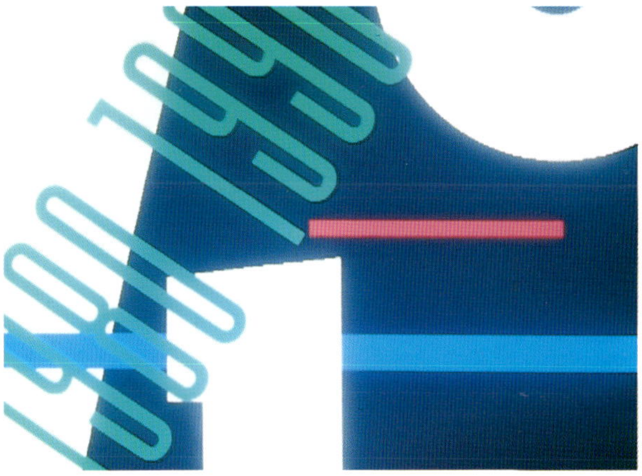

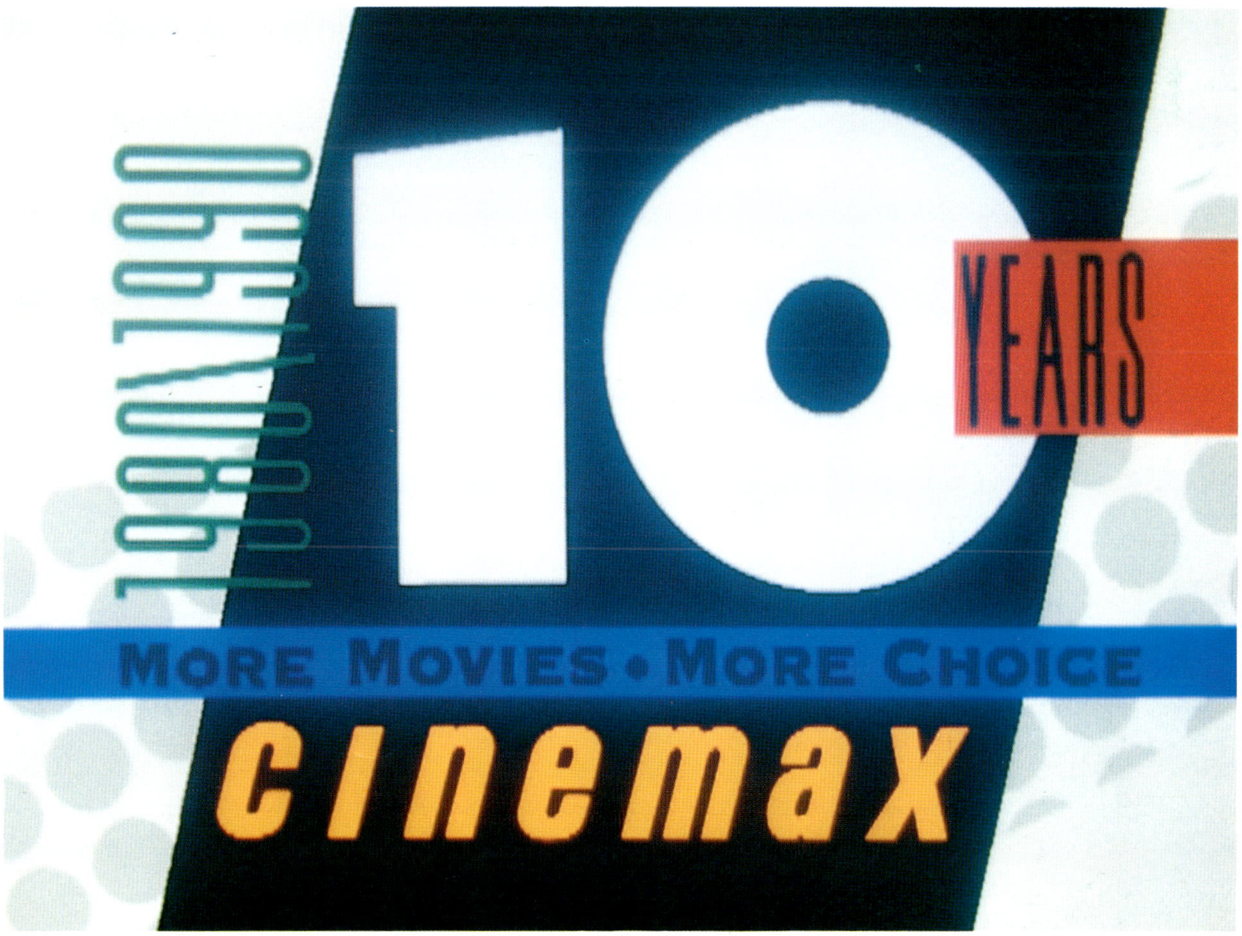
1980/1990
10
YEARS
MORE MOVIES • MORE CHOICE
cinemax

Manitoba Television Network

350 River Road, Portage La Prairie, Manitoba, Canada RIN 3N9

Sofa Spud

Designed for the Manitoba Television Network as a video introduction to a comic editorial on "Bundy's Late Night Review" hosted by Kevin Dunn.

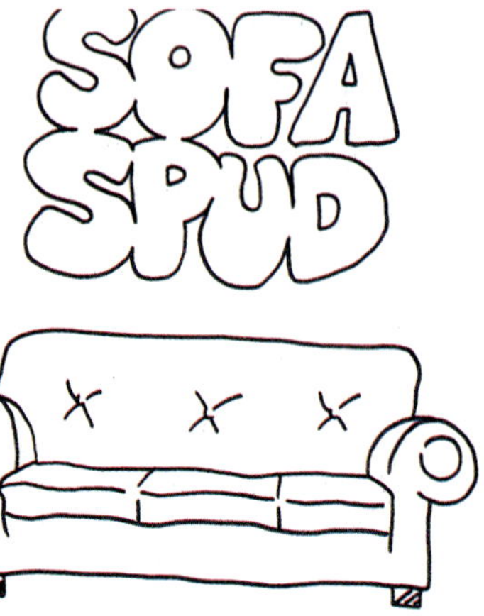

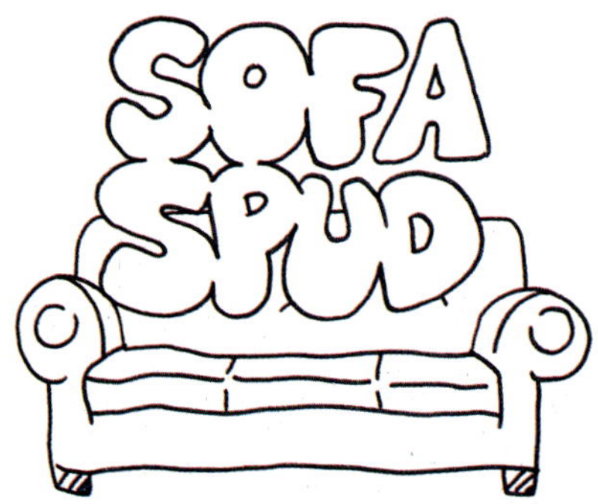

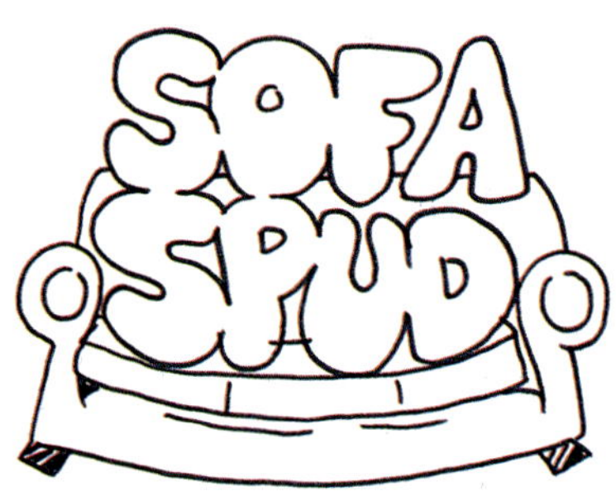

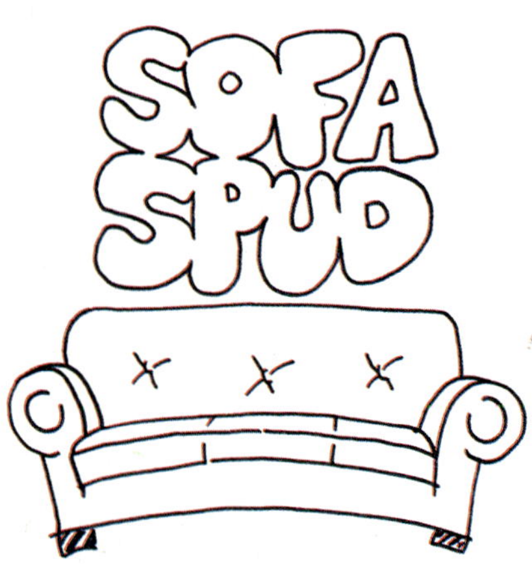

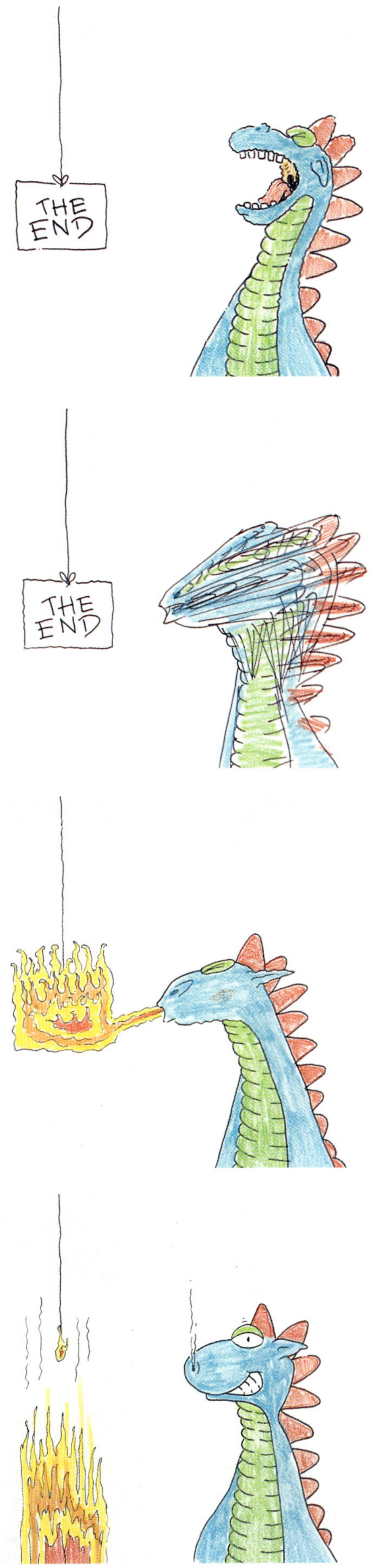

Kid's Club Dragon

Designed for the Manitoba Television Network as a video extra to a weekly children's puppet program.

Max TV Man

Designed as a video introduction for the Manitoba Television Network's sales presentation featuring MTN's fall lineup and promotional activities.

All of the graphics were created by hand drawing hundreds of animation cells. Each cell was shot in video and edited frame by frame with a Sony BVE 900 editor. A DVE was employed to enlarge or move separate pictures. Each individual video graphic design consisted of over 100 individual cells.

All of the material is a great example of a time consuming but relatively inexpensive method to achieve highly professional looking results.

Design Firm	Ad Type Graphics
Graphic Artist	Adam Rickner
Producer	Kevin Dunn
Video Editor	Tony Wytinck
Created at	Ad Type Graphics
Completed at	MTN

Length of Time to Complete Work—8 hours each project

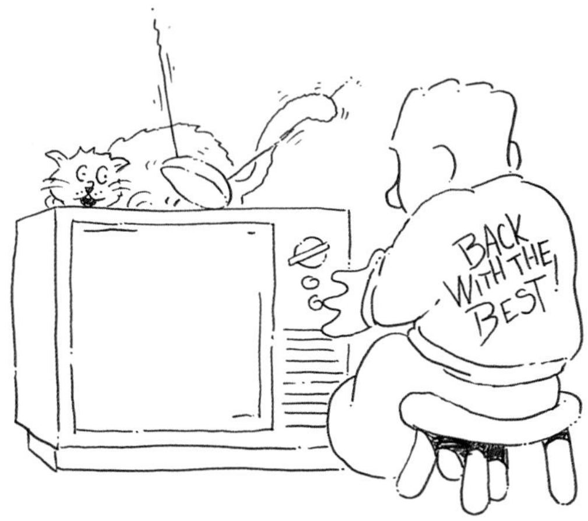

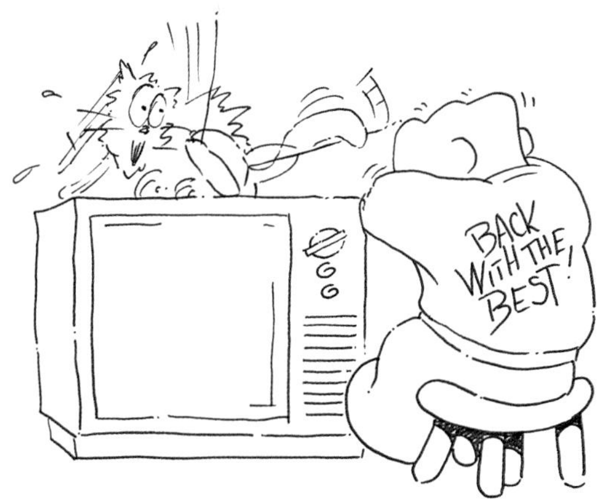

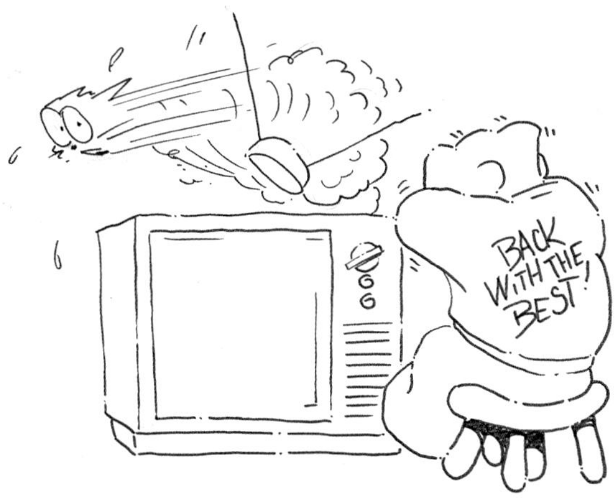

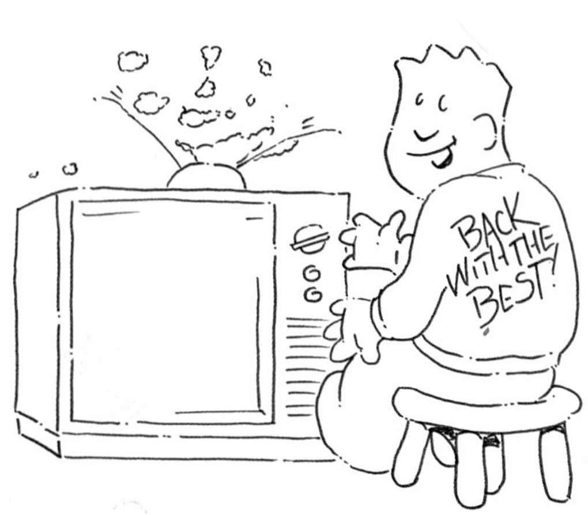

Charles Marsella

HBO Studio Productions, 120a E. 23rd Street, New York, NY 10010

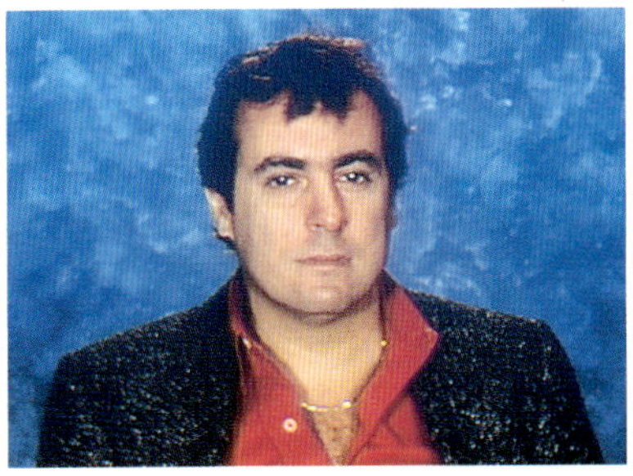

Charles Marsella, HBO Studio Productions, New York, NY

Charles Marsella has designed for a great number of video projects including programs, sporting events and show openings. He has spent 12 of his 17 years in the business at HBO where he is an expert on specialized technical equipment. He has received numerous award nominations for his work.

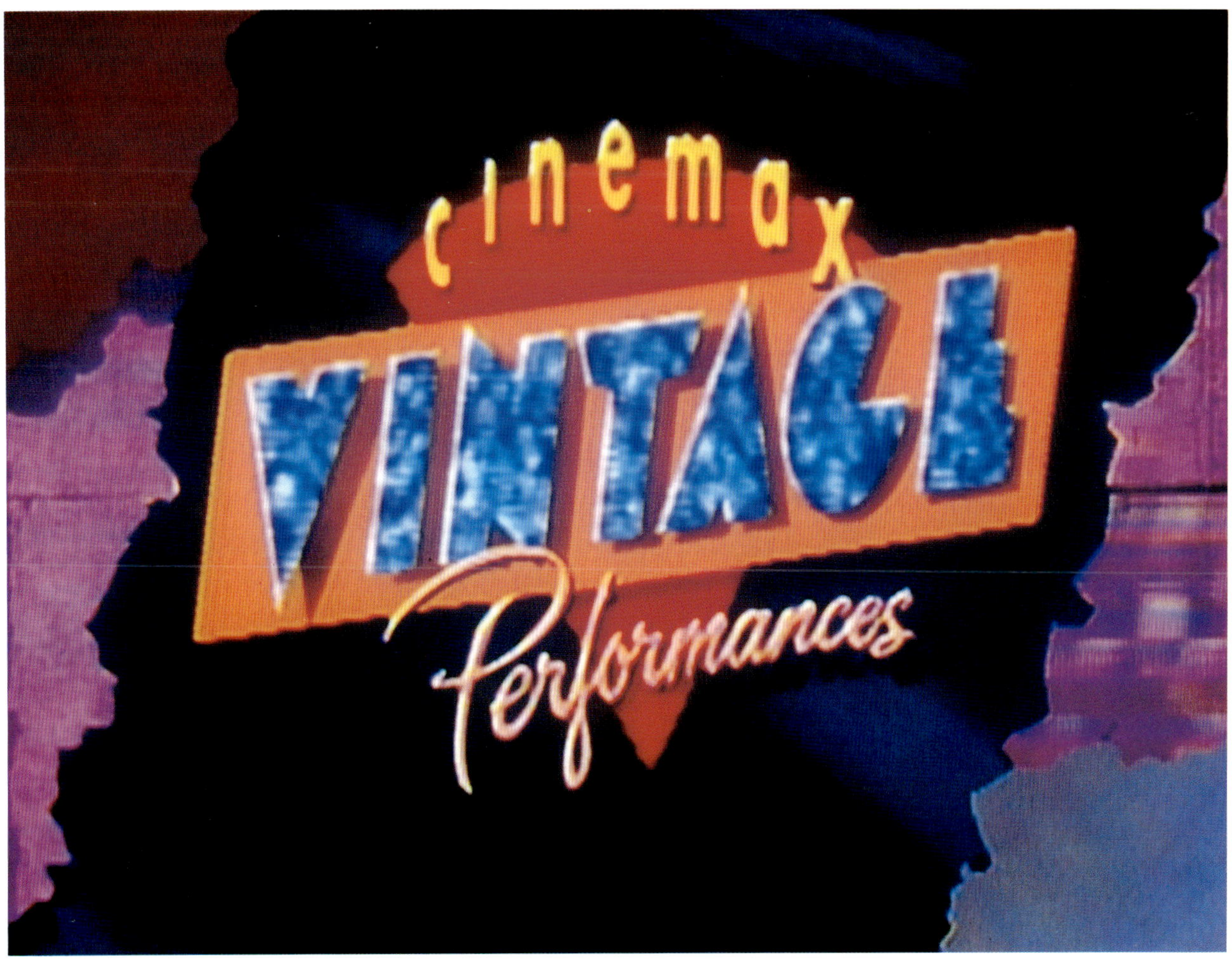

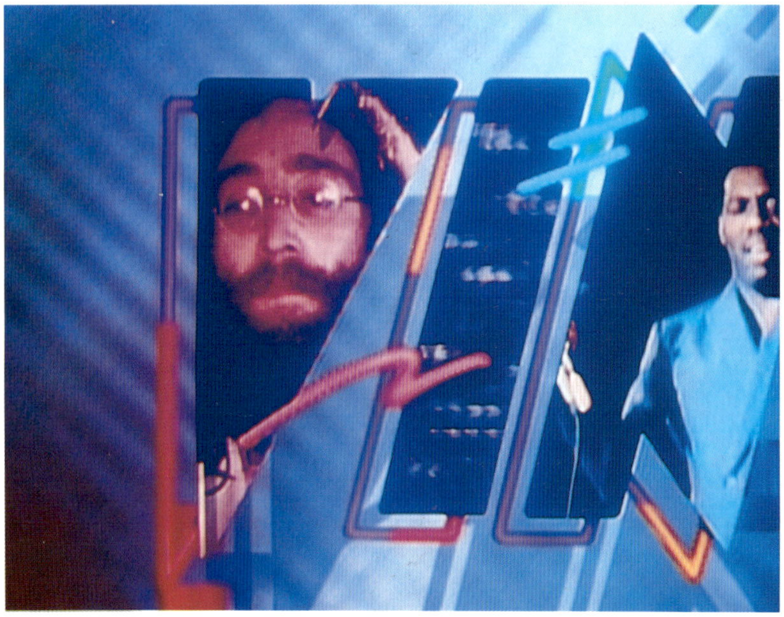

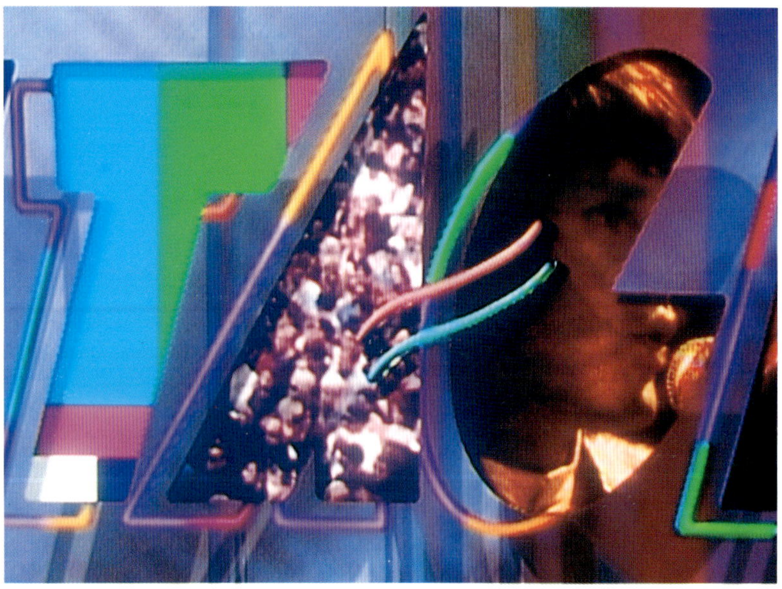

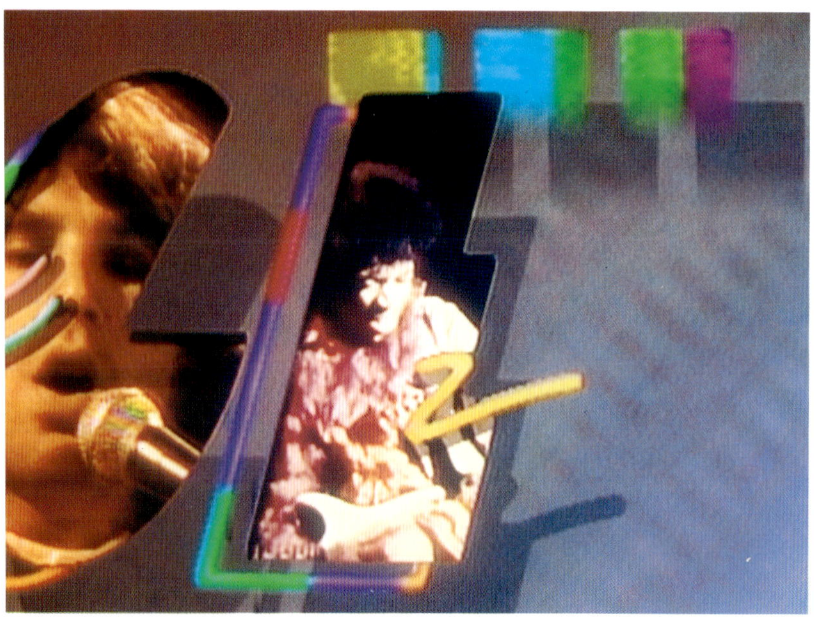

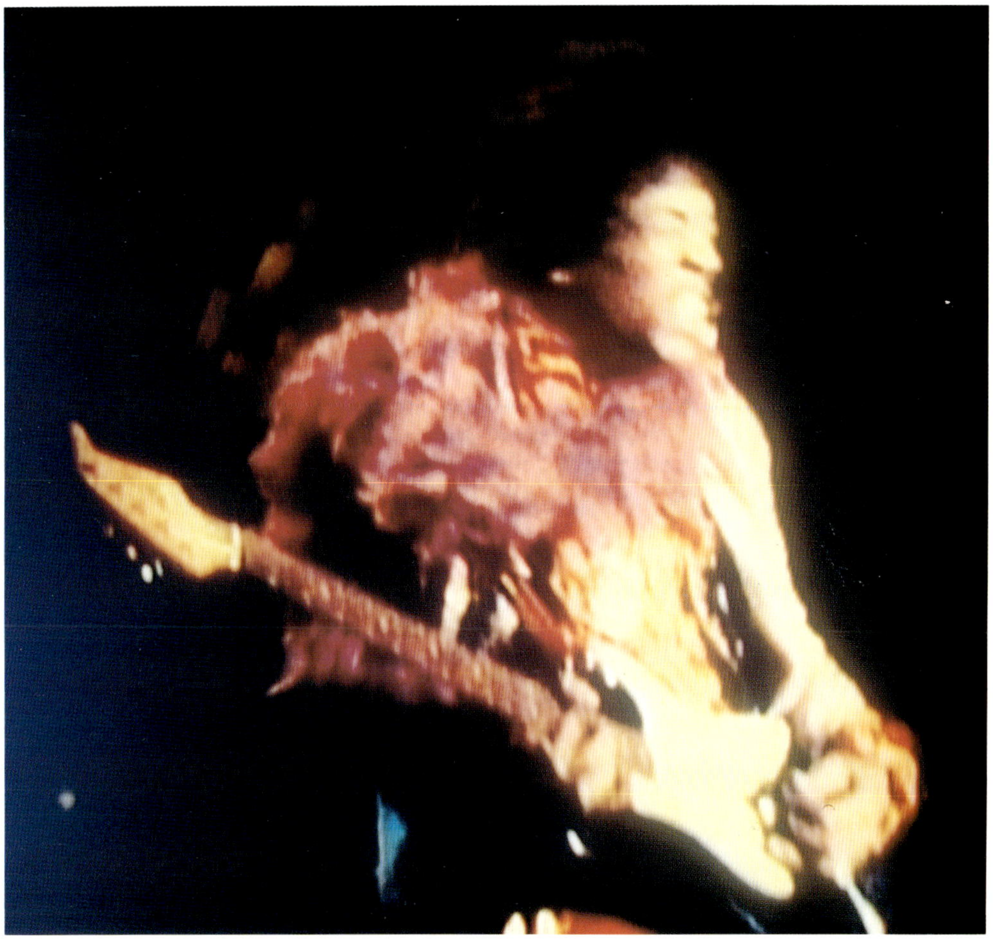

Cinemax Vintage Performances, Jimi Hendrix Open

Designed as a show open for Paul Fuentes of Cinemax.

Created by animating Paintbox frames with 2 channel ADO 3000, Grass Valley 300 Switcher and Abekas A 62.

Created By	Paul Fuentes, Charles Marsella, Henry Baker
Designer	Paul Fuentes
Effects Supervisor	Charles Marsella
Graphic Artist	Henry Baker
Video Editor	Charles Marsella
Created and Completed at	HBO Studio Productions

Length of Time to Complete Work—16 hours

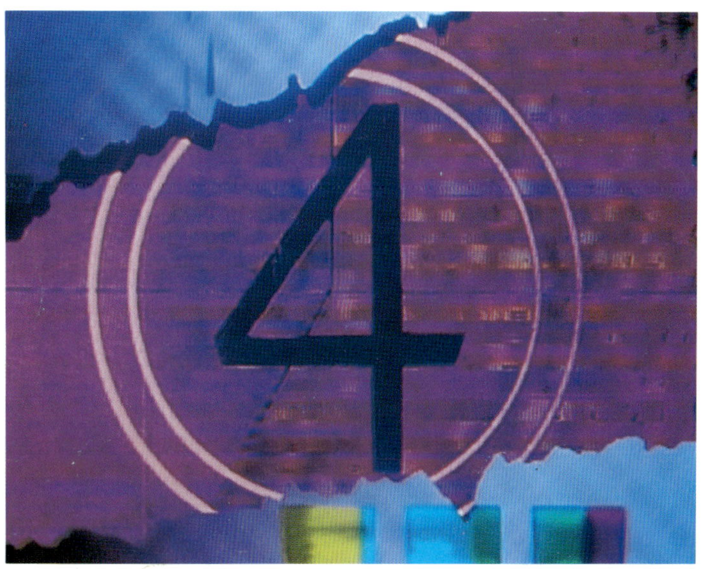

MVP Communications, Inc.

1075 Rankin, Troy, MI 48083

MVP Communications of Troy, Michigan is a full-service video production facility. Their divisions include, a Video Division, TV News Division, A Presentation Services Division, a Promotion and Display Division, an American Videowall Division and an MVP Imprints Division. Here then, are excellent examples of video graphic design in these areas.

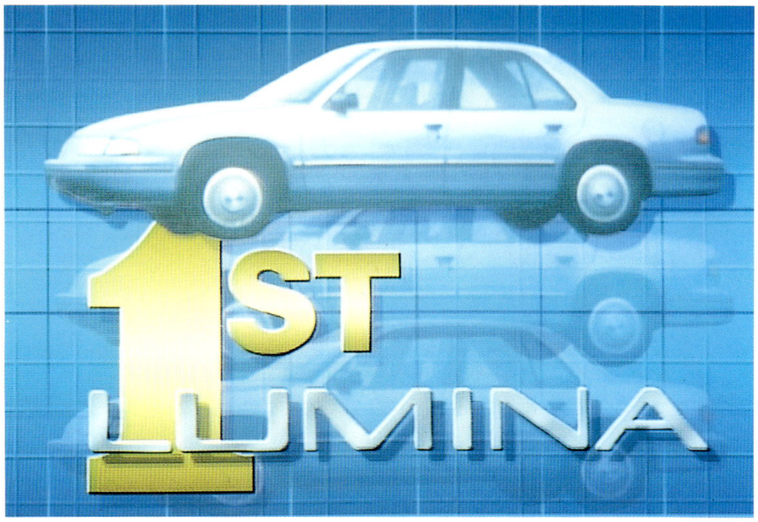

Team Chevrolet Today

Designed to update employees on job-related issues and events for Arlene Reindel, Public Relations, Chevrolet Motor Division, Warren, MI.

Created by inputting black-and-white logos, video freeze frames and Chyron fonts into the Dubner DPS — 1. These were then manipulated and stenciled onto computer-generated backgrounds. Electronic equipment used included a studio camera, Dubner DPS-1 paint box, Betacam SP recorder/editor and Chyron.

Designer	Laurie Peyok
Creative Director	Laurie Peyok
Art Director	Laurie Peyok
Graphic Artist	Laurie Peyok
Producer	Gary Smith
Created and Completed at	MVP Communications

Length of Time to Complete Work—2–4 hours per graphic

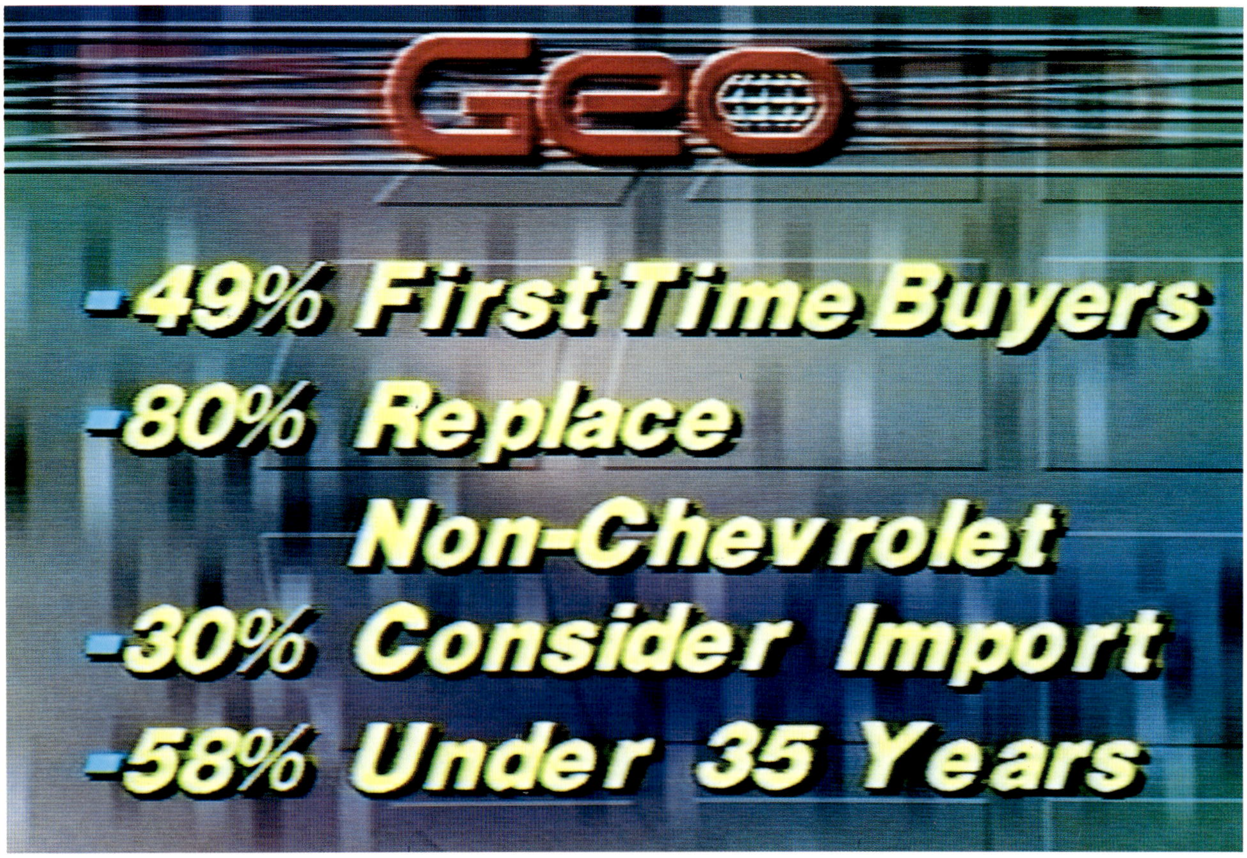

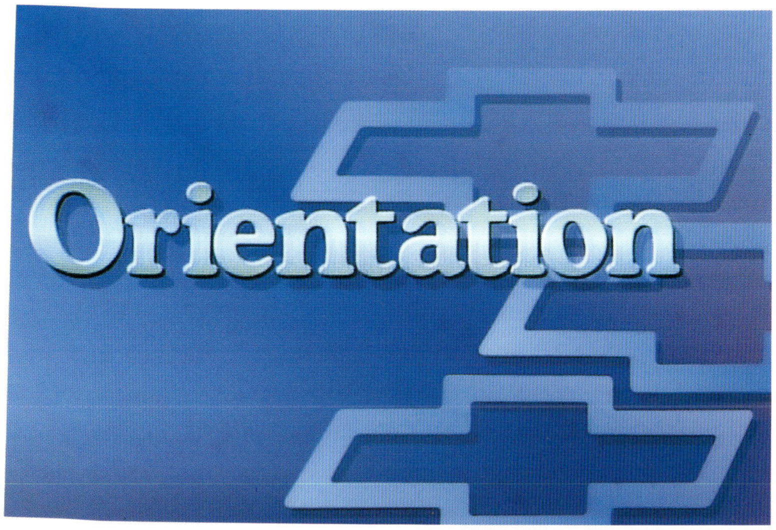
Orientation

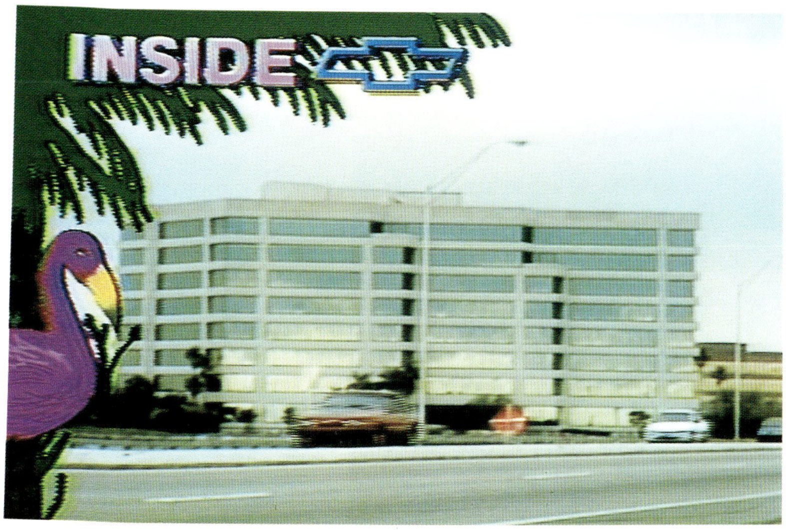
INSIDE

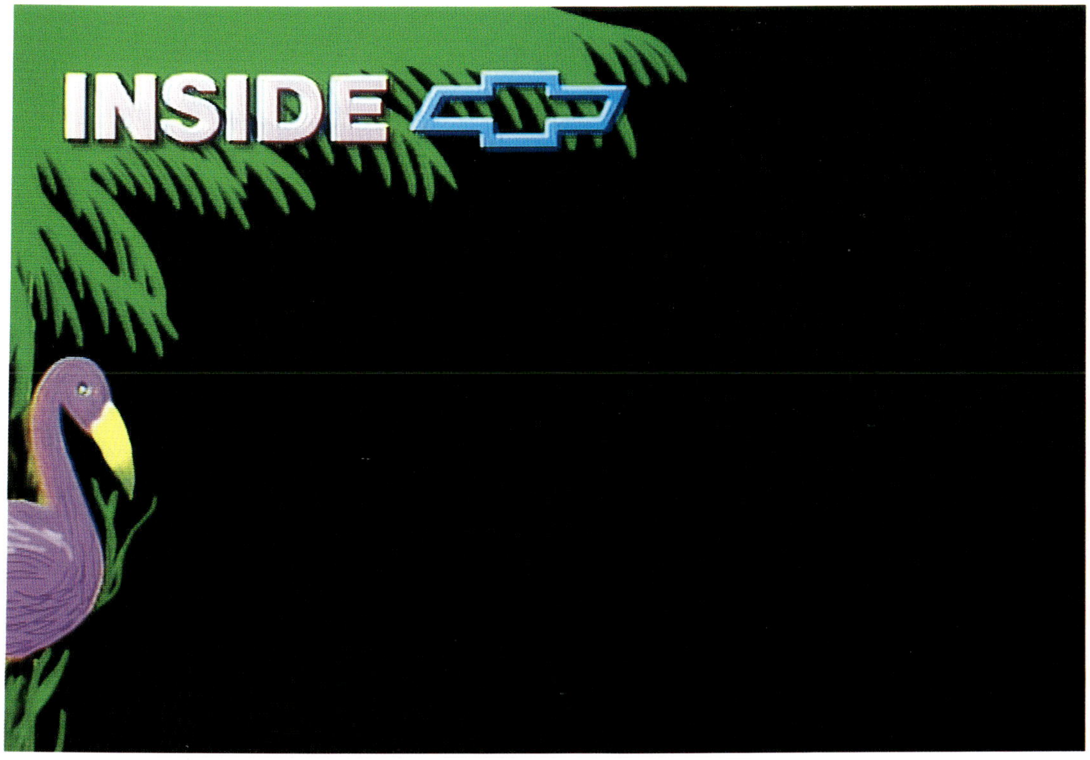
INSIDE

Chevrolet Satellite Network

Designed to explain a new satellite network to Chevrolet dealers for Arlene Reindel, Chevrolet Motor Division, Public Relations Staff, Warren, MI.

Created by inputting black-and-white logos and video freeze frames into the Dubner DPS – 1. They were then colorized and airbrushed, color corrected and otherwise altered. At that point they were stenciled onto computer-generated backgrounds.

Designer	Laurie Peyok
Creative Director	Laurie Peyok
Art Director	Laurie Peyok
Graphic Artist	Laurie Peyok
Producer	Gary Smith
Video Editor	Bill Robbins
Created and Completed at	MVP Communications, Inc.

Length of Time of Complete Work—2–3 hours per graphic

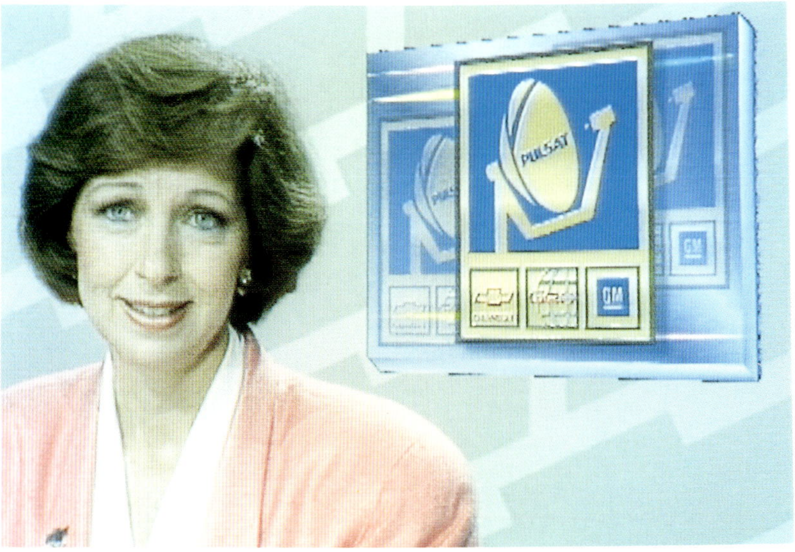

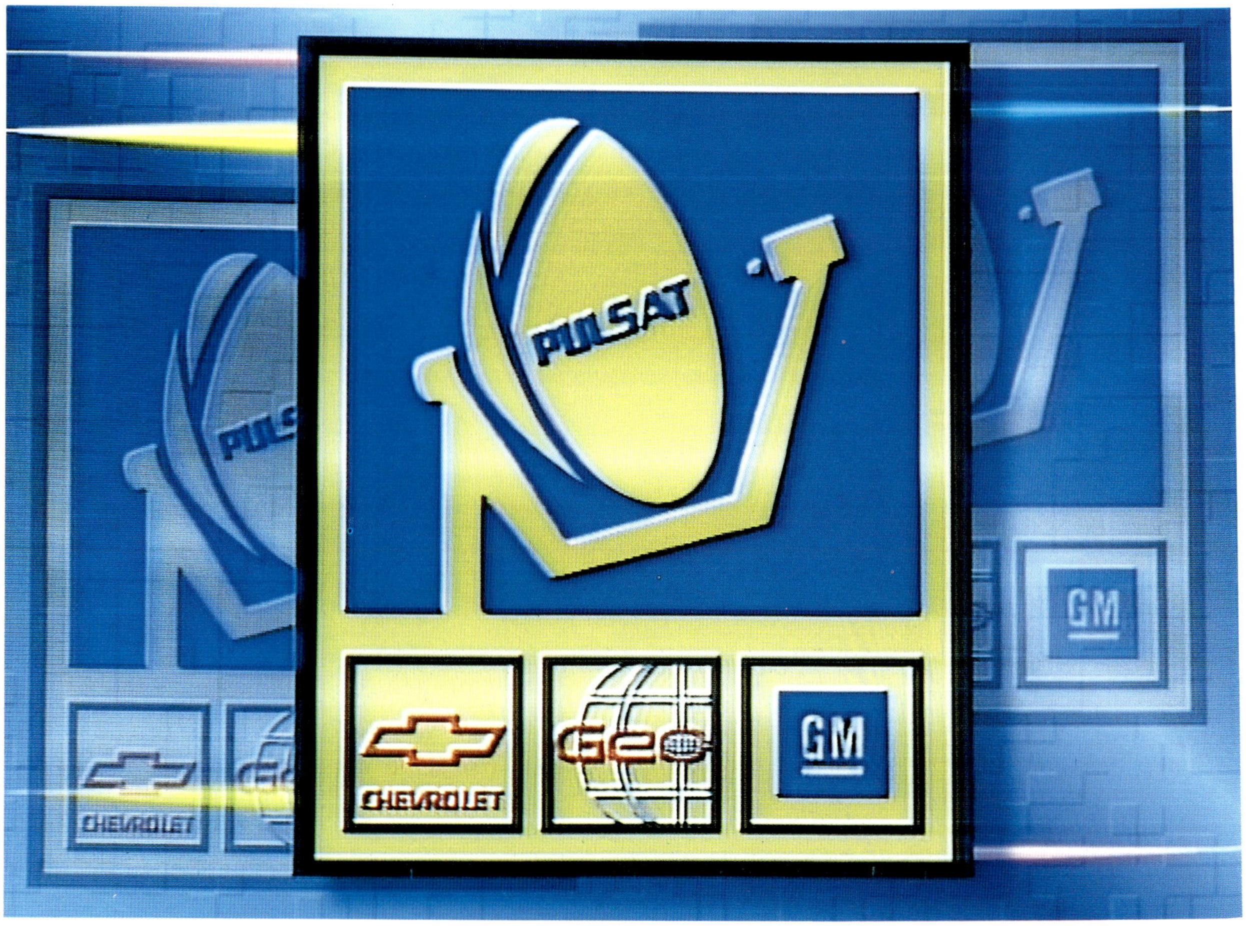

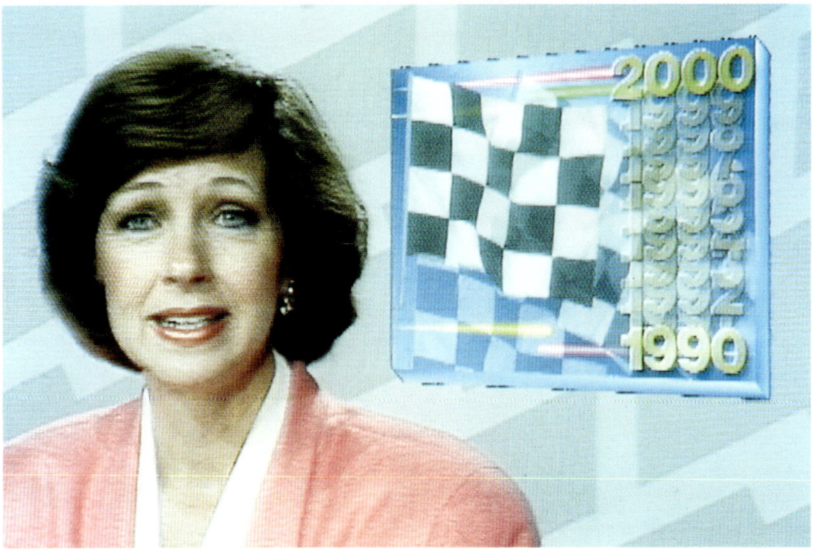
2000
1990

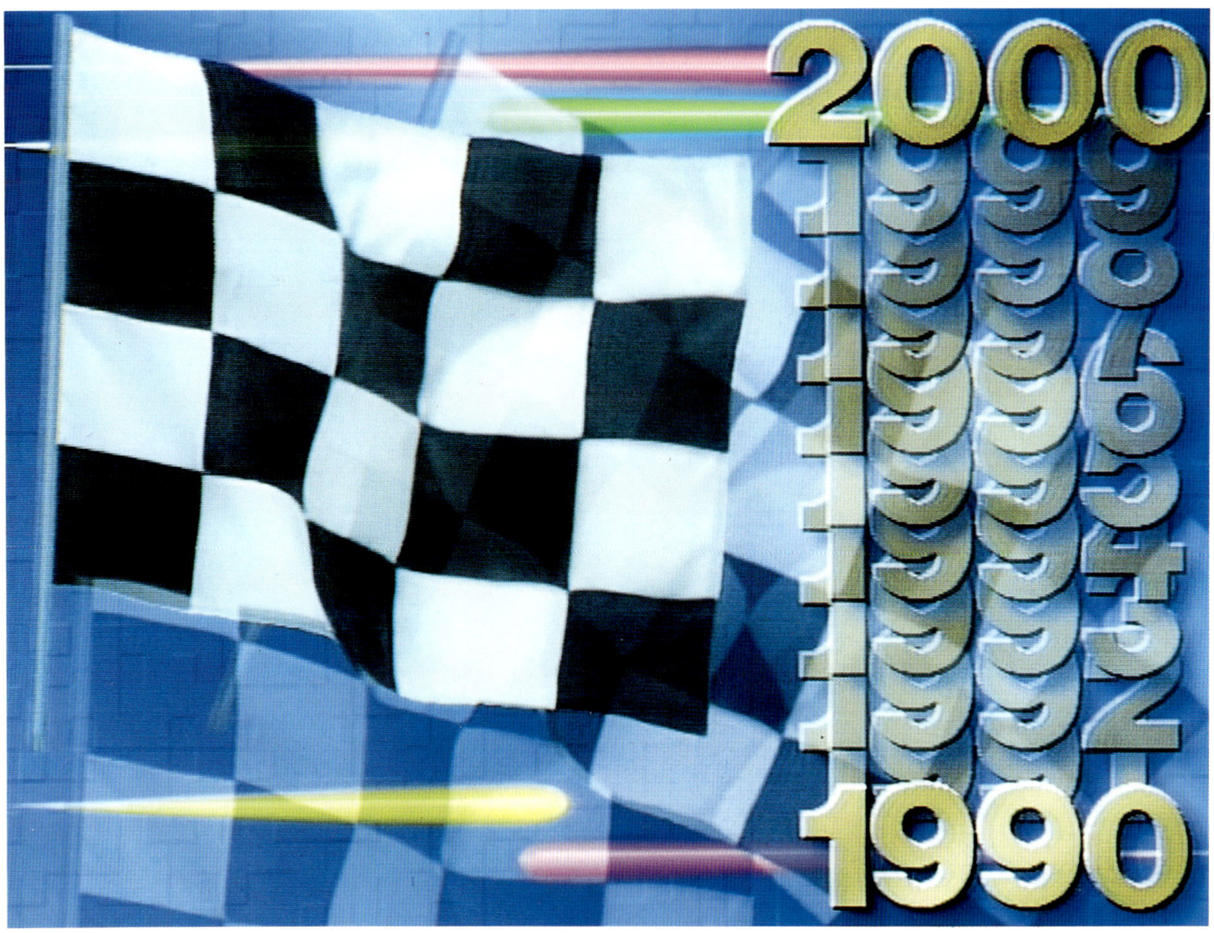
2000
1990

ONE PASS

1 China Basin Building, San Francisco, CA 94107

ONE PASS LOGO ANIMATION

Designed as an opening for the One Pass demo reel.

The work was brought into being entirely from a business card. All elements were created in the Paintbox. The Encore was used for all element motion and the Harry provided a component digital editing environment to composite edit the master. Since the Encore could only move a 2-D image in a 3-D space, many layers of tracking moves were needed to emulate 3-D animation. The pyramid, floor block and all lighting and shadow mapping were essentially done by linking together 2-D planes in their proper orientation in 3-D space. The illusion of the pyramid passing over the One Pass name subtly refers to the relationship of One Pass to the Editel Group.

Created, Designed and Executed by	Bart Giovannetti
Created and Completed at	One Pass

Length of Time to Complete Work—1 week

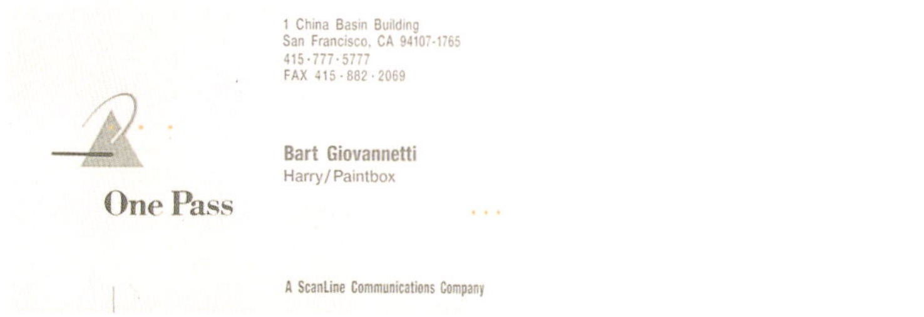

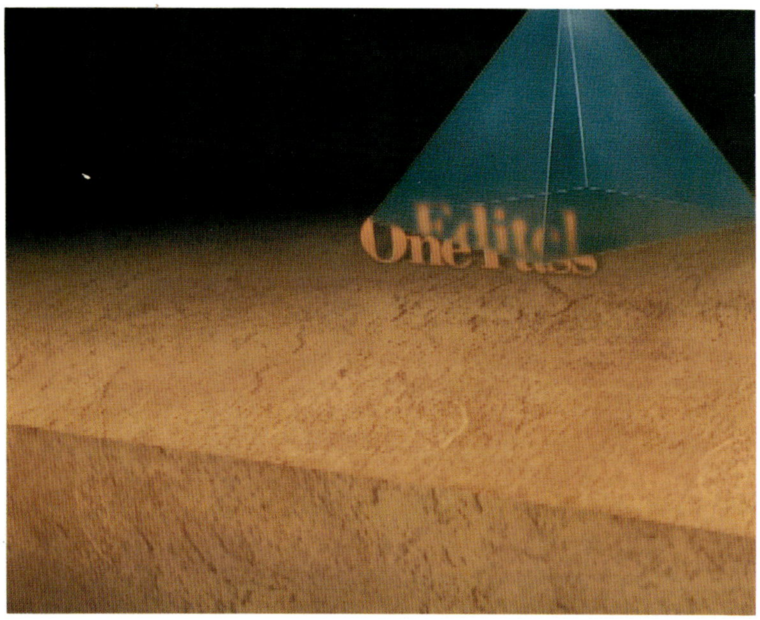

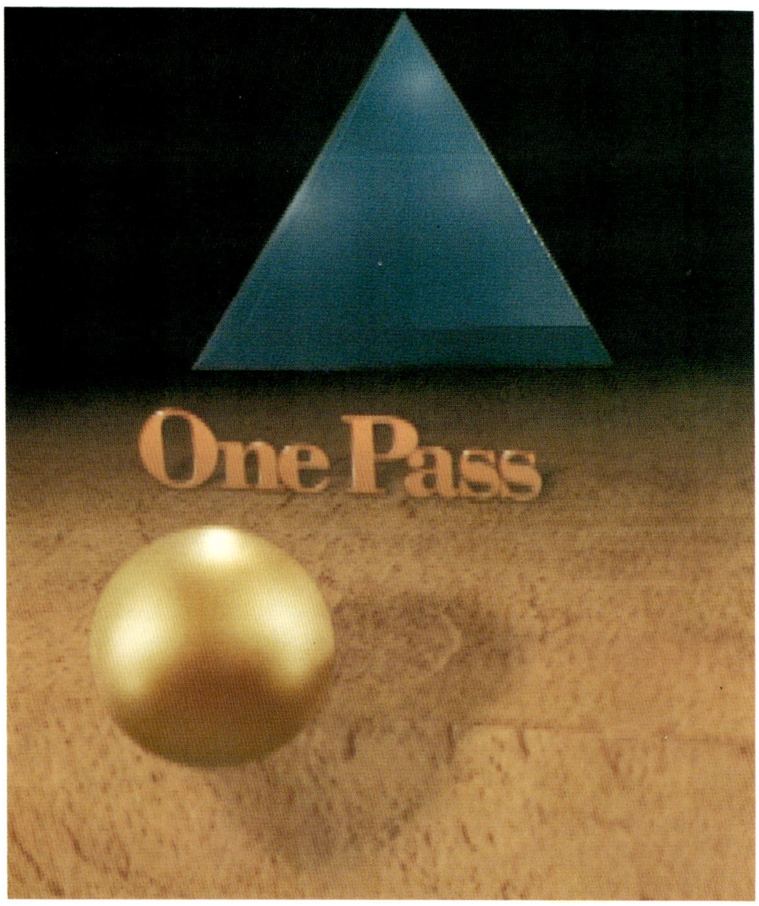

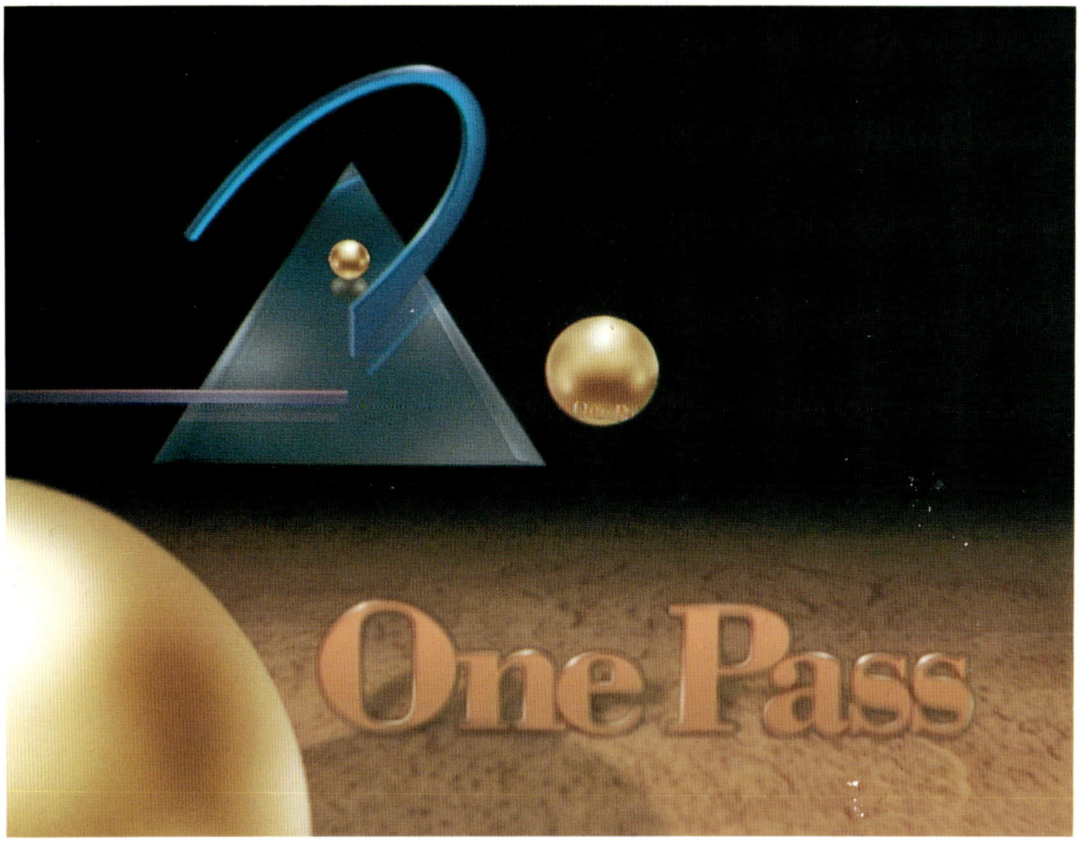
One Pass

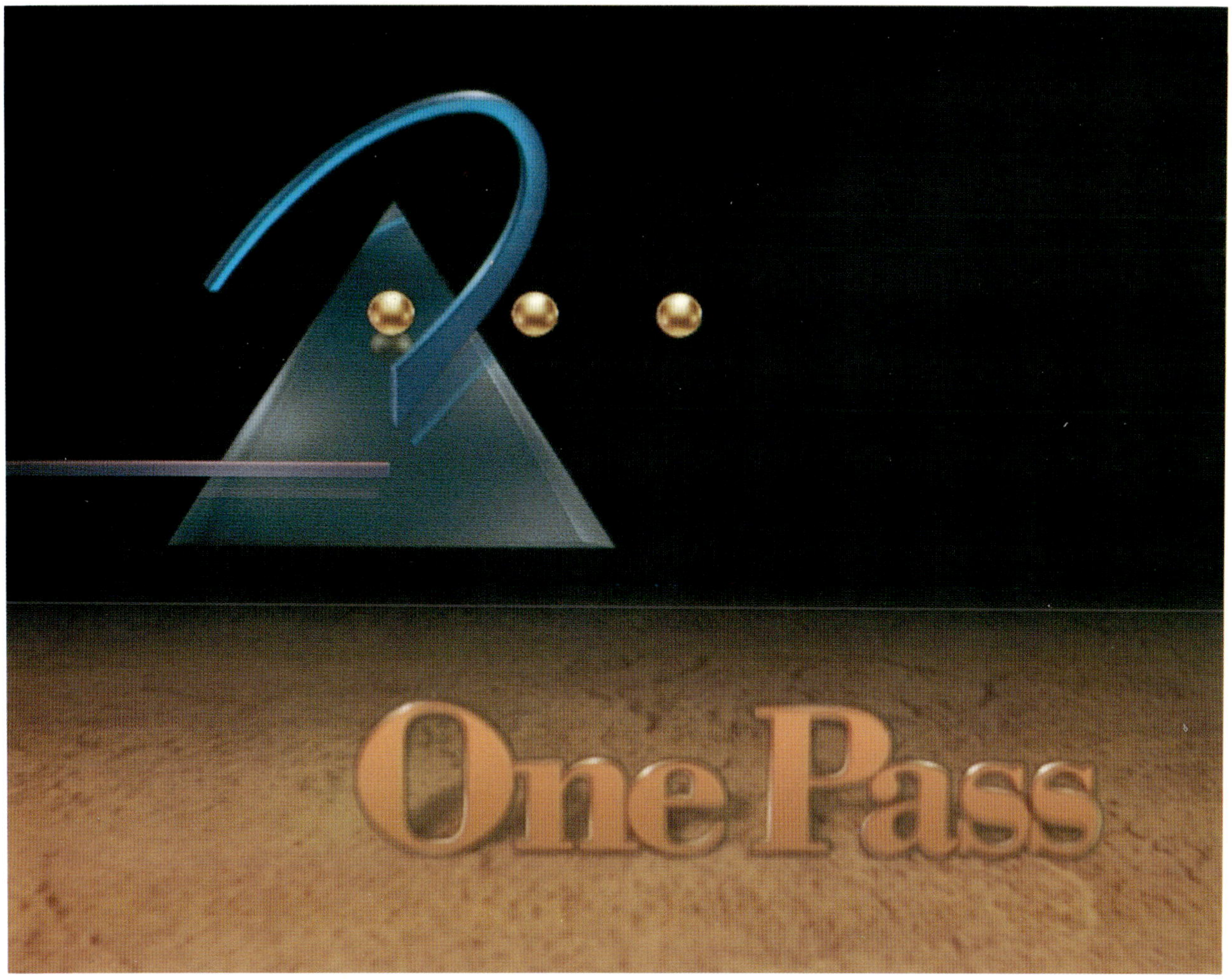
One Pass

KNTV News Design

Developed as a fresh television news look for Bob Anderson, Promotions Manager of KNTV, San Jose, CA.

Designed to incorporate visual images associated with the computer and communications technologies which are familiar to the TV station's marketplace which is made up of people employed in the advanced technology fields of the Silicon Valley area. Obtuse or open angles instead of right angles were used exclusively. These represent the through-ways utilized for electron flow within computer chips. Design images representing high speed data transmission were used to reinforce the stations image of being constantly integrated with local and worldwide information sources which link the audience to the news events that impact their lives.

Created by Nicholas Koenig, who did the design and Paintbox generated storyboards.

Length of Time to Complete Work—1 week

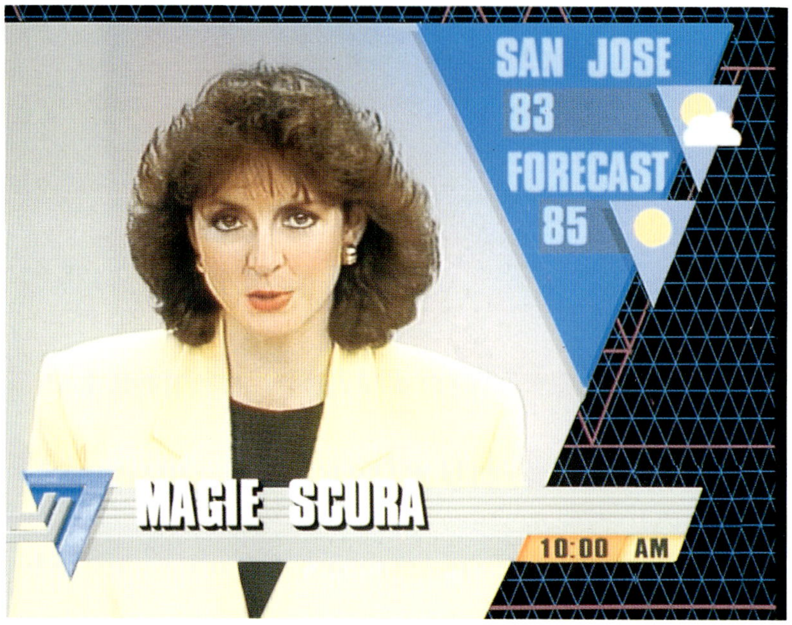

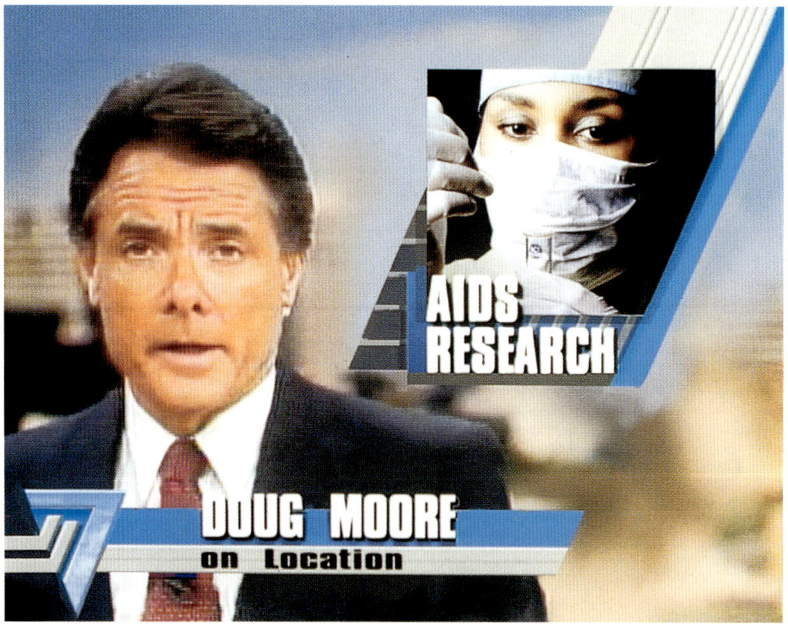

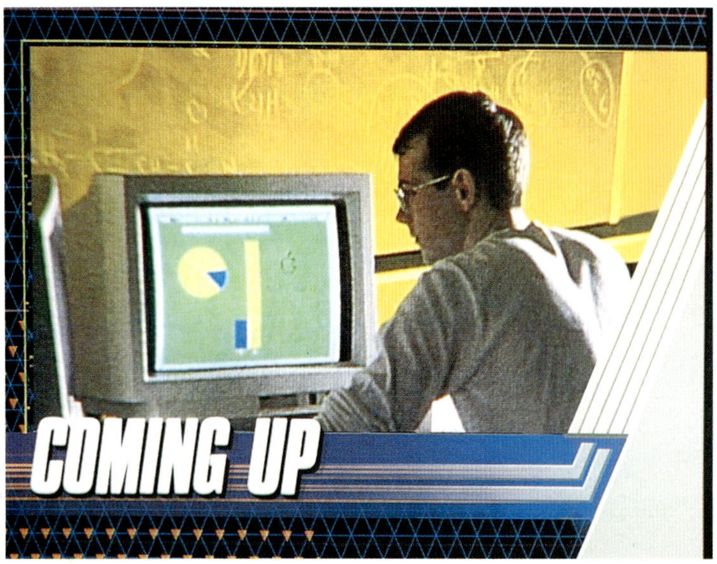

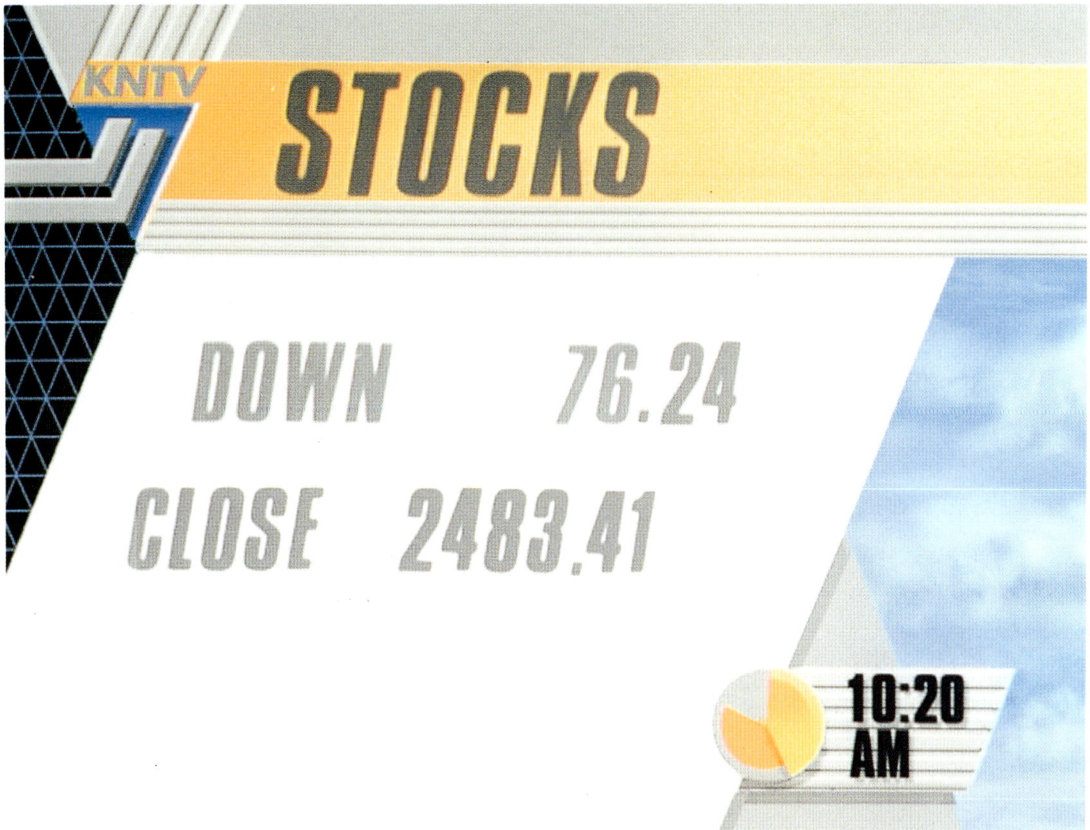
KNTV
STOCKS
DOWN 76.24
CLOSE 2483.41
10:20
AM

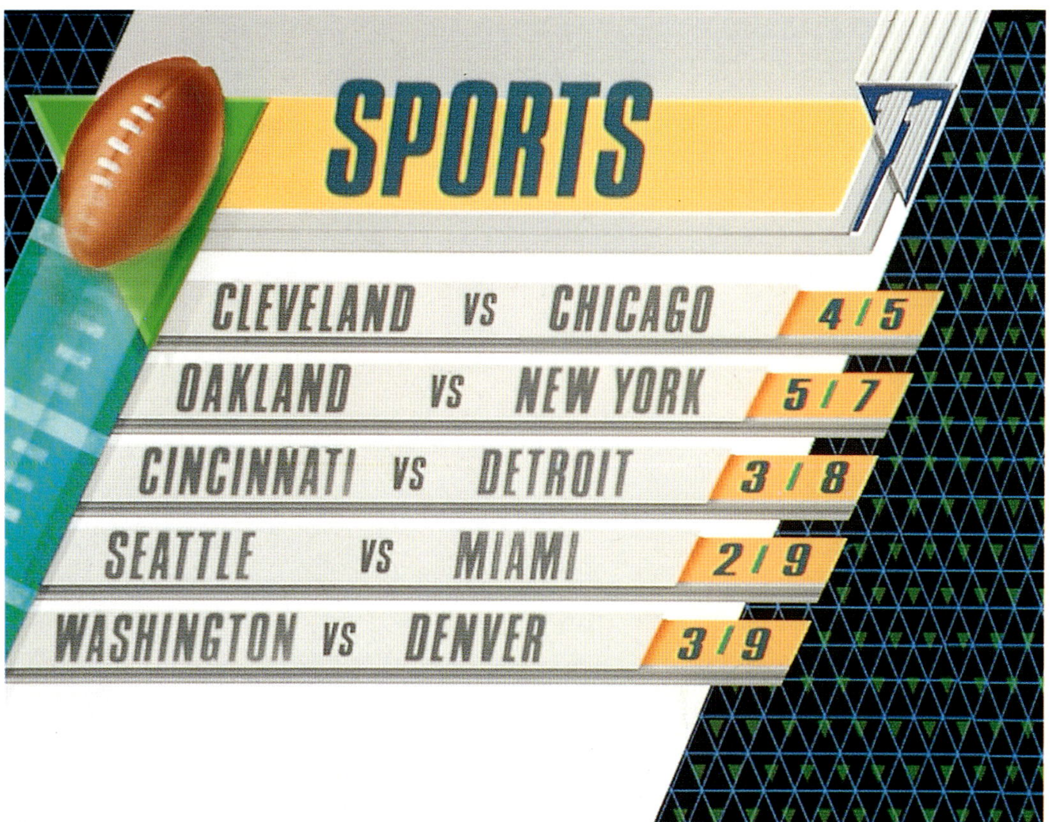
SPORTS
CLEVELAND vs CHICAGO 4/5
OAKLAND vs NEW YORK 5/7
CINCINNATI vs DETROIT 3/8
SEATTLE vs MIAMI 2/9
WASHINGTON vs DENVER 3/9

Pulse Communications

2830 Ramada Way, Green Bay, WI 54304

Pulse Communications started as the dream of its president, Dave Moorman. Dave began in the broadcast industry as a producer and director 20 years ago. He saw the need in the area for a complete video design facility and also wanted to keep the business from leaving the region. He soon moved into the commercial area, where he developed on air graphics, directed award-winning programs and supervised on location live televised events. The experience that Dave brings to Pulse Communications shows in the enthusiasm of his Pulse team leadership.

Greyhound Week :30 Open

Created as a thirty-second opening for a thirty-minute television show for Jay Van Zeeland, Fox Valley Greyhound Park, Kaykauna, WI.

Seven seconds of 3-D animation was built and then 11 frames of video was rotoscoped. The title was then composited with an ADO. Equipment used to create the opening was Artstar 3-D paint and animation system, ADO 2000 and BVE 9000 computerized editing system.

Created By	Jay Van Zeeland, Scott Koffarnus, Kerry Strom, Kregg Shilbauer
Design Firm	Pulse Communications
Designer	Scott Koffarnus
Creative Director	Kerry Strom
Art Director	Scott Koffarnus
Effects Supervisor	Scott Koffarnus
Graphic Artist	Scott Koffarnus
Producer	Jay Van Zeeland
Video Editor	Kregg Shilbauer
Created and completed at	Pulse Communications

Length of Time to Complete Work—65 hours

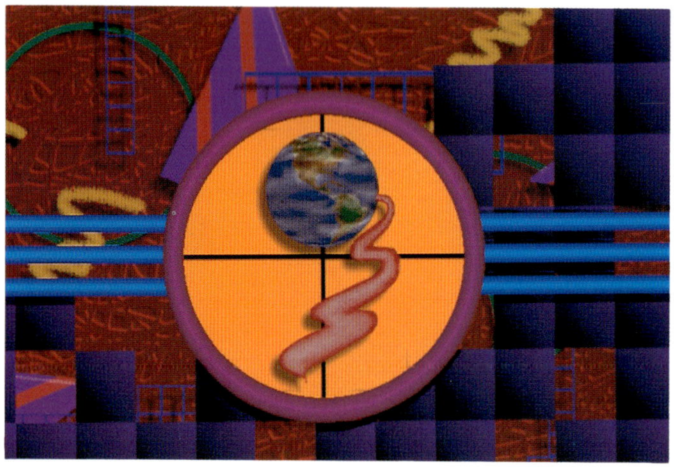

Countdown #1

Designed as a lead-in countdown for all Pulse Communications videos and commercials.

The base art was completed by doing a 24 bit rolling background page and an 8 bit foreground color cycling page in blue neon. The numbers were composited in editing with a clock wipe. The work was done on an Artstar and Sony BVE 9000 computerized editor.

Created By	Scott Koffarnus and Kregg Shilbauer
Design Firm	Pulse Communications
Designer	Scott Koffarnus
Art Director	Scott Koffarnus
Graphic Artist	Scott Koffarnus
Created and completed at	Pulse Communications

Length of Time to Complete Work—16 hours

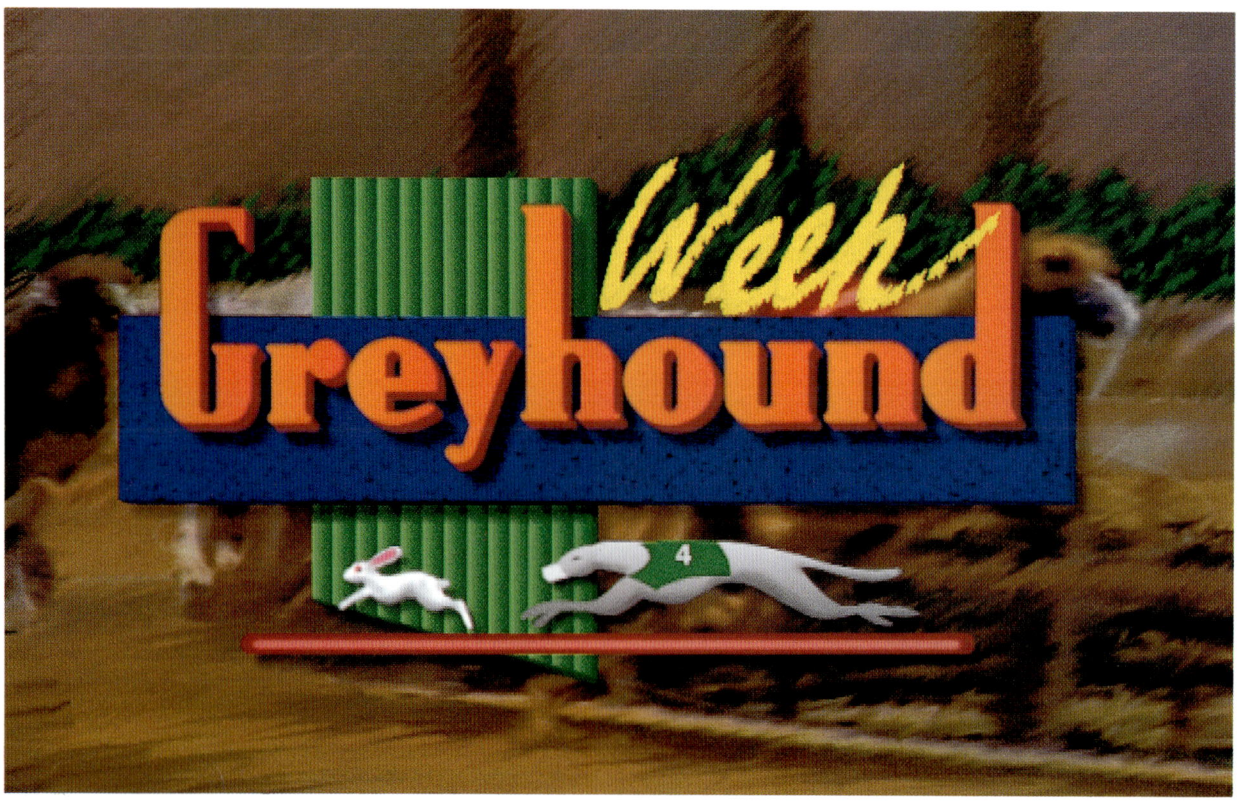

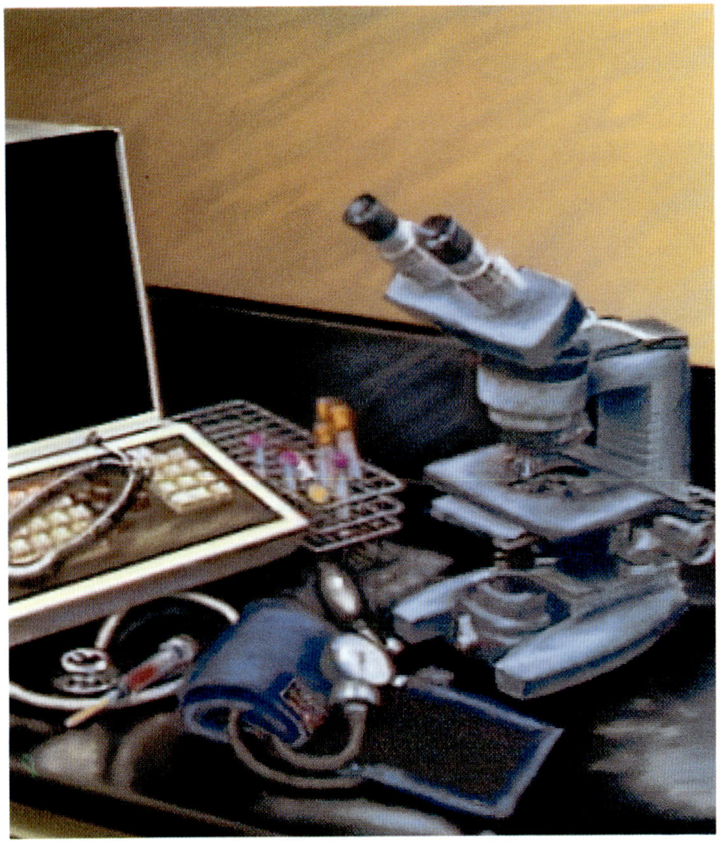

Transitional Page, St. Vincent Hospital Video

Designed as a transitional page within a five-minute nurse recruiting tape done for Jim Reck, St. Vincent Hospital, Green Bay, WI.

A single frame of video was rotoscoped and electronically painted to be used as the transition page. The sequence shows the video being flown out of the monitor via a DVE move to a full frame of video, at which point a Chyron was added.

Created By	Jim Reck, Kerry Strom, Scott Koffranus, Kreg Shilbauer
Design Firm	Pulse Communications
Designer	Scott Koffarnus
Creative Director	Kerry Strom
Art Director	Scott Koffarnus
Effects Supervisor	Kerry Strom
Graphic Artist	Scott Koffarnus
Producer	Jim Reck
Video Editor	Kreg Shilbauer
Assistant Video Editor	Duane White
Created and completed at	Pulse Communications

Length of Time to Complete Work—this page—2 hours, entire video design—30 hours

Employee Assistance Program

Designed as an in-house informational for the Wisconsin Public Service Corporation

The work was created on the Artstar, first creating the embossed background with the cut and paste program, then using the paint program to create the glass for the text.

Created By	Scott Koffranus
Design Firm	Pulse Communications/WPS
Creative Director	Kerry Strom
Art Director	Scott Koffranus
Graphic Artist	Scott Koffranus
Created and completed at	Pulse Communications

Length of Time to Complete Work—4 hours

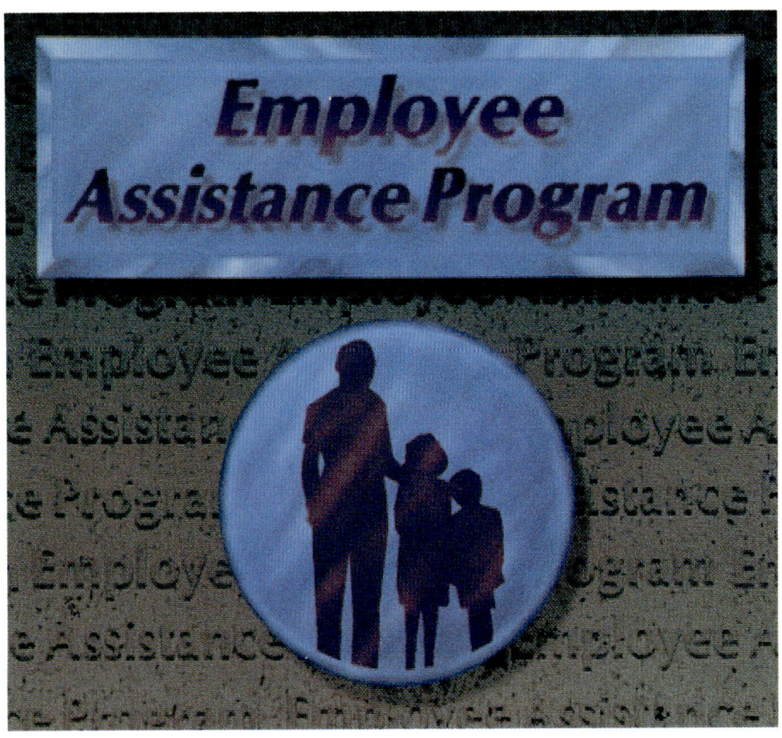

MARC ROSENBERG

Home Box Office, 1114 Avenue of the Americas, New York, NY 10036

Marc Rosenberg is Senior Designer at Home Box Office. He has also held the same position and that of Graphics Producer at other top firms. His awards include Emmy Finalist; Clios; Art Directors and BDA—Gold, Silver and Bronze. He holds a BFA from the Rhode Island School of Design.

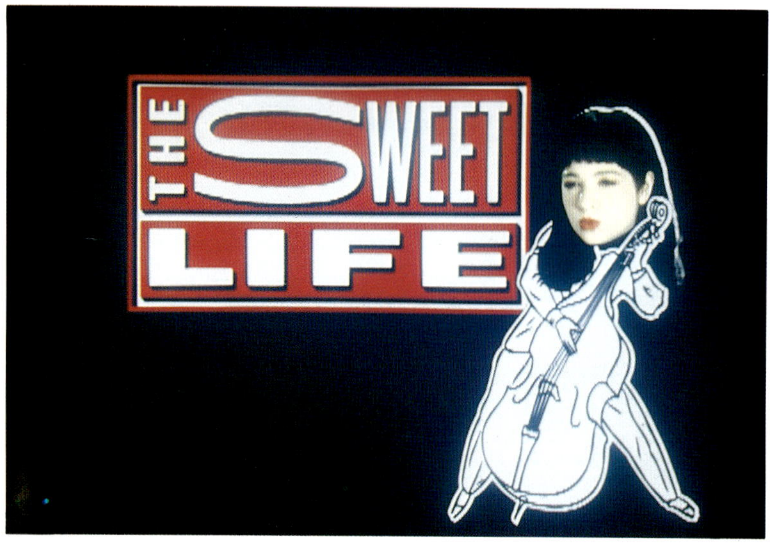

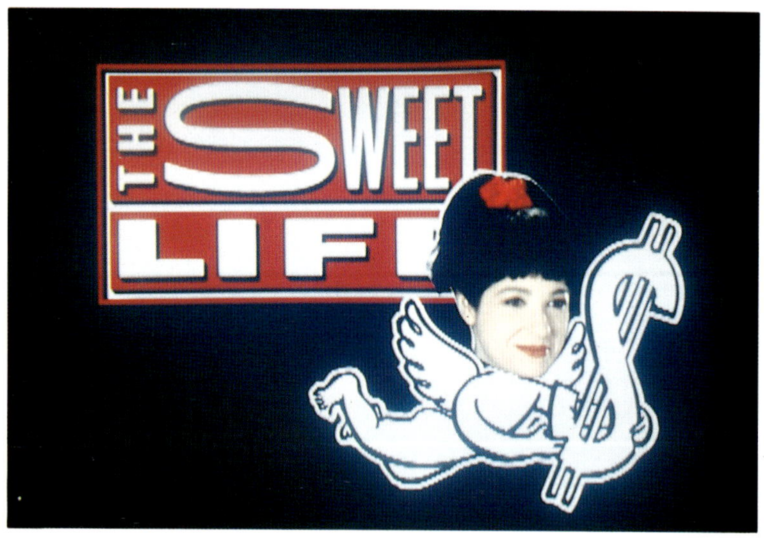

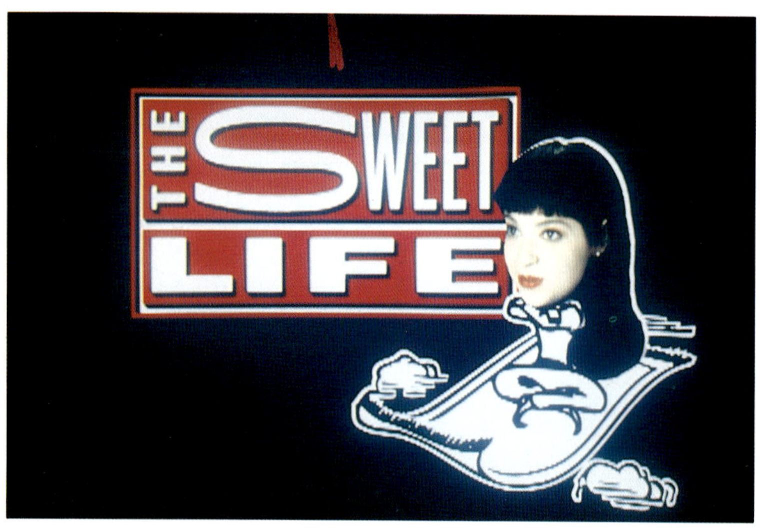

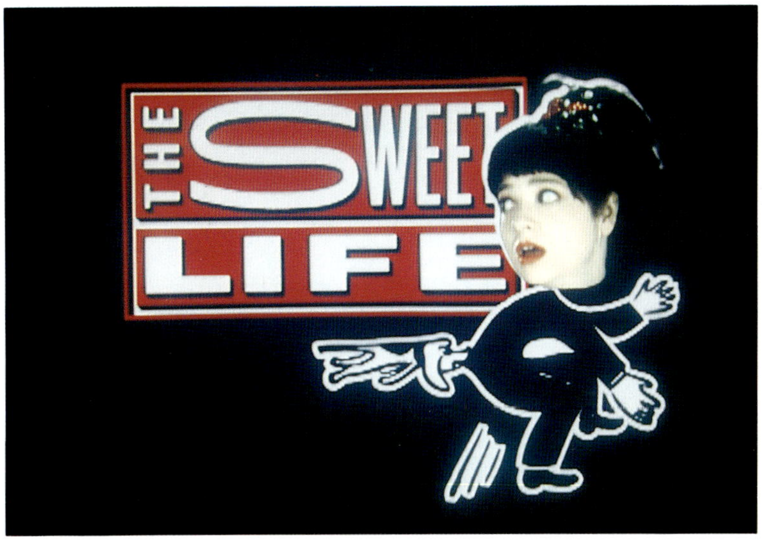

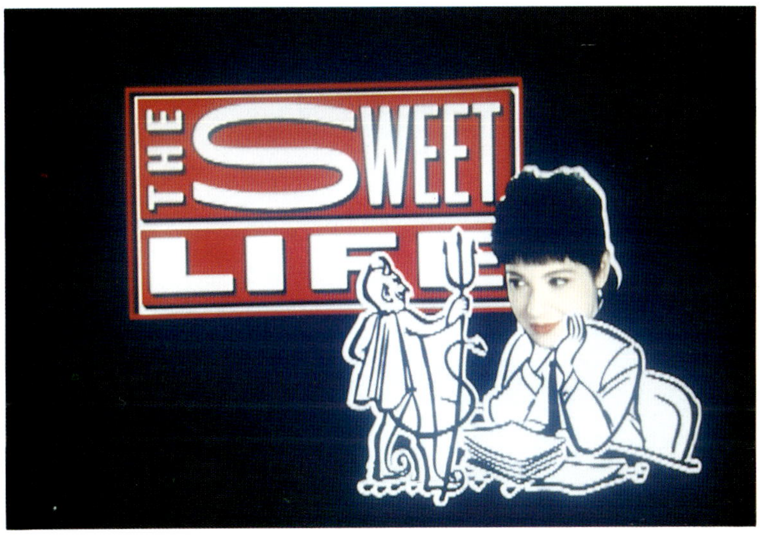

"THE SWEET LIFE" BUMPERS

Designed as bumpers for a comedy show on The Comedy Channel for HBO.

Created by shooting the heads with Ultimate and combining them with Paintbox elements. The work was animated on the Harry.

Created By	Marc Rosenberg, Henry Baker
Designer	Marc Rosenberg
Art Director	Marc Rosenberg
Harry Operator	Henry Baker
Producer	Marc Rosenberg
Created and Completed at	HBO Studios

Length of Time to Complete Work—2 weeks

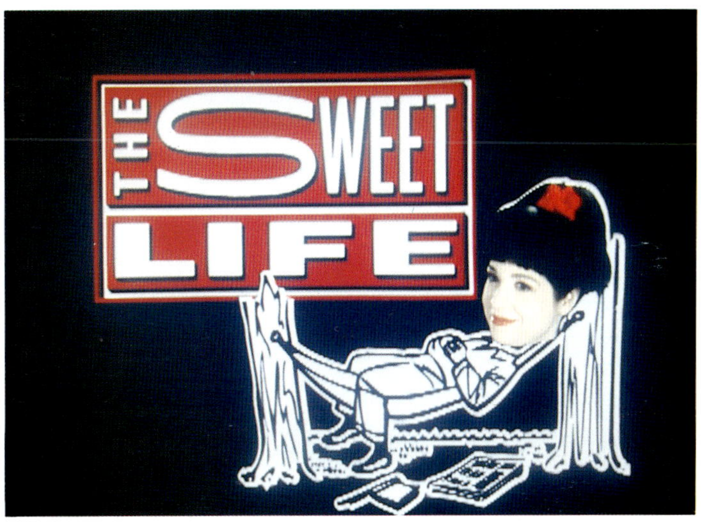

Darlene Ruess

The Tape House, 216 East 45th Street, New York, NY 10017

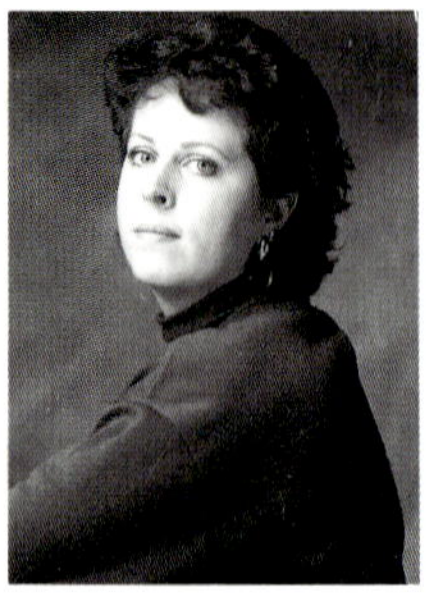

Darlene Ruess

Darlene Ruess is the senior effects designer for The Tape House in New York, NY. She is a graduate of The School of Visual Arts and received an Emmy Award nomination.

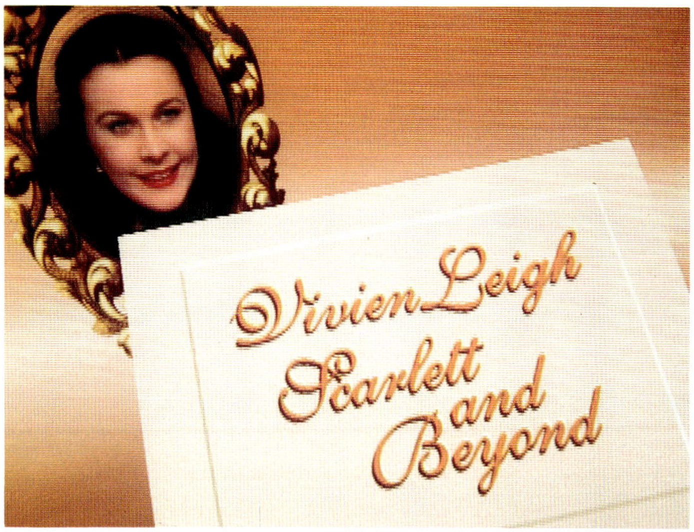

Vivien Leigh—Scarlet and Beyond

Show opening created for Gene Feldman and Wombat Productions, New York, NY.

Created by loading a 1" tape of Vivien Leigh into the Harry. Black-and-white art work was scanned and colorized in the Paintbox. The background and frame were also created in the Paintbox. The elements were moved with the Encore.

Created By	Gene Feldman, Suzette Winter, Ted Lowery, Darlene Ruess, Mark Polyocan
Designer	Darlene Ruess
Creative Director/ Producer	Gene Feldman
Art Director	Ted Lowery
Effects Supervisor	Mark Polyocan
Producer	Suzette Winter
Created and completed at	The Tape House

Length of Time to Complete Work—4 hours

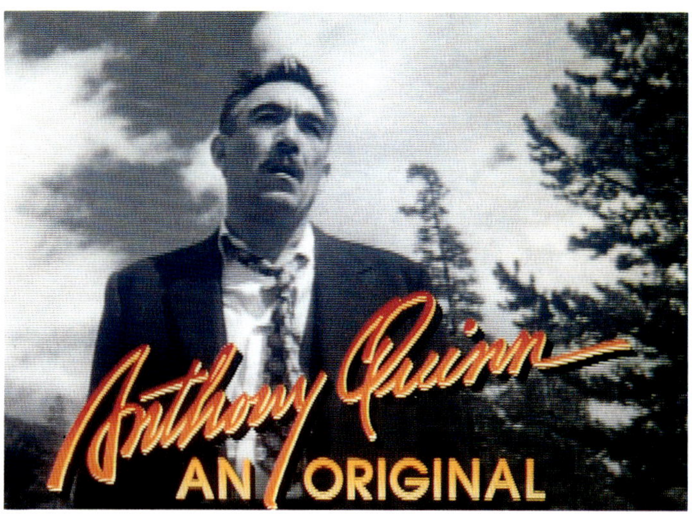

Anthony Quinn—An Original

A show opening created for Gene Feldman and Wombat Productions, New York, NY.

Created by loading Anthony Quinn footage into the Abekas A-60 from 1" tape. Black-and-white art work of type was loaded from a camera. The animation was created over the footage in the A-60.

Created By	Gene Feldman, Suzette Winter, Ted Lowery, Darlene Ruess, Mark Polyocan
Designer	Darlene Ruess
Creative Director/ Producer	Gene Feldman
Art Director	Ted Lowery
Effects Supervisor	Mark Polyocan
Producer	Suzette Winter
Created and completed at	The Tape House

Length of Time to Complete Work—3 hours

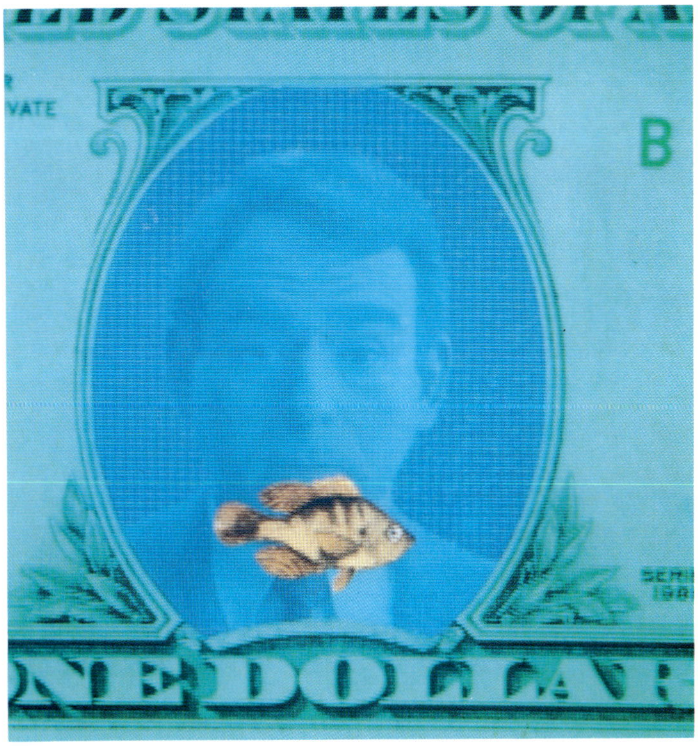

EZ $64—Carolina Power and Light

Created as a television commercial for Ed Noyes, Colossal Pictures, New York, NY and Silver Advertising

Created by adding footage of live action over the Prism in film to tape transfer. The bill stretching effect was accomplished by extensive tracking with the Harry. The bill's texture was accomplished by shooting a grid and layering it over the man in the Harry. The work was finished on the Kaleidoscope.

Created By	Eli Noyes, Mark Reusch, Darlene Ruess, Tree O'Donnell, Judd Parson, Milan Boncich, John Russo, Steve Davis
Design Firm	Colossal Pictures
Creative Director	Eli Noyes/John Russo
Art Director	Steve Davis
Effects Supervisor	Tree O'Donnell
Copywriter	Mabon Childs
Director of Photography	John Krauss
Animation Director	Johann Edstrom
Graphic Artist, Paintbox, Harry	Darlene Ruess
Producer	Mark Reusch/Prudence Fenton
Video Editor	Judd Parson
Film to Tape Colorist	Milan Boncich
Agency Producer	John Pace
Created at	Colossal Pictures
Completed at	The Tape House

Length of Time to Complete Work—2 weeks

MTV—Awake on the Wild Side

Created as an MTV program opening for Steve Oaks and Broadcast Arts, New York, NY.

Created by first transferring film footage of animals and animation elements on the Rank Cintel. The live action and animation was composited in the Harry and in the edit suite using the Paintbox, Encore and D-1.

Created By	Kim Johnson, Paul Golden, Milan Boncich, Judd Parson, Darlene Ruess, David Berkner, Abby Teruhle, Peter Dougherty
Design Firm	Broadcast Arts
Creative Director	Kim Johnson
Effects Supervisor	Abby Terkuhle, Peter Dougherty
Graphic Artist/Paintbox	Darlene Ruess, David Berkner
Producer	Paul Golden
Video Editor	Judd Parson
Film to Tape Colorist	Milan Boncich
Created at	Broadcast Arts
Completed at	The Tape House

Length of Time to Complete Work—2 days

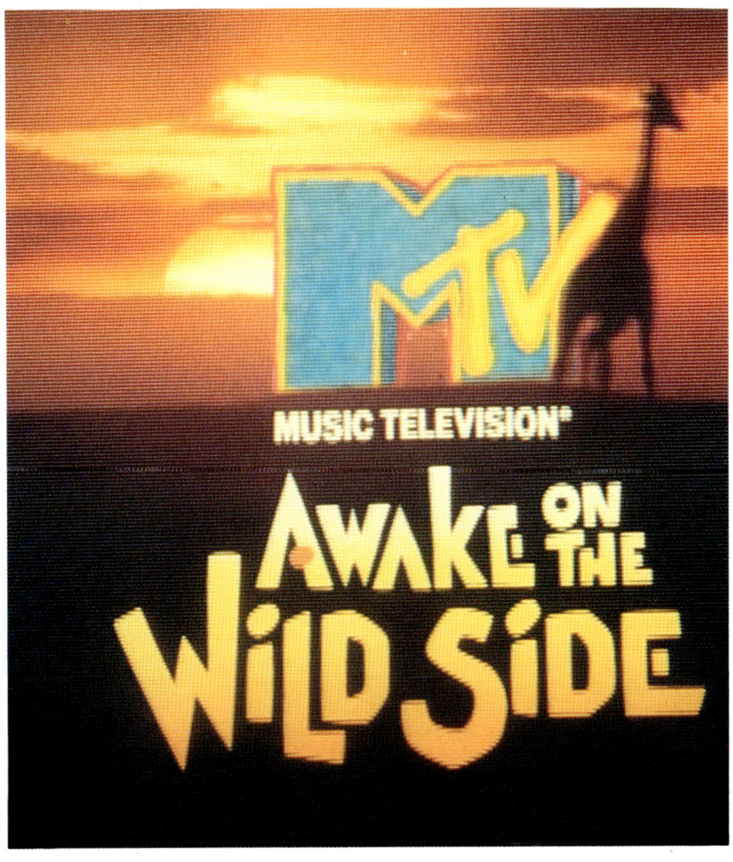

RVI/RUTT VIDEO, INC.

137 E. 25th Street, New York, NY 10010

RVI/Rutt Video, Inc. has been in the post production/graphics business for 12 years. RVI/ Rutt Video president, Steve Rutt, a pioneer in video graphic design, built one of the first ever computer graphics systems in the mid '70s.

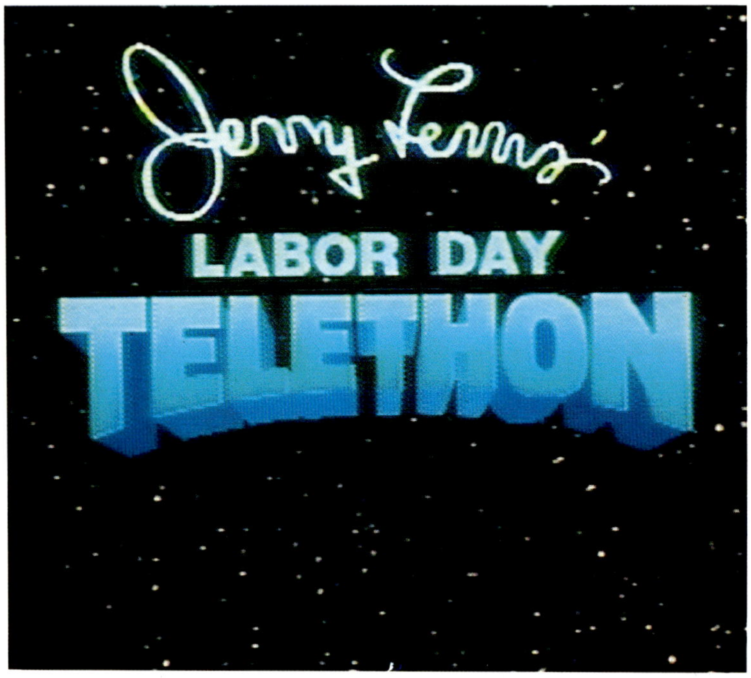

JERRY LEWIS TELETHON

Designed for Tom Wertz, producer, Jerry Lewis Telethon.

Edited by Hal Schild at RVI/Rutt Video using ADO, Grass 300 switcher, Sony 2000 1", and Dubner CBG Computer Graphics. The Dubner created the 3-D lettering, animation of title and the frames around the stars. A separate fill and matte roll was created for the many individual versions produced.

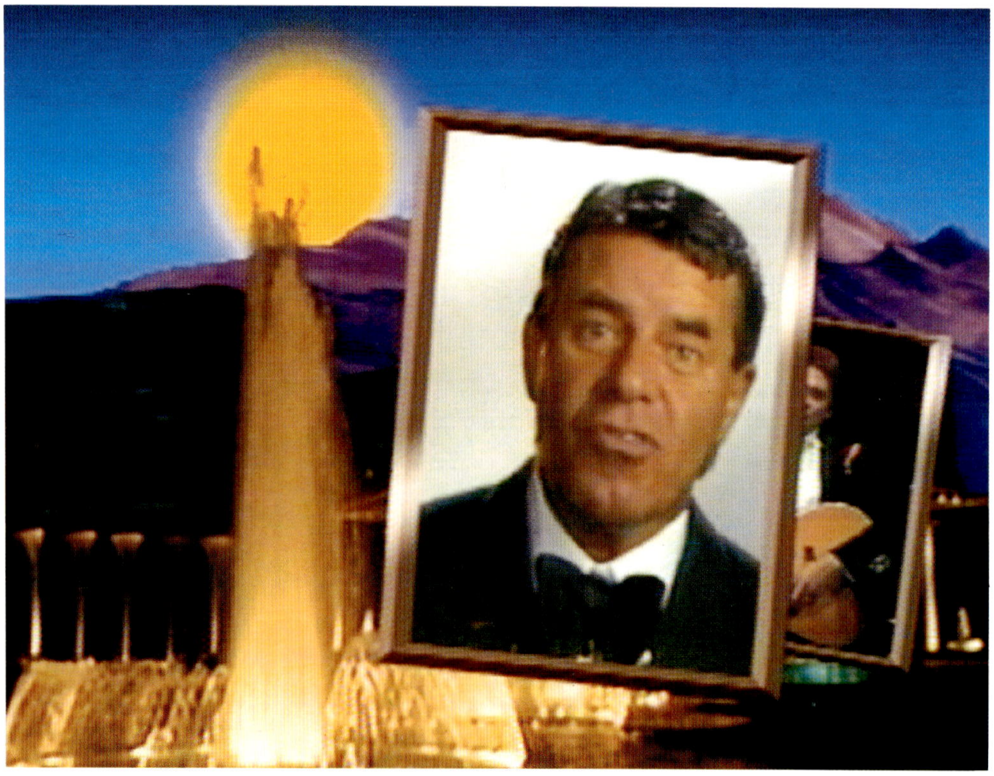

WORLD PREMIERE MOVIE

Designed for David Fantaci, VP of Post Production Services, LBS Communications, New York, NY.

Edited by Hal Schild, RVI/Rutt Video using Chyron Superscribe and Sony D2. The logo was scanned into the Superscribe and an ADO was used to animate.

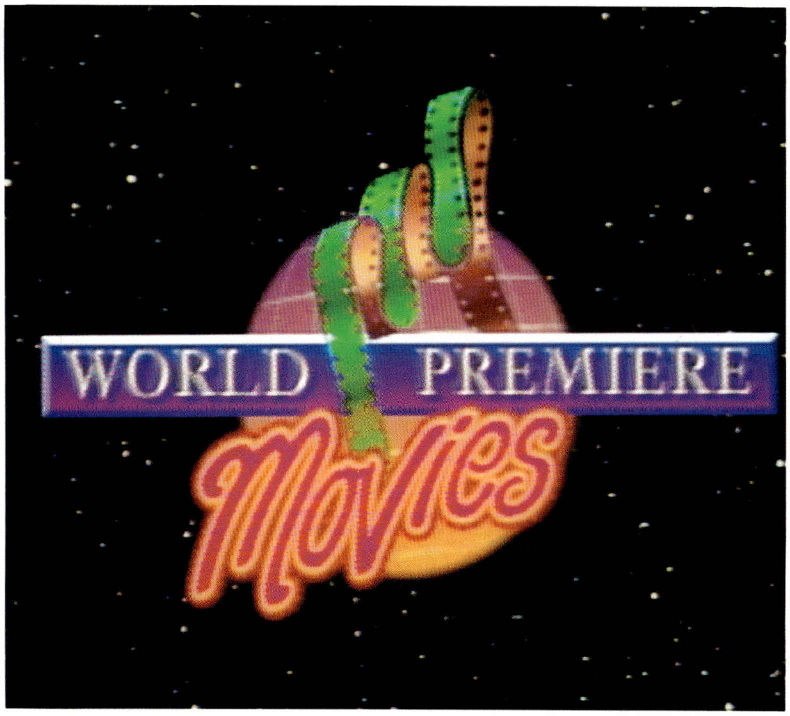

LEXINGTON ENTERTAINMENT GROUP

Designed for David Fantaci, Lexington Broadcast Services.

Edited in D2 at RVI/Rutt Video by Hal Schid who used the Superscribe to design the logo and an ADO to fly in the different elements.

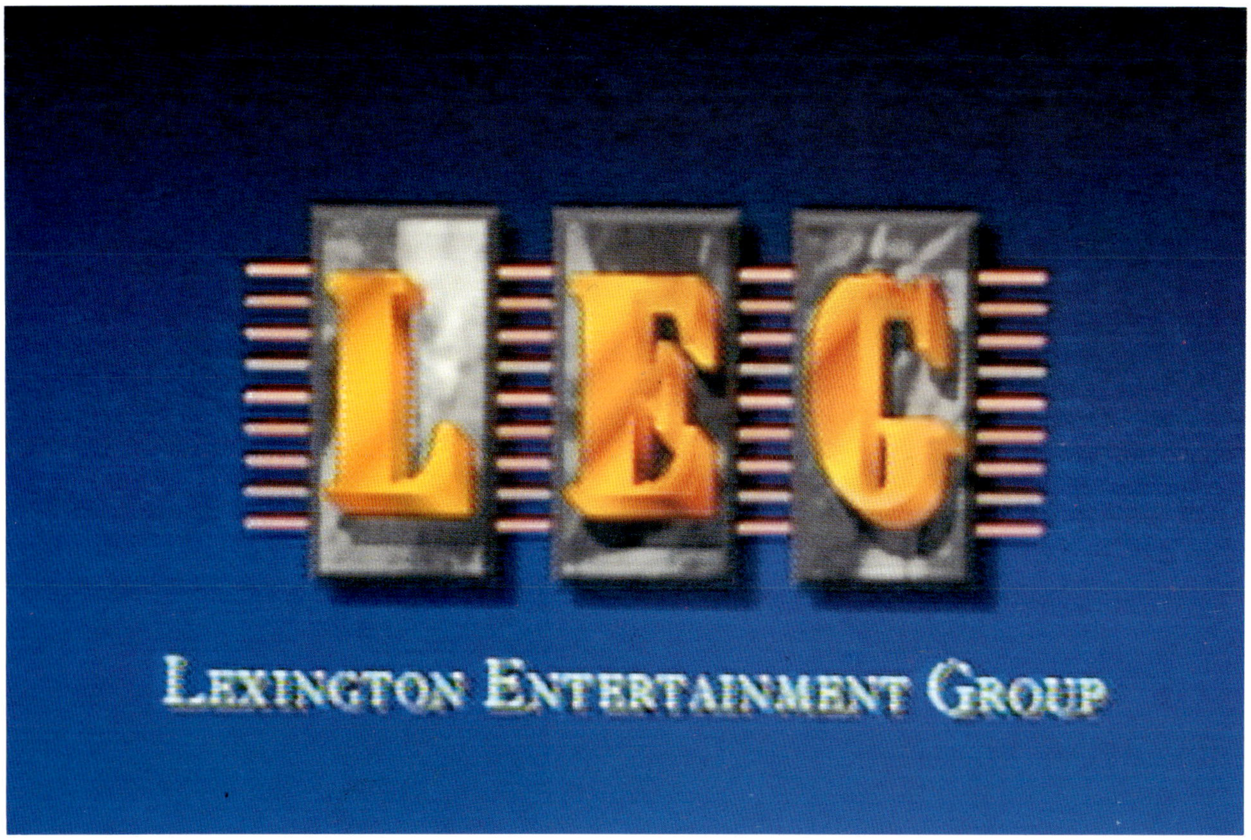

JOAO PAULO SCHLITTLER

HBO On Air Promotion Design, 1114 Ave. of the Americas, New York, NY 10036

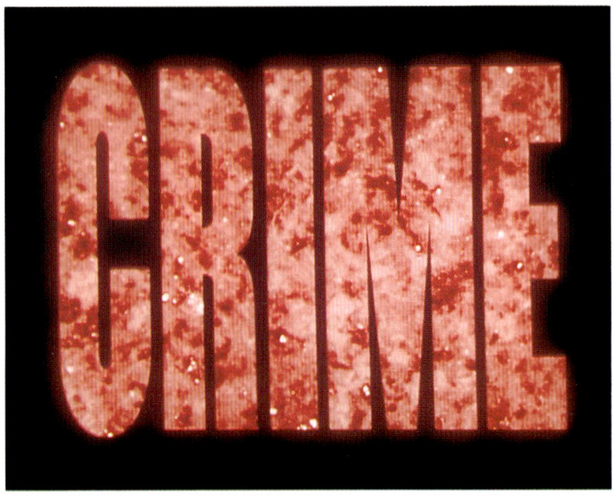

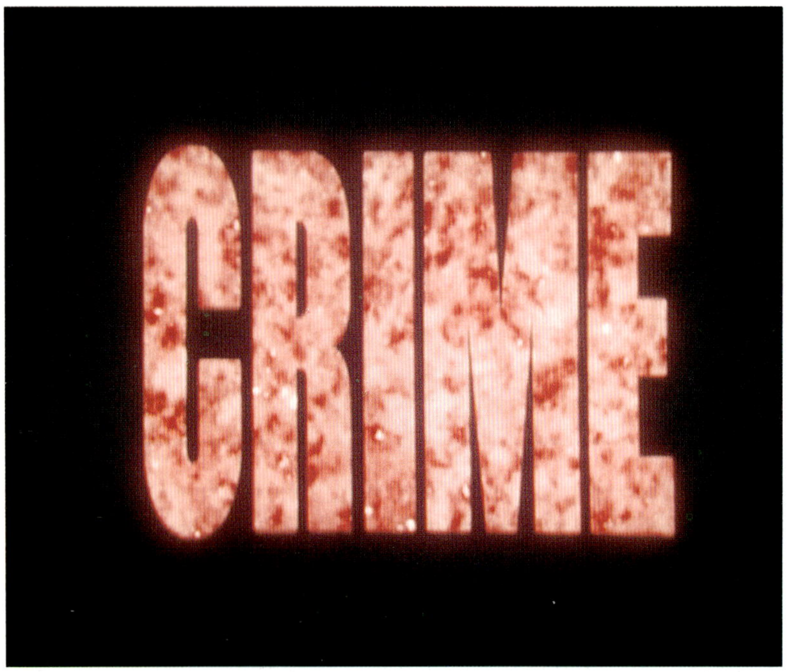

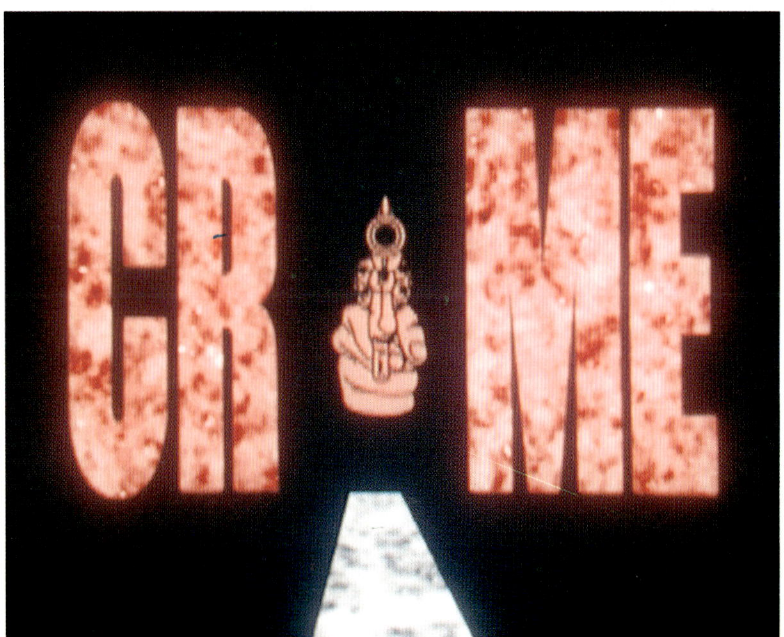

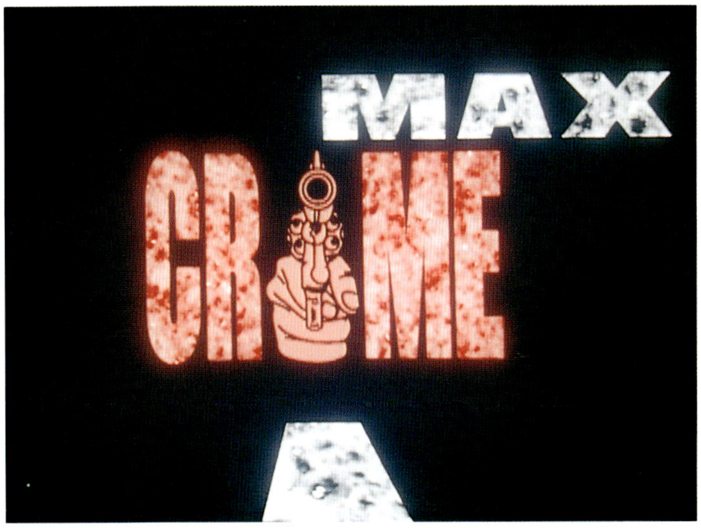

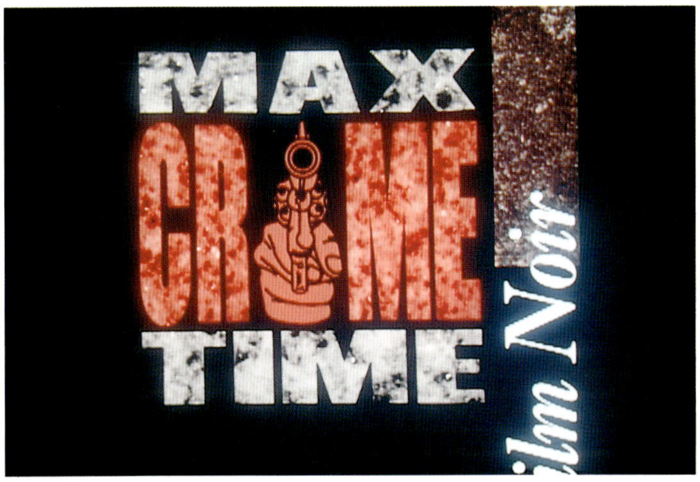

Max Crime Time

Designed as an on air promotion of "Film Noir" style crime movies on Cinemax for Cinemax, New York, NY.

Created in Sony D1 by first using a Macintosh II for designing type and illustration. A Quantel Paintbox added the color and texture. The animation was done on a Quantel Harry.

Created By	J.P. Schlittler, Henry Baker, Orest Woronewych
Designer	Joao Paulo Schlittler
Creative Director	Orest Woronewych
Graphic Artist	Henry Baker
Producer	J.P. Schlittler
Video Editor	Henry Baker
Created at	HBO On Air Design
Completed at	HBO Studio

Length of Time to Complete Work—1 month

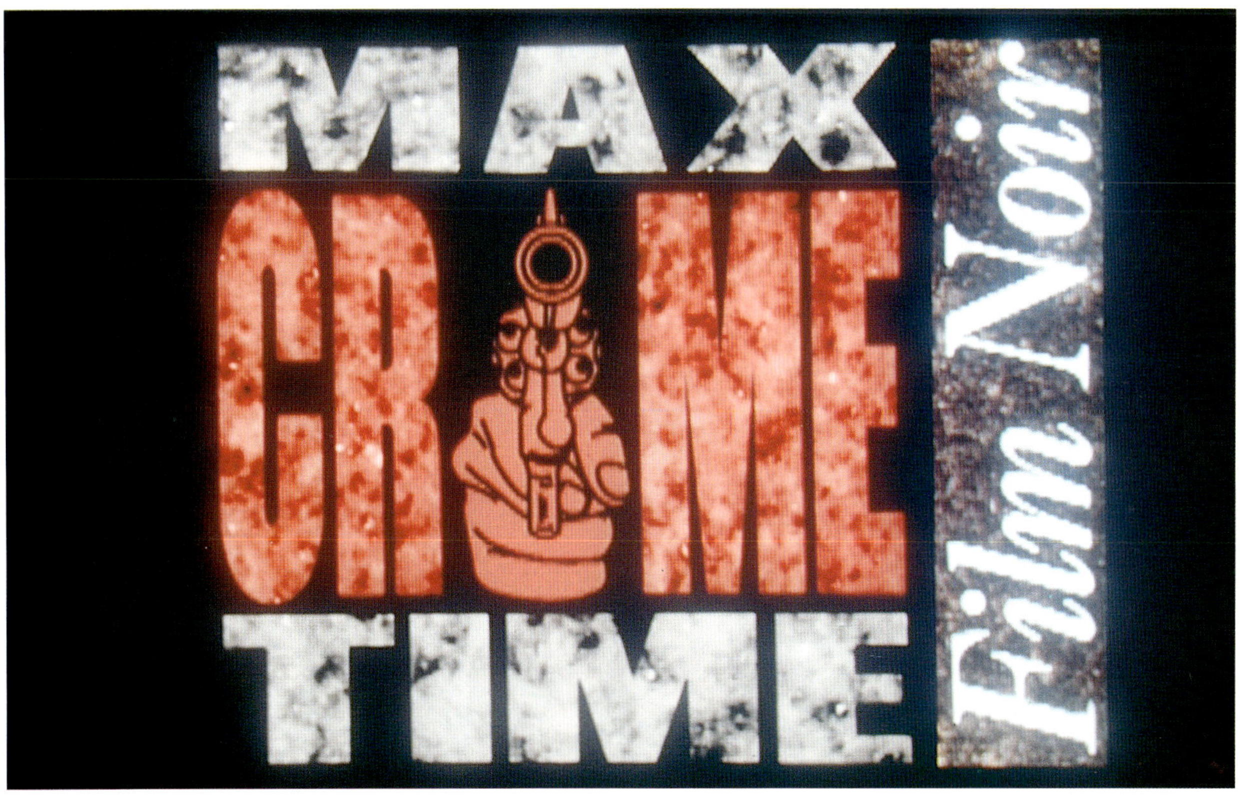

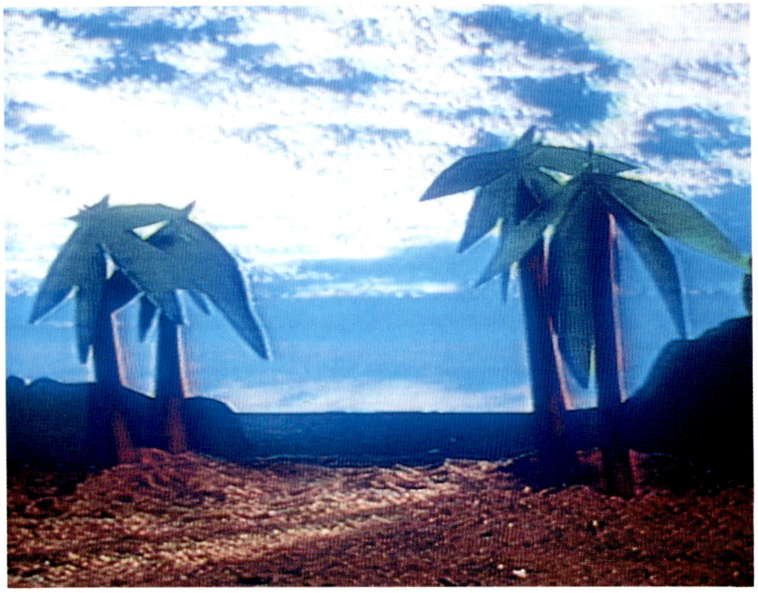

Prisioneiros Do Paraiso (Prisoners of Paradise)

Designed as an open for an independent video production for Conecta Video, Sao Paolo, Brazil.

Created with an Ikegami camera, Sony S.E.G. and Sony 5000 series recorders in an on line room. A cel effects generator was used for freezing, compressing and chroma keying for video compositing.

Created By	Joao Paulo Schlittler, Ricardo Martirani
Designer	Joao Paulo Schlittler
Effects Supervisor	Joao Paulo Schlittler
Producer	Ricardo Martirani
Video Editor	Ricardo Martirani
Assistant Video Editor	Andre Pinho
Created and Completed at	Conecta Video

Length of Time to Complete Work—1 month

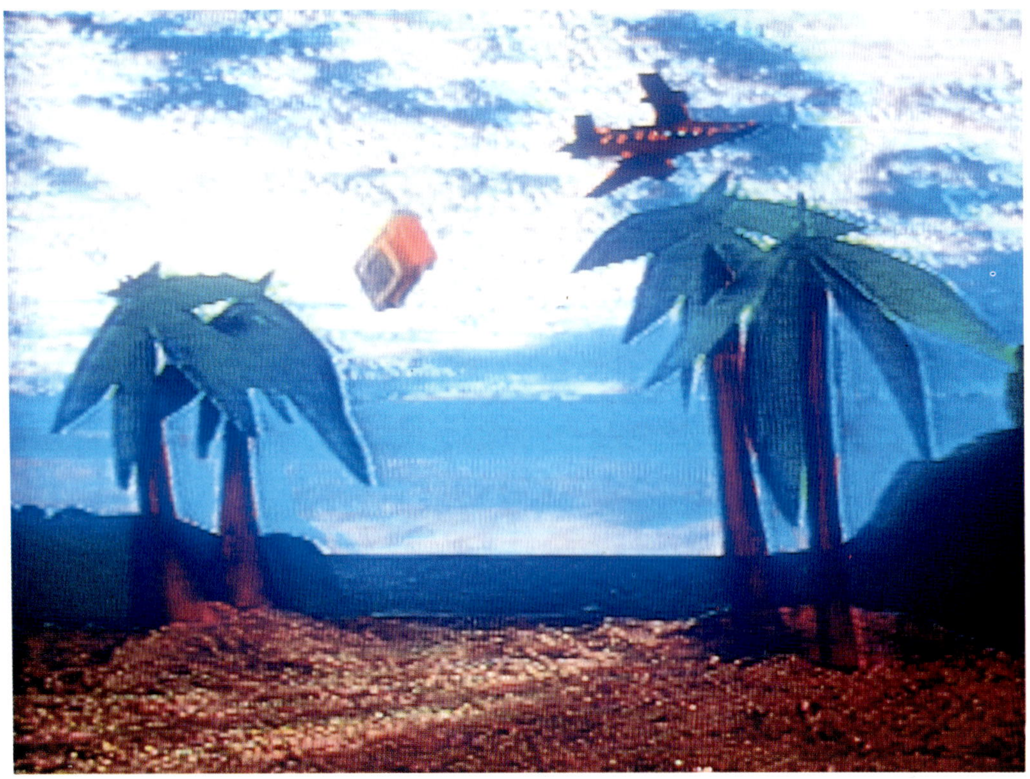

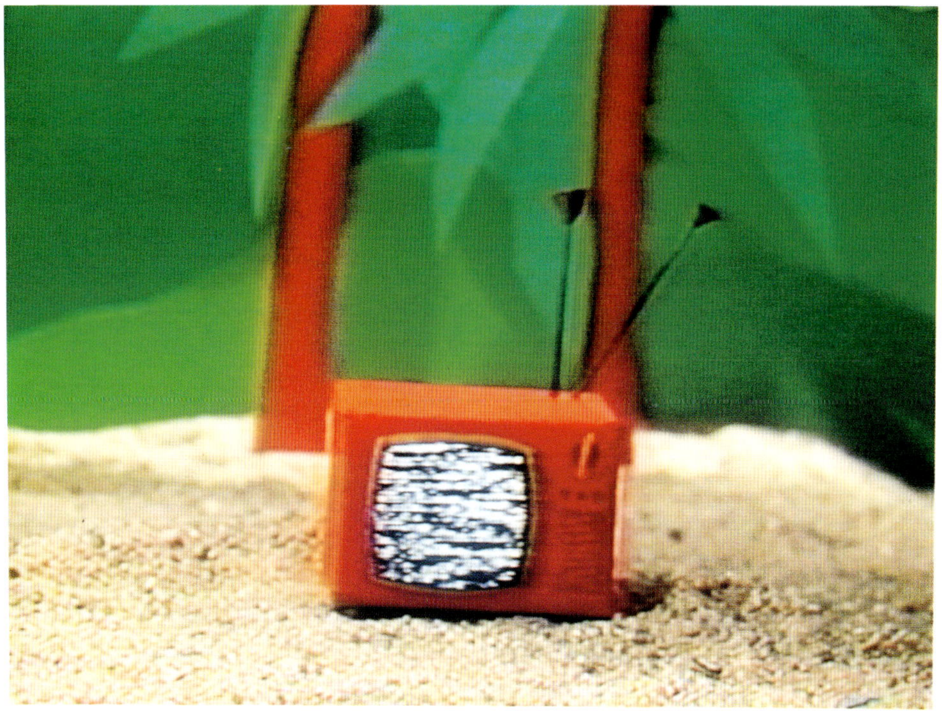

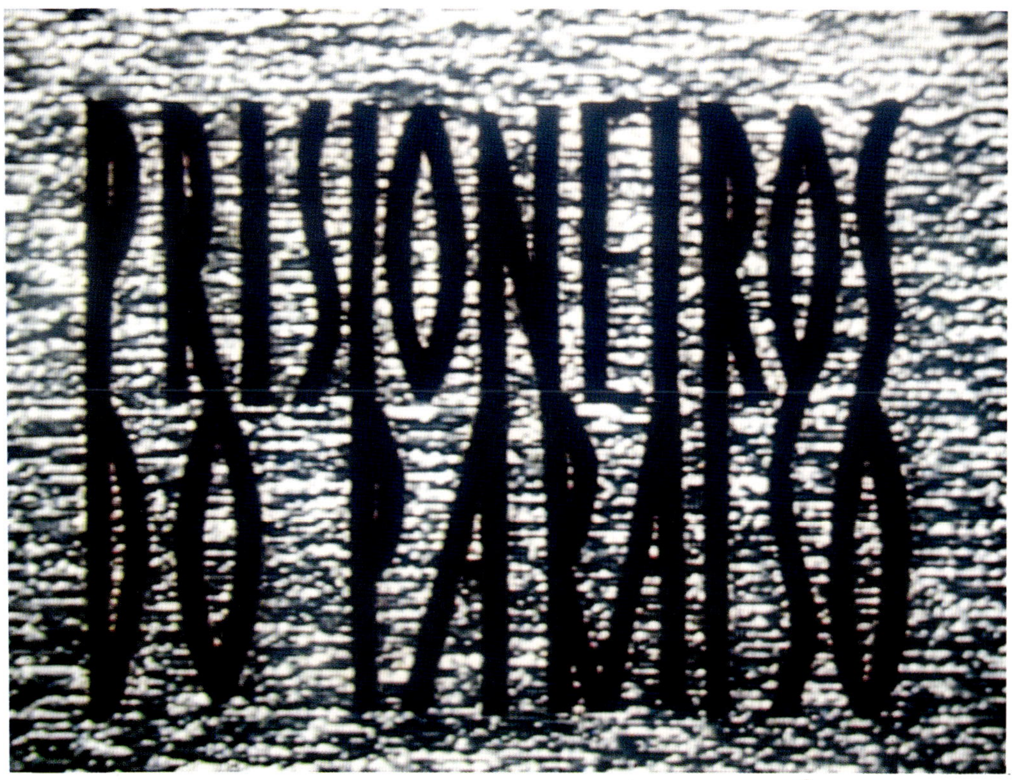
PRISIONEIROS
DO PARAISO

Schwartzberg & Company

12700 Ventura Blvd., Studio City, CA 91604

Louis Schwartzberg started his Energy Productions in 1974. He introduced the Timescape Image Library and has over a million feet of the world's premiere time lapse and custom footage which has been used extensively commercially and theatrically. He has created and directed special visual effects for an unbelievable number of features which include "Karate Kid II" and "Altered States." He has directed and created for countless commercials, television programs and music videos. Among his many awards are Clio; International Film and Television Festival—Gold and Bronze; Monitor; Telly; and Eastman. He has a BA and MFA from UCLA, Theater Arts/Motion Picture Division.

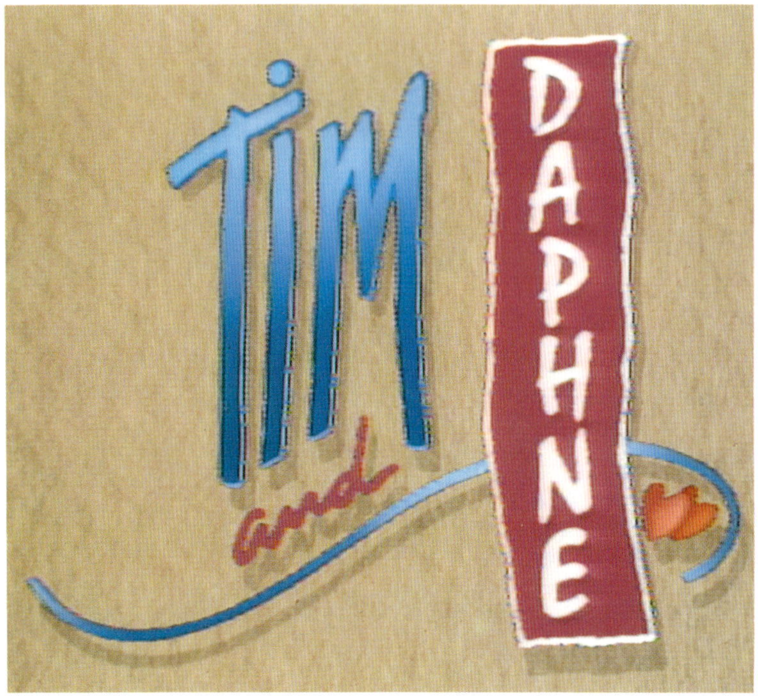

Tim & Daphne

Designed as an opening title for the Tim & Daphne television show.

Created for Freddie Chapman at King World Productions, West Los Angeles, CA on a Quantel Paintbox.

Created By	Louis Schwartzberg, Terri Yarbrow, Tony Basile
Designer	Terri Yarbrow
Creative Director	Louis Schwartzberg
Art Director	Terri Yarbrow
Effects Supervisor	Louis Schwartzberg
Graphic Artist	Tony Robbins
Producer	Tony Basile
Video Editor	Andrew Hanges
Created and Completed at	Varitel Video

Length of Time to Complete Work—2 weeks

Candid Camera

Designed as main title for Candid Camera.

Created for Bianca Pino at King World, West Los Angeles, CA, using a Quantel Paintbox and Harry.

Created By	Louis Schwartzberg, Terri Yarbrow, Tony Basile
Designer	Terri Yarbrow
Creative Director	Louis Schwartzberg
Art Director	Terri Yarbrow
Effects Supervisor	Louis Schwartzberg
Graphic Artist	Tony Robbins, Terri Friedman
Producer	Tony Basile
Video Editor	Andrew Hanges
Created and Completed at	Varitel Video

Length of Time to Complete Work—2 weeks

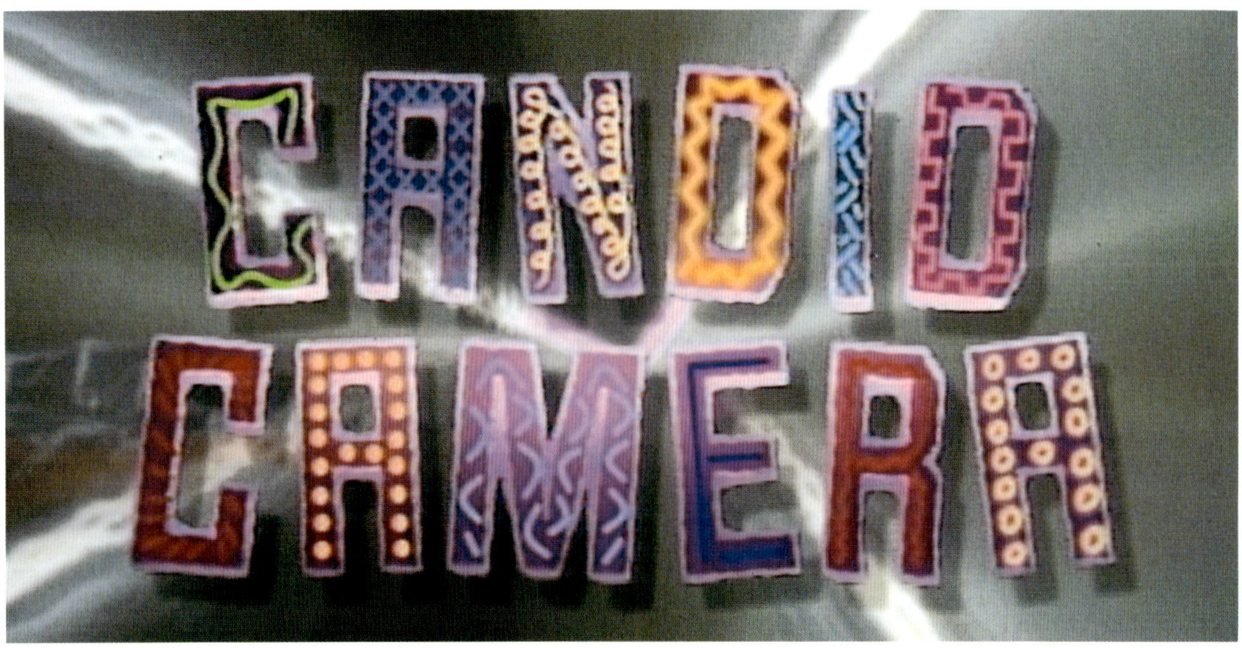

Seti Video Communications

10 E. 40th Street, New York, NY 10016

Ray Seti, president of Seti Video Communications, has been an animator for over 30 years. Seti Video Communications deals directly with the production of commercials as well as medical and business presentations through the use of live action, graphic computers and animation. Ray Seti was the head of the highly successful Sunflower Films and one of the founders of Trilogy Design. He is a past president of the New York Screen Cartoonists, and was one of the first animators to adapt his artistry to the fields of electronic graphics and computer animation. He has been quoted as saying, "Some animators figured computers were going to replace them. My approach was to throw away the pencils and paper and learn something new." Ray feels the challenge for the future is to use the new technologies to create new looks. His many awards include a Clio and both Gold and Silver awards at The International Film & TV Festival of New York.

"Bury it in the Yard"
30 second video commercial for Purina Biscuits

Advertising Agency—Martin Marshall Jaccoma Mitchell, New York, NY

All the frames were animated by hand, inked and opaqued. They were then shot frame by frame on top of a hand-painted background. The final result was transferred to video tape and titles were added with a Super Scribe. An ADO was used to place the Purina logo.

Created By	Ray Seti, Ken Walker, Ron Dias, George Jaccoma, Hugh Hough
Design Firm	Seti Video Communications
Designer	Ray Seti, Ken Walker
Creative Director	George Jaccoma
Art Director	Hugh Hough
Producer	Ray Seti

Length of Time to Complete Work—3 months

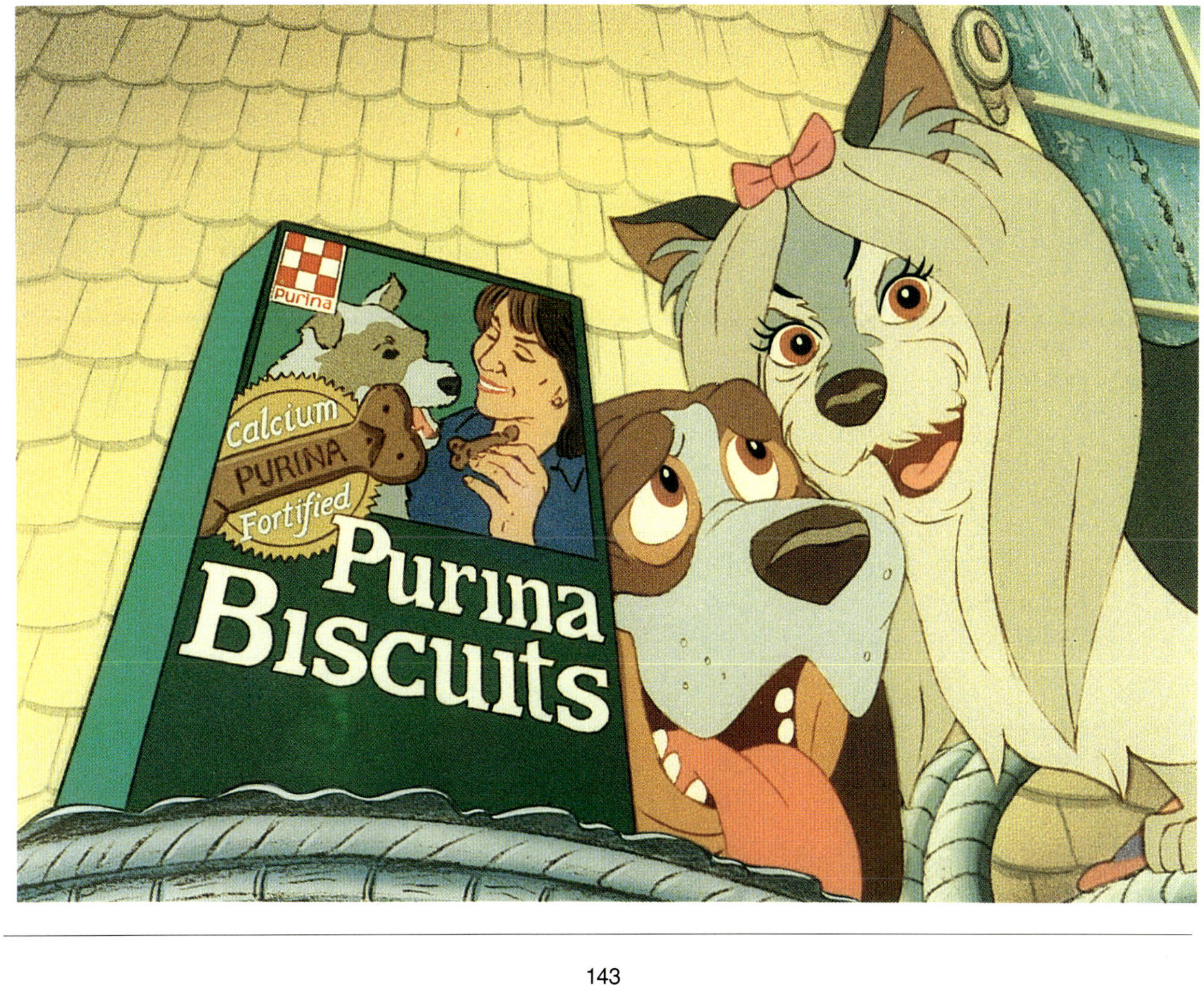

Jill Taffet

HBO On Air Promotion, 1100 Avenue of the Americas, New York, NY 10036

Jill Taffet is Art Director/Designer for HBO On Air Promotion and has held similar positions with other well-known firms including her own. She has a BFA from Cooper Union for the Advancement of Science and Art.

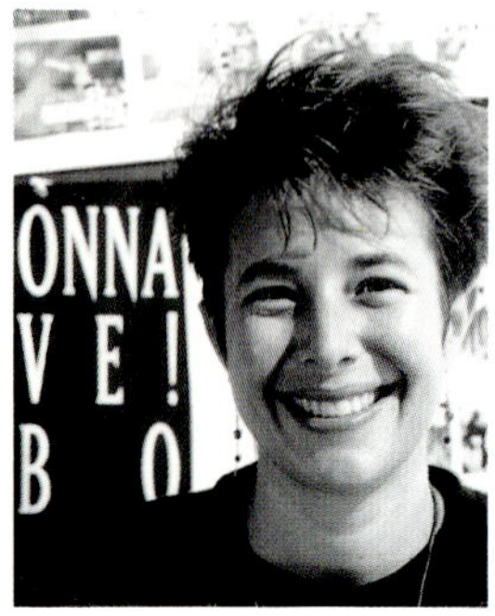

Jill Taffet

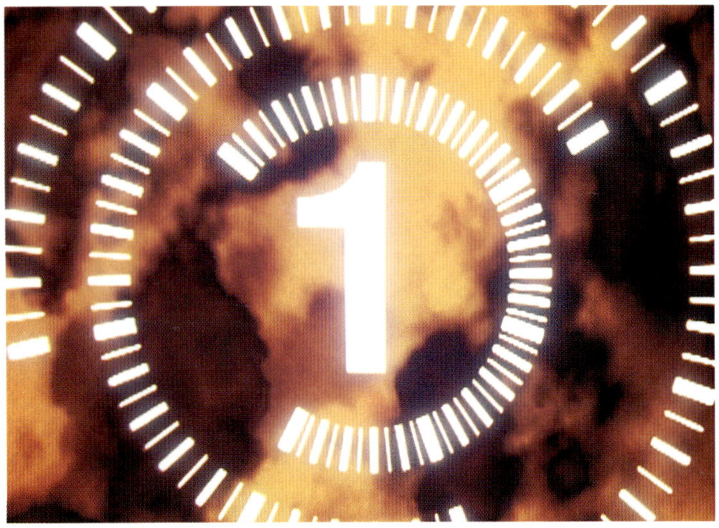

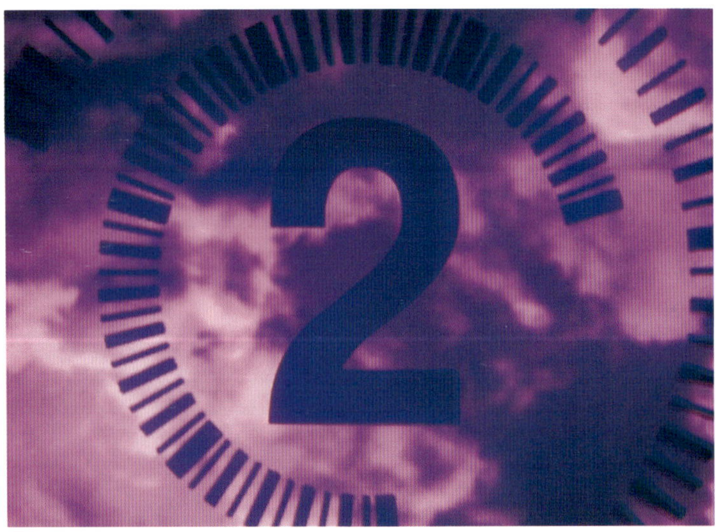

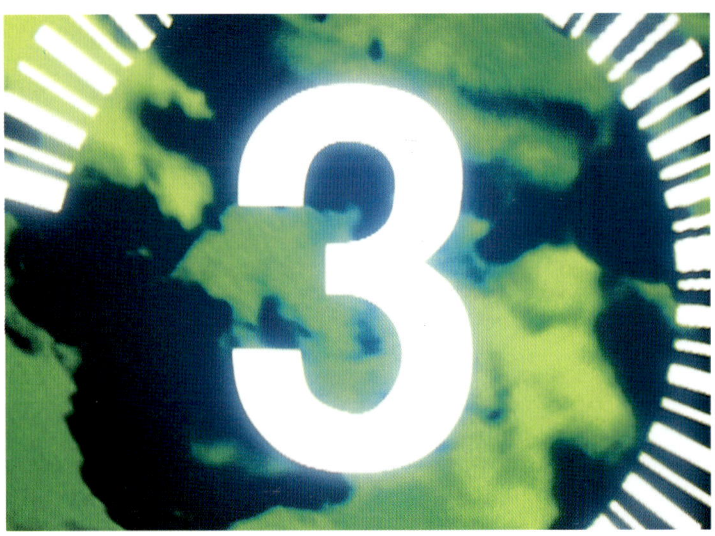

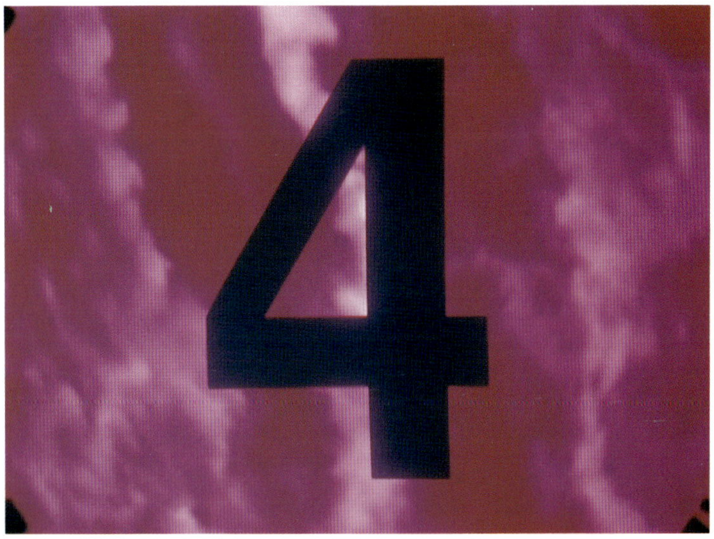

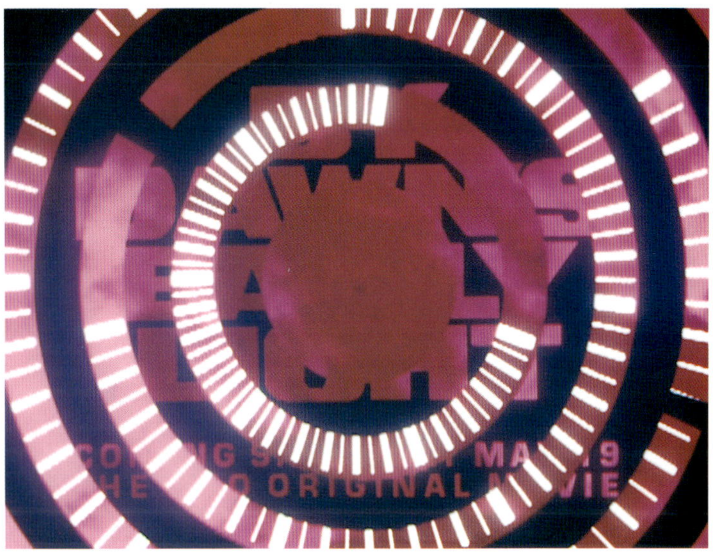

Dawn's Early Light Graphic Tease

Designed to promote the HBO original movie, "Dawn's Early Light" for HBO On Air Promotion, New York, NY.

Created on the Quantel Paintbox, Harry, and Kaleidoscope

Design Firm	HBO On Air Promotion
Designer	Jill Taffet
Creative Director	Orest Woronewych
Art Director	Jill Taffet
Effects Supervisor	Jill Taffet
Producer	Jill Taffet, Audrey Hall
Video Editor	Henry Baker
Created at	HBO Studios

Length of Time to Complete Work—1 day

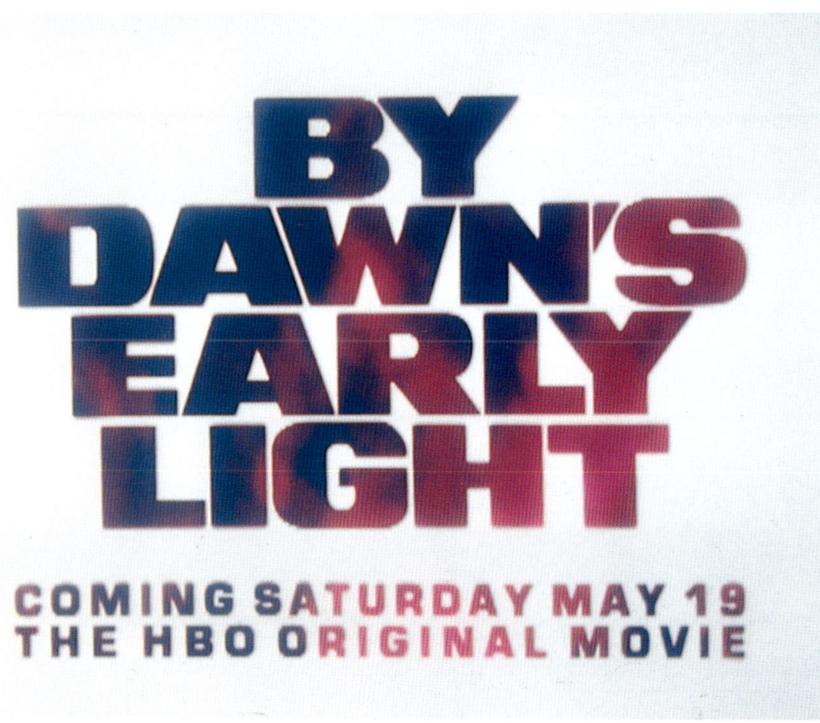

1990 Boxing Image

Designed for HBO On Air Promotion, New York, NY

Created on the Quantel Harry and Paintbox, Kaleidoscope and in the Digital Finishing Suite.

Design Firm	HBO On Air Promotion
Designer	Jill Taffet
Creative Director	Orest Woronewych
Art Director	Jill Taffet
Effects Supervisor	Jill Taffet
Producer	Jill Taffet, Che Che Mata
Video Editor	Peter Consiglio, Peter Savigny, Bill Mahler
Created at	HBO Studio, Compugraph

Length of Time to Complete Work—3 days

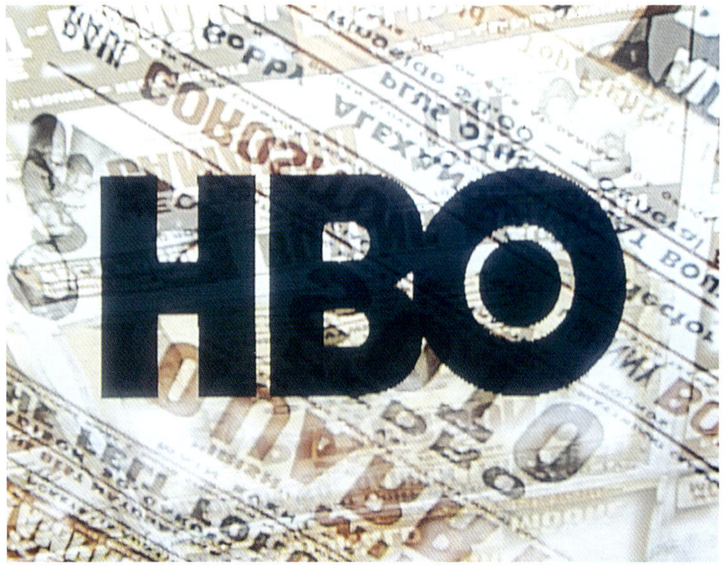

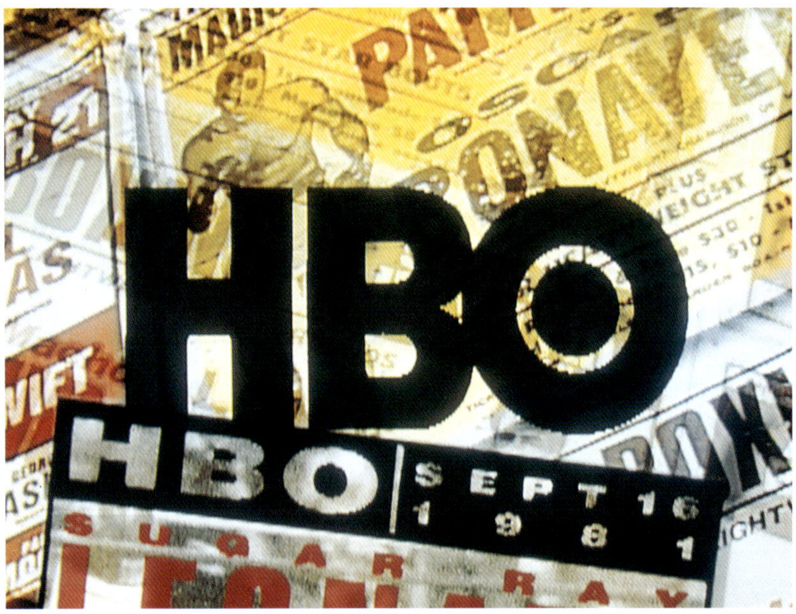

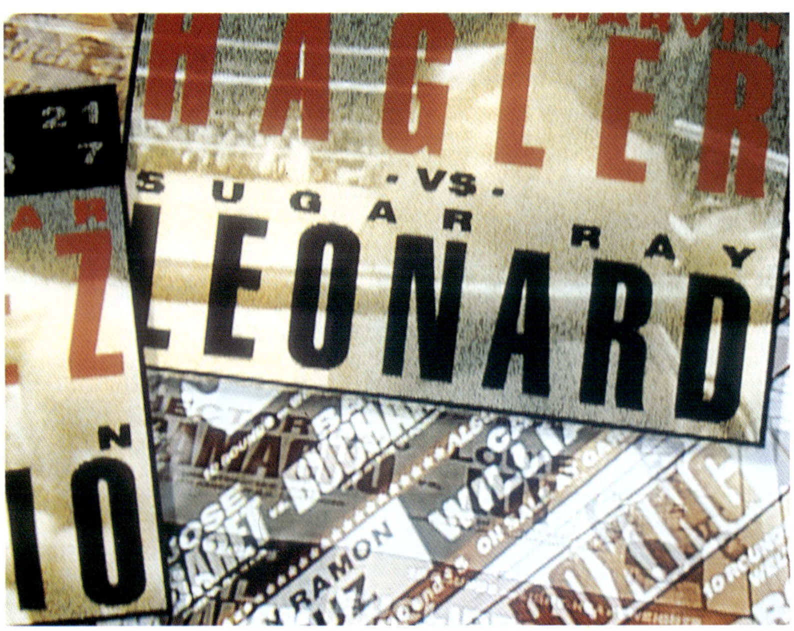

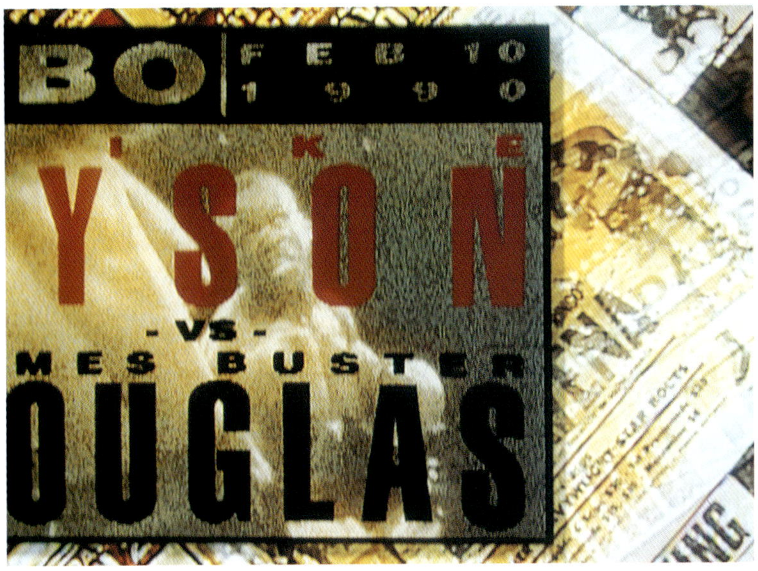
BO
FEB 10
1990
YSON
- VS -
MES BUSTER
OUGLAS

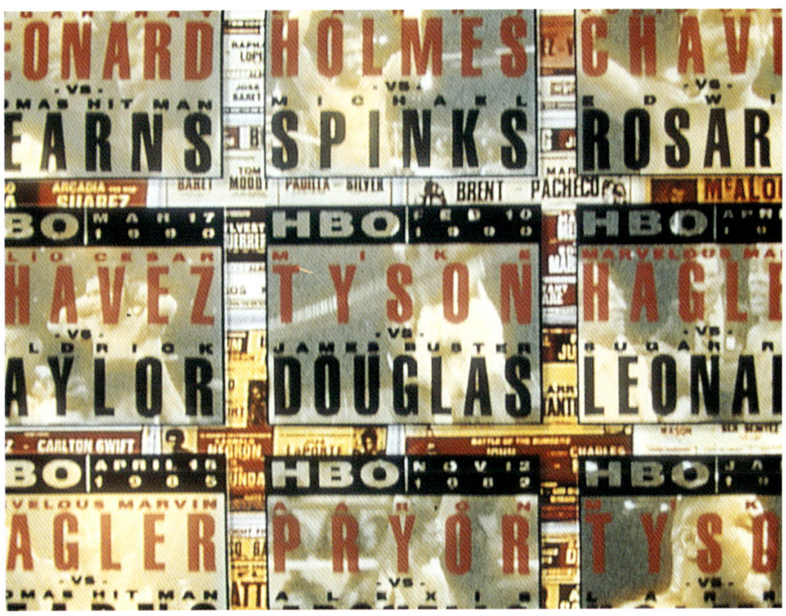
ONARD
HOLMES
-VS-
EARNS
SPINKS
ROSAR
HBO
FEB 10
1990
HAVEZ
TYSON
-VS-
JAMES BUSTER
AYLOR
DOUGLAS
AGLER
PRYOR

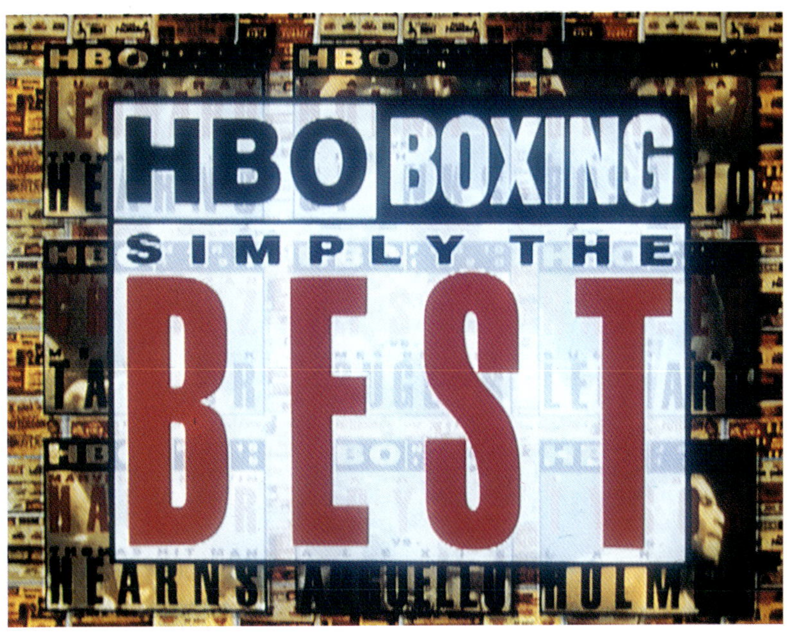
HBO BOXING
SIMPLY THE
BEST
HEARNS

TELEMATION/TAMPA

PO box 9090, Clearwater, FL 34618

V.P., General Manager	Dominic Ambrosio
Director of Operations	Larry Rackley
Design Firm	Telemation/Tampa's GRAfx POLICE
Graphic Designers	Vince Pedulla, Jim Regan
Graphic Artists	Vince Pedulla, Jim Regan
Paintbox Artist	Vince Pedulla
3-D Animator	Jim Regan
Designers	Vince Pedulla, Jim Regan
Video Editors	Steve Beverly, Michael Patterson, Paula Peterson, Ed Staffenberg
Created and Completed at	Telemation/Tampa

DESIGNER ROW

Created as a fashion ad using the Quantel Paintbox. The client wanted a very warm hand drawn look but could only provide a video of the model. A frame of video was grabbed and treated in the chalk mode of the Paintbox. The background elements were drawn away and the model's colors were picked up by the Paintbox palette and shaded down to pastel tones. The image was placed over a background of the client's logo and blended in.

Length of Time to Complete Work—3 hours

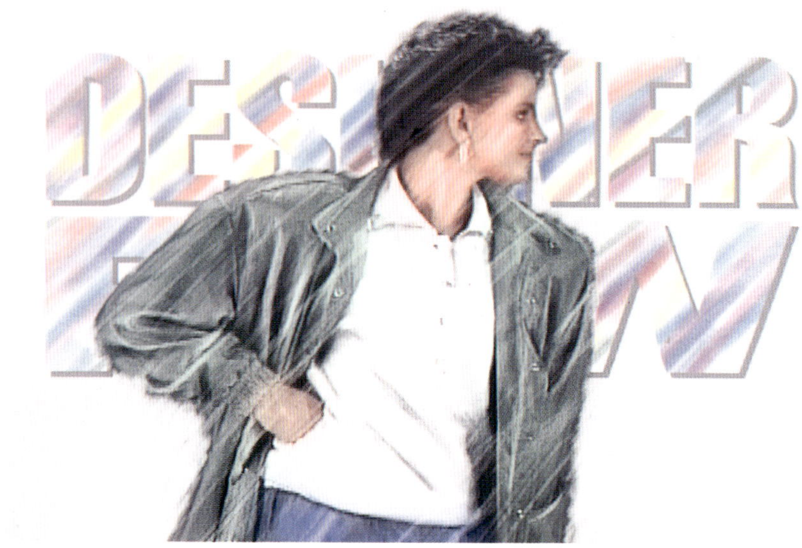

GRAFX POLICE

Created as a logo using the Quantel Paintbox to squeeze and squash the letters, drop in colors and textures and set it against backgrounds.

Length of Time to Complete Work—3 hours

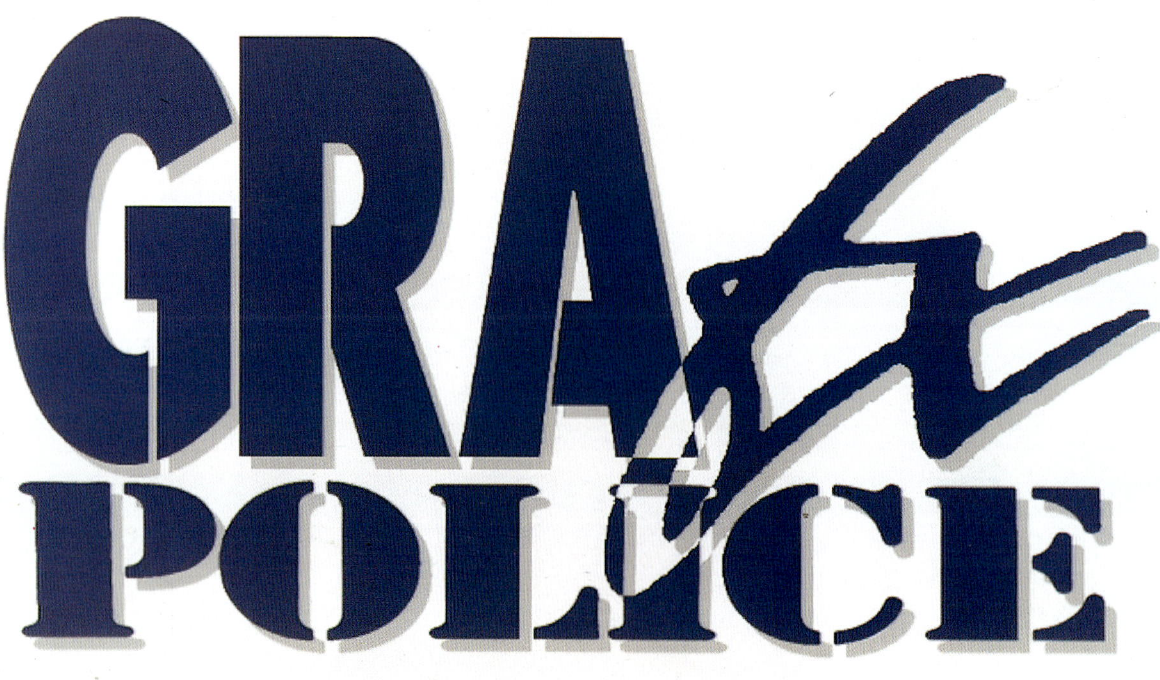

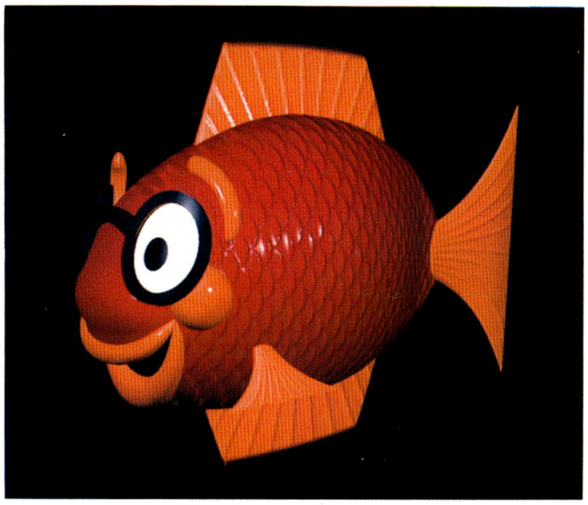

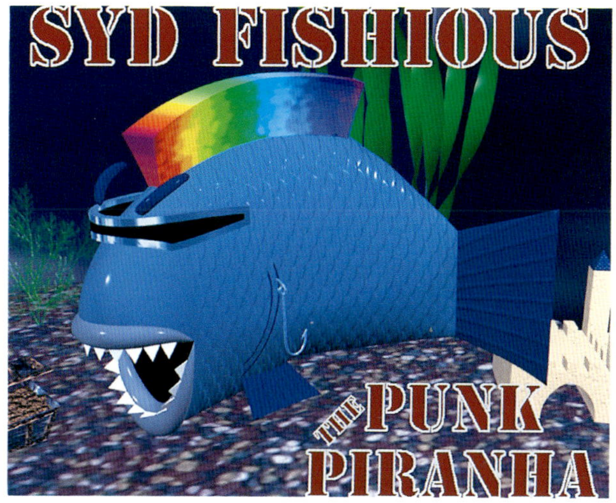

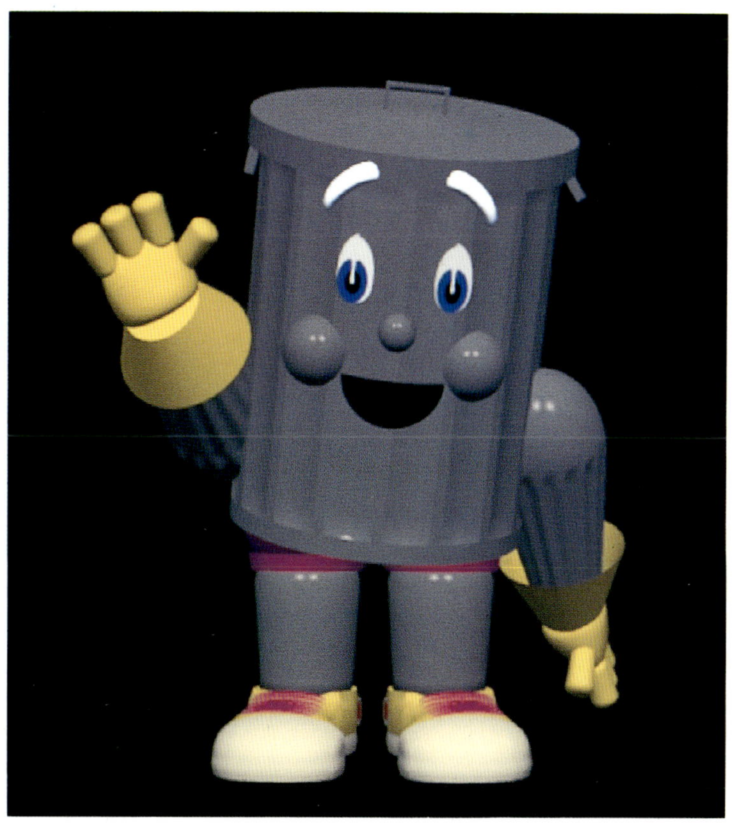

BUSTER, SYD, MR. SPARKLE

Created as characters using Wavefront Technologies Advanced Visualizer Software and SGI 4D-70 hardware. Buster and Syd are completely three dimensional, articulate and capable of a broad range of expressions. They are able to move about in a computer generated 3-D aquarium complete with computer generated 3-D gravel and computer generated 3-D moving plants.

Length of Time to Complete Work—2 weeks each character

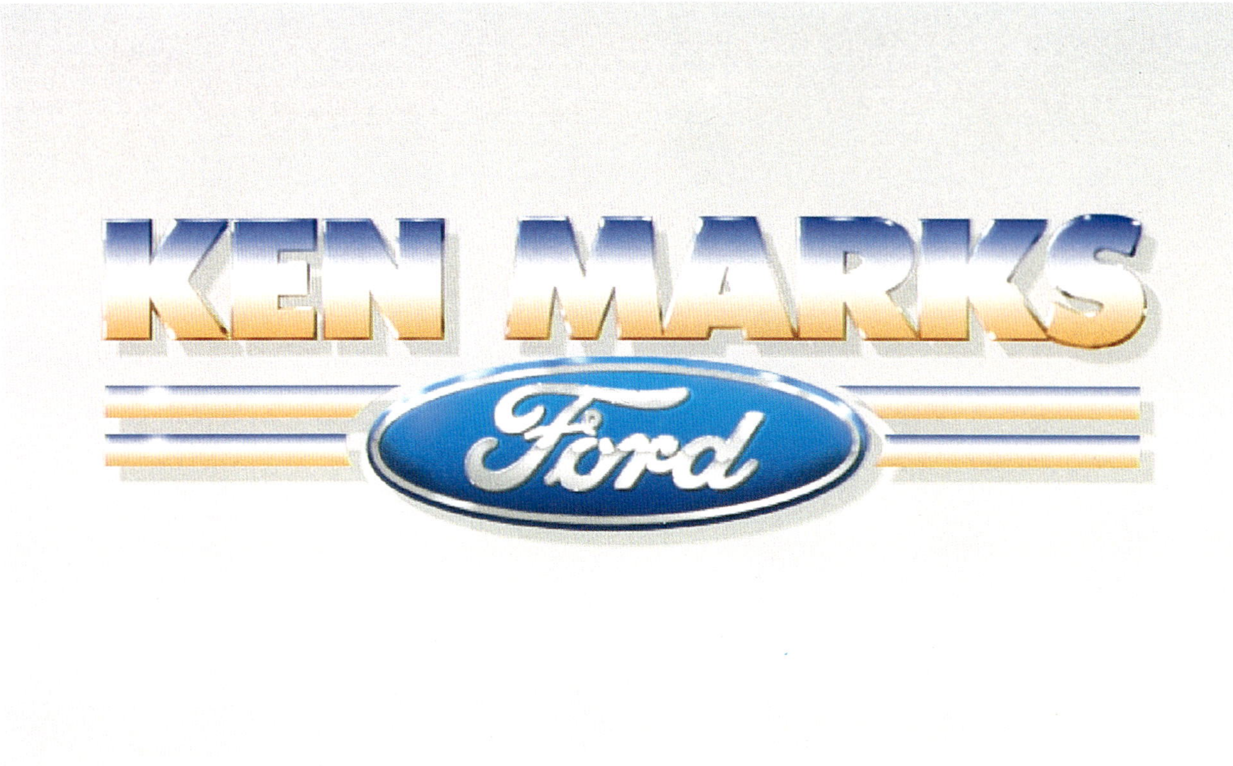

KEN MARKS FORD

Created as a logo from an actual license plate using the Quantel Paintbox.

Length of Time to Complete Work—2 hours

SCIENCE HELPER

Created as a logo design in a program open animation using Wavefront Software and SGI Hardware with and such techniques as texture mapping, hierarchical motion and image composition.

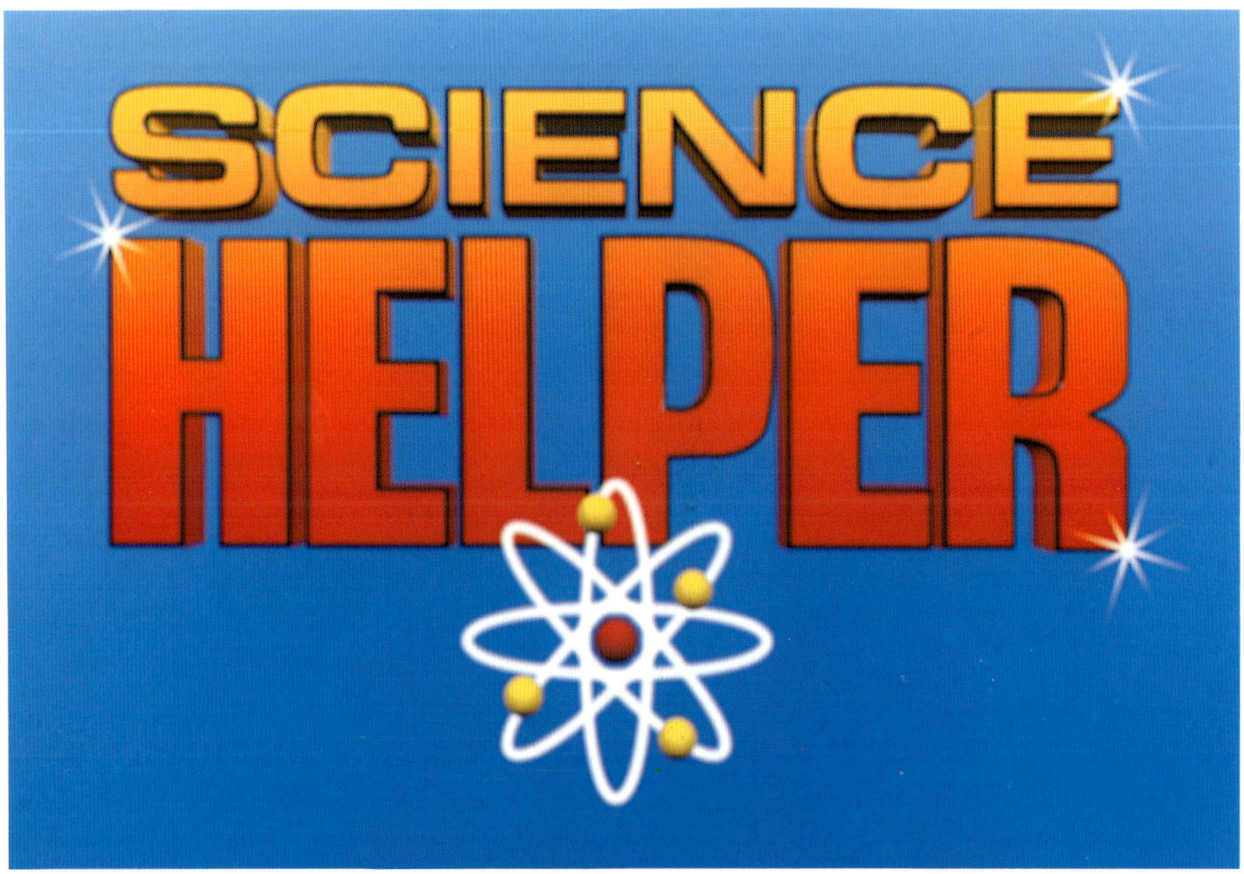

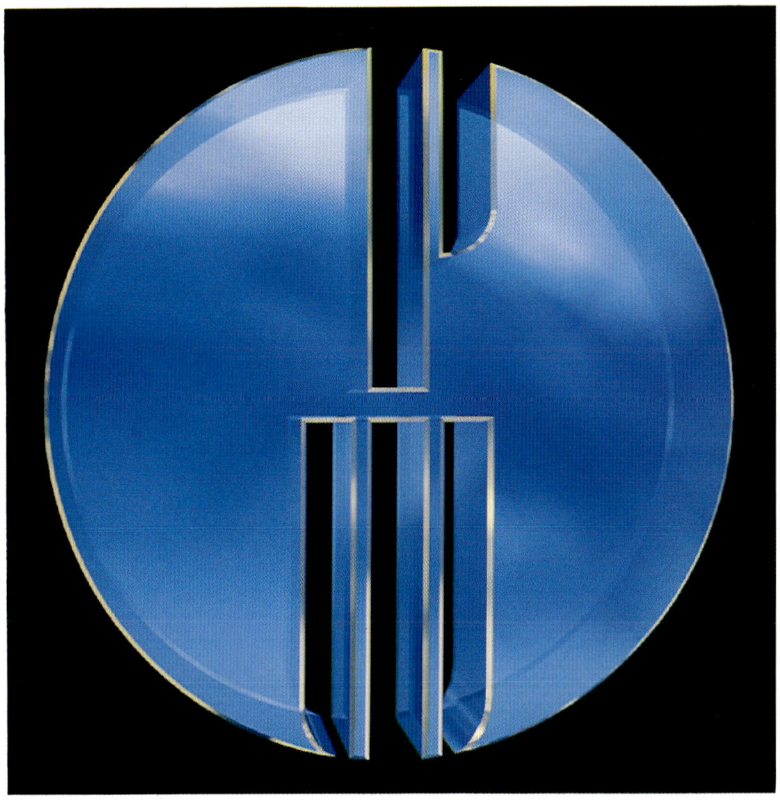

Price Waterhouse Logo

Created as a logo utilizing Wavefront Software and Silicon Graphics Hardware. Flat art work was used to digitize the basic outline of the logo into the computer, then the outline was beveled and extruded to create the finished logo design. The glass effect was created using a varying degree of transparency on the logo as well as using reflection mapping.

Amoco Split Second

Created as an open from several slides of a building and a stat of the logo. The three dimensional moving open was developed on Paintbox and edited using the A-62 Digital Disk Recorder.

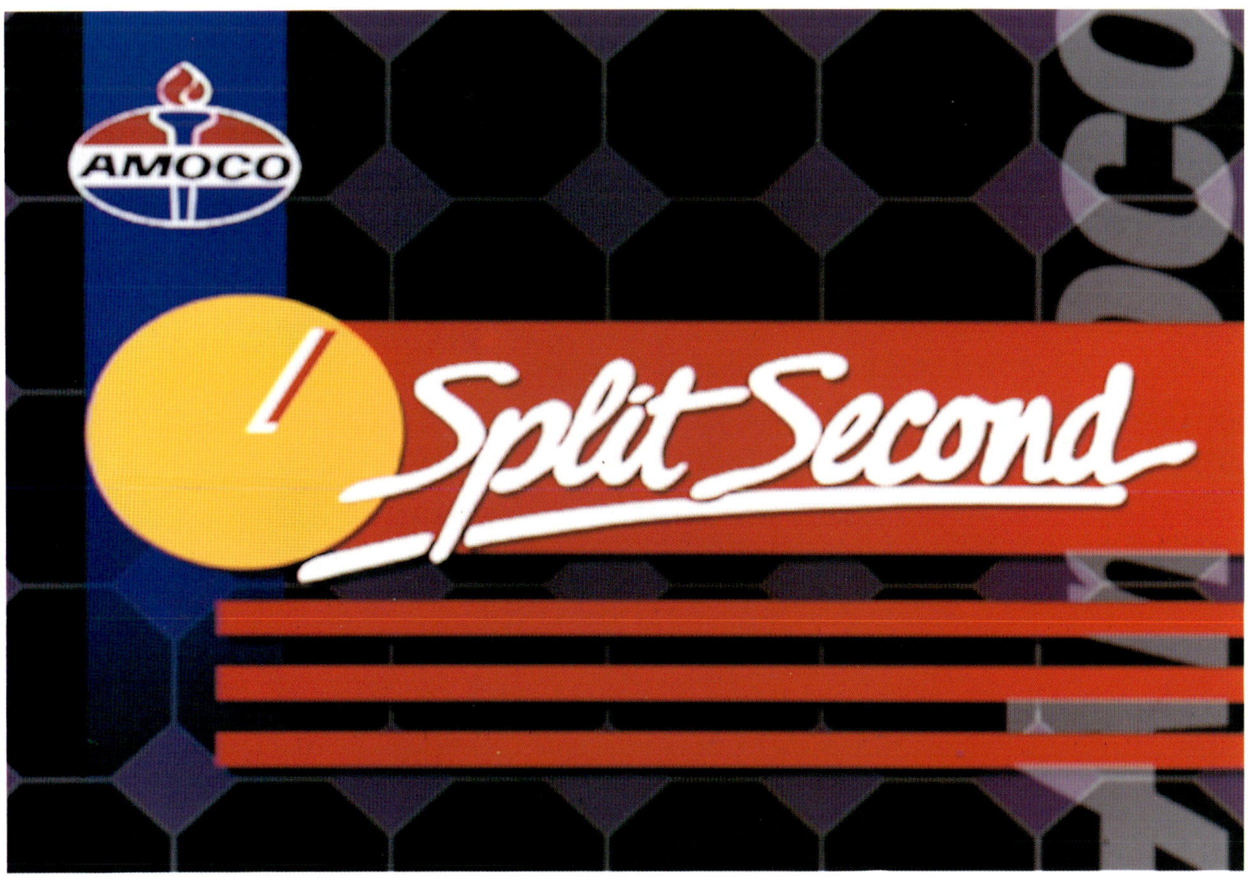

TV 22 WYOU

415 Lackawanna Avenue, Scranton, PA 18593

The overall on air look of a television station is originated at the in-house art department, if a station is lucky enough to have one. WYOU Television in Scranton, PA has such a department, and Ro. Rayner is its Art Director. This material is a fantastic example of WYOU's on air graphics and commercial production. Most of the material is news and promotion related for WYOU. MLFS, Victory Fund and Stallions were generated for commercial clients. The on air graphics were all generated using the ARTSTAR computerized paint and 3-D system. Those involved in the project, had only 2 months to learn a new graphic system and create a new and fresh news image for the television station. During that time period over 75 graphics were generated.

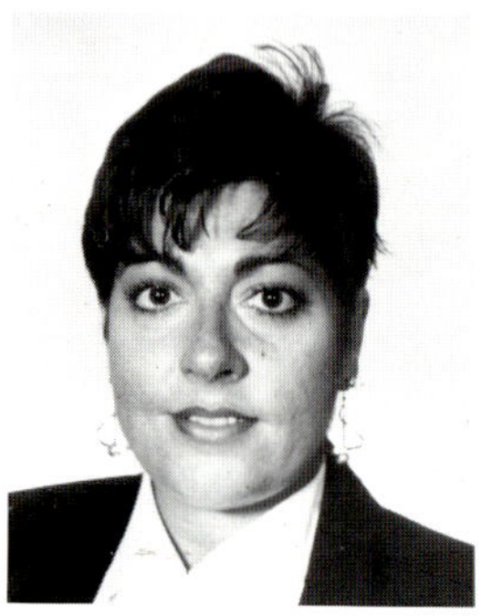

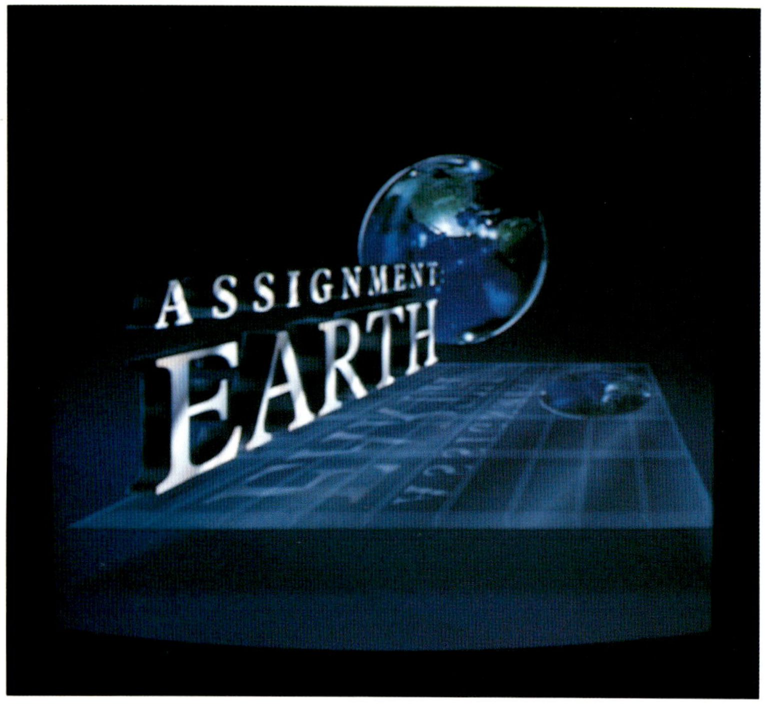

NEWS 22
Special Series

Assignment Earth

RO. RAYNOR

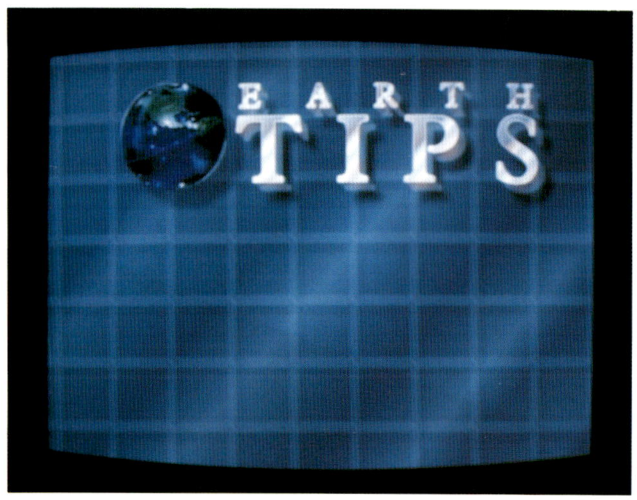

NEWS 22
Special Series

Earth Tips

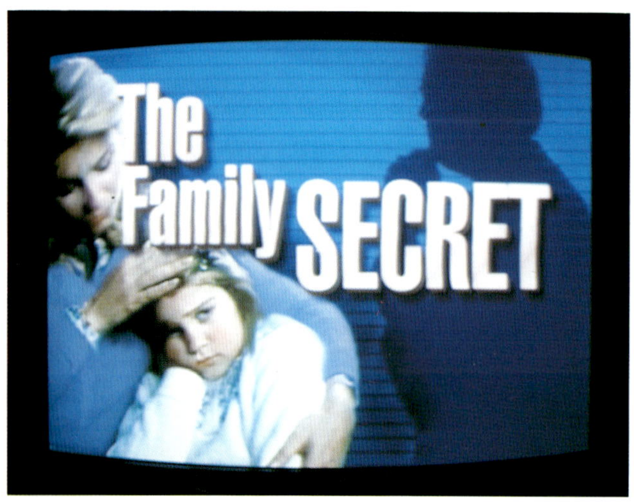

NEWS 22
Special Series

The Family Secret

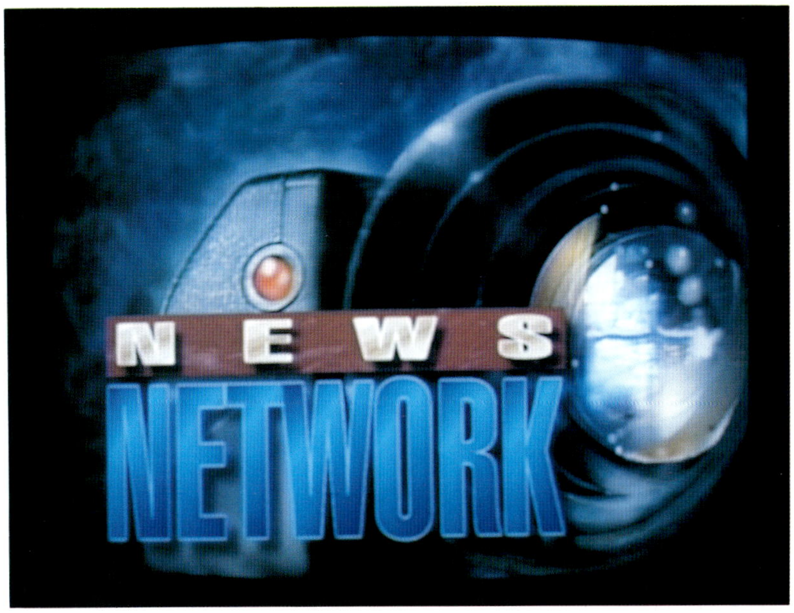

News 22
Special Series

News Network

News 22
Special Feature

Live From Your Own Hometown

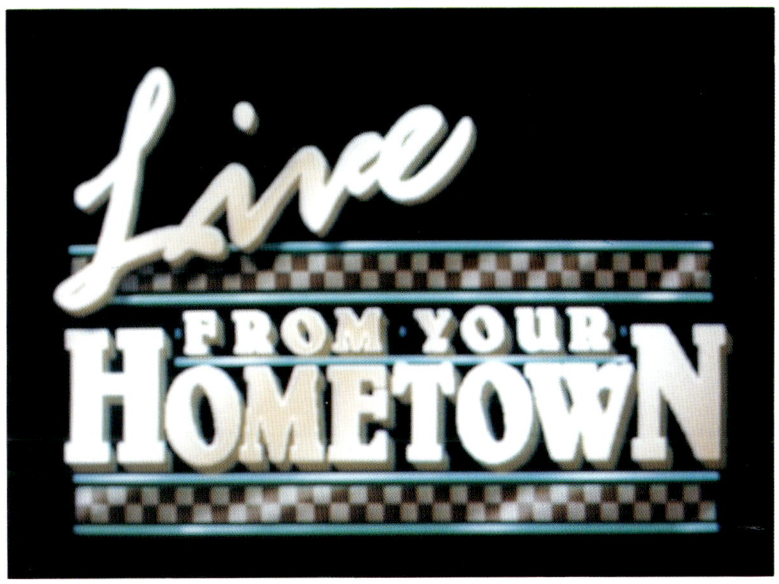

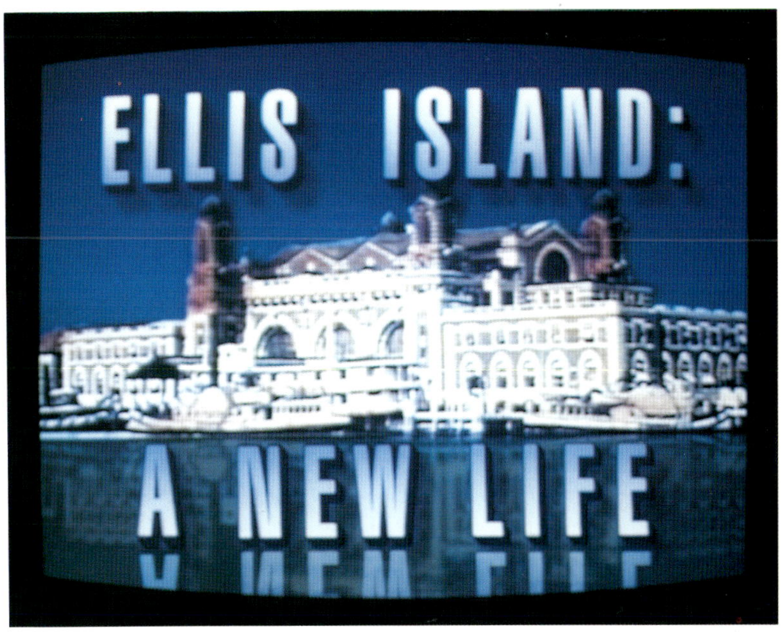

News 22
Special Feature

Ellis Island: A New Life

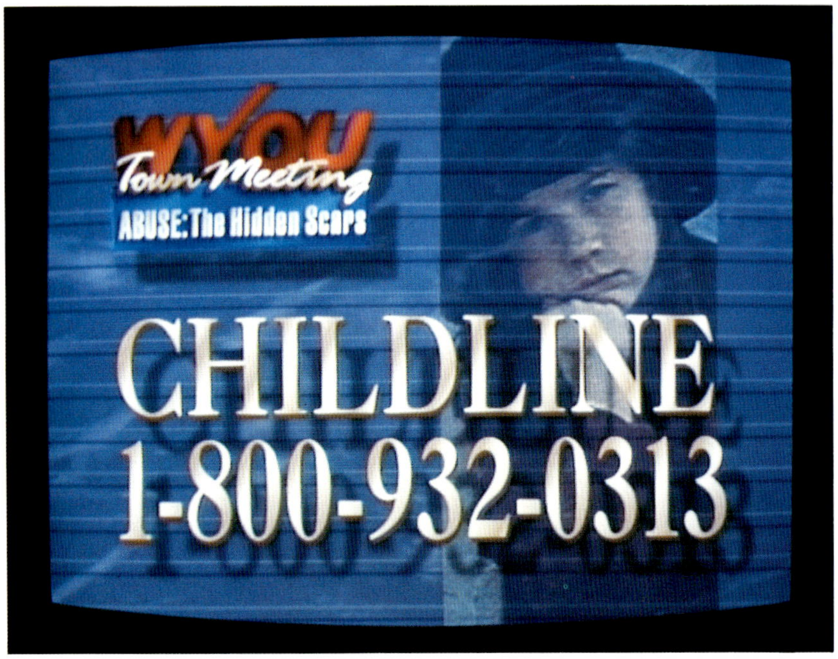

NEWS 22
News Special

Town Meeting

NEWS 22
News Special

Town Meeting

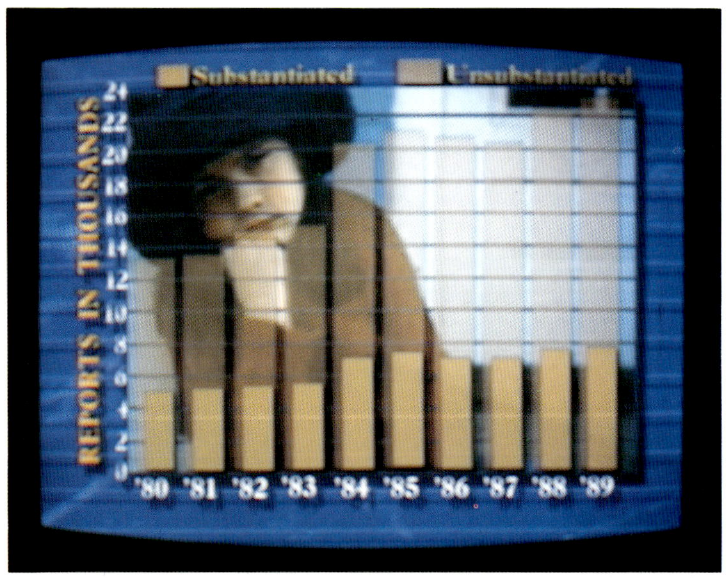

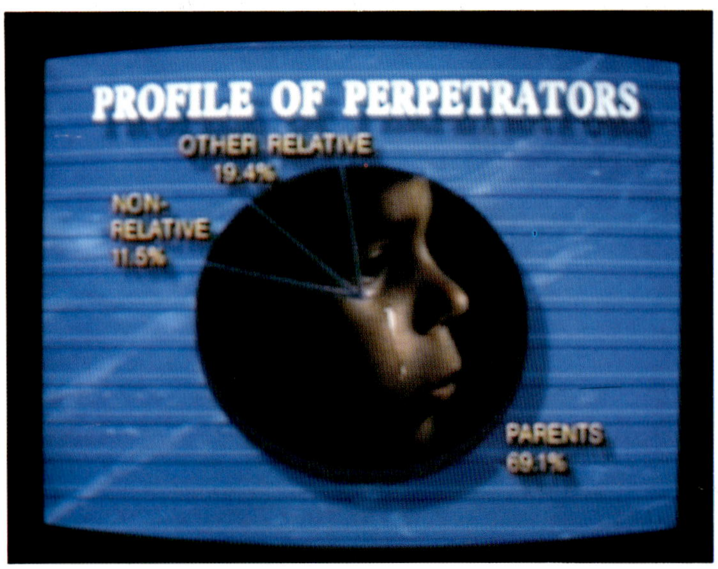

NEWS 22
News Special

Town Meeting

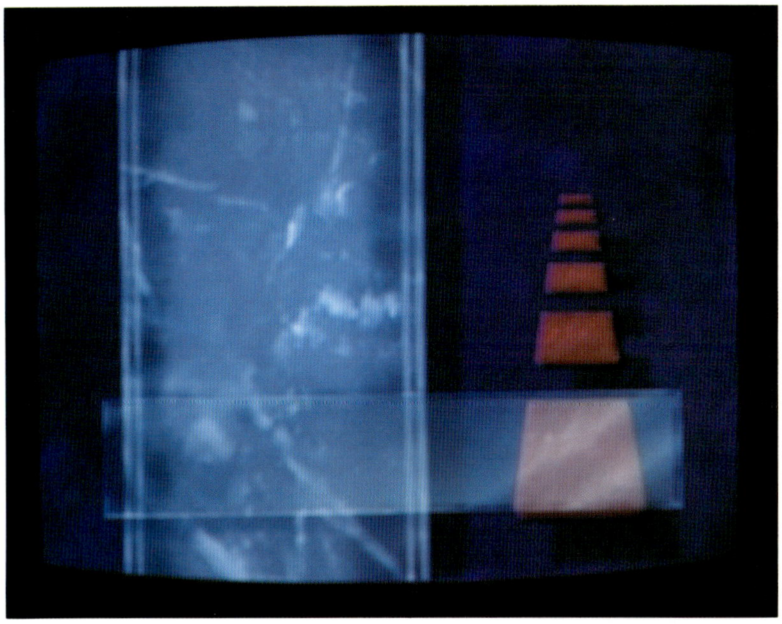

News 22
Photo Insert Graphic

News 22
Weather Graphic

After School Forecast

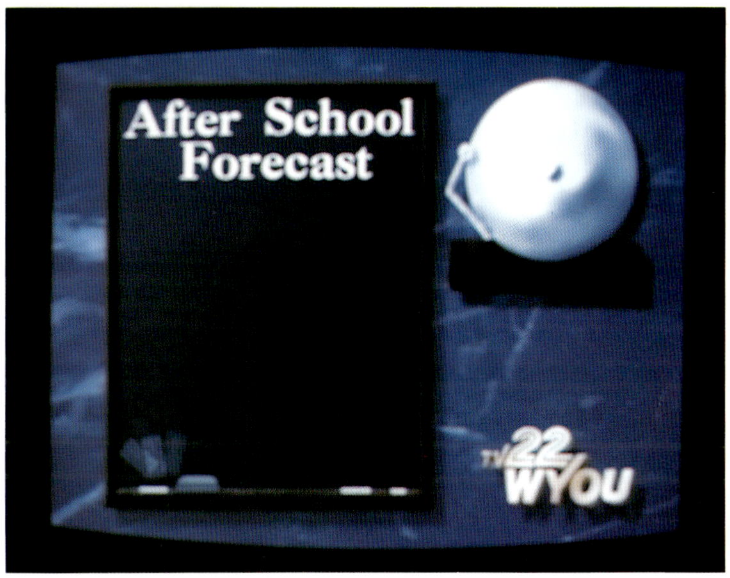

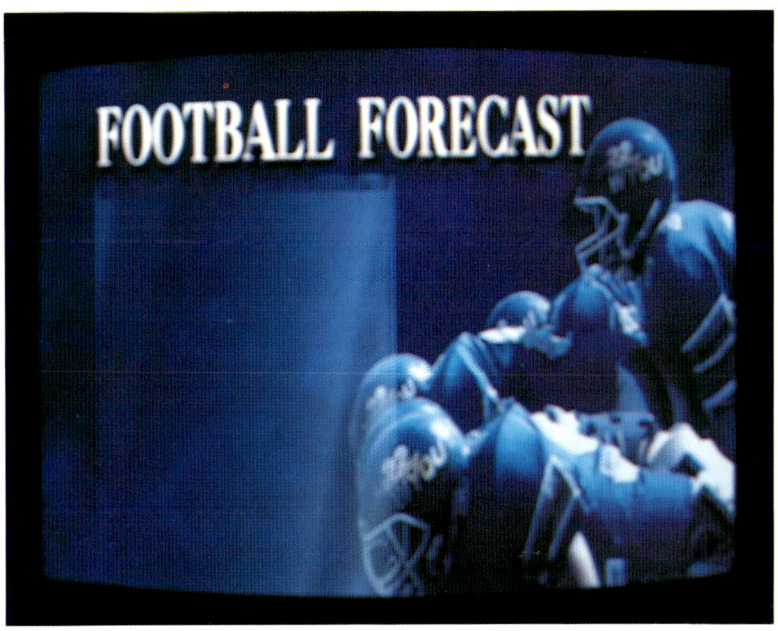

News 22
Weather Graphic

Football Forecast

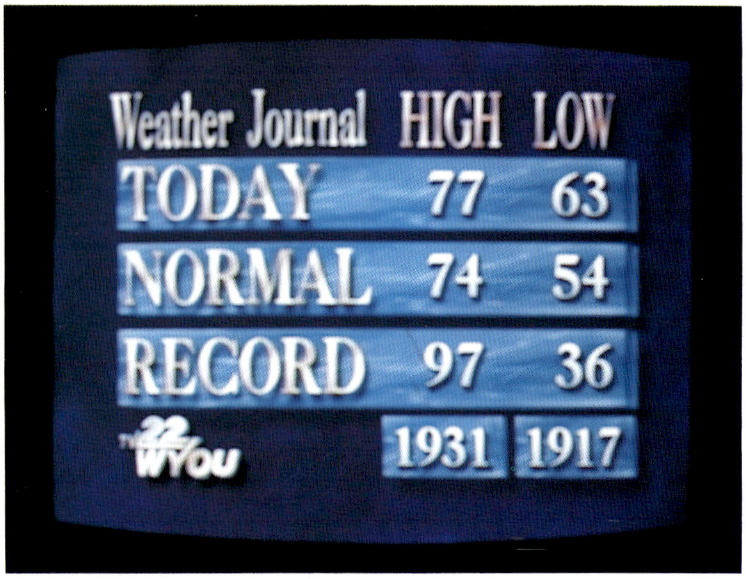

NEWS 22
Weather Graphic

High/Low

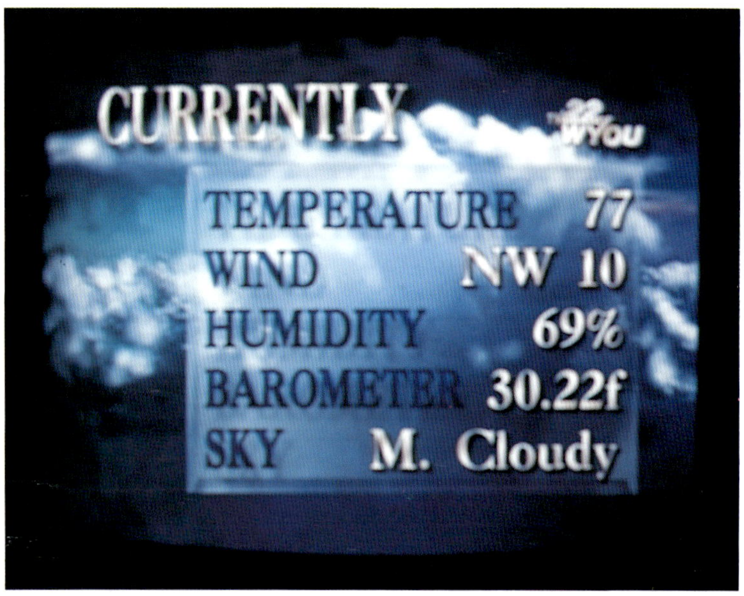

NEWS 22
Weather Graphic

Currently

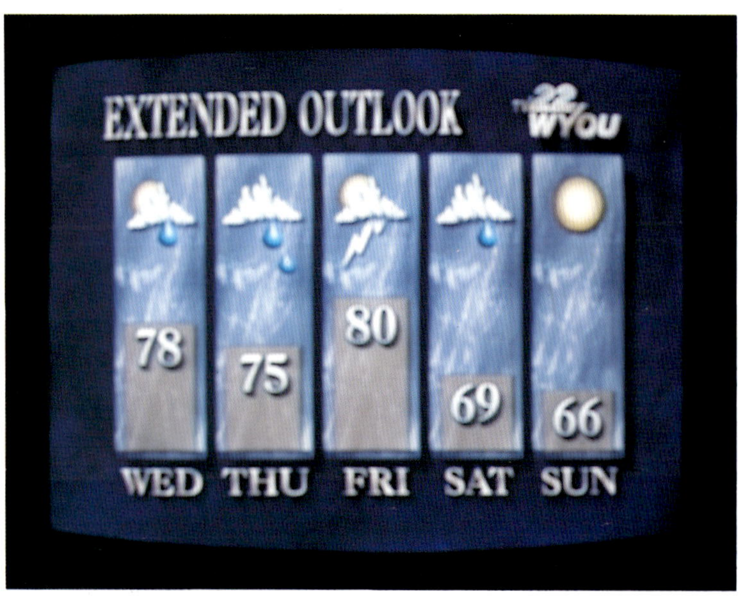

NEWS 22
Weather Graphic

Extended Outlook

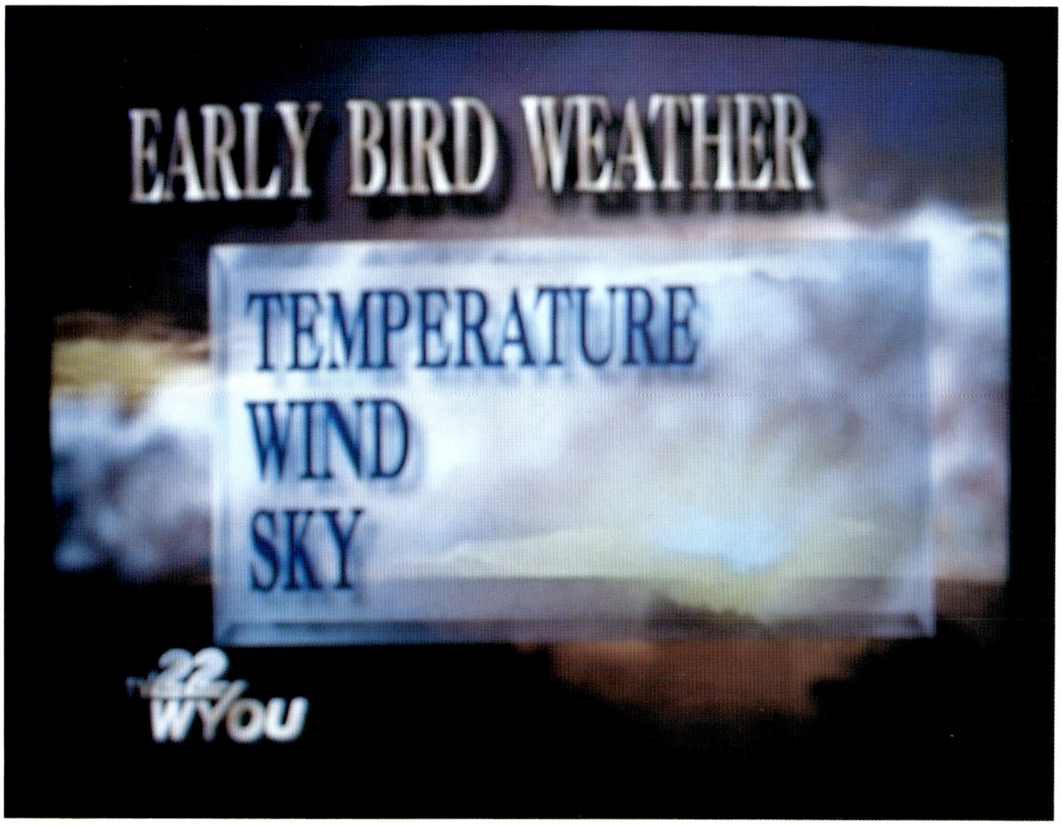

News 22
Weather Graphic

Early Bird

News 22
Weather Graphic

Shorecast

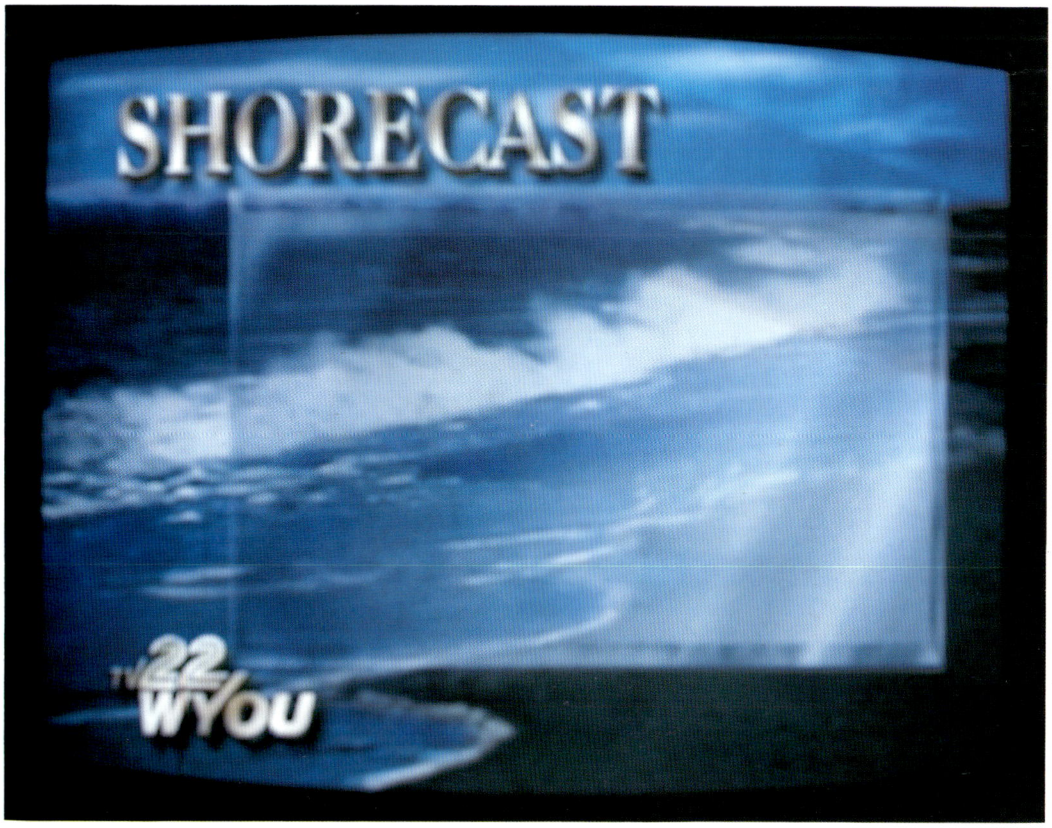

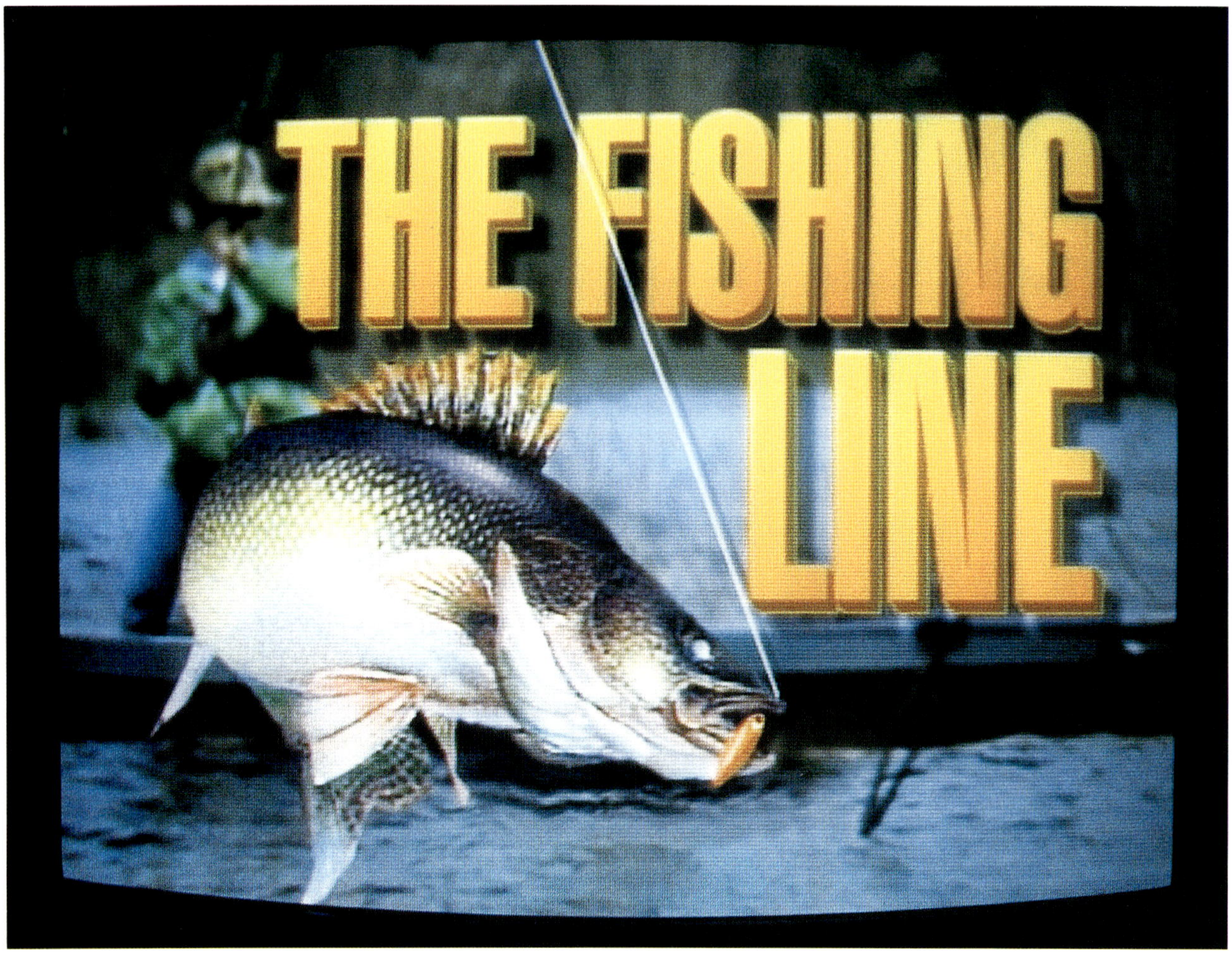

NEWS 22
Weekly Feature

The Fishing Line

News 22
Weekly Feature

Athlete of the Week

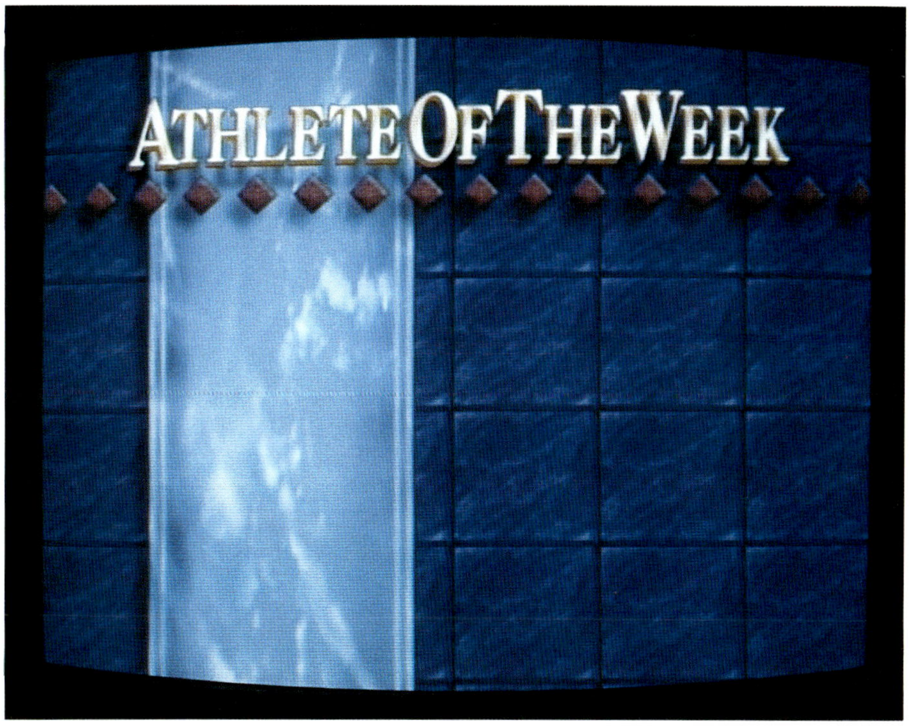

News 22
Consumer Feature

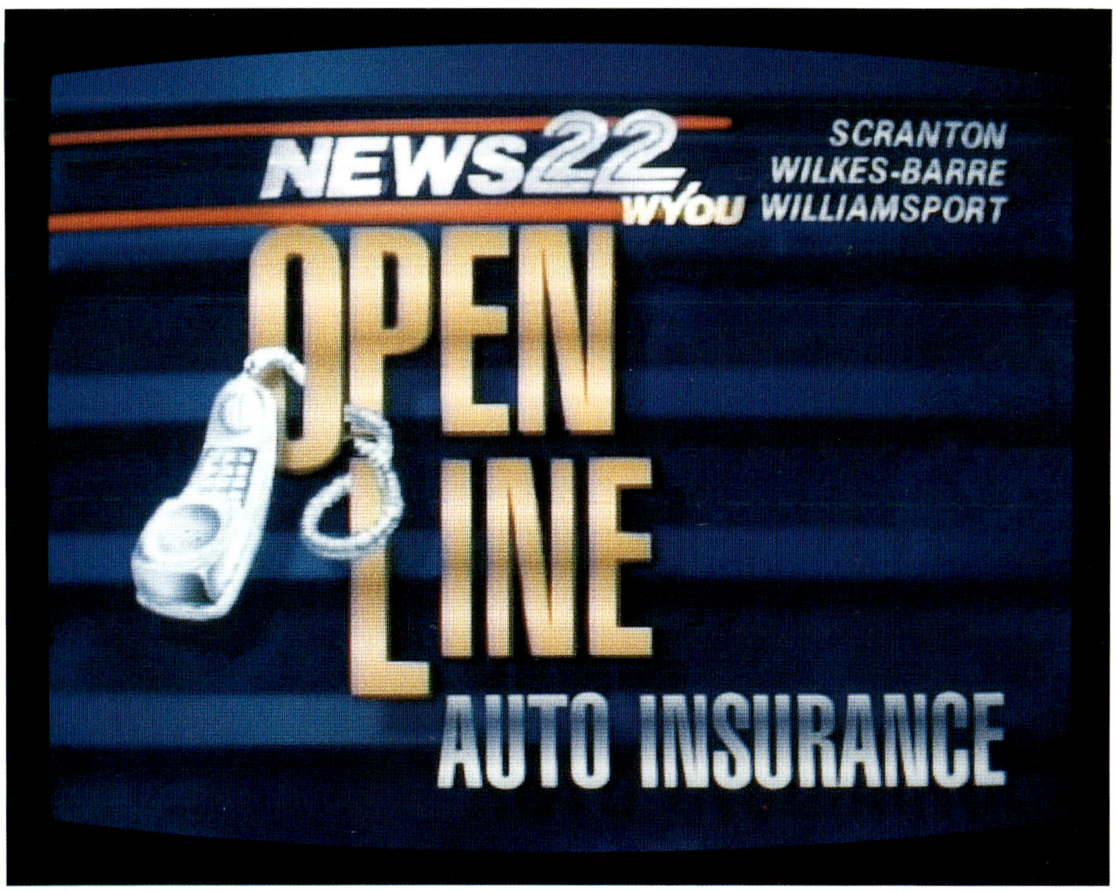

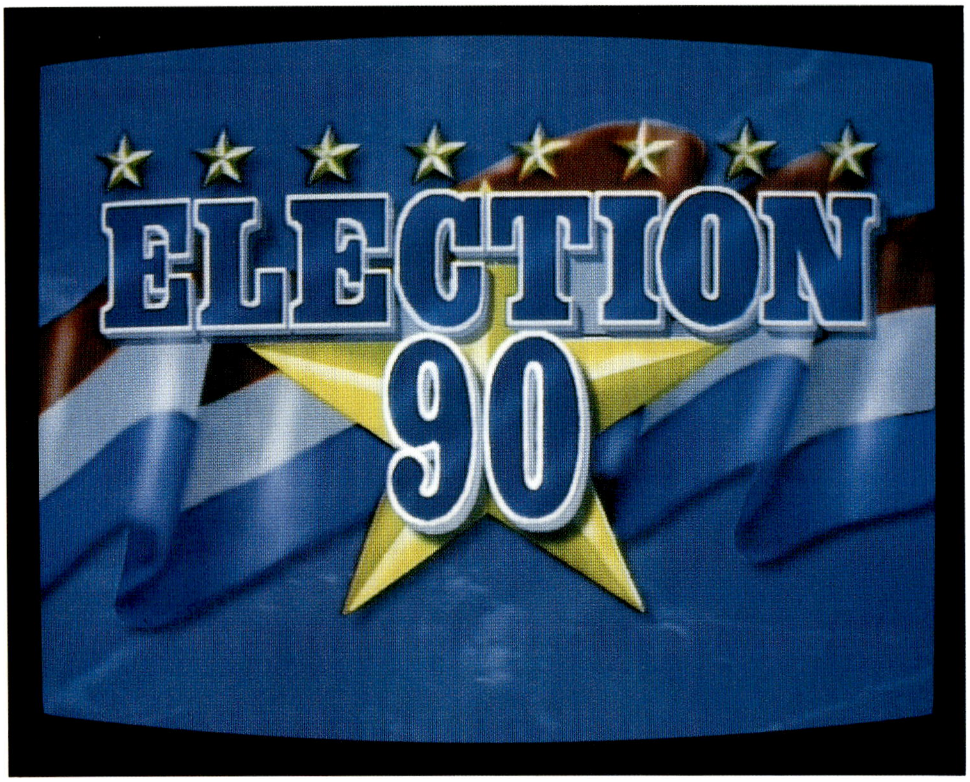

News 22
Election 90

News 22
Election 90

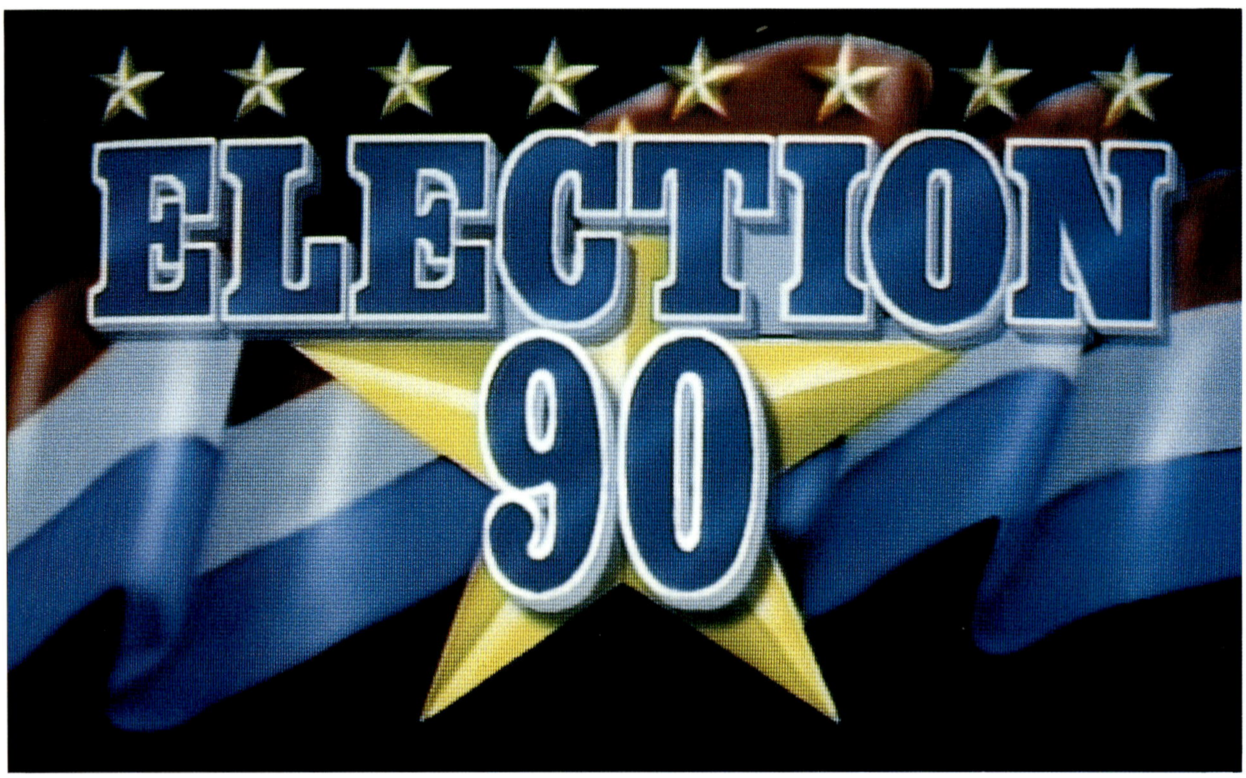

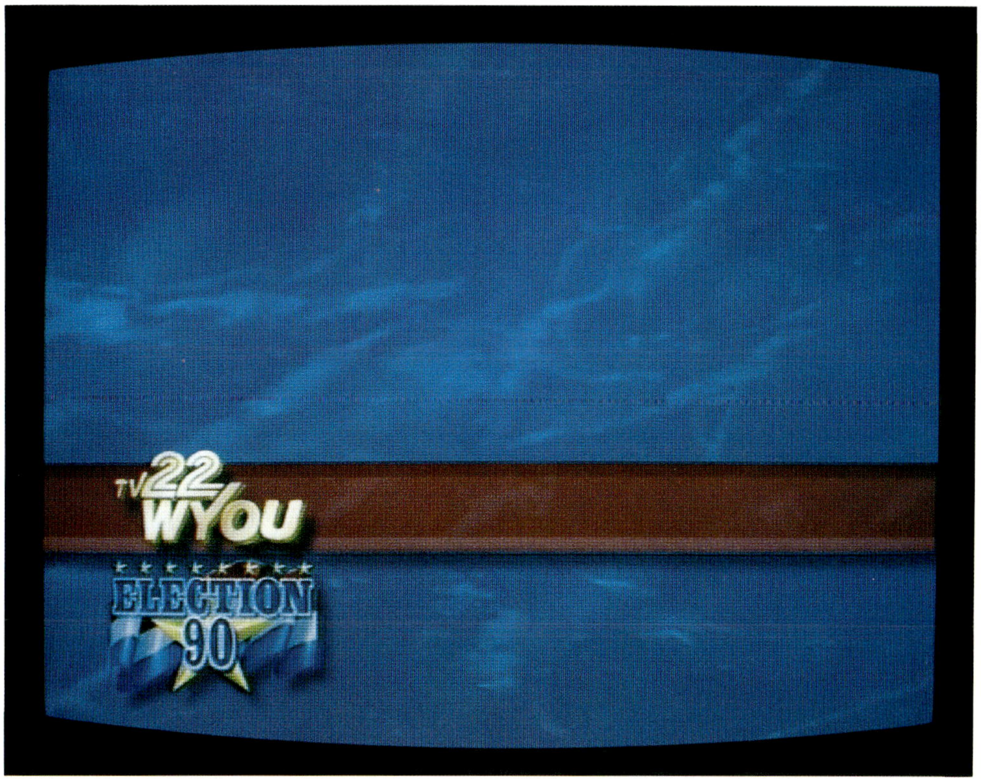

NEWS 22
Election 90

Totals Graphic

NEWS 22
Election 90

Precinct Percentage Graphic

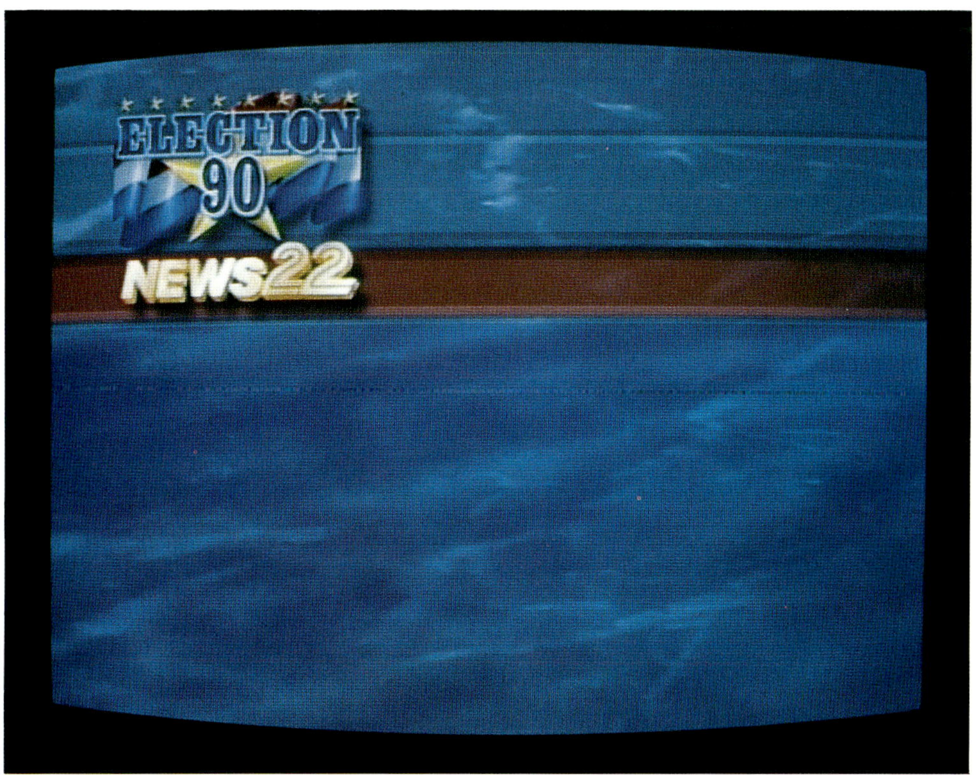

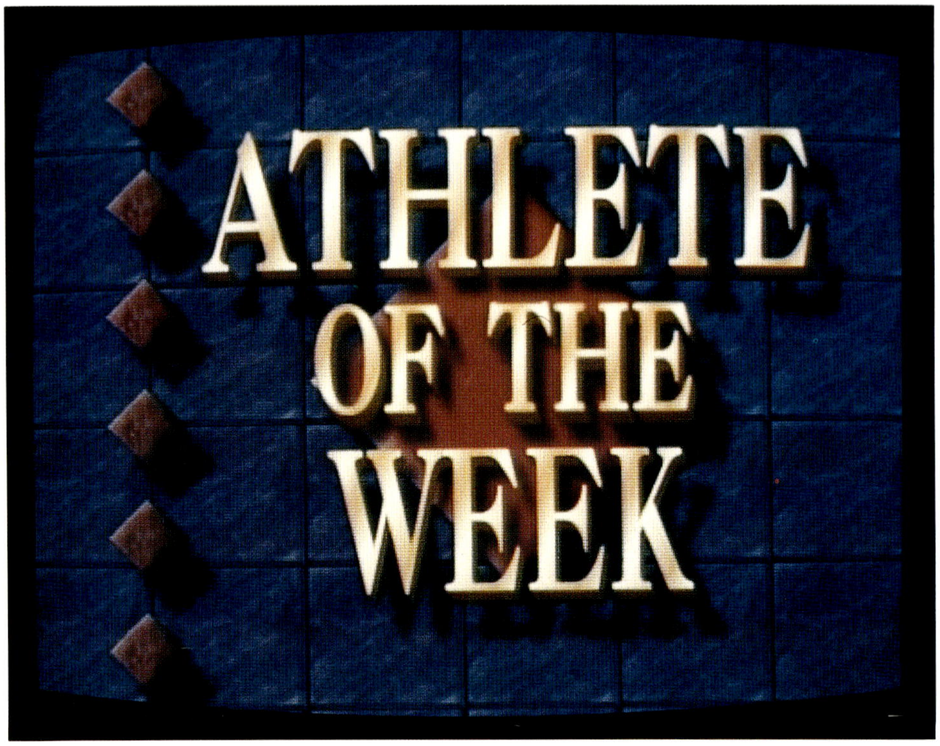

News 22
Sports

Athlete of the Week

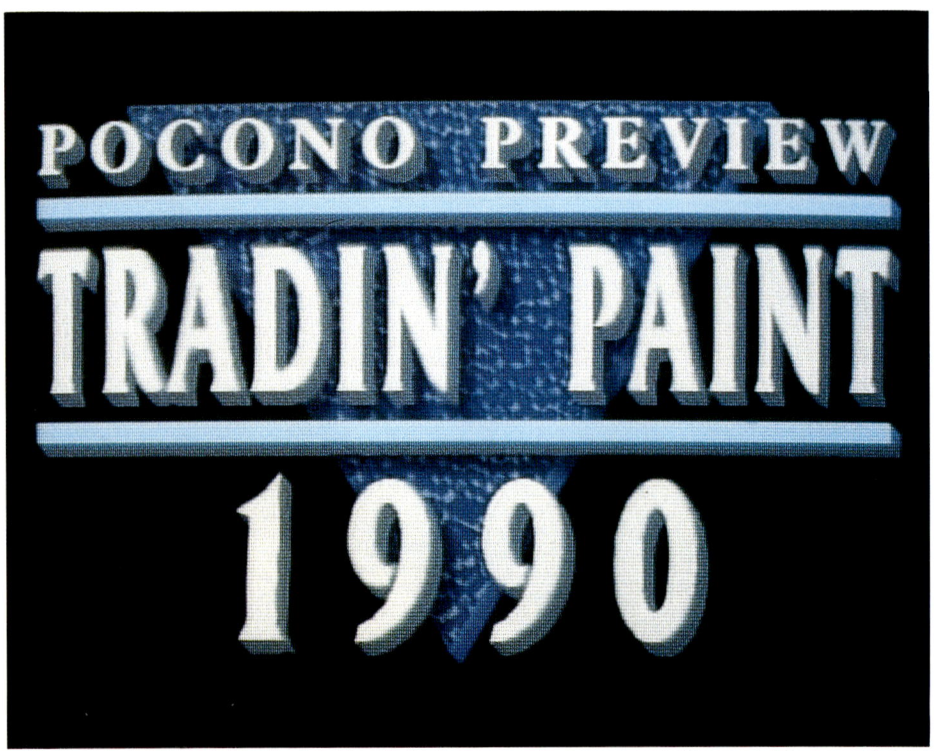

News 22
Sports

Special

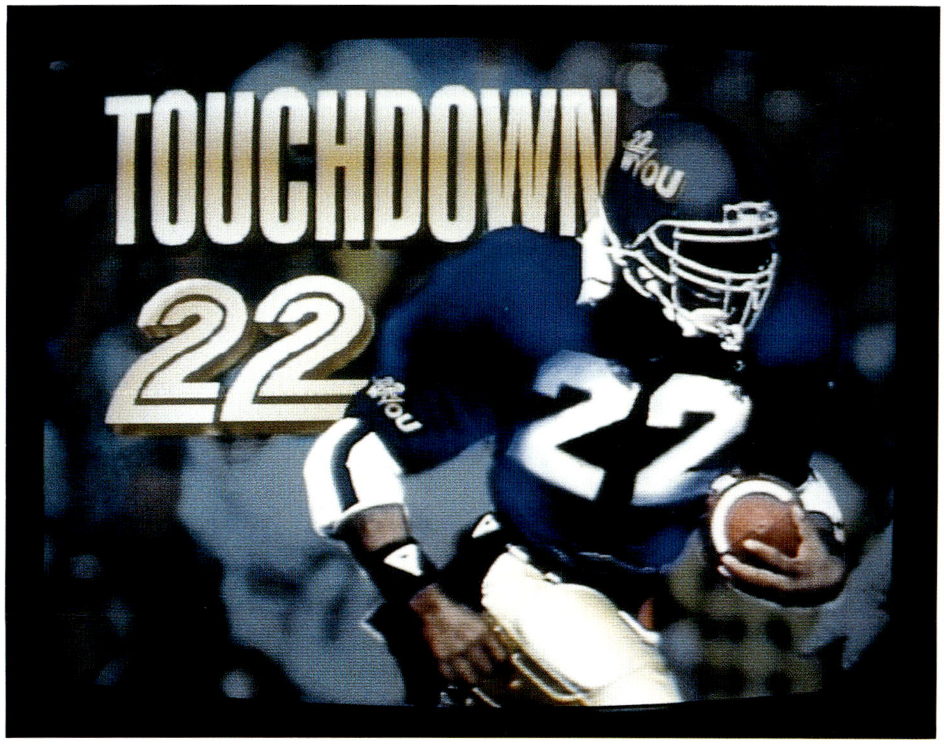

News 22
Sports

Weekly Sports Feature

News 22
Sports

Scoreboard

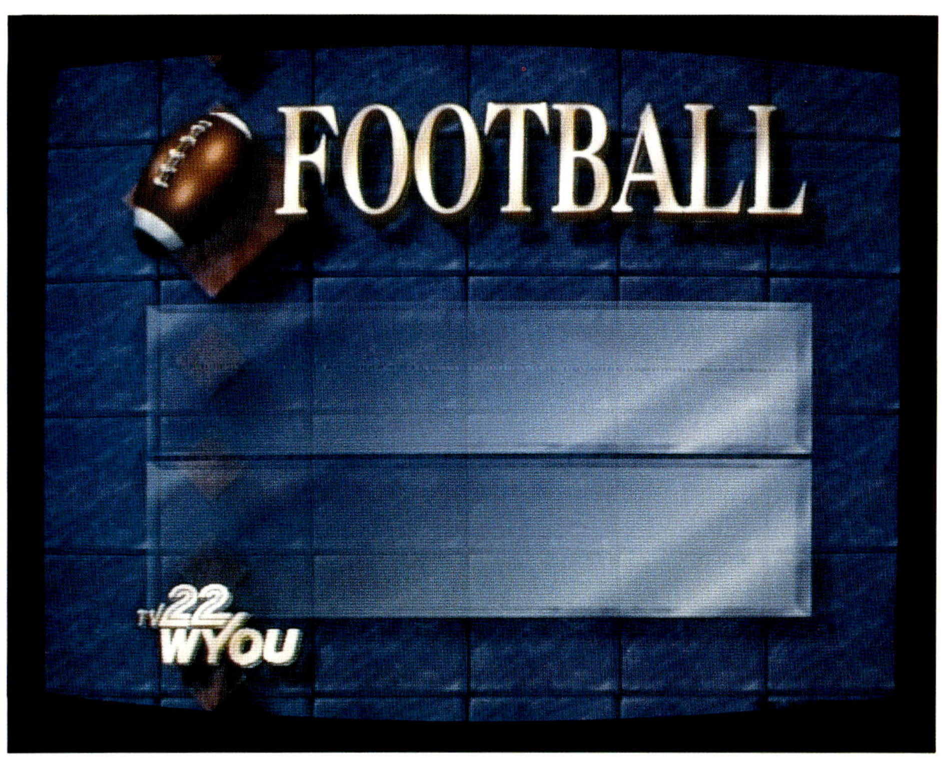

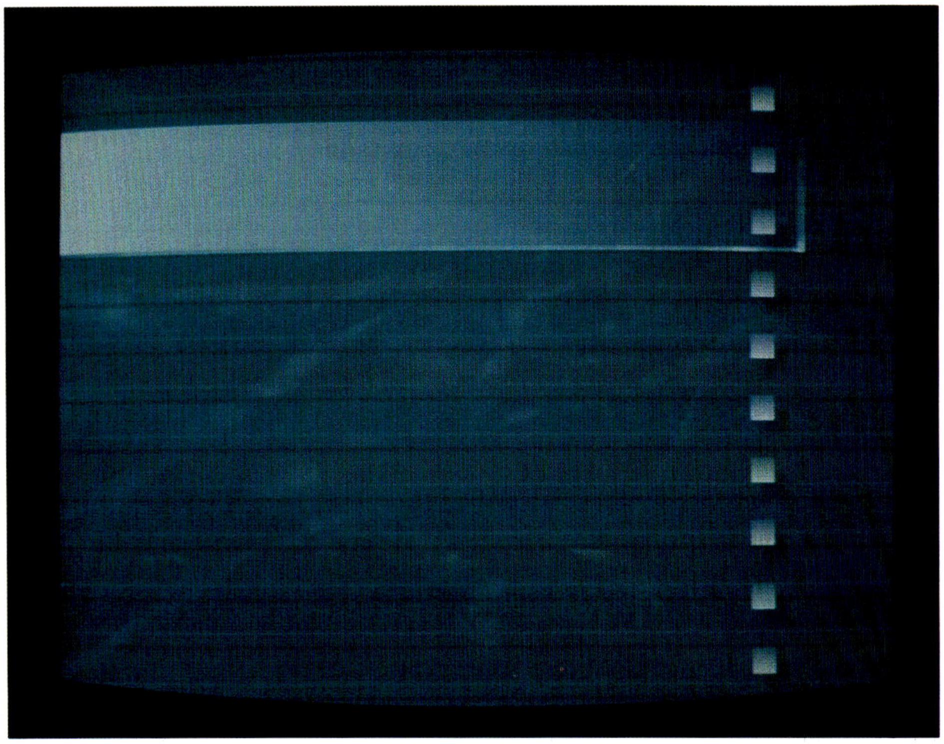

WYOU
Commercial Production

MLFS Scoreboard

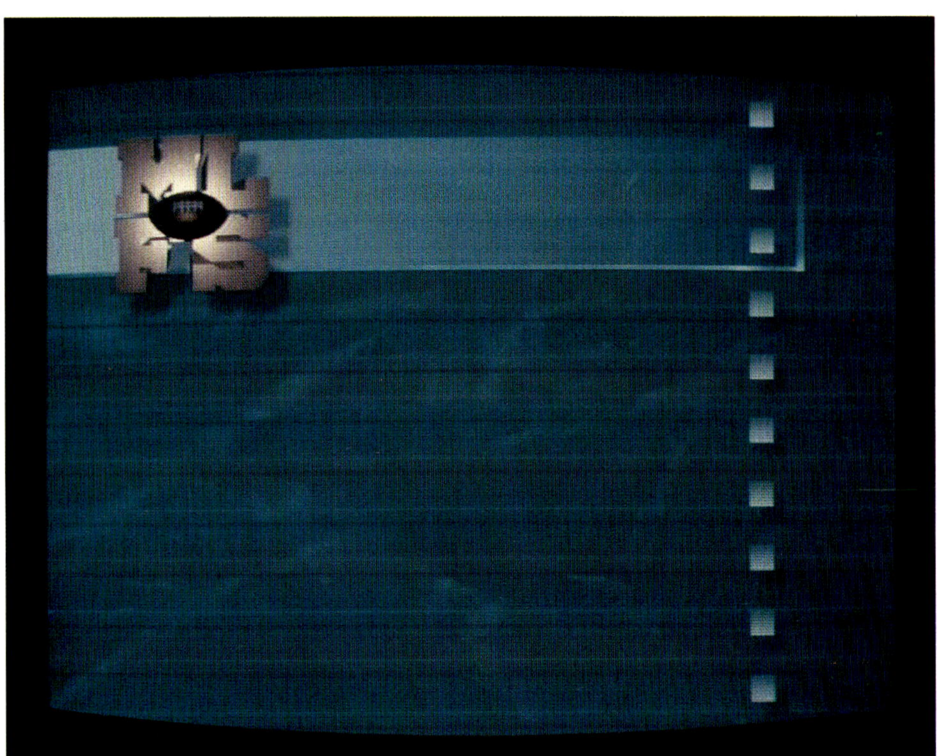

WYOU
Commercial Production

MLFS Scoreboard

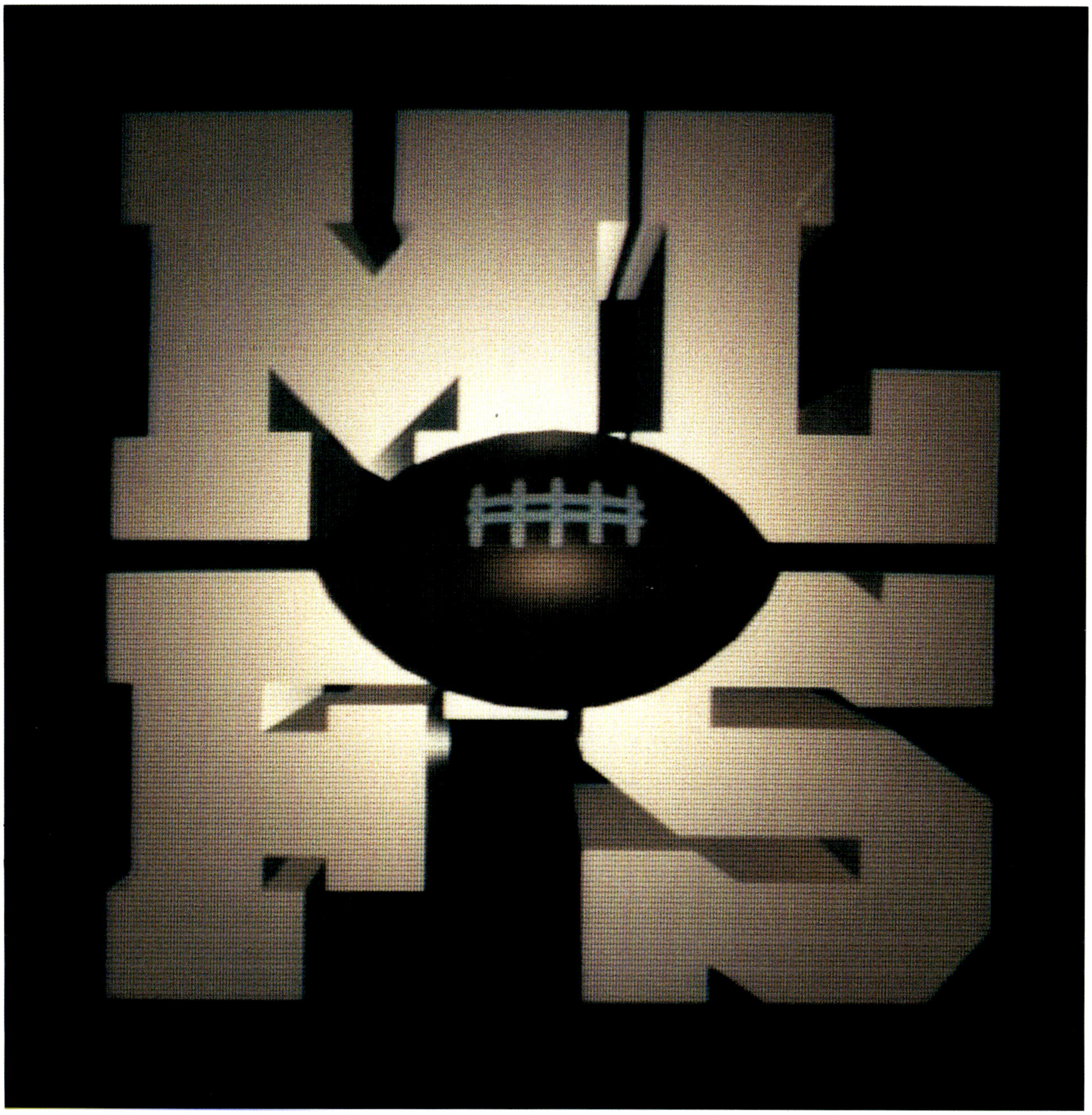

WYOU
Commercial Production

MLFS 3D Logo

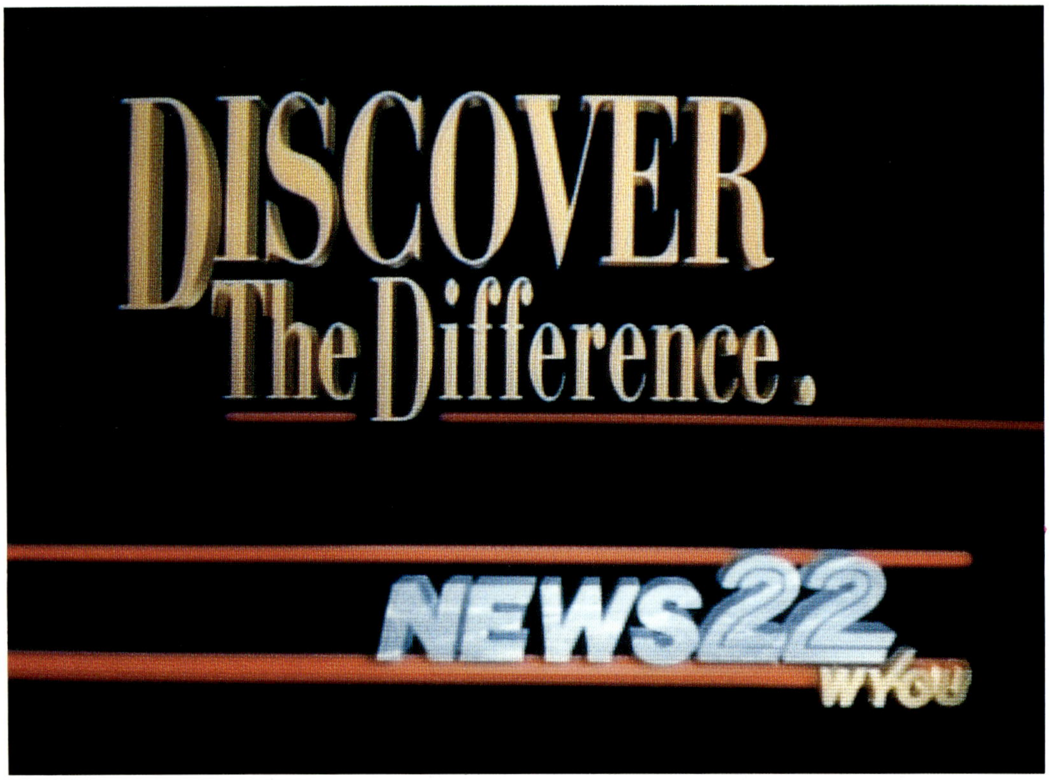

WYOU
Full Screen Promotion

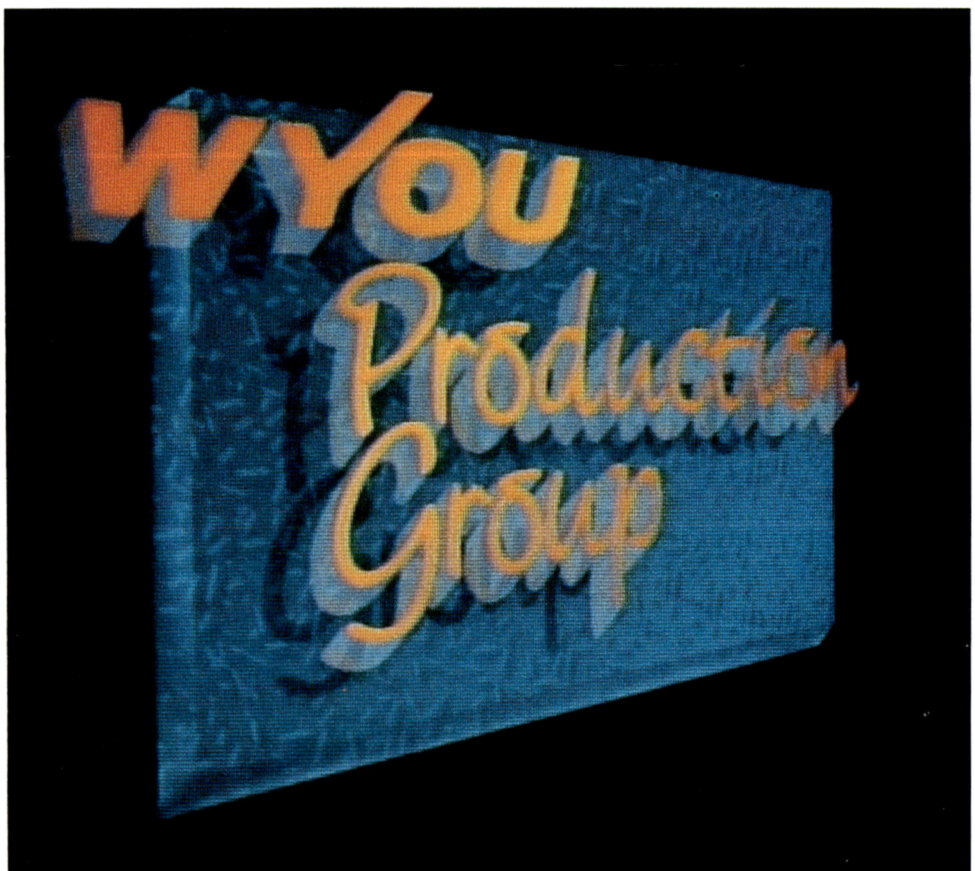

WYOU
Logo Design Promotion

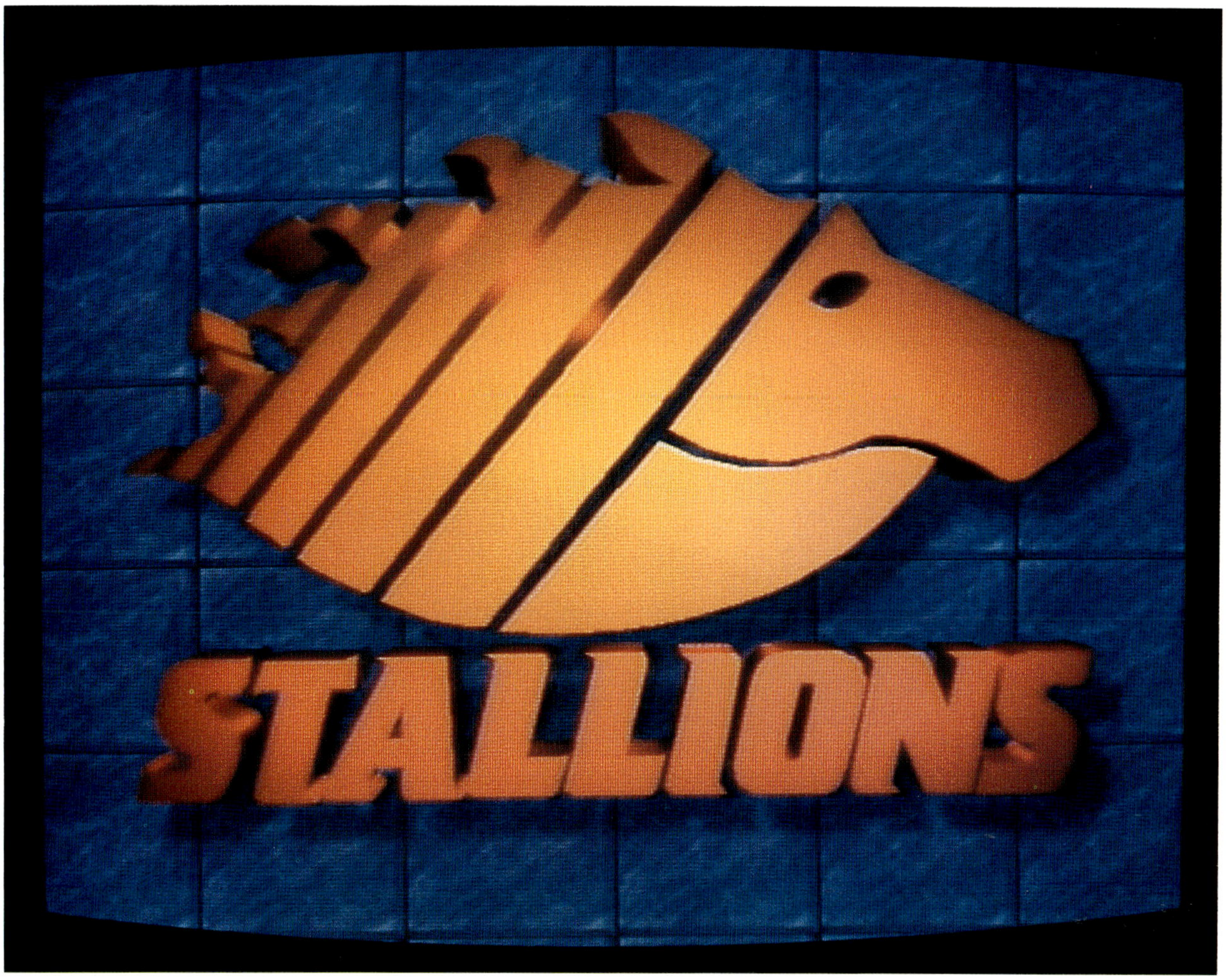

WYOU
Commercial Production

Stallions 3D Logo

WYOU
Commercial Production

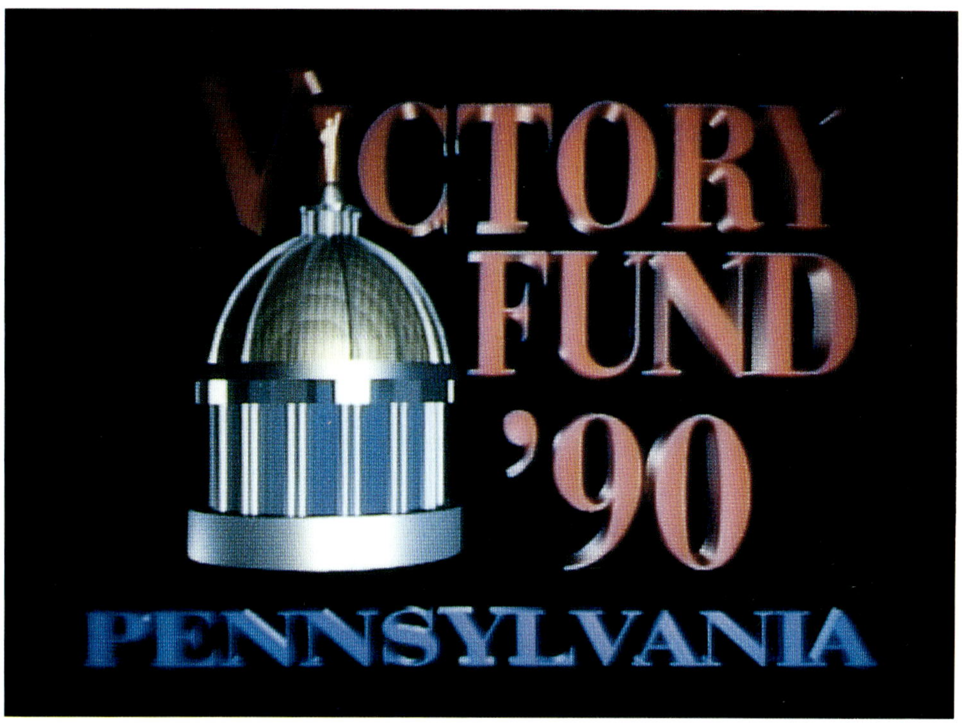

Unitel Video

515 West 57th Street, New York, NY 10019

Quisine Raptide Opening Graphics

Designed for Charles Pinsky, New York, NY to be used as opening graphics for Maryland Public Television's 30-minute cooking show with Pierre Franey.

The first frame was created tile by tile in the A-62 and objects were shot live tabletop and positioned with the ADO. Once built, a global ADO move was used to pan around the picture. From there, the opening presents the host of the show, Pierre Franey, in various situations that allowed seamless transitions by use of the Paintbox, ADO and A62.

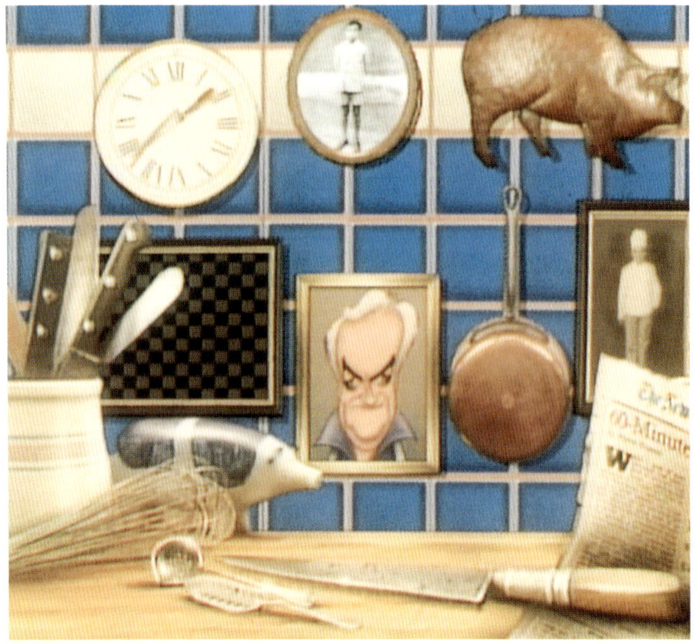

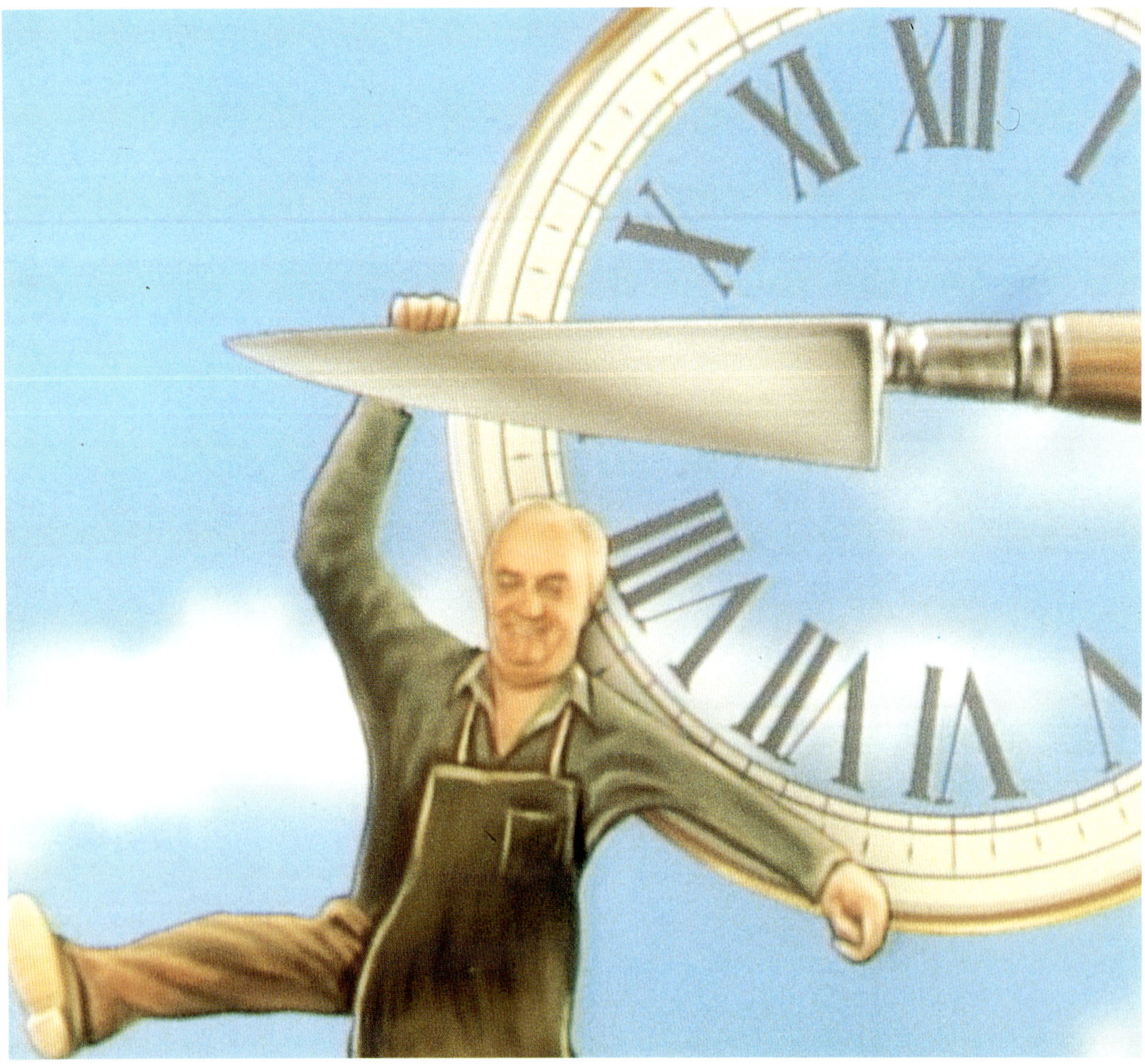

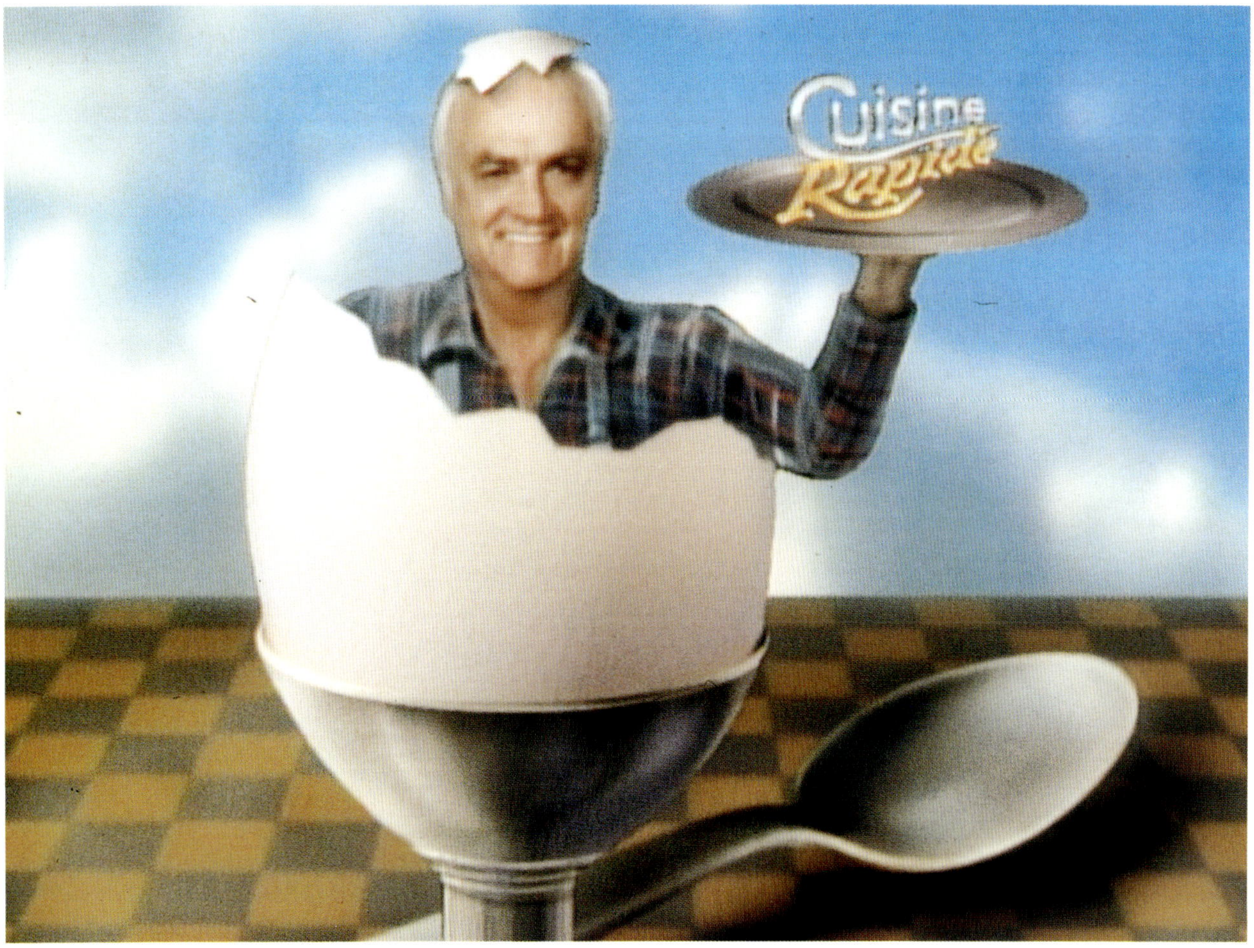

Created By	Charles Pinsky, Mike McCall, David Geisler, John Tierney, David Rosen
Design Firm	Unitel Graphics
Designer	David Geisler
Creative Director	David Geisler
Director	Charles Pinsky
Graphic Artist	David Rosen
Producer	Mike McCall
Video Editor	John Tierney
Created and Completed at	Unitel Video

Length of Time to Complete Work—40 hours on Paintbox, 10 hours editing

The VideoCenter Of NJ, Inc.

228 Park Avenue, East Rutherford, NJ 07073

The VideoCenter of NJ, Inc. is a remote production, post production and graphics facility that evolved in 1984 from a successful technical services company formed in 1981. The company principals are Frank O'Connell, Bob Camitta and Bob Schaffner.

Frank O'Connell, a pioneer in color television, has received a Presidential citation as project engineer for the Presidential Inaugural Balls as well as three Emmy Awards as Outstanding Technical Director for his work with "Live From Lincoln Center" and "Great Performances."

Bob Camitta, who is D.P./Director for the company also is an Emmy Award winner. His credits include "The Tony Awards," "Night of 1,000 Stars" and numerous rock and music concerts.

Bob Schaffner has countless record album credits to his name and pioneered the introduction of digital multitrack audio recording.

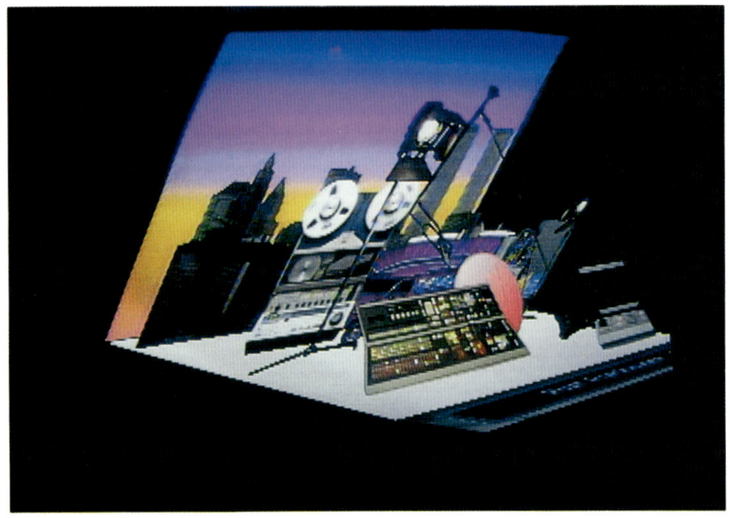

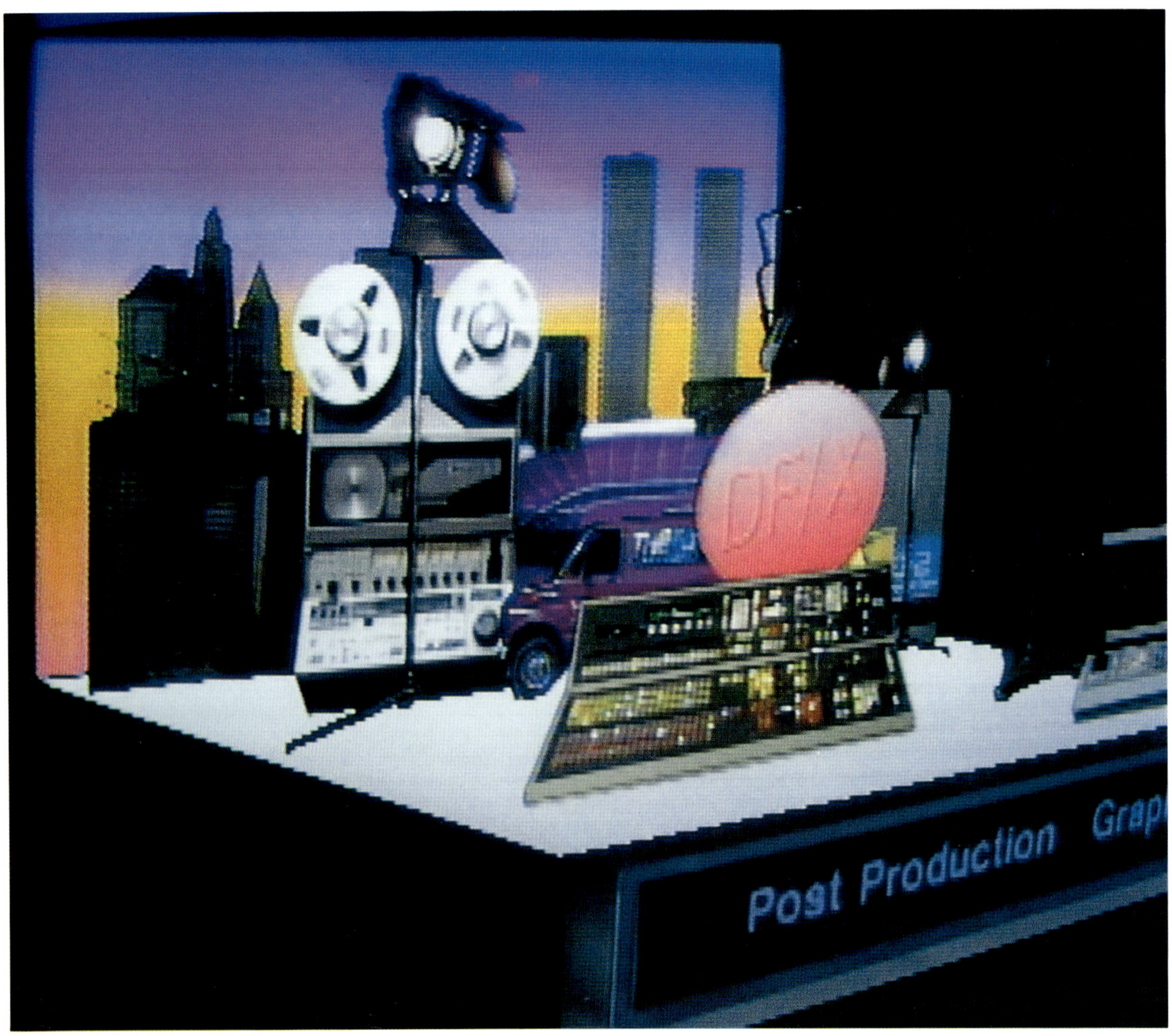

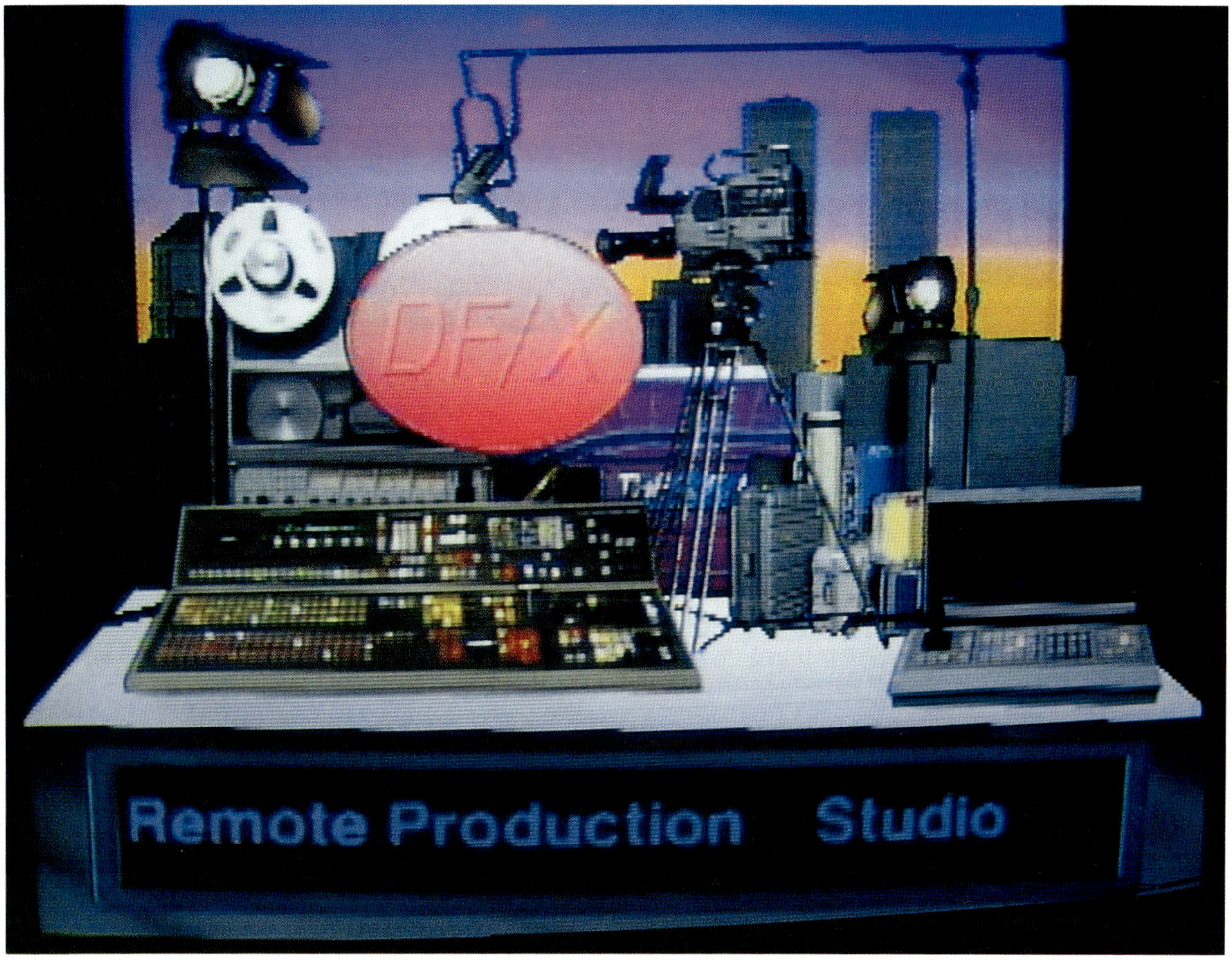

The VideoCenter Pop Out Card

Designed to show and promote the graphics and effects capabilities of The VideoCenter of NJ.

Created by shooting various pieces of equipment live on video tape and then capturing the images in the DFX Composium. An ADO, Abekas A 52 and Dubner character generator were used to touch up, paint, rotate and create 3-D relationships.

Created By	Mike Reilly, Theresa Nicholson
Designer	Mike Reilly
Graphic Artist	Theresa Nicholson
Video Editor	Mike Reilly
Created and Completed at	The VideoCenter of NJ

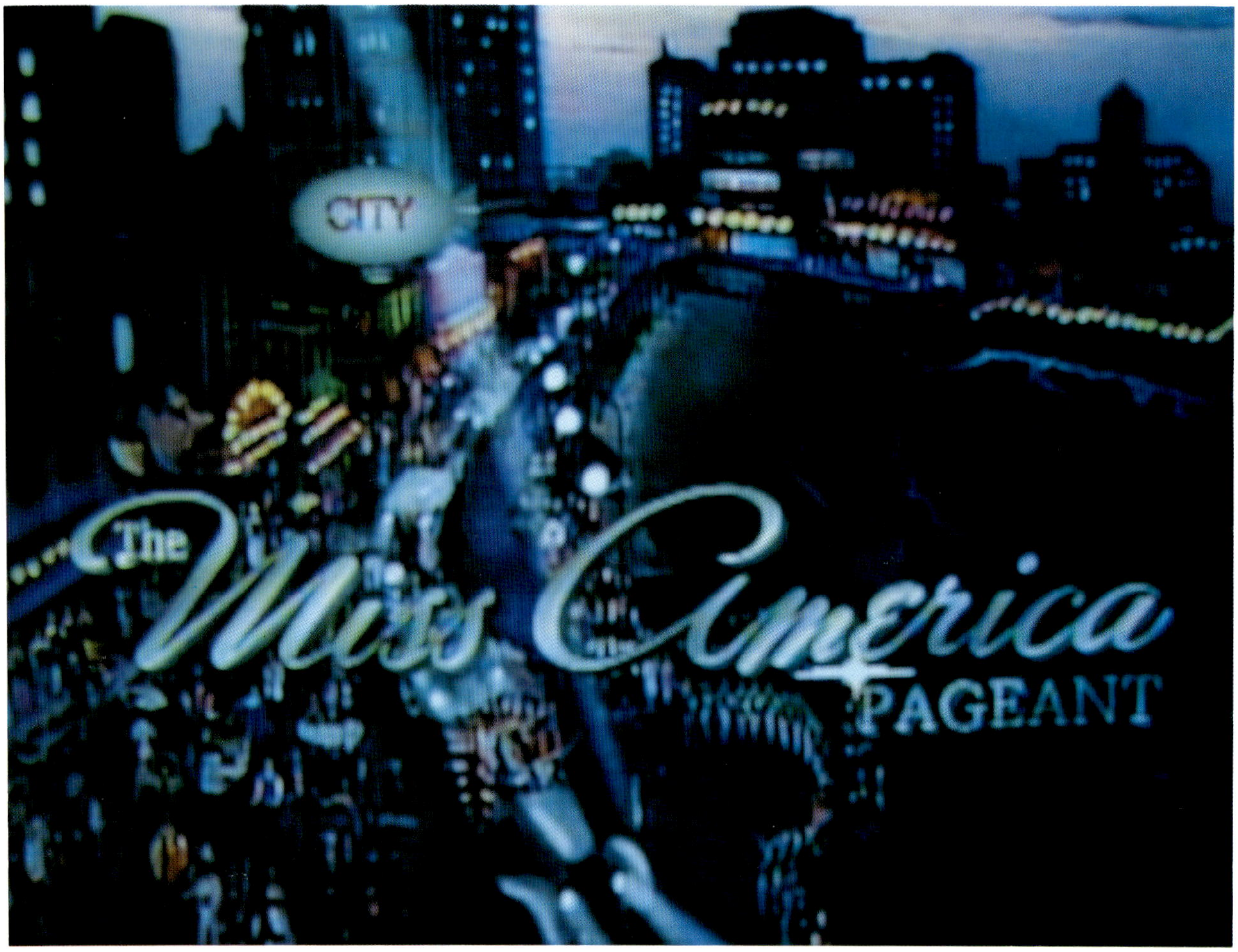

Miss America '89 Commercial Billboard

Designed as a television commercial bumper for The Miss America Pageant, Atlantic City, NJ.

Created by shooting on video, a poster designed by Melanie Taylor Kent and then altering it to a night scene in the DFX Composium. The lights were made via masks in the DFX and the searchlight moves were done with an ADO. The titles and sparkles were created with a Dubner DPS and Dubner CBG II. The blimp and its moving titles were done via DFX, ADO and Abekas.

Created By	Theresa Nicholson, Mike Reilly, John Koushouris
Designer	Theresa Nicholson
Creative Director	Frank O'Connell
Graphic Artist	Theresa Nicholson
Producer	John Koushouris
Video Editor	Mike Reilly
Created and Completed at	The VideoCenter of NJ

Length of Time to Complete Work — 1 day

Wide World Of Golf

Designed as segment bumpers for the "Wide World of Golf" video magazine section title pages, for Bob Lanning, Video Magazine International, Liberty Corner, NJ.

Created with camera captured elements which were redeveloped via multiple channels in the DFX Composium. The composited effects were rendered in Beta SP.

Created By	Bob Lanning, Cathy Graham, Theresa Nicholson
Designer	Theresa Nicholson
Graphic Artist	Theresa Nicholson
Producer	Bob Lanning, Cathy Graham
Video Editor	Mike Reilly, Rich de Martino
Created and Completed at	The VideoCenter of NJ

Length of Time to Complete Each Work—3 hours

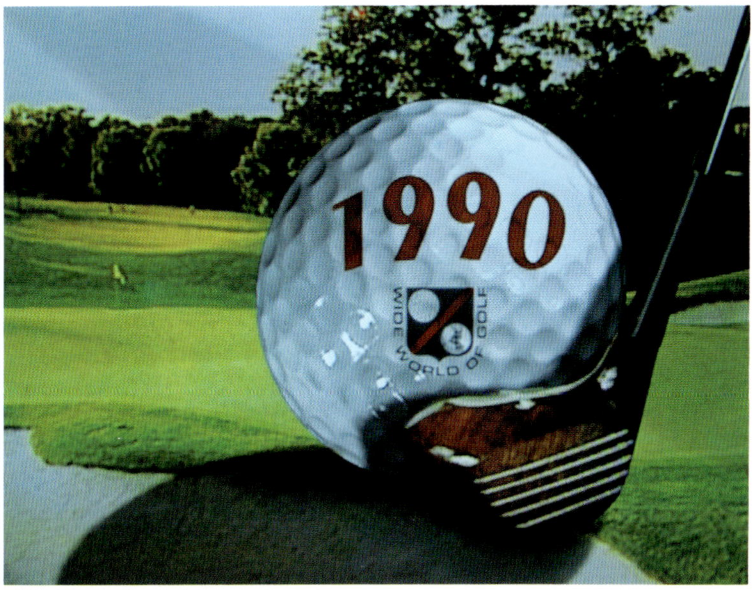

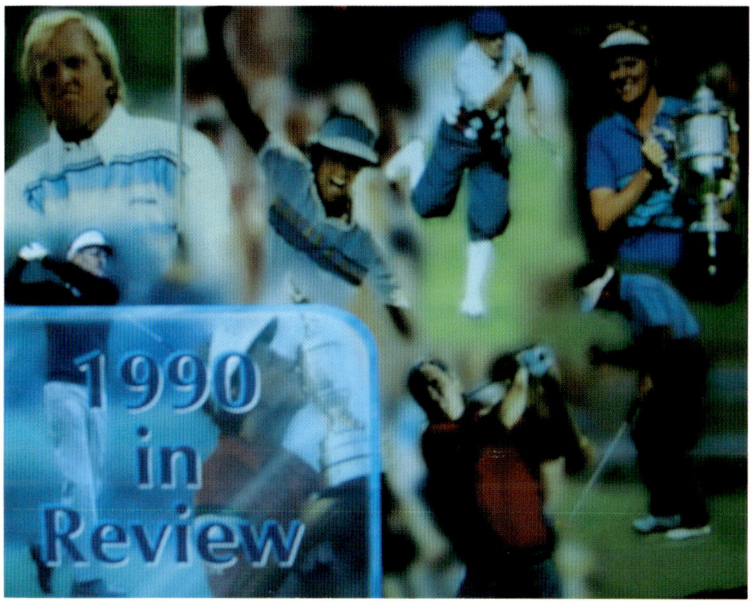

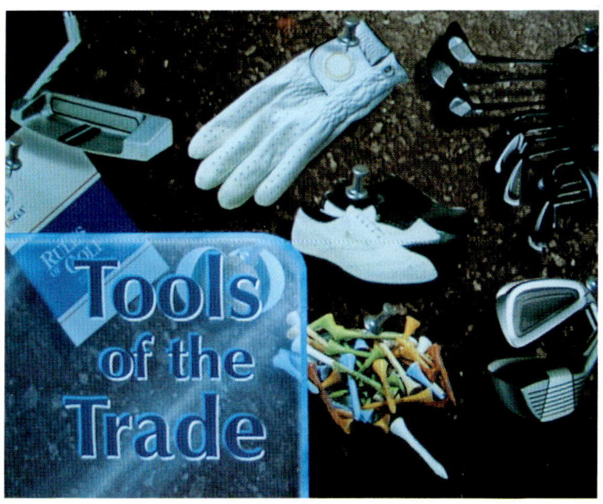

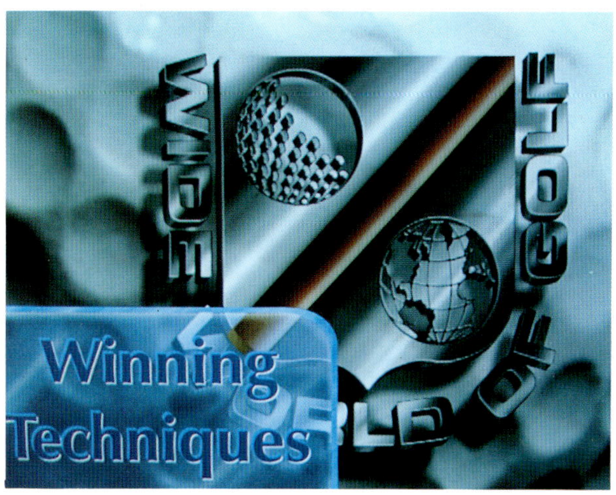

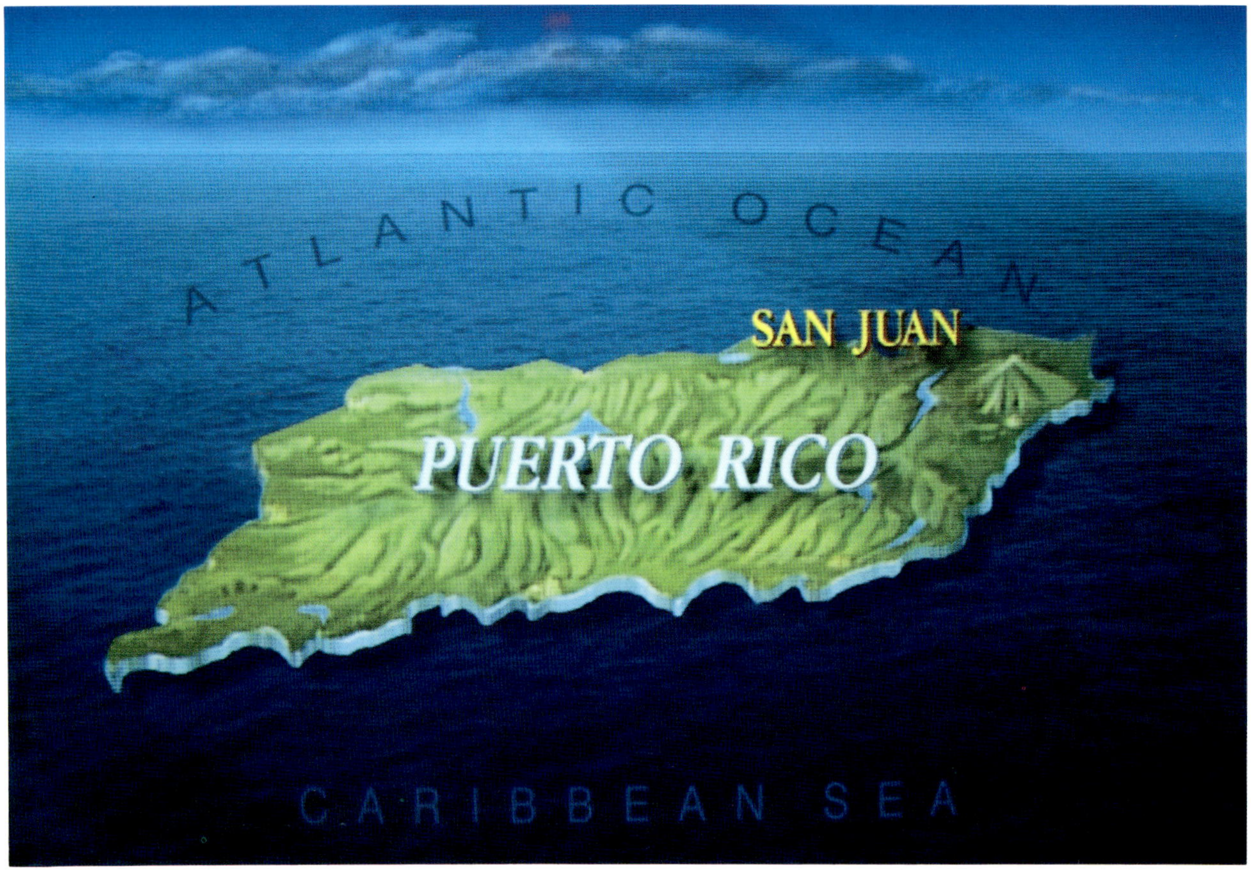

JOHNSON & JOHNSON—PUERTO RICO

Designed for a video program about tax laws and U.S. possessions for John Sheahan, Johnson & Johnson, New Brunswick, NJ.

Created on a DFX Composium work station utilizing the paint, type and video capture capabilities. The images were hand drawn and altered through the DVE within the DFX. The hicon channel was used to move the objects and cut and paste them.

Created By	Theresa Nicholson, Gary Vandenburg
Designer	Theresa Nicholson
Graphic Artist	Theresa Nicholson
Producer	John Sheahan
Video Editor	Gary Vandenburg
Created at	The VideoCenter of NJ
Completed at	Johnson & Johnson

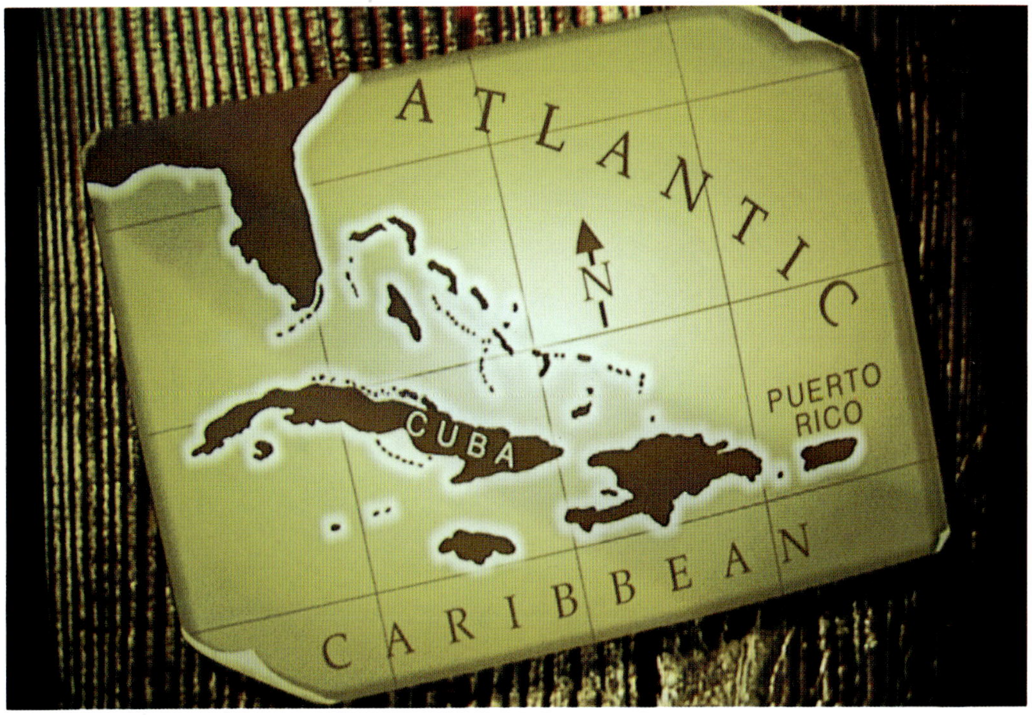
ATLANTIC
N
PUERTO RICO
CUBA
CARIBBEAN

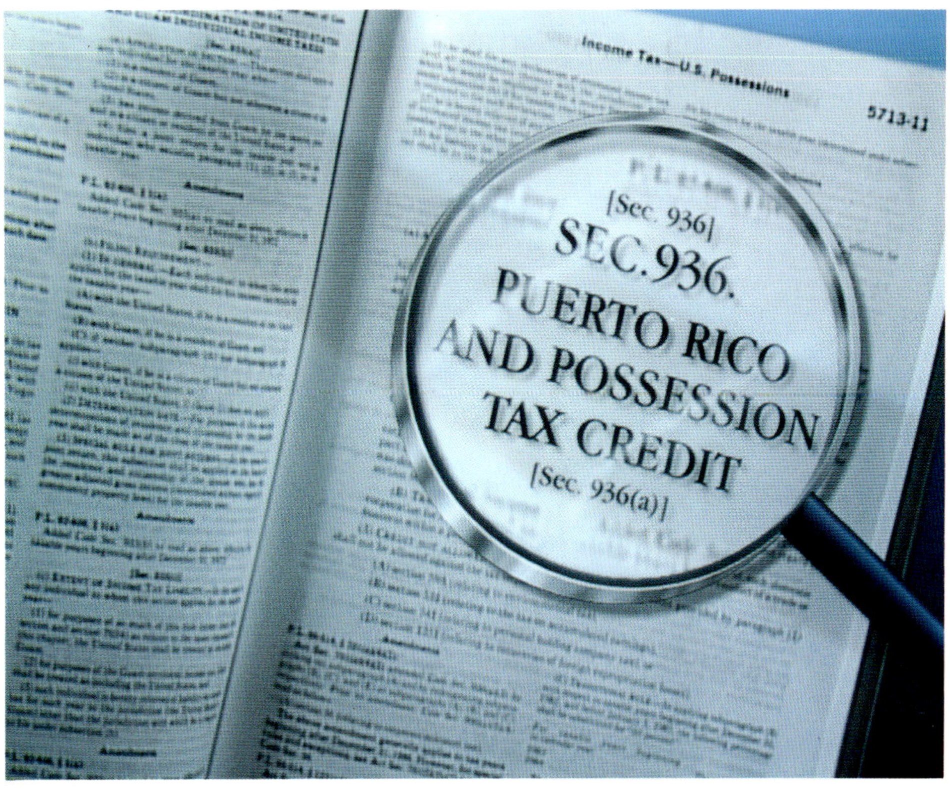
Income Tax—U.S. Possessions
5713-11
[Sec. 936]
SEC.936.
PUERTO RICO
AND POSSESSION
TAX CREDIT
[Sec. 936(a)]

WANDER COMMUNICATIONS, INC.

534 E. 84th Street-Suite 5W, New York, NY 10028

OCCASIONAL VIDEO LOGO

Designed as a corporate logo for special event coverage video.

Created by reproducing a business card and then feeding the image into a Dubner Graphics Factory where it was manipulated.

Created By	John Stapsy of Aerial Image and Andrew Wander of Wander Communications
Design Firm	Aerial Image
Designer	Andrew Wander
Creative Director	Andrew Wander
Art Director	Andrew Wander
Effects Supervisor	Linda Bernstein
Graphic Artist	David Wander
Producer	Andrew Wander
Created and Completed at	Aerial Image, NY

Length of Time to Complete Work—8 hours

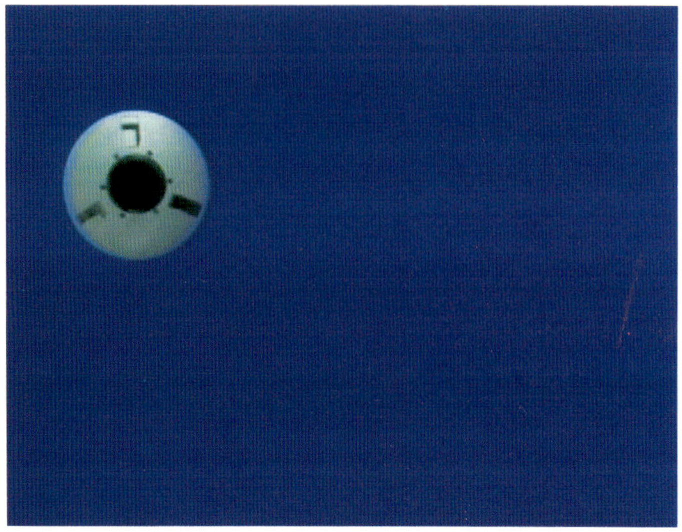

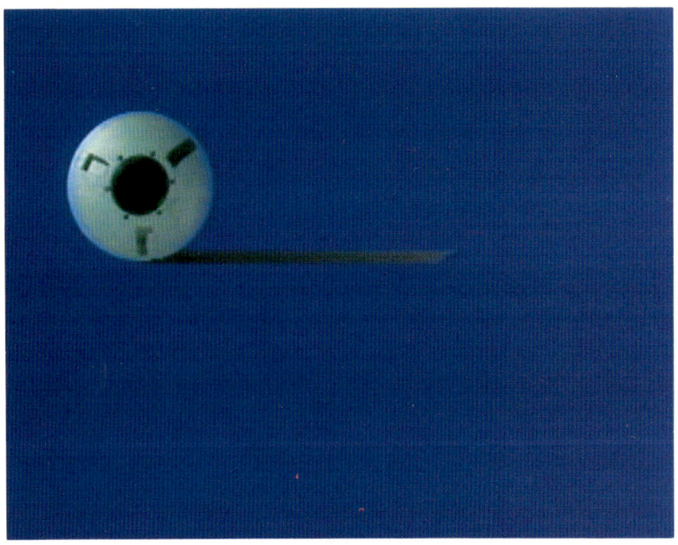

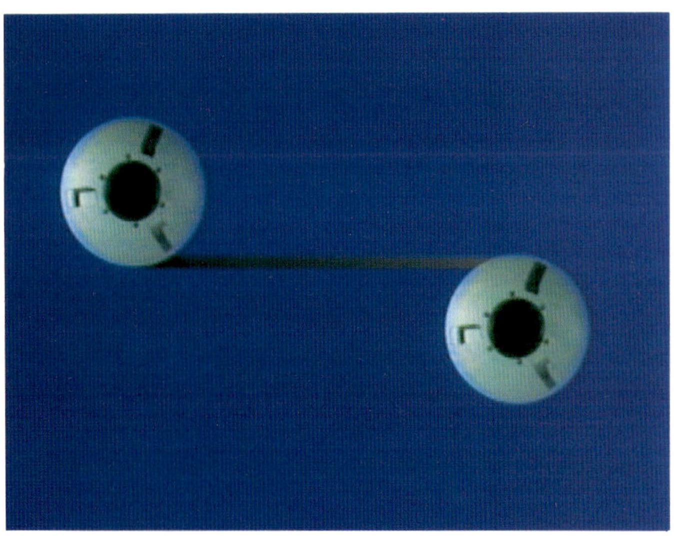

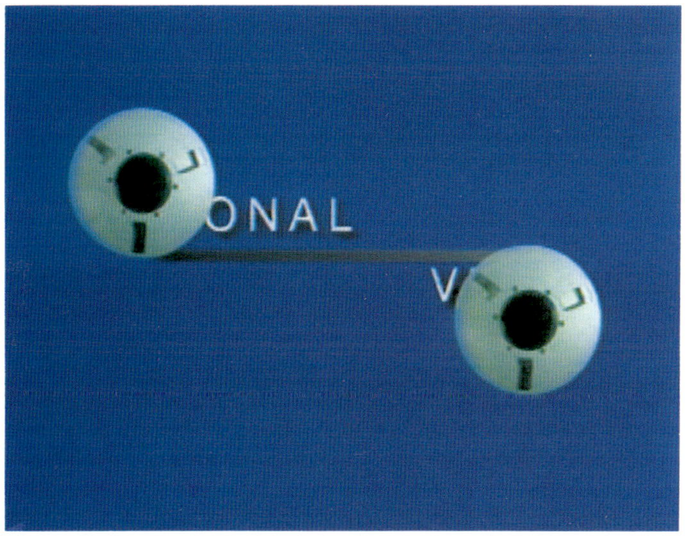
ONAL
V

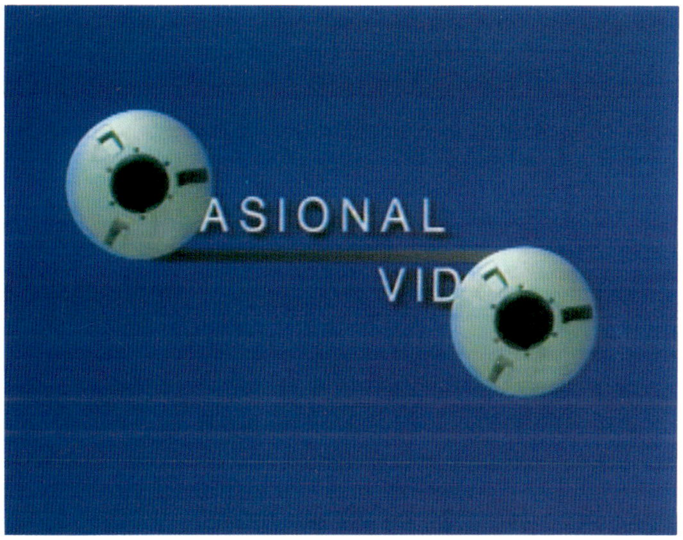
ASIONAL
VID

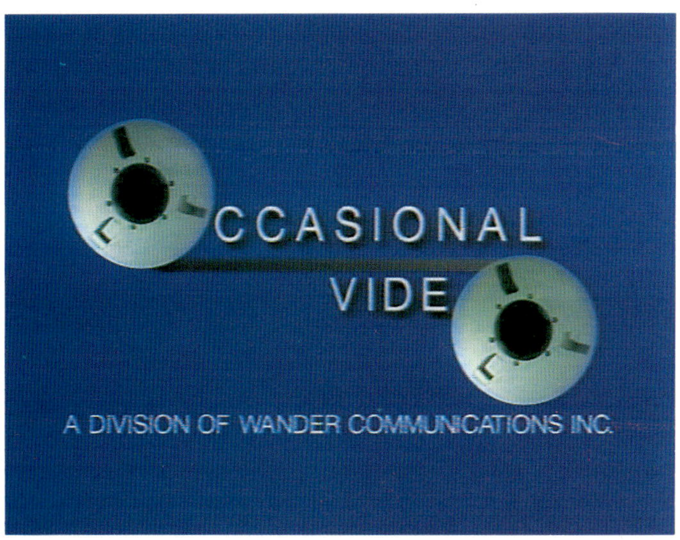
CCASIONAL
VIDE
A DIVISION OF WANDER COMMUNICATIONS INC.

WVLA–TV

5220 Essen Lane, Baton Rouge, LA 70809

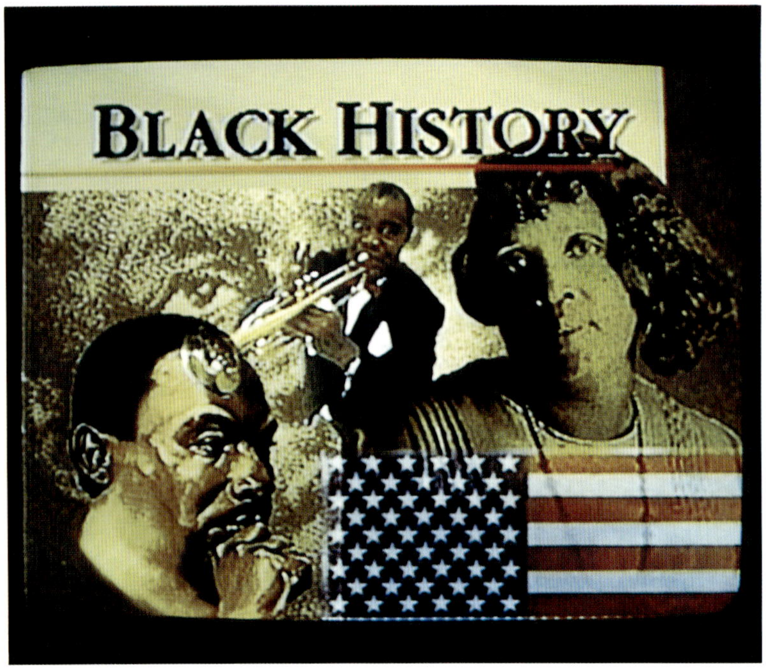

BLACK HISTORY

Designed for a television program and created on an Aurora Paint Box, in house, at WVLA-TV

Created By	Jay Ruiz
Designer	Jay Ruiz
Art Director	Jay Ruiz
Producer	Bob Davidge

Created in house, at WVLA-TV

Length of Time to Complete Work—5 hours

LOUISIANA'S CRISIS: COASTAL WETLANDS

Designed for a WVLA-TV television program, "Coastal Wetlands Special." Created on an Aurora Paint Box, the greatest obstacle was to achieve the sand effect.

Created By	Jay Ruiz and Ed Lakin
Designer	Jay Ruiz
Creative Director	Ed Lakin
Art Director	Jay Ruiz

Created in house, at WVLA-TV

Length of Time to Complete Work—7 hours

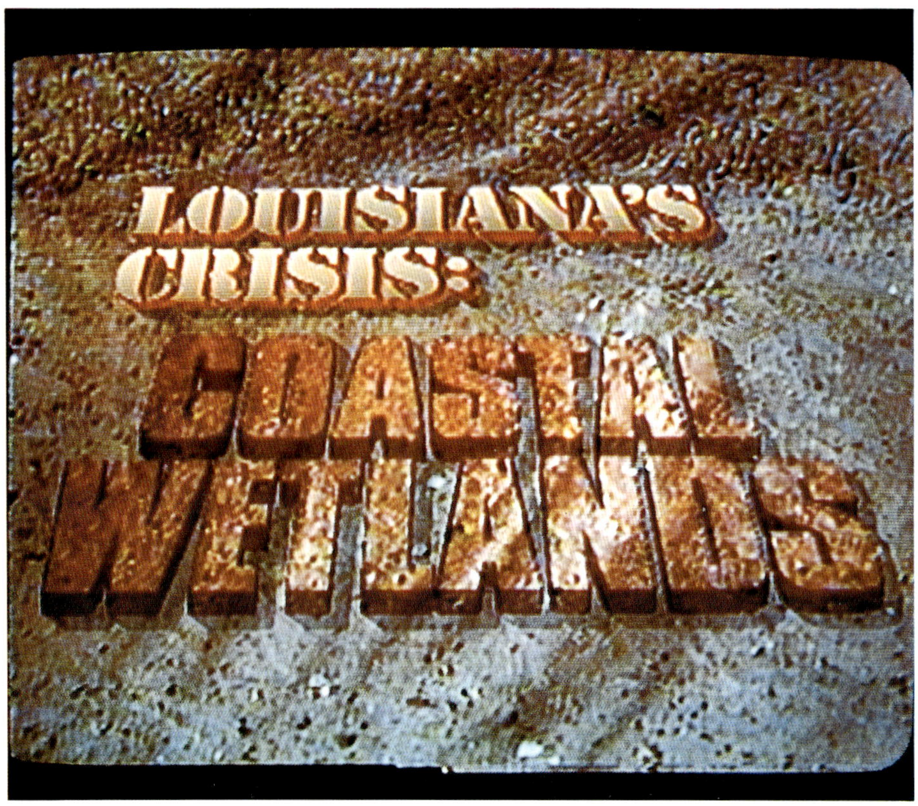

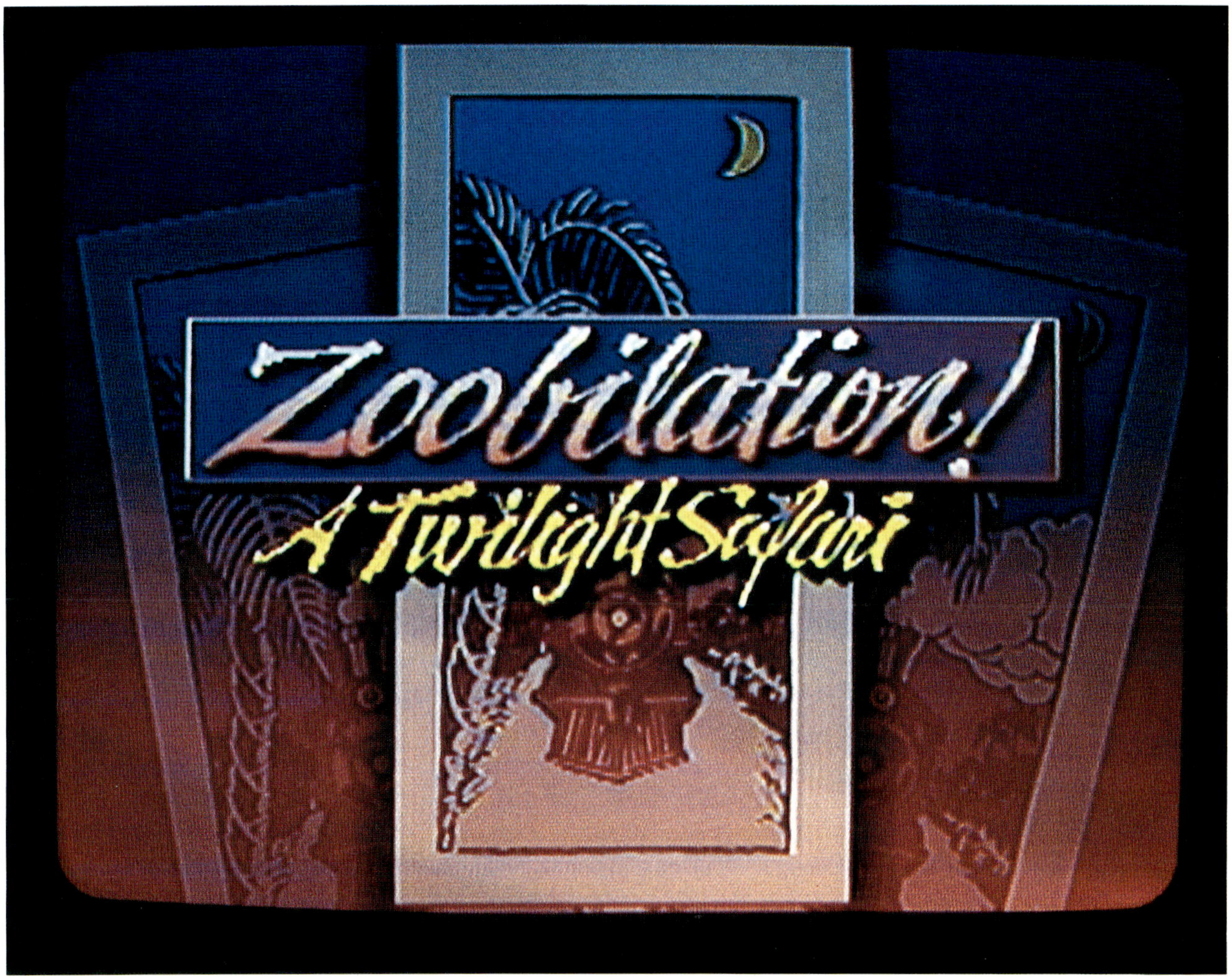

ZOOBILATION

Designed for The Baton Rouge Zoo to promote an event to raise funds for the zoo.

Created By	Jay Ruiz
Designer	Jay Ruiz
Art Director	Jay Ruiz

Created, in house at WVLA-TV

Length of Time to Complete Work—5 hours

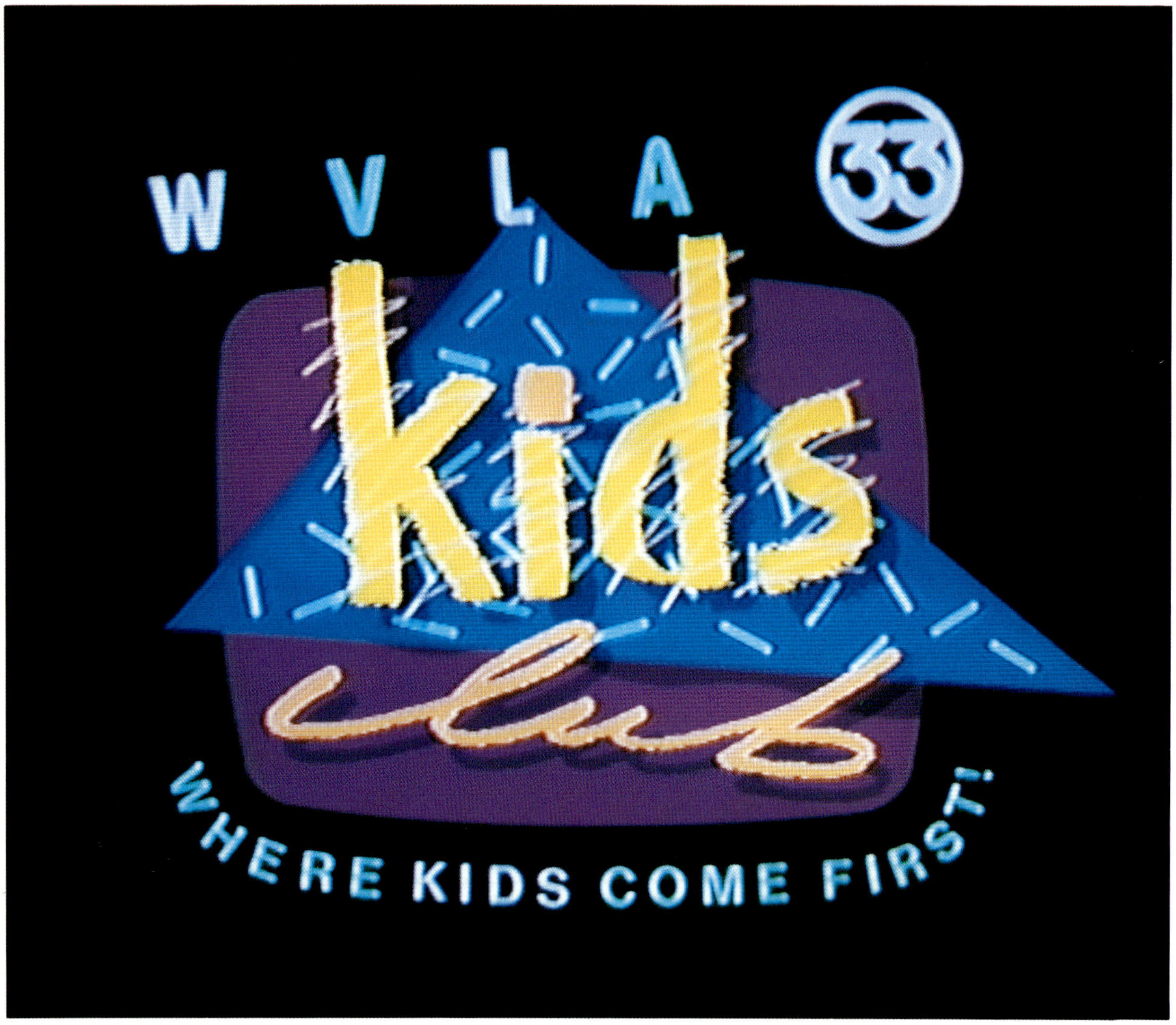

WVLA Kids Club

Designed for on air television promotion, and created on an Aurora Paint Box

Designer	Jay Ruiz
Creative Director	Ed Lakin
Art Director	Jay Ruiz

Created in house, at WVLA-TV

Length of Time to Complete Work—10 hours

Community Mail Box

Created on an Aurora Paint Box for WVLA and designed to promote public service events, listing projects and happenings around the city.

Designer	Jay Ruiz/Ed Lakin
Art Director	Jay Ruiz

Created, in house at WVLA-TV

Length of Time to Complete Work—6 hours

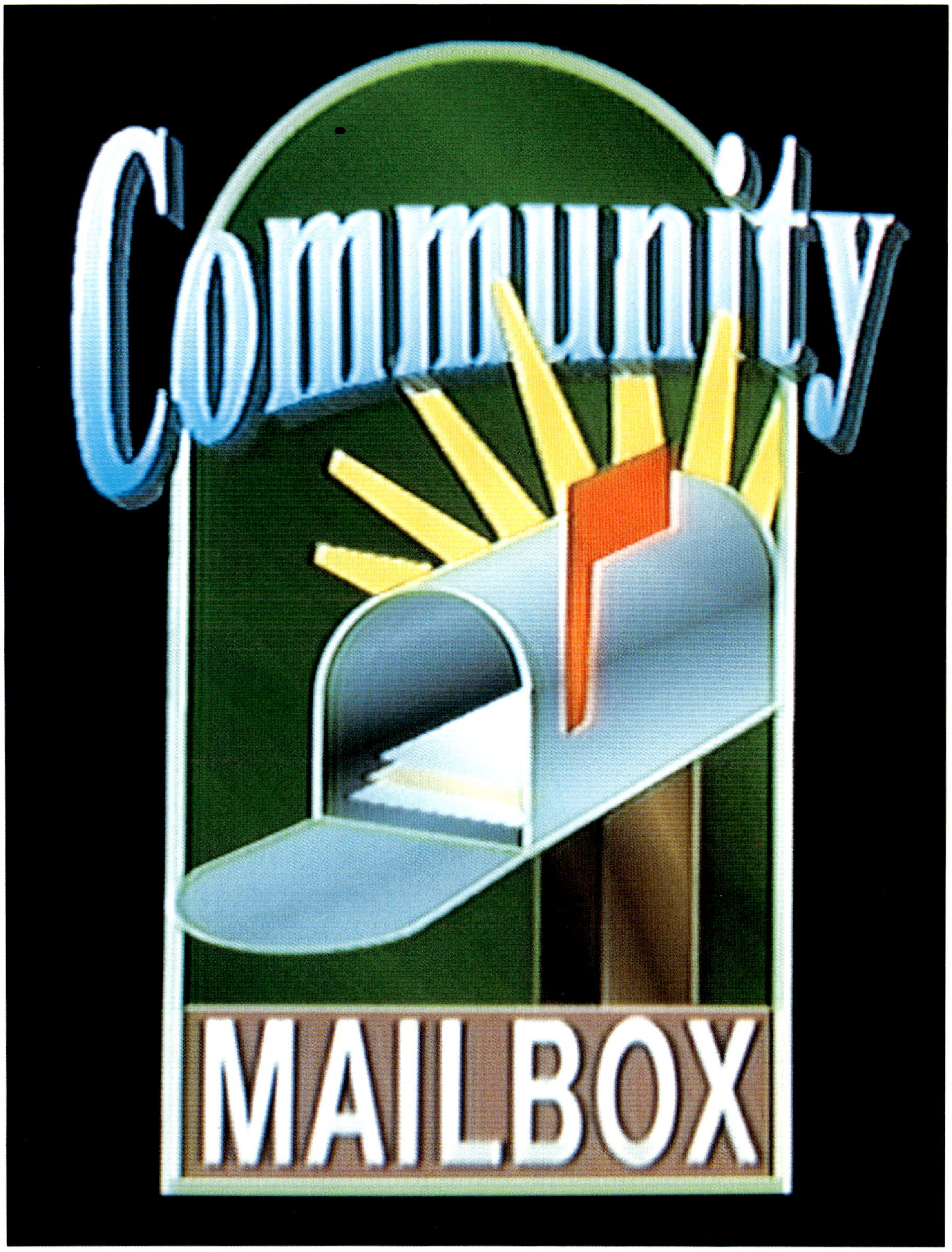

INDEX